What Every Mormon (and Non-Mormon) Should Know

Examining Mormon History, Doctrine and Claims

Edmond C. Gruss and Lane A. Thuet

Copyright © 2006
by Edmond C. Gruss and Lane A. Thuet

*What Every Mormon (and Non-Mormon) Should Know:
Examining Mormon History, Doctrine and Claims*
by Edmond C. Gruss and Lane A. Thuet

Printed in the United States of America

ISBN 1-60034-162-4

All rights reserved solely by the author. The author guarantees all contents are original and do not infringe upon the legal rights of any other person or work. No part of this book may be reproduced in any form without permission in writing from the author, except in the case of brief quotations embodied in critical articles or reviews. The views expressed in this book are not necessarily those of the publisher.

Unless otherwise indicated, all Scripture quotations are taken from the Authorized King James Version of the Bible. Copyright © 1964 by B. B. Kirkbride Bible Co., Inc.

Scripture quotations noted as NIV are from the New International Version of the Bible. Copyright © 1985 by The Zondervan Corporation.

Scripture quotations noted as NASB are from the New American Standard Bible. Copyright © 1977 by The Lockman Foundation.

www.xulonpress.com

What Every Mormon (and Non-Mormon) Should Know

Contents

Introduction xiii

1. Mormons—Attacked or Attackers? 15

2. The First Vision 33

3. The Great Apostasy 51

4. The Book of Mormon—Text Research 77

5. The Book of Mormon—Further Research 101

6. Joseph Smith's Abilities as a Translator 153

7. Prophetic Claims 173

8. Amazing Predictions? 211

9. Changing Mormon Truths 229

10. The Mormon Godhead 281

11. The Mormon Priesthood 315

12. The Mormon Testimony 333

13. The Mormon Gospel 355

Appendices
    A. The Testimony of Lane Thuet 369

B. Short Biographies of Quoted
   LDS Leaders 395

Notes..411

Select Bibliography 523

Ministries Involved with Mormonism............529

Acknowledgments

Any study of this length and detail is only made possible because of the prior publications and contributions of many people. All cannot be named here, but are mentioned in the text and/or endnotes where they deserve credit for their work.

A special debt of gratitude is given for those who have dedicated their lives to studying and researching the claims of the Church of Jesus Christ of Latter-day Saints, and publishing their findings. Their publications have been most valuable to us in this project. Most notably are the writings and publications of Bill McKeever, founder and director of Mormonism Research Ministry (www.mrm.org); and Jerald and Sandra Tanner, cofounders of Utah Lighthouse Ministry (www.utlm.org).

We are also very grateful for the assistance of several others who have graciously taken the time to assist us by previewing this manuscript and making valuable suggestions to improve it. We are indebted to Dr. John Hotchkiss, who spent many hours going over the manuscript. His attention to detail, his knowledge of the Bible and his expertise in English improved the text dramatically, for which we are truly appreciative. Our gratitude also goes out to Ryan Gruss, Bill McKeever, Donna Morley, Amos Clemmons and Sharon Fullmer for their assistance. We thank you and pray that God will bless all your righteous efforts.

Publications and Miscellaneous Information

Many of the works cited throughout this book have been reprinted several times. The unfortunate result is that occasionally the page citations will vary from edition to edition. Therefore, a page citation we give may apply only to the edition that is specifically quoted in this work. The first citation in each chapter of this book, from any volume, notes which edition we used.

In most instances, when we could not obtain an original publication from which we cite, photocopies of the original sources were obtained. Also, because of the fact that many early Mormon records have been reprinted or quoted in later publications, some quotations we use might also be found in a number of additional sources.

There has also been a tendency for the Mormon Church leaders to alter or delete potentially embarrassing passages from publications without indicating any change in the text (see Chapter 9 for more details on this subject). Hence, a later edition of an LDS source may not contain quotations exactly as cited in this work.

Verify the Information

We specifically ask everyone who can double check this information to do so themselves, rather than blindly taking our word, or anyone else's, on these subjects. While many of the references in this book are to nineteenth century documents or books that are very rare today, they can usually be verified without much difficulty. In most cases, copies of quoted sources can be found in libraries that have large collections of rare early Mormon writings. In and around Salt Lake City, good locations are The Church of Jesus Christ of Latter-day Saints, Historians Office; The Salt Lake City Public Library; The Utah State Historical Society; The University of Utah Marriott Library; and The Brigham Young University Lee Library. In Los Angeles: The City of Los Angeles Central Public Library; and The Huntington Library. In New York: The New York City Public Library. In Washington, D.C.: The Library of Congress.

Many libraries have microfilm services that will provide copies of early documents for a few cents per page.

A very valuable source for obtaining copies of many nineteenth-century documents and publications that relate to Mormon history is Utah Lighthouse Ministry.

Organization Names

The Church of Jesus Christ of Latter-day Saints is the official name of the organization we investigate in this work. It is also commonly referred to as the LDS Church, or the Mormon Church, on occasion. If we mention a teaching or practice of "Mormonism," we mean the official teachings and practices of the leadership for that organization.

The Reorganized Church of Jesus Christ of Latter-day Saints is an offshoot organization based in Independence, Missouri. It has since changed its name officially to the Community of Christ. We occasionally refer to this organization in our study.

King James Version of the Bible

In most instances, when the Bible is cited, quotations are from the King James Version because it is the official version that the Mormon Church uses and distributes to its membership. The Church strictly uses this version because it was used by founding prophet, Joseph Smith, Jr. (See Bruce McConkie, *Mormon Doctrine* [Salt Lake City: Bookcraft, 1966], 421-23). Whenever another version of the Bible is quoted, it will be noted in the citation.

Emphasis, Notations and Brackets

Unless otherwise noted, all **boldface type** found in quoted and non-quoted material is added for emphasis. Quotations *italicized* were either emphasized or italicized in the original source. Comments or clarifications added to quotations will be noted with brackets [ ]. Bracketed material already in quotations will be noted in the citation.

Often we cite from works such as *Early Mormon Documents* (Dan Vogel, 5 vols. [Salt Lake City: Signature Books, 1996-2003]); or *The Papers of Joseph Smith* (Dean C. Jessee, 2 vols. [Salt Lake City: Deseret Book, 1989-1992]). Works such as these reproduce the text of documents with all original notations (such as strikethroughs, additions and incorrect spelling) included. Whenever we cite from these sources, we use the original spelling and notations as well.

Introduction

Joseph Smith's Claim –
I have more to boast of than ever any man had. I am the only man that has ever been able to keep a whole church together since the days of Adam.... Neither Paul, John, Peter, nor Jesus ever did it. I boast that no man ever did such a work as I.
– *History of the Church*, 6:408-09

By Edmond Gruss

There is no way to express my feelings more accurately—I am impressed. Over the years I have read and studied LDS materials, visited historical sites and stopped at Visitor Centers from Honolulu, Hawaii, to Palmyra, New York. At the end of 2004 there were 122 spectacular temples in operation worldwide, costing untold millions of dollars to construct, with another 11 in various stages of construction.[1]

Through my reading of such publications as the *Deseret News—* [LDS] *Church Section, Ensign, BYU Studies,* books by Mormon and non-Mormon authors, and in the past, as a member of The Society for Early Historic Archaeology at BYU, I have followed with interest the latest developments in the Church. From these contacts and others I have learned that many prominent persons in the entertainment industry, business, sports, education, government and other walks of life are active members of The Church of Jesus Christ of Latter-day Saints. The non-Mormon could easily be envious of what he or she sees in the LDS Church. It is a rapidly growing church with over 12 million members.[2]

An article in the 13 November 2000 *U.S. News & World Report* said that the LDS Church was "one of the world's richest[3] and fastest growing religious movements."[4] More recently, Barnes and Noble included the *Book of Mormon* on its list of "Twenty Books That Changed America."[5] This inclusion was not an endorsement of Mormonism, but a selection based on the social impact of the book.[6]

The LDS Church demonstrates its concern: in helping its own, in striving to build up the family, in requiring strong moral values and in maintaining programs for its youth. It stresses lay involvement in church and missionary activities. It places a strong emphasis on education and temperate living. I also admire the stories of Mormon accomplishments that were realized in spite of difficulties and persecution. I could go on and mention other commendable things that are well known.

Over the years I have talked with LDS missionaries[7] and Church members and have often been impressed with their zeal and dedication. These discussions were sometimes punctuated with the comment, "You would make a good Mormon!" In my response I said that although much of what I saw in the LDS Church was admirable, I could not accept most of its claims and doctrines. This usually brought the question, "What do you mean?" In this book, both Lane Thuet (who was raised as a Mormon)[8] and I will review some of the things which we have stated in our replies to this and similar questions. In addition, we will present many other findings from our extensive research.

Our purpose is to examine many of the claims and teachings of Joseph Smith and the Church of Jesus Christ of Latter-day Saints[9] through the study of historical records and other relevant materials, to determine whether these support their assertions. Rather than stating ourselves what Mormon doctrines and beliefs are, we cite what LDS leaders, writers, and other informed scholars have said regarding these subjects. We do not wish any to think we are disparaging Joseph Smith or Mormons in any way. We only wish to examine (test) everything, then to "hold fast that which is good."[10]

Again, while I am impressed by much of what I see in the LDS Church, I am reminded of this insightful statement by author Charles Larson: "However, the ultimate promise of a religious system lies not in its *life-style*—its buildings, programs, or fraternity—but in its ability to reconcile us to God."[11] This is the ultimate test.

Chapter 1
Mormons—Attacked or Attackers?

Joseph Smith's Claim –
> I soon found, however, that my telling the story had excited a great deal of prejudice against me among professors of religion, and was the cause of great persecution, which continued to increase ... and this was common among all the sects—all united to persecute me.
> – *History of the Church*, 1:7

Criticizing Other Religions

Why Not Leave Them Alone?

At the outset, there is one important question that should be taken up. In contacts with Latter-day Saint (LDS) missionaries and Church members, they frequently ask, "Why do some people criticize or attack the Mormon Church?" Even some non-LDS have wondered, "Why not just leave Mormons and Mormonism alone? They do not criticize other churches." In response, a few misconceptions need to be pointed out. Doctrinal reasons will be discussed later.

Why Do Some Attack the Mormon (LDS) Church?

First, we do not attack Mormons, and we do not criticize their doctrines out of hate. The Bible teaches that all those who do not have faith in the blood of Jesus Christ shed on the cross will be condemned to eternal punishment.[1] There is no greater punishment than that. When compared to Bible teachings, Mormons do not have this saving faith. If we were motivated by hate, then, we would leave them alone so that they would end up condemned. Instead, we are motivated by love and concern for the Mormon people, and wish to see them come to a saving knowledge of the truth.

Second, the Mormon Church actively sends out missionaries to convert members of Christian denominations. We are responding by reaching out to Mormons with the gospel message of the Bible. We are serving as missionaries to the Mormons.

Finally, the LDS Church was founded upon the conviction—still taught—that **all other churches are false, apostate, without authority,** and that the Mormon Church alone is "**the only true Church.**"[2] This is verified by statements in the *Book of Mormon*, the *History of the Church*, the *Journal of Discourses*, the *Doctrine and Covenants* and various other Church publications, as well as by Mormon authorities. The materials used by Mormon missionaries in their proselytizing activities show that this belief has not changed. In fact, in the LDS Church General Conference for October 1985, Apostle Boyd K. Packer said, "It is our firm conviction that The Church of Jesus Christ of Latter-day Saints is, as the revelations state, '**the only true** and living church **upon the face of the whole earth.**'"[3]

Certainly anyone can understand that for churches or individuals to be critical of Mormonism and this claim is not unwarranted or unreasonable. They are only rejecting LDS claims and defending what they believe to be true in response to a clear attack.

Furthermore, the Bible directs all professing Christians to "earnestly contend for the faith"[4] and to "be ready always to give an answer to every man that asketh you a reason of the hope that is in you...."[5]

Does the Mormon Church Attack Other Churches?

"Why do you attack our church?" Mormons often complain that critics are guilty of Mormon "bashing." While the Mormon Church denies that it attacks other churches, this practice has actually characterized the LDS Church throughout its history.

In his booklet, *Does the Mormon Church Attack Orthodox Christianity?* John R. Farkas, a former Mormon, summarized what he found after researching this question.

I firmly believe that **the Mormon church from its very beginning until now, has attacked the orthodox Christian church.... this attack is official** and supported by many of the leaders of the Mormon church **past and present**.... My conclusion that the Mormon church has and **still does attack orthodox Christianity** is based solely upon Mormon publications and rituals.... **By name it has attacked all the major denominations** at some point in time.[6] The following is a summary of the statements made by the Mormon church and Mormon leaders through the years: all churches are wrong; Satan sits at the head of Christian churches; none of the Christian churches have authority to act in God's name; none is inspired; none can save souls; marriages performed in them are illegal and children by those marriages are illegitimate;[7] the Roman Catholic Church is the mother of harlots; the Protestants are the harlot's daughter and apostate; the churches are the "whore of Babylon"; the Bible has parts removed or is mistranslated; the false Christian gods bear the same name as the true Gods of the Bible—Beyond this they have little resemblance (to true Christianity).[8]

All of these statements are easily verified. The rest of Farkas' booklet includes a detailed index of references, followed by all the photocopies from the LDS publications upon which the summary is based.

As Christian apologist Bill McKeever said, "Mormonism has always insisted that all churches are wrong...." McKeever referred to the LDS missionary message, noting that to

> make such a statement and not think that this is somehow "belittling" shows how oblivious many Mormons are to this offensive claim. **Every time a Mormon insists that the church needed to be restored or that the church fell into apostasy, or that the Mormon Church is the "only true church,"** they belittle every Christian's beliefs.... To insist that only the LDS church is true is to insist all other churches must be false.[9]

What about the positive things that Mormon leaders have sometimes stated about mainstream Christian churches? Farkas continues:

> The good things the Mormon church has said about the orthodox Christian church over the years can in no way offset the hostility and the attacks it has showered upon Christianity through its official publications, books by top leaders and in its temple rituals from the founding of the Mormon church until now. The severity and magnitude of the attacks only tell me that **much of the Mormon church's good comments probably were made for public relations.**[10]

Jerald and Sandra Tanner comment: "Although the present-day leaders of the Mormon Church are **becoming more subtle in their attack** on other churches, **they still teach** that the Mormon Church **is the only true church** and that all others are in a state of apostasy."[11] And LaMar Petersen observes: "Missionaries are now instructed to avoid pejorative statements against other churches, such as 'mother of abominations,' 'whore of all the earth,' 'mother of harlots,' and other offensive designations. **But such unfortunate words cannot be erased from LDS scriptures.**"[12]

Mormon Attacks on All Other Churches

The following brief review presents specific examples of where and how the LDS Church has denigrated non-LDS churches and their members.

Mormon Missionary Handbooks

What do Mormon missionaries communicate to potential converts, as set forth in their official manuals? The following material is quoted from four official Mormon missionary handbooks.

A Uniform System For Teaching Investigators (1961).

> Elder: I know that **the Church of Jesus Christ was taken completely from the earth**. Once this true Church had been lost, other churches began; they continued to use his name and some of his teachings. **These are the modern Catholic and Protestant churches.** (17)
>
> Elder: In comparison with the true church of Jesus Christ then, what about these other churches [Catholic or Protestant]? Brown [potential convert]: They are false....
> **There was a complete apostasy and my church is false.** (18)

The Uniform System For Teaching Families (1973).

After reading Joseph Smith's first vision testimony, the missionaries add theirs:

> We testify that God the Father and his Son Jesus Christ appeared to Joseph Smith and spoke to him.... (*Companion adds his testimony....*) (C-9)
>
> *Missionary:* Answering his question, the Savior told Joseph Smith that he should **join none of the churches** and explained why. He said **they had a form of godliness but taught the doctrines of men and not of God.** Mr. Brown, how does this help you to understand why the churches today teach so many conflicting doctrines? (C-11)

Uniform System For Teaching the Gospel (1986).

Discussion 3 of this System is titled *The Restoration*. A *Study Guide* brochure, by the same title, is prepared for the investigator (potential convert). The following is quoted from the *Study Guide:*

The True Church of Jesus Christ ...
We must come unto Christ by being baptized into his Church. **Only in The Church of Jesus Christ of Latter-day Saints** can we find all the truths that will help us return to our Father in Heaven. **Only in the true Church of Christ** can we find the authority to perform the necessary gospel ordinances. (5)

From the missionary discussions:

They [God the Father and Jesus Christ] told Joseph **not to join any of the churches because the churches were teaching incorrect doctrines.** The people understood many Christian principles that helped them lead good lives. But they also misunderstood some basic and vital truths because **these truths had been lost centuries before.** (3-8)

The Lord testified that this is "the **only true and living church upon the face of the whole earth.**"(D&C 1:30). (3-11)

Testify:... Your knowledge that this is **the true Church of Christ.** (3-11)

Find Out—
- Whether the investigators recognize the need to belong to the **true Church of Christ.**
- Whether they accept **The Church of Jesus Christ of Latter-day Saints as the only true Church of Jesus Christ.**

Testify: Express your feelings about—...
- Your assurance that **The Church of Jesus Christ of Latter-day Saints is the only true Church of Jesus Christ.**
- The need to belong to the **only true Church.** (3-12)

"Preach My Gospel" (2004).

Lesson 1 is entitled *The Message of the Restoration of the Gospel of Jesus Christ*. The lesson teaches:

> With the death of the Apostles, priesthood keys and the presiding priesthood authority **were taken from the earth**.... over time **the doctrines were corrupted**, and unauthorized changes were made in Church organization and priesthood ordinances.... Much of the knowledge of the true character and nature of God the Father, His Son Jesus Christ, and the Holy Ghost **was lost. The doctrines ... became distorted or forgotten**.... **This apostasy eventually led to the emergence of many churches**.... They recognized that many of the doctrines and ordinances of the gospel had been changed or lost. They sought for greater spiritual light, and many spoke of the need for a restoration of truth. (35)

What can one conclude from these statements about LDS attitudes toward **all** other churches?

Joseph Smith's Testimony

Mormons often quote a portion of Joseph Smith's testimony, included in the *Pearl of Great Price*, in their proselytizing work (as shown above). Verse 19, and a portion of verse 20, from this testimony is quoted below.

> I was answered that I must **join none of them**, for they were **all wrong;** and the Personage who addressed me said that all their **creeds were an abomination** in his sight; that those **professors were all corrupt**; that: "they draw near to me with their lips, but their **hearts are far from me**, they **teach for doctrines the commandments of men**,[13] **having a form of godliness, but they deny the power thereof**." He again **forbade me to join any of them**....

The last part of verse 19 is footnoted to 2 Timothy 3:5 in the Bible, which reads: "Having a form of godliness, but denying the power thereof: from such turn away." The Introduction to *History of the Church* cites the 2 Timothy 3:1-5 passage as one reference to "The Testimony of Prophecy to the Universal Apostasy."[14] What is being said of **all other churches and their members** in Joseph Smith's testimony and by Mormons when this passage is applied to non-LDS churches and members?

In these verses there is a "depravity list" of no less than 18 vices. It would be difficult to find any greater condemnation of other churches than by applying this to them.

2. For men shall be lovers of their own selves, covetous, boasters, proud, blasphemers, disobedient to parents, unthankful, unholy,
3. Without natural affection, trucebreakers, false accusers, incontinent, fierce, despisers of those that are good,
4. Traitors, heady, highminded, lovers of pleasures more than lovers of God;
5. Having a form of godliness, but denying the power thereof: from such turn away.

Many additional references from the Bible have also been cited in LDS literature as references to The Great Apostasy[15] and as applicable to all non-Mormon churches. Why, then, is it wrong for Christians to defend themselves against such attacks? Those who put the blame on the Christians are simply uninformed.

The Temple Endowment Ceremony

The small portion of the Temple Endowment ceremony quoted below was current in 1989. At this point in the ceremony Lucifer (the Devil) appears as the one who employed the non-LDS ministers. The following dialogue is a verbatim transcription. The leadership of the LDS Church changed the temple ceremony in April 1990,[16] and those changes (also from a transcription) are indicated in brackets.

After Adam and Eve have been removed from the Garden of Eden and sent into the "lone and dreary world" (i.e.: this world), Adam prays, and in response Lucifer appears.

> **Adam**: Who are you?
> **Lucifer**: I am the God of this world.
> **Adam**: You, the God of this world?
> **Lucifer**: Yes, what do you want?
> **Adam**: I am looking for messengers.
> **Lucifer**: Oh, you want someone to preach to you. You want religion, do You? **[next six words removed]** I will have preachers here presently.
> **[16 words added]** There will be many willing to preach to you the philosophies of men mingled with scripture.
> **[All the following has been removed]**
> **Lucifer**: Good morning sir!
> **Sectarian Minister**: Good morning! ... A fine congregation!
> **Lucifer**: Yes, they are very good people. They are concerned about religion. Are you a preacher?
> **Sectarian Minister**: I am.
> **Lucifer**: Have you been to college and received training for the ministry?
> **Sectarian Minister**: Certainly! A man cannot preach unless he has been trained for the ministry.
> **Lucifer**: Do you preach the orthodox religion?
> **Sectarian Minister**: Yes, that is what I preach.
> **Lucifer**: If you preach your orthodox religion to these people, and convert them, I will pay you well.
> **Sectarian Minister**: I will do my best....[17]

As the Tanners conclude, before the changes, "this portion of the ceremony made it perfectly clear that in the eyes of the Mormon leaders the orthodox Christian religion is the Devil's religion."[18] But, as they point out, "Unfortunately, the removal of the portion of the temple ceremony which implies that Christian ministers are working for the Devil does not really solve the problem. The

Mormon Church still retains Joseph Smith's story of the First Vision in the *Pearl of Great Price*...."[19]

Joseph Smith's testimony, which condemns all other churches, continues to be the central message in the Mormon conversion program. First Nephi 14:10 from the *Book of Mormon* has often been quoted by Mormon leaders:

> And he said unto me: Behold there are save **two churches only; the one is the church of the Lamb of God, and the other is the church of the devil**; wherefore, whoso belongeth not to the church of the Lamb of God belongeth to that great church, which is the mother of abominations; and she is the whore of all the earth.

George Q. Cannon, former First Counselor to the LDS First Presidency, explains:

> After the Church of Jesus Christ of Latter-day Saints was organized, there were **only two churches upon the earth**. They were known respectively as **the Church of the Lamb of God and Babylon. The various organizations which are called churches throughout Christendom**, though differing in their creeds and organizations, have **one common origin. They all belong to Babylon.**[20]

What does it mean to "belong to Babylon?" In discussing "Babylon," Bruce McConkie writes: "As Babylon of old fell to her utter destruction and ruin, **so the great and abominable church together with all wickedness shall be utterly destroyed when the Lord comes.**"[21]

Statements Made by LDS Leaders and in Church Publications

Should these Mormon statements offend Christians? It is not difficult to see why they would. Here are even more quotations from their leaders about those outside the LDS Church.

Prophet Joseph Smith, Jr.:

What is it that inspires professors of Christianity generally with a hope of salvation? **It is that smooth, sophisticated influence of the devil**, by which he deceives the whole world.²²

President Brigham Young:

Every spirit that confesses that Joseph Smith is a Prophet, that he lived and died a Prophet and that the *Book of Mormon* is true, is of God, and **every spirit that does not is of anti-Christ.**²³

The Christian world, I discovered, was like the captain and crew of a vessel on the ocean without a compass, and tossed to and fro whithersoever the wind listed to blow them. When the light came to me, I saw that **all the so-called Christian world was groveling in darkness.**²⁴

Brother Taylor has just said that the **religions of the day were hatched in hell. The eggs were laid in hell**, hatched on its borders, and then kicked on to the earth. They may be **called cockatrices** [a mythical serpent that has the power to kill by its glance], for they sting wherever they go.²⁵

With regard to true theology, **a more ignorant people never lived** than the present so-called Christian world.²⁶

Apostle Orson Pratt:

Q. After the Church of Christ fled from earth to heaven, what was left?
A. A set of **wicked Apostates, murderers, and idolaters**, who, after having made war with the saints ... were left to follow the **wicked imaginations of their own corrupt hearts**, and to build up churches by human authority, and to follow after the **cunning craftiness of uninspired men**....²⁷

... any person who receives Baptism or the Lord's supper from their hands will highly offend God, for he looks upon them as **the most corrupt of all people**. Both Catholics and Protestants are nothing less than the ***"whore of Babylon" whom the Lord denounces by the mouth of John the Revelator as having corrupted all the earth by their fornications and wickedness***. And any person who shall be so wicked as to receive a holy ordinance of the gospel from the ministers of any of these **apostate churches will be sent down to hell with them**, unless they repent of the unholy and impious act.[28]

Apostle Heber C. Kimball:

Christians—those poor, miserable priests Brother Brigham was speaking about—**some of them are the biggest whoremasters there are on the earth**, and at the same time preaching righteousness to the children of men. The poor devils, they could not get up here and preach an oral discourse, to save themselves from hell; they are preaching their fathers' sermons—preaching sermons that were written a hundred years before they were born.[29]

Apostle John Taylor:

The transactions of men are even more outrageous against the Lord, and the only excuse for them is their ignorance. What! are Christians ignorant? Yes, **as ignorant of the things of God as the brute beast**.[30]

We talk about Christianity, but it is **a perfect pack of nonsense.... the Devil could not invent a better engine to spread his work** than the Christianity of the nineteenth century.[31]

What does the Christian world know about God? **Nothing**.... Why, so far as the things of God are concerned, they are the veriest fools; they know neither God nor the things of God.³²

Apostle (later President) Joseph F. Smith:

... but the time came when **Paganism was engrafted into Christianity, and at last Christianity was converted into Paganism** rather than converting the Pagans. And subsequently the Priesthood was taken from among men, this authority was re-called into the heavens....³³

Apostle Daniel H. Wells:

Many who have thus been foundering are honest people; but the so-called system of Christianity **is not only an error and a snare, but is a monstrous iniquity fastened upon the children of men** throughout the earth. No wonder that people become infidel. The inconsistent and incongruous nature of the system is enough to make **any being who reasons infidel.**³⁴

Apostle (later President) Joseph Fielding Smith:

For hundreds of years the world *was wrapped in a veil of spiritual darkness, until there was not one fundamental truth belonging to the plan of salvation that was not, in the year 1820, so obscured by false tradition and ceremonies, borrowed from paganism, as to make it unrecognizable; or else it was entirely denied....* Joseph Smith declared that in the year 1820 the Lord revealed to him that **all the "Christian" churches were in error, teaching for commandments the doctrines of men.**³⁵

Apostle (later President) Spencer W. Kimball:

In the category of **taking the name of the lord in vain**, we might include the use by unauthorized persons of the name of

Deity in performing ordinances.... **Presumptuous and blasphemous are they who purport to baptize, bless, marry, or perform other sacraments in the name of the Lord while in fact lacking his specific authorization.** And no one can obtain God's authority from reading the Bible or from just a desire to serve the Lord, no matter how pure his motives.[36]

Apostle (later President) Ezra Taft Benson:

This is the Church and kingdom of God, **the only true Church upon the face of the earth**, according to the Lord's own words (see D & C 1:30) ["... the only true and living church upon the face of the whole earth, with which I, the Lord, am well pleased ..."].[37]

There is no other way, because this is the only true message and **the only true church upon the face of the whole earth.**[38]

President Gordon B. Hinckley:

The Lord said that **this is the only true and living church upon the face of the earth** with which He is well pleased (see D&C 1:30). I didn't say that. Those are His words. The Prophet Joseph was told that **the other sects were wrong** (see Joseph Smith—History 1:19). Those are not my words. Those are the Lord's words. But **they are hard words for those of other faiths.**[39]

The Ensign:[40]

Of historical and theological significance is the fact that in Paul's prophecy the church structure survives. But God is not at its head, making that church—following the appearance in it of Satan—no longer the church of God.

To say that **Satan sits in the place of God in Christianity** after the time of the Apostles is not to say that all that is in it is satanic.... Still, "the power of God unto salvation" (Rom. 1:16) **is absent from all but the Church of Jesus Christ of Latter-day Saints**, which the Lord himself has proclaimed to be "the only true and living church upon the face of the whole earth" (D&C 1:30).[41]

Apostle Bruce R. McConkie[42] wrote the book *Mormon Doctrine*, which is a dictionary of Mormon beliefs. The following quotations are from that work under the subjects indicated.

"Baptism":
> As with other doctrines and ordinances, **apostate substitutes** of the real thing are found both among pagans and **supposed Christians**. (p. 72)

"Broad-mindedness":
> When inquiring and scientific minds delve into the **narrow and bigoted creeds of the apostate sects of Christendom**, it is not surprising that they rebel against those dogmas falsely set forth as the tenets of true religion. (107)

"Christendom":
> That portion of the world in which **so-called Christianity prevails**—as distinguished from heathen or Mohammedan lands—is called *Christendom*. The term also applies to the whole body of **supposed Christian believers**; as now constituted this body is properly termed *apostate Christendom*. (131)

"Christianity":
> *Christianity* is the religion of the Christians. Hence, true and acceptable Christianity is found among the saints who have the fullness of the gospel, and **a perverted Christianity holds sway among the so-called Christians of apostate Christendom**. (132)

"Church of Jesus Christ of Latter-day Saints":
This Church is "**the only true and living church upon the face of the whole earth**" (D. & C. 1:30), the **only organization authorized by the Almighty** to preach his gospel and administer the ordinances of salvation, the only Church which has power to save and exalt men in the hereafter. (136)

"Church of the Devil":
The titles *church of the devil* and *great and abominable church* are used to **identify all churches or organizations of whatever name or nature**—whether political, philosophical, educational, economic, social, fraternal, civic, or religious—which are designed to take men on a course that leads away from God and his laws and thus from salvation in the kingdom of God.... **There is no salvation outside this one true Church, the Church of Jesus Christ.** (137-38)

"False Christs":
And **virtually all the millions of apostate Christendom have abased themselves before the mythical throne of a mythical Christ** whom they vainly suppose to be a spirit essence who is incorporeal, uncreated, immaterial, and three-in-one with the Father and Holy Spirit. (269)

"Liars":
Those who believe in false doctrines are thus guilty of believing a lie, and those who propagate these untruths are guilty of lying. For instance: **The creeds of apostate Christendom teach untruths** about God, and the scriptures say that those who accept these creeds "**have inherited lies.**" (Jer. 16:16-21.) Those who accept any of the doctrines of the apostate churches are said to "**believe a lie.**" (2 Thess. 2:1-12.) The process of apostasy consists in changing the "truth of God into a lie." (Rom 1:25.) (440-41)

Here are statements from two of McConkie's more recent books:

What is the church of the devil in our day, and where is the seat of her power? ... It is all of the systems, both Christian and non-Christian, that have perverted the pure and perfect gospel; ... It is communism; it is Islam; it is Buddhism; **it is modern Christianity in all its parts.**[43]

The gods of Christendom, for instance, are gods who were created by men in the creeds of an apostate people. There is little profit or peace in serving them, and certainly there is **no salvation available through them.**[44]

Conclusion

In their book *Mormon America: The Power and the Promise* (1999), journalists Richard and Joan Ostling comment,

> The Saints [i.e.: Mormon members] universally resent it when outsiders consign them to non-Christian or semi-Christian status. They consider the very "Are Mormons Christians?" question an insult. At the same time, however, their own scriptures virtually forbid Saints to recognize that the great churches of Christianity—Catholic, Orthodox, or Protestant—have any authentic claim to be Christian. [BYU's Stephen] Robinson, for example, has written that the non-Mormons may have "opportunities to accept the gospel in the postmortal life," but that "the historical church no longer possessed the gospel" after the Great Apostasy.[45]

From these many statements, it is clear that the Mormon Church does not "leave Christians alone." From the very beginning, the Mormon Church has attacked other churches and sent missionaries to them in hopes of converting their members. Those who are labeled "LDS critics" or "anti-Mormons" are usually nothing more than Christians defending the historic Christian faith against these attacks.

Chapter 2
The First Vision

Joseph Smith's Claim –
> ... I had beheld a vision.... I had actually seen a light, and in the midst of that light I saw two personages, and they did in reality speak to me; and though I was hated and persecuted for saying that I had seen a vision, yet it was true.... I had seen a vision; I knew it, and I knew that God knew it, and I could not deny it....
> – *History of the Church*, 1:7-8

The Beginning of Mormonism

Which Church Is True?

According to LDS scripture, when Joseph Smith was 14 years old,[1] he was confused as to which church was true. He claimed this confusion was sparked by an 1820 religious revival in his neighborhood of Palmyra, New York. His heart was powerfully impressed one night when he read James 1:5, and subsequently he went into the woods near his house to pray that God would tell him which of all the Christian sects was right. According to the account, as he began to pray, he was nearly overcome by "some power" of "astonishing influence" that prevented him from speaking. As he called out to God, he was miraculously delivered by two beings, one of whom identified the other as *"My Beloved Son."* The beings are therefore identified as God the Father and Jesus Christ. Joseph Smith said that he was told the following: "I was answered that I must join none of them, for they were all wrong; and the Personage who addressed me said that all their creeds were an abomination in his sight; that those professors were all corrupt...."[2]

This story is referred to within the LDS Church as the first vision. It was this vision that ultimately led Joseph Smith to organize what is known today as The Church of Jesus Christ of Latter-day Saints. Whenever LDS missionaries meet with potential converts, their message always includes the first vision story. LDS scholar James Allen writes, "In 1961 the official missionary plan of the Church required all missionaries to use the [first vision] story in their first lesson as part of the dialogue...."[3]

Cornerstone of the Church

Today, this vision is taught to be the cornerstone upon which the LDS Church is built. In fact, the ninth president of the Mormon Church, David O. McKay, said that "the appearing of the Father and the Son to Joseph Smith **is the foundation of this Church.**"[4] Early LDS Apostle John Widtsoe also affirms this: "The First Vision of 1820 **is of first importance** in the history of Joseph Smith. Upon its reality rest the truth and value of his subsequent work."[5] According to the *Salt Lake Tribune*, current LDS President Gordon B. Hinckley agreed: "LDS faithful believe it all began when 14-year-old Joseph Smith, the church's founder, had a vision of God and Jesus Christ in a grove of trees in 1820. 'Our whole strength rests on the validity of that vision,' Hinckley declared. 'It either occurred or it did not occur. **If it did not, then this work is a fraud.**'"[6] He also wrote, "**Without it** as a foundation stone for our faith and organization, **we have nothing**.... it is an **essential foundation stone, a cornerstone**, without which the Church could not be 'fitly framed together.'"[7]

On another occasion, Hinckley said,

> **Every claim that we make** concerning divine authority, **every truth that we offer** concerning the validity of this work, all **finds its root in the First Vision** of the boy prophet. Without it we would not have anything much to say.... **That becomes the hinge pin** on which this whole cause turns. **If the First Vision was true**, if it actually happened, **then the Book of Mormon is true**. Then we have the priesthood. Then we have the Church organization and all of the other keys and blessings of authority which we say we have. **If the**

First Vision did not occur, then we are involved in a great sham. It is just that simple.[8]

In the introduction to the book *Studies of the Book of Mormon*, Sterling McMurrin states:

> In a unique way the Mormons even today have tied their faith to their historical roots. They insist that **the truth of their religion**, the authority of their priesthood, and the divine foundations of their Church **depend entirely on the factual truth** of certain of their historical claims. The truth of two of those claims is held to be **absolutely crucial. If Joseph Smith's vision of the Father and Son was not in fact an objective, veridical experience ... then the Church and its priesthood and Mormonism as a religion are abject frauds.** This is the position in which the Church has, by its own official pronouncements, voluntarily placed itself.[9]

However, this strong stand on the first vision has not always been the case. LDS writer Grant Palmer writes, "We might expect that after the church's organization in early 1830, Joseph would cite the first vision as the source of his call since it came directly from Jesus Christ. **He does not.**"[10] In 1966, James Allen published an article about this matter. He writes,

> ...**none of the available contemporary writings** about Joseph Smith in the 1830's, **none of the publications** of the Church in that decade, and **no contemporary journal or correspondence** yet discovered **mentions the story of the first vision**.... As far as Mormon literature is concerned, **there was apparently no reference to Joseph Smith's first vision in any published material in the 1830's**.... From all this it would appear that the general church membership did not receive information about the first vision **until the 1840's** and that the story certainly did not hold the prominent place in Mormon thought that it does today.[11]

Other researchers at the time found no references to the vision, either. Fawn Brodie, after having researched voluminous papers, diaries and writings from Joseph's family and hometown, writes,

> Joseph's first published autobiographical sketch of 1834, already noted, contained no whisper of an event [the first vision] that, if it had happened, would have been the most soul-shattering experience of his whole youth.... **If something happened that spring morning** in 1820, **it passed totally unnoticed** in Joseph's home town, and apparently did not even fix itself in the minds of members of his own family.[12]

In a supplement added to her revised biography of Smith years later, she adds:

> Despite dedicated searching of early newspapers and manuscripts during the past twenty-five years, **no one has yet found any document** written before the publication of the Book of Mormon in 1830 **which mentions Joseph Smith's first vision** of God and Jesus Christ....[13]

Since then, as we will show in this Chapter, documents have been either discovered and/or released by the LDS Church which do show some references to the first vision having been made. However, they bring the vision into a new and curious light. Joseph Smith claimed that his vision **caused a great deal of notice and attention** from everyone around him. In fact, he claimed that all the religious groups of his town united in their efforts to persecute him because of the vision.[14] It is interesting to note that the documentation shows otherwise.

Grant Palmer agrees, writing,

> There is **no evidence of prejudice** resulting from his first vision. If his report that "all the sects ... united to persecute me" were accurate, one would expect to find some hint of this in the local newspapers, narratives by ardent critics, and

in the affidavits D. P. Hurlburt gathered in 1833.[15] The record is nevertheless silent on this issue. **No one**, friend or foe, in New York or Pennsylvania remembers either that there was "great persecution" **or even that Joseph claimed to have had a vision. Not even his family remembers it.**[16]

Is the first vision, then, really the foundation of the LDS Church? If so, why would there have been so little prominence or knowledge of the event in the first 10 years of the official Church history? Why did no one in the membership seem to know about the vision in those early years? It seems that such an astonishing event as God and Jesus appearing to someone would be of major importance, and should have been the very center of discussion and conversion. Looking further into the available information, some additional interesting facts about this reported vision come to light.

Only One Story?

Preston Nibley, a descendant of an early LDS apostle, once wrote *"Joseph Smith lived a little more than twenty-four years after this first vision. During this time he told **but one story**...."*[17] So important is this vision that it is published as scripture to the Mormon people in *The Pearl of Great Price*. This official version of the vision was copied from the early LDS publication *Times and Seasons*, which originally published it on 1 April 1842.[18] Joseph Smith wrote this account of the vision himself in 1838—18 years after it allegedly happened.

However, contrary to what Nibley claimed, this is **not** the only version of the story that Joseph ever told. For most of the Church's history, this account was rarely disputed or questioned. The most vocal critics were Jerald and Sandra Tanner, who had raised some doubts as to whether or not the vision was genuine. But then in 1965, a BYU student, Paul Cheesman, was working on a study of this vision for his thesis when he came across **a completely different version** in the LDS Church Historian's office.[19] In his research, he noted that the accounts differed in significant details. This was a very surprising development, because until that time, there had been only one version publicly known—the official version. As Cheesman looked deeper, he found other early accounts of the vision that also differed in their details.

This finding led others to start looking into the matter, and surprisingly, many differing accounts of the vision were brought to light. **At least 11 versions of this first vision are now known to exist.**

The Differing Versions

Version 1[20]

Grant Palmer writes that "the earliest allusion, oral or written, to the first vision is the brief mention that was transcribed in June 1830 and originally printed in the *Book of Commandments* (XXIV:6/D&C 20:5)."[21] Upon reading this section, we see that it is not actually labeled as an account of the first vision, but further reading shows that it truly is.

The chapter claims to be an account of "the rise of the church of Christ in these last days."[22] Verse 6 states that Joseph Smith "**had received a remission of his sins**" but then had become "entangled again in the vanities of the world." The following verse goes on to say that Joseph had truly repented; therefore "God ministered unto him **by an holy angel** ... and **gave unto him commandments....**"[23]

No mention is made of Joseph Smith's age at the time. No mention is made as to why Joseph was praying, though it could safely be assumed he wanted forgiveness of his sins. No mention is made of any other religious group or that Joseph should not join them. Instead, Joseph is merely given some unidentified commandments. The most conspicuous difference between the official version of the first vision and this account, however, is that **God the Father and Jesus Christ did not appear** to young Joseph. Instead, only one personage, who is identified merely as "an holy angel," visited him.[24]

This account refers to the first vision story. This fact is verified by a letter that Joseph Smith's mother, Lucy Smith, wrote to her brother, Solomon Mack, on 6 January 1831. Not only does her letter verify that Joseph received forgiveness of sins and that it was only a "holy Angel" that came to him, but she adds that it was this vision that led to the translation of the *Book of Mormon*.[25]

Version 2[26]

The earliest known full account of the first vision was also the only known account to be written in Joseph Smith's own handwriting, in the form of a letter. The actual time of its writing is uncertain because the document itself is not dated. Some writers date it about 1833, which would have been 13 years after the event had taken place,[27] and others a year earlier.[28] This version was the one made public by Paul Cheesman in 1965.[29] This account had been in the hands of LDS leaders for over 130 years, but was kept hidden, presumably because it differs so greatly from the official version.

In this account, Smith claimed that **he was 16 years old** when he prayed. He also claimed that **he already knew that all churches were wrong** from reading the Bible. **His purpose in praying was to seek forgiveness** from his sins. In answer to his prayer, **Jesus alone visited him** and forgave his sins. Some of the details of this vision agree with the version published in the *Book of Commandments*—such as that his sins were forgiven—while the identification of the messenger has been upgraded to the Lord Jesus Himself.

This account raises some disturbing questions. For example, why did Joseph wait 12-13 years to record the fact that he was visited by a heavenly being? Most people would immediately record such an event in their journal, especially if it were Jesus that had visited. The fact that Joseph waited so long to write about it causes us to question whether the vision was real, or perhaps just a vaguely remembered dream.

That the age of his visitation is two years off could be a simple mistake. The fact that he claimed he already knew all churches were wrong, however, is an obvious inconsistency. In the official version, that was Joseph's whole purpose in going to pray: "My object in going to inquire of the Lord was to know which of all the sects was right, that I might know which to join."[30] He even states specifically in the official version that "**at this time it had never entered into my heart** that all were wrong."[31]

The most troublesome difference is that only one personage—Jesus—visited Joseph in this account. It is inconceivable that he would somehow forget that God the Father had been there also, or that he would leave out that vital detail.

Version 3[32]

In February 1835, the LDS publication *Messenger and Advocate* printed a letter written by Oliver Cowdery to W. W. Phelps, giving an account of the first vision. The purpose of the letter was to make absolutely certain that the account of the vision was printed correctly in all its details. In fact, it was to correct an error in the story from a previous printing.

In this account, Joseph was **17 years old**. The **date of the Christian revival** was listed as **1823**. **No mention is made of James 1:5**. Instead, Joseph claimed **he had been wondering if there was a God** and **if his sins could be forgiven**. His **reason for praying was to ask if God did exist** and if he was accepted by Him. After *"11 or 12 hours"* in **prayer**, he was visited by *"a messenger from God"* who said he was sent **"by commandment of the Lord"** to forgive Joseph's sins.

While this vision is identified in the *Messenger and Advocate* as the "first vision" of Joseph Smith, it was later revised and republished, this time as a **second** vision from an angel named "Moroni," a vision that was supposedly preparatory to Joseph Smith receiving the golden plates for translation.

Some might disregard this as a secondhand account of the story, since it did not come directly from Joseph Smith himself. However, Oliver Cowdery claimed that Joseph Smith helped him to write the letter.[33] Cowdery was Joseph Smith's close confidant and secretary.[34] Because he was a witness to many of the key events in LDS history, he would certainly know the details of this vision.

However, this version carries a great deal of weight for a number of additional reasons. First, it should be noted that this account was printed in an LDS publication over which Joseph Smith kept a careful watch. Second, it was printed during the lifetime of Joseph Smith, which is significant because he never made any statements against its accuracy. Since he was well known for correcting the errors of those under his charge, this indicates his approval of the information printed. Finally, we can accept this account as correct because it was later copied **unchanged** into Joseph Smith's *Manuscript History of the Church*[35] and subsequently into the LDS publication *Times and Seasons*.[36] Since it was copied with Joseph Smith's approval into other LDS publications and records without any changes, the account must have been considered accurate and valid. This adds major significance to the differing details of this version.

In this version, the difference in Smith's age is more pronounced. We also have a different date for the revival that is intimately connected with the vision. This time, Joseph's purpose in praying had nothing to do with which church was correct. Instead, he wanted to know whether or not there actually was a God. And, whereas the official version states that Joseph received a response to his prayer **immediately** upon kneeling down,[37] this time it took **more than 11 or 12 hours** in prayer. There is no accounting for such a vast difference in response time. When we add to all of this the most obvious difference—that he was not answered by God the Father or Jesus Christ, but by an angel identified as "Moroni"—we are left with serious doubts as to whether the first vision really took place, or was invented later and embellished.

This third version strikes a serious blow to the validity and truthfulness of the first vision. And the fact that this account was later revised and identified as a second vision lessens the story's credibility even further. Could Cowdery have simply gotten confused about which was Joseph's first vision? It is possible that some details might have been mixed up, but it is unlikely that major points—such as the reason for praying, his age, the response time, and the fact that in this account it was not Jesus or God that came—would be so different.

Version 4[38]

On 9 November 1835, Joseph Smith dictated his own account of the first vision for his personal diary. There is some question among scholars, even those who are LDS, as to who the scribe was for this part of the diary. Some believe it was Warren Parrish,[39] but others believe it was Warren Cowdery.[40] Regardless of which man wrote the account, it appears in the official diary of the Prophet, and was dictated by him directly. LDS scholars accept this journal entry as accurate and valid. Curiously enough, **this account of the first vision was purposely left out** when the information was transferred into the official *History of the Church*. The only reasonable explanation for the omission is that the details of the vision contradict the official version.

In this account, which was first published in *Dialogue: A Journal of Mormon Thought*,[41] **the evil power** that overcomes Joseph **is mentioned for the very first time**. In all previous published accounts (listed above), no evil power was ever mentioned. **Joseph also does not claim that the messengers were God and Jesus.** Instead, he simply states that **many angels visited him.** He also claims that at the time of the vision, he was 14 years old.

The problems with this version are obvious. Previously, Joseph said that he prayed and simply received an answer. This time, however, the story is more mysterious because there is something trying to prevent him from praying or from getting an answer: an evil power. His prayer is still answered, but there is a conspicuous absence of God the Father and Jesus Christ from the account. It is merely "many angels" that visit him. As with the previous account, it is impossible to believe that Joseph would have forgotten that the messenger was Jesus, as he said in his first handwritten account.

Version 5[42]

In 1837, William Appleby[43] recorded in his diary the vision story as related by Orson Pratt. In this version, the revival was not until **1822, Joseph was 17**, and **the visitors were not God and Jesus,** but beings who identified themselves only as **angels** who claimed to have **forgiven Joseph's sins**. This account is a thirdhand account, which raises the question whether the details given are accurate at all. However, it seems curious that such an important detail as Jesus having visited Joseph Smith would be left out, while other seemingly nonessential details were included.

Normally, a thirdhand account such as this would not carry much weight. But other statements of LDS leaders throughout the early years of the LDS Church have verified the differing details of this version. Brigham Young, Wilford Woodruff, John Taylor, George Q. Cannon, Orson Hyde, and George A. Smith all state that Joseph was visited not by God or Jesus but by angels.[44] Even Joseph Smith's own diary recorded that this vision was merely a "visitation of angels."[45] Such corroborative information makes this account worthy of consideration. It shows that Appleby recorded the information correctly, and that Orson Pratt was giving the details as he had heard them from Joseph. Since so many early leaders who were close to Joseph Smith gave the details the same in their accounts, they are very likely to have all gotten the same information from him.

In addition, the discourses and statements of the early LDS apostles and prophets (as published in many books by the LDS Church) along with early historical events of interest to the Mormon Church were mainly recorded in the diaries and journals of the early Mormons. The LDS Church considers these thirdhand accounts to be valid enough to accept them for inspirational material wherever they see fit. It would be inconsistent for the Mormons to accept only those accounts that support their teachings, but to flatly disregard all those with which they disagree. Orson Pratt was an eyewitness to the early events of Mormonism and to the life of Joseph Smith. Therefore, his version of the events is important for consideration.

Version 6[46]

This is the officially accepted version of the first vision, published in *Times and Seasons* on 1 April 1842. While not published until 1842, the account was ostensibly written in 1838, according to the LDS *History of the Church*.[47] Other LDS writers list the date of the original manuscript as 1839.[48]

In this account, Joseph was 14 when he received his first vision. After pondering James 1:5, he retired to the woods in an effort to pray. **His purpose** for praying **was to know which of all the** churches was correct. **The very moment he knelt down** to pray, he was overcome by the **dark power** of an enemy. He is released from the power by a light from heaven. **Two personages visit** him, one identifying the other as **"My Beloved Son."** He was told **not to join any of the churches**, for they were **all wrong**.

Version 7[49]

On 18 April 1841, Joseph Smith's brother, William Smith, told the first vision story to James Murdock. This account is published in the *Congregational Observer 2*, dated 3 July 1841. It gives Joseph's **age as 17** when he received the vision, and **rather than God and Jesus appearing** to him, William states that **it was only a "glorious angel."**

Admittedly, this account is another thirdhand account, and William could certainly have been mistaken about Joseph's age. But we must also consider that other accounts have placed his age at 17 as well, corroborating William's information. But even if he were mistaken about Joseph's age, it is not likely that he would forget that God Himself and Jesus Christ had visited his brother, unless William had never been told that.

This account is also substantiated by other sources. For example, in the early LDS publication *Times and Seasons*,[50] Oliver Cowdery stated specifically that Joseph Smith was 17 at the time of the first vision, and placed the year of the vision in 1823. And in at least seven places in the *Journal of Discourses*,[51] early LDS leaders agreed that it was only an unidentified angel that visited Joseph, not God and Jesus. In fact, Brigham Young even states **specifically** that the Lord did not visit young Joseph. In reference to this first vision, Young says, "**The Lord did not come** with the armies of heaven ... But **He did send His angel** to this same obscure person, Joseph Smith jun ... and informed him that he should not join any of the religions of the day, for they were all wrong...."[52]

William Smith's account was also printed in part in the Reorganized LDS Church[53] publication *The Saint's Herald*.[54] No corrections or retractions of the information published there were ever printed. Keeping in mind that both the Salt Lake City LDS

Church and the Missouri RLDS Church share the same history for the early years of their existence, what one Church has recorded about initial events in their history is significant to both, especially in matters pertaining to the life of Joseph Smith. Contradictions regarding his vision would affect the credibility of both groups.

In 1883, William Smith published a book about Mormonism, and again he shared the details of the first vision. Again he claims that the heavenly visitor was only an unnamed angel.[55]

Finally, LDS scholars deemed this account worthy of consideration. Dean Jessee discussed it in *BYU Studies* in the Spring 1969 issue.[56] James Allen also mentioned it in a 1966 article for *Dialogue: A Journal of Mormon Thought.*[57] While Jessee speculates as to why the account differs in the details, he never doubts the veracity of the information. Therefore, we are also at liberty to scrutinize the account as historically valid.

Version 8[58]

On 1 March 1842, the *Times and Seasons* published the contents of a letter written by Joseph Smith to John Wentworth.[59] This was published one month before the account that is accepted as the official version today.

In this account, Joseph Smith did not give his age. **He mentioned no evil power** overcoming him. Finally, **he said two personages visited** him, though **he never identified them.**

It is significant that he did not mention the evil power that played so prominently in the story, adding—as it does—that edge of mystery, drama and fear. But it is even more significant that he neglected to mention that the personages visiting him were supposedly God the Father and Jesus Christ. That is one detail we would certainly expect to be included.

Version 9[60]

In August of 1843, Joseph Smith gave an interview to David White[61] of the *Pittsburgh Weekly Gazette*, who printed Joseph's recounting of the first vision on 15 September 1843. The interview was reprinted in the *New York Spectator* on 23 September 1843.

In this version, Joseph said he was 14 years old, and there was **no mention of any dark power trying to overcome him**. **Two personages** are mentioned, one who introduced the other as his "beloved Son."

Version 10[62]

Joseph Smith wrote a chapter on Mormonism for the book *He Pasa Ekklesia: An Original History of the Religious Denominations at Present Existing in the United States,*[63] published in 1844. In it, he also shares the first vision story.

In this account, Joseph says he was 14 years old. This time, rather than heavenly visitors coming to him, he claims he was **taken away in a vision**. **No evil power** is mentioned. **Two personages** come to him, though **neither is identified, nor does either one identify the other** in any manner. He was told that **all religious denominations were teaching incorrect doctrines**, and that **none were acknowledged by God** as his Church. He said he was "**expressly commanded**" not to go after any of them. Finally, **he was promised that the fulness of the gospel would eventually be revealed to him.**

Version 11[64]

On 24 May 1844, Alexander Niebaur[65] recorded the first vision in his journal as Joseph Smith had told it to him.

In this account, many of the details are the same as in the official version. However, the personage that visits him is **said to have blue eyes**, and **later another personage comes** to his side. One introduces the other as "My Beloved Son." But in this account, **Joseph was not told that all of the Christian sects were wrong**. Instead, he was **specifically told that the Methodists were not God's people.**

Why Varying Stories?

We are left, then, with various stories of this vital event. Joseph never did tell "but one story" of the first vision; he told several, as already shown by the published accounts and verified by statements of early LDS leaders. There is no way to tell, then, if the details are reliable, or if the vision itself really happened.

Was it one angel[66] or several[67] that visited Joseph? What was the identity of the heavenly visitor—was it Jesus alone,[68] Peter,[69] Nephi,[70] Moroni,[71] or was it Jesus and God?[72] Was he 14,[73] 16[74] or 17[75] years old when it happened? Was his reason for praying to get forgiveness,[76] to determine if there was a God[77] or to find out which religion was correct?[78] Was he overcome by a dark and evil power,[79] or not?[80]

Above all, we have to wonder why there are so many differing accounts? Fawn Brodie puts forth one theory. She writes,

> The awesome vision he described in later years was probably **the elaboration of some half-remembered dream** stimulated by the early revival excitement.... Or it may have been **sheer invention**, created some time after 1830 when the need arose for a magnificent tradition to cancel out the stories of his fortune-telling and money digging.[81]

Joseph Smith's mother believed that the whole first vision came about because of a family conversation. After the family had discussed the varying church beliefs, she claims that Joseph went up to his room and was "pondering in his mind which of the churches were the true one...." She then says that an angel appeared to him and told him all churches on earth were false and then informed him about the gold plates buried nearby.[82]

Grant Palmer also found the differing details of these vision accounts suspect. Even more strange was the fact that the first vision was conspicuously absent for so many years of the early LDS Church history. He writes, "These omissions are peculiar.... After twelve years of reflection, to then omit the role his 1820 vision played in the

Restoration ... suggests that when he rewrote his history in 1838, he reinterpreted his experience to satisfy institutional needs."[83]

What possible "institutional needs" could there have been? Brodie lists some, among them the accounts of Joseph Smith's involvement in fortune telling and money digging.[84] Palmer mentions the large apostasy from the Church in the mid-1830s as another possible reason,[85] and quotes Dean Jessee, "During this time of apostasy, approximately three hundred left the Church, representing about 15 percent of the Kirtland membership."[86]

Palmer adds that "three of the apostles no longer believed in the Book of Mormon and two more were out of favor with the church. All three witnesses to the Book of Mormon and three of the eight had defected. The entire Whitmer clan had left the church." Based on these facts, he concludes,

> Fearing the possible unraveling of the church, Joseph Smith took to reestablishing his authority. During this week of 7-13 April [1838], he contemplated rewriting his history. On April 26 he renamed the church [The Church of Jesus Christ of Latter-day Saints]. The next day he started dictating a new first vision narrative ... a revised and more impressive version of his epiphany....[87]

It was this newly dictated account that was so impressive and so detailed that became the officially accepted version of the first vision.

Conclusion

LDS scholar Marvin S. Hill studied the changes in the first vision accounts, and admitted that the 1838-39 account, which is currently presented as the "official version," was "streamlined for publication." That way it would be "more logical and compelling" for readers.[88] When Hill published a book on the subject seven years later, he conceded that "when Smith dictated a more polished version in 1838, **it was altered** in many details **and more elaborate**."[89]

Gordon B. Hinckley writes,

This transcendent experience [the first vision] opened the marvelous work of restoration.... For more than a century and a half, enemies, critics, and some would-be scholars have worn out their lives **trying to disprove** the validity of that vision. Of course **they cannot understand it**. The things of God are understood by the Spirit of God.... Much has been written, much will be written, in an effort to explain it away. The finite mind cannot comprehend it. But the testimony of the Holy Spirit ... bears witness that it is true, that **it happened as Joseph Smith said it happened**....[90]

To which, though, of all the different ways Joseph Smith said the vision happened is the Holy Spirit supposedly testifying? Understanding the first vision story is not difficult for anyone. In fact, it is not even difficult to understand why there are so many different versions of the account—because it is not true. It is a tale that was embellished over the years. Even some Mormon researchers agree that it was a story that evolved over time. Minister and LDS history researcher Wesley P. Walters writes,

> ... we received a letter from Dale Morgan, noted researcher and historian ... a descendant of Orson Pratt and highly respected as a historian by Mormons and non-Mormons alike.... Dale Morgan had reached the same conclusion as this writer regarding Joseph's early history ... that "it very readily becomes apparent **that the idea of a visitation from the Father and the Son was a late improvisation, no part at all of his original design**." He came to see that Joseph's early history has very little in it of base reality. There is **"progressive distortion of reality" as Joseph retells the story**.[91]

All these first vision accounts lead to the inevitable conclusion that the official version of it is, at best, unreliable. Smith may have had some kind of a dream or vision in his younger years, but he expanded it and/or changed the details each time he retold it.

It is likely that Joseph needed to make a better case for his assertion that he alone was called to restore the truth of the gospel to the earth. To establish his claim, he pointed to an early vision he allegedly had. In order to give the story more impact, he added elements to the original version, such as the evil power overcoming him and that it was God the Father and Jesus Christ who came in response. In the end, of all his accounts, it was this polished and heart-rending version that the LDS Church promotes today as fact.

However, the evidence shows clearly that this vision is not what today's Mormons believe it to be. Joseph may have had an experience early in his life, but if so, the details of it were embellished, exaggerated and enhanced as time went on. Even LDS writers and scholars have come to the same conclusion. The fact that it has been altered and expanded leaves no other conclusion than that it is a fable Smith created to try to establish his claim to divine authority.

Chapter 3
The Great Apostasy

Joseph Smith's Claim –
> ... the Gentiles received the covenant, and were grafted in ... but have departed from the faith that was once delivered to the Saints, and have broken the covenant....Have not the pride, high-mindedness, and unbelief of the Gentiles, provoked the Holy One of Israel to withdraw His Holy Spirit from them, and send forth His judgments to scourge them for their wickedness? This is certainly the case.... we may look at the Christian world and see the apostasy there has been from the apostolic platform....
> – *Teachings of the Prophet Joseph Smith*, 15

The Falling Away of the Christian Church

Complete Apostasy

Joseph Smith taught that there had been a total and complete apostasy (or falling away) of the Christian Church. In Mormonism, this is often called The Great Apostasy. This apostasy was the reason Smith was to "restore" the true gospel of Jesus Christ and reorganize the Church upon the earth.

As non-Mormon Lloyd Sharp states: "Of all the doctrines taught by the Mormon Church, **none is as key** to their beliefs **as the teaching of a total apostasy** of the early Christian Church. Indeed, there would be **no need** for the Mormon Church **if there was not a total apostasy**."[1] LDS Historian B. H. Roberts agrees, writing, "**Nothing less than a complete apostasy** from the Christian religion **would warrant the establishment** of the Church of Jesus Christ of Latter-day Saints."[2] LDS apologist Kent Jackson also affirms this, saying,

"**This is a fundamental belief** of our religion: if there had not been an apostasy, there would have been no need for a restoration."[3]

Retrospective Apostasy

In discussion with missionaries from the LDS Church, or members in general, it is usually brought out that the first time Joseph Smith learned of a complete apostasy was when he received his first vision. According to the official account, Joseph went to pray "to know which of all the sects was right." He said that when he knelt down to pray in the grove, "at this time **it had never entered into my heart** that all [Christian sects] were wrong."[4] Simple reading of the account shows otherwise, because just a few verses earlier he claims he was pondering on the subject and wondered, "Who of all these parties are right; or, **are they all wrong together**"?[5]

But as seen in Chapter 2, **the first vision was a story that grew and developed over time**. Its details emerged and were elaborated as the Mormon Church grew. Did the teaching of a complete apostasy emerge over time as well, or was it Smith's claim from the very beginning? The available evidence leaves doubt that Smith claimed it all along. It is possible that he claimed there had been a general apostasy in the Christian Church—this was a fairly common view of Christianity at the time and the prevailing opinion of Smith's family.[6] The belief of a complete apostasy was not incorporated into the first vision story, however, until around 1832 or 1833.

The early revelations given through Smith do not mention a complete apostasy. In fact, some of them teach that the church still existed, but needed reform. For example, in a revelation dated March 1829, God informed Smith that "if the people of this generation harden not their hearts, **I will work a reformation among them**...."[7] "Reformation" could certainly imply a partial apostasy, but not a complete one. By 1830, however, it was being taught that there needed to be a "restoration of all things."[8] Of course, if the Church needed to be "restored," it must have been entirely lost.

The first time that an account of the first vision mentions a complete apostasy was in the 1832-1833 account.[9] Though the official version says that Smith had never before thought all churches could be wrong, in this account he had already decided that fact for himself. He writes, "by Searching the Scriptures I found that mand <mankind> did not come unto the Lord but that **they had apostatised** from the true and liveing faith and **there was no society or denomination that built upon the Gospel of Jesus Christ** as recorded in the new testament...."[10]

Grant Palmer writes that "Joseph [Smith] concluded prior to 1820 that none of the churches was right."[11] This is most likely true. Certainly the *Book of Mormon* manuscript teaches a complete apostasy. This would reflect Smith's personal views back at that time. Second Nephi 28:12 says, "Because of pride, and because of false teachers, and false doctrine, their churches have become corrupted...." Mormon 8:28 adds, "Yea, it shall come in a day when the power of God shall be denied, and churches become defiled and be lifted up in the pride of their hearts...."

But even so, Joseph must have had some doubts about all religions being wrong, for he requested to join the Methodist Church in Harmony, Pennsylvania, in the summer of 1828.[12] As Palmer observes,

> Had Lucy [Smith] **heard her son say that Jesus Christ personally instructed him** "to go not after them [Christian denominations]" and **to not "join any" church because** "all" of the ministers, creeds, and churches "**were an abomination in his sight**," she and her several children certainly would not have joined the Presbyterians and worshipped with them from 1825 until 1828. **Nor is it probable that Joseph would have participated with the Methodists** between 1820-28.[13]

In 1829, hints about an apostasy could be seen in revelations to the Church. Hyrum Smith was told, "you need not suppose that you are called to preach until you are called: wait a little longer, **until you shall have my word, my Rock, my church, and my gospel**, that you may know of a surety my doctrine...."[14] Joseph revealed that "**the world is ripening in iniquity**, and it must needs be, that the children of men are stirred up unto repentance...."[15]

By 1830, the apostasy was being clearly mentioned in revelations: "... I say unto you that ye are called to lift up your voices ... to declare my gospel unto **a crooked and perverse generation** ... **my vineyard has become corrupted every whit; and there is none which doeth good** save it be a few; and **they err** in many instances because of priestcrafts, **all having corrupt minds**."[16] "And it shall come to pass that there shall be a great work in the land, even among **the Gentiles, for their folly and their abominations** shall be made manifest in the eyes of all people."[17]

Smith was definitely teaching about a complete apostasy by 1831. In a letter to her older brother, Joseph's mother writes that "we can see the situation in which the world now stands that the eyes of the whole world are blinded, that **the churches have all become corrupted**, yea **every church** upon the face of the earth; that **the Gospel of Christ is nowhere preached**. [T]his is the situation which the world is now in...."[18] In a revelation to Joseph later that year, the following is recorded, "And the anger of the Lord is kindled ... and it shall fall upon the inhabitants of the earth.... **For they have strayed from mine ordinances**, and have **broken mine everlasting covenant**; **They seek not the Lord** to establish his righteousness, but **every man walketh in his own way**...."[19]

While the teaching of a general Christian apostasy had probably taken root in Joseph Smith's mind early, it was not expressed as a **complete apostasy** until some time later. It was also not coupled with the first vision until the later 1830s.[20] As Smith taught a complete apostasy of the Christian church more openly, his claim to a restored authority was more readily accepted. Merging his teaching of the apostasy with the account of his first vision, then, gave his claim more weight.

Complete Apostasy Taught Ever Since

Once this teaching was openly given by Joseph Smith as doctrine and had been retroactively added to the Church's history, it was widely accepted and believed. Mormon leaders have taught it as unquestioned truth ever since.

James E. Talmage:

We affirm that the great apostasy was foretold by the Savior Himself while He lived as a Man among men, and by His inspired prophets both before and after the period of His earthly probation.[21]

Joseph Fielding Smith:

It is true that the time came when **there was no one left** in mortal life **with authority** to organize and set in order the kingdom of God.... During the dark period after the death of all but one of the apostles and their rightful successors holding the divine authority, **there was no person on the earth who was authorized to restore the Holy Priesthood**.... after false teachings and organizations had been introduced, the time came when **the pure gospel of Jesus was not found among men on the earth**; false ordinances and doctrine had been substituted for the divine truth in all parts of the earth....[22]

Spencer W. Kimball:

It [the Church] **was lost**—the gospel with its powers and blessings—sometime after the Savior's crucifixion and the loss of his apostles. The laws were changed, the ordinances were changed, and the everlasting covenant was broken.... There was a long period of centuries when **the gospel was not available to people on this earth**, because it had been changed.[23]

Mark E. Petersen:

Then with his warning these chosen servants of the Lord, these authorities of the early day Church, went forth as commanded by the Lord, and they tasted of the opposition in all things. There was opposition within the Church, and there was opposition out of the Church. Persecution both within and without increased. **The spirit of apostasy spread, and finally apostasy overcame the Church.** The leaders of the Church were destroyed, and taken out of the ministry. The people were left in darkness, and gross darkness covered their minds, and **we had a complete apostasy** from the truth.[24]

Ezra Taft Benson:

Not only by history, which is quite conclusive, but through prophecy also we have been informed definitely that **there was and there would be a complete apostasy from the truth**. Many of the early reformers recognized this fact as they struck out against the false teachings and practises of their day.[25]

Bruce R. McConkie:

There is to be **absolute, total, complete apostasy** after John's day and before the angelic ministrations commence. **The falling away shall be complete, the apostasy universal.** Gross darkness shall be everywhere. **The gospel shall not be found in any nation**, among any kindred; no tongue shall teach its truths, and no people rejoice in its blessings, for all these shall receive it as a result of the angelic ministrations.[26]

Complete Apostasy Not Biblical

In the LDS manual *Duties and Blessings of the Priesthood*, it is stated that

> for some time after Jesus ascended to heaven, the Church continued to teach the truth and thousands of people from many cities joined the Church. However, in time, history

repeated itself. Some who had joined the Church refused to obey the laws and ordinances of the gospel and changed them to suit their own ways of thinking. At the same time, many members, including the Apostles and other priesthood leaders, were persecuted and killed. As these men were killed and others fell away from the truth, **the Church lost the authority of the priesthood.** The time came when **the priesthood no longer remained** in the Church.... churches which were organized during the great apostasy **did not have the priesthood.** As a result, they could not receive direction from God or perform the ordinances of salvation.[27]

Wilford Woodruff taught, "There was **no man on the face of the earth** [in Joseph Smith's time], nor had not been for the last seventeen centuries, **who had power and authority from God** to go forth and administer in one of the ordinances of the house of God."[28] The belief in **a complete and total apostasy of the Christian Church**, then, becomes the very basis for the LDS priesthood claims. If there was no complete apostasy, then there was no need for this restoration.

In fact, the introduction to the *History of the Church* states that "**nothing less than a complete apostasy** from the Christian religion **would warrant the establishment** of the Church of Jesus Christ of Latter-day Saints."[29] James E. Talmage affirms this, "**If the alleged apostasy** of the primitive Church **was not a reality**, the Church of Jesus Christ of Latter-day Saints **is not the divine institution** its name proclaims."[30]

Any honest student of the Bible and history will readily accept the fact that an apostasy has taken place. The Apostle Paul did give warning concerning the coming apostasy,[31] which had already begun in New Testament times.[32] In defense of Smith's claim of complete apostasy, Mormons point to many Bible passages. Among them, the most prominent are Amos 8:11-12; Isaiah 60:2; Matthew 24:3-13; Acts 20:29-30; Galatians 1:6-9; 2 Thessalonians 2:1-3; 2 Timothy 3:1-5 and 4:3-4.[33]

Do these references cited really support their claim? Christian writer James Holding points out that it is always assumed, not proved, that any reference to a false teaching, or a rebellion, or to an apostasy, is *de facto* evidence of "the" apostasy that Mormon apologists claim took place. **Upon investigation, the citations prove to be** either to a false teaching with known content **that does not correspond to the apostasy** ... or else have **no specific referent** as to the content or nature of the apostasy.... It is illegitimate to argue that the occurrence of one apostasy proves the existence of another specific apostasy....[34]

A study of these passages shows that Holding is right: they do not teach what the Mormon Church claims.

Amos 8:11-12

Behold, the days come, saith the Lord GOD, that I will send a famine in the land, not a famine of bread, nor a thirst for water, but of hearing the words of the LORD: And they shall wander from sea to sea, and from the north even to the east, they shall run to and fro to seek the word of the LORD, and shall not find it.

Mormons explain that the "famine" of "hearing the words of the LORD" refers to a period of complete apostasy after the time of Christ, wherein the true gospel had been corrupted and as a result had been taken from the earth. James Talmage tells us that this passage is "applicable to the period when there should be no Church of Christ to be found, and when, in consequence there should be lamentation and suffering...."[35] Apostle Richard Lyman, after quoting Amos 8:11, comments, "Thus there is predicted **a time when the gospel of Jesus Christ cannot be found** anywhere."[36]

Is this what Amos was really referring to? He was preaching during a time when the Israelites had become secure and smug both politically and spiritually. They were positive that God favored them, so they became complacent. The whole nation was characterized by three attitudes identified in Chapter 6: they were "complacent,"[37] felt "secure"[38] and had "pride."[39] They had fallen into this condition many times before. Each time, God chastened them. When they found themselves in distress, they always turned back to the Lord for a prophetic word of guidance and hope. This time, though, when God's punishment would come, God would remain silent. True to His word, when Israel went into captivity in Assyria nearly 40 years later, no word from the Lord could be found.[40]

This prophecy cannot apply to the period of Church history referred to by Mormons for several reasons. This was a prophecy to Israel for her rebellion, while the Church after Christ's ascension was sent mainly to the Gentiles. Also, the "word of the Lord," the Scriptures, were not lost during the period Mormons call the Great Apostasy. In fact, there was far more of God's Word available to them than even Israel had when this prophecy was given. Finally, the period of famine was to end with God restoring Israel.

Amos 9:14-15 makes this clear:

> And I will bring again the captivity of my people of Israel,[41] and they shall build the waste cities, and inhabit them; and they shall plant vineyards, and drink the wine thereof; they shall also make gardens, and eat the fruit of them. And I will plant them upon their land, and they shall no more be pulled up out of their land which I have given them, saith the LORD thy God.

This did not happen in 1830 through Joseph Smith. It happened over a period of time beginning under the reign of Cyrus (559-530 BC) and took over 100 years.[42]

Isaiah 60:2

> For, behold, the darkness shall cover the earth, and gross darkness the people: but the LORD shall arise upon thee, and his glory shall be seen upon thee.

Mormons believe that the "darkness" here refers to a period of time when God's word and authority are completely lost to the earth. LDS leader Thomas Monson explains it this way, referring to Isaiah's prophecy: "The bright daylight of enlightenment slipped away, and the lengthening shadows of a black night enshrouded the earth. One word and one word alone describes **the dismal state that prevailed: apostasy.**"[43]

Bruce McConkie makes reference to this Isaiah passage, saying,

> When the gospel sun went down almost two millennia ago, **when the priesthood was taken away** and a dreary dusk descended in the congregations that once had known light, when **light and truth no longer shone forth from heaven**, and when those on earth no longer were taught and directed by apostles and prophets, then spiritual darkness reigned. Darkness covered the earth and **gross darkness** the minds of the people.[44]

As with many Mormon explanations, their interpretation of this verse fails to understand the context. Isaiah is using this passage to explain to Israel that she alone of all the nations possesses the light of God. Verse 2 contrasts Israel's chosen position with the state of the world, which is in darkness. But, Isaiah promises, the light will come to them also. Verse 3 says, "And the Gentiles shall come to thy light, and kings to the brightness of thy rising." Since this passage is comparing Israel to the world, it could not be referring to a state of complete apostasy in a yet unformed church.

Acts 20:29-30

> For I know this, that after my departing shall grievous wolves enter in among you, not sparing the flock. Also of your own selves shall men arise, speaking perverse things, to draw away disciples after them.

LDS writer Richard Anderson explains the LDS view on this verse when he writes,

The real threat to the Church was not opposition **but inner corrosion**. Here Paul's last prophecy on the Church fits his last recorded speech on the subject, Acts 20. Both carry the same pessimism about the Church's future and the same mechanism **for its failure**. What made Paul's Ephesian farewell heartrending to him was not his leaving **but his realizing that the great flock he had gathered would be divided and spoiled**. There would be successors to the apostles, **but not true successors**, for after Paul left would come "savage wolves ... not sparing the flock" (Acts 20:29, *NKJB*).[45]

Ezra Taft Benson adds:

As the restored Church, **we affirm that with the passing of the apostolic age, the Church drifted into a condition of apostasy**, that succession in the priesthood was broken, and that the Church, as an earthly organization operating under divine direction and having authority to officiate in spiritual ordinances, **ceased to exist**.... We affirm also that all this was foreseen and predicted by the apostles when they were living, yea, and by the Master in his day. The apostasy had started during the days of the Apostles.... You are acquainted with the quotation in Paul's reference to the situation as he met with the elders of Ephesus for the last time when he said, "For I know this, that after my departing shall grievous wolves enter in among you, not sparing the flock." (Acts 20:29.)[46]

Once again, these explanations fail to understand the context of the passage. Benson does correctly mention that in this passage, Paul is speaking specifically to the elders of the Church in Ephesus.[47] But Benson then draws the wrong conclusion as to the scope of the message. Paul is warning those elders of something that was going to happen in their own church, not all over the world. Though the **warning** certainly applies to every church to watch for such things, the **prophecy** was specific to the Church in Ephesus.

John MacArthur[48] writes,

> True to Paul's prediction, false teachers did come in among the flock at Ephesus and attack it (cf. Rev. 2:2).... In his letters to Timothy (who was then the pastor of the Ephesian church), Paul condemned the false teachers who had arisen from within the Ephesian congregation (1 Tim. 1:2-7; 2 Tim. 3:1-9), even naming some of them (1 Tim. 1:20; 2 Tim. 1:15; 2:17).[49]

Translator and commentator David Williams[50] adds, "In the previous verse [Acts 20:29] the danger was from without. Here, [Acts 20:30] Paul speaks of the danger from within—of teachers who would arise from among the Ephesians themselves to seduce the congregation."[51]

This passage speaks of attacks on a specific congregation, the Ephesian Church, even though such attacks are possible on all churches. In fact, the Ephesian Church even withstood these attacks and survived, according to Revelation 2:1-3.[52]

2 Thessalonians 2:3

> Let no man deceive you by any means: for that day shall not come, except there come a falling away first, and that man of sin be revealed, the son of perdition;

Assistant LDS Church Historian Andrew Jenson writes, "**The Church**, which was established on the earth by Jesus Christ and his Apostles anciently, **ceased in course of time to exist**, through the martyrdom of many of its chief representatives and the final 'falling away' of the remnant of its members, as predicted by the Apostle Paul (2 Thess. 2:3).... "[53] Joseph Fielding Smith explains, "The apostasy did not come suddenly. It was a gradual development and commenced while some of the apostles were still living. Paul ... warned the members of the Church in Thessalonica not to be deceived regarding the ushering in of the second advent of Jesus Christ |2 Thess. 2:3|."[54]

This LDS argument is reading into the Biblical text something that is not there. In context, Paul is writing to the Thessalonians to correct an error in their belief. Many of them had feared that they had somehow missed the "day of the Lord."[55] Paul is explaining to them in verse 3 that they did not miss it, for there are still specific events that have to happen first. He names two: a "falling away" and that a "man of sin be revealed."

What is this "falling away?" It is not a generalized apostasy. Paul uses the definite article in this verse, so that it means not **an** apostasy, but **the** apostasy. There have always been apostate churches and individuals. MacArthur explains, "Such generalized apostasy, because it is always present, cannot signify a particular time period. Therefore, it cannot be the specific event Paul has in mind."[56] What then is Paul referring to?

The Greek word used here is *apostasia*.[57] Concerning this word, Greek linguist Spiros Zodhiates writes that it "does not refer to the Christians who would depart from the faith, but those who would reject Christ."[58] Williams explains, "Some have understood the *apostasia* as a falling away within the church, but the word expresses not so much apathy as deliberate opposition, and it is better to see this as a reference to events outside the church which, however, will profoundly affect the church."[59]

This is not a falling away from the Church, so it cannot refer to a "Great Apostasy," as Mormons define it. Since this word refers to a deliberate defiance against Christ, it must be a specific event. Paul tells us which event by coupling it with the "man of sin" being "revealed." That revelation will take place when he "opposeth and exalteth himself above all that is called God, or that is worshipped; so that he as God sitteth in the temple of God, shewing himself that he is God."[60]

This is the same event mentioned in Revelation 13:1-17. All those who worship this "man of sin," taking his side instead of Jesus', will be in open rebellion against Christ. They will be the ones committing this *apostasia*. Could some of them come out of the Church? Certainly, but it still will not be a complete apostasy, because the ones who leave to side with the antichrist would not have been true believers in the first place.⁶¹ That is the event that Paul is speaking of in 2 Thessalonians 2:3.

MacArthur observes, "Paul's point is clear. The apostasy, Antichrist's blasphemous self-deification and desecration of the Temple, is a unique, unmistakable event that precedes the Day of the Lord. Since that clearly has not happened, the Day of the Lord cannot have arrived."⁶² Instead of a general apostasy **from within** the Church, Paul is speaking of a specific opposition to Christ yet to come **from outside** the Church.

How should the other verses mentioned be understood in context? The Matthew 24:3-13 passage speaks of many signs that will happen before the return of Christ. Apostasy is mentioned, but not a complete apostasy, as verse 13 indicates, "But he that shall endure unto the end, the same shall be saved." Galatians 1:6-9 refers to a specific problem in the Galatian Church, not to the entire worldwide Church. The 2 Timothy 3:1-5 and 4:3-4 passages also speak of the conditions of the end times, but never state that there would be a complete and total apostasy.

In the overall analysis of the many Bible verses Mormons use to support their claim of universal apostasy, we find that **not one** of them speaks of the apostasy as being total and complete. Many of them do not even apply to the Church or to the Church Age. Mormonism's claim of a complete apostasy is left, then, with no Biblical support.

Bible Passages Ignored

In order to accept the Mormon claim of a complete apostasy, many other Bible verses must be completely ignored. Consider the following passages:

Matthew 16:18

And I say also unto thee, That thou art Peter, and upon this rock I will build my church; and **the gates of hell shall not prevail against it.**

If the Church fell into complete apostasy a century later, then "the gates of hell" would have prevailed against Jesus' Church and this promise would be false.

John 10:28-29

And I give unto them eternal life; and they shall never perish, **neither shall any man pluck them out** of my hand. **My Father,** which gave them me, is **greater than all; and no man is able to pluck them out of my Father's hand.**

If God is truly greater than all, He could certainly hold His Church together and not allow it to fall into complete apostasy.

Romans 11:1-5

I say then, **Hath God cast away his people? God forbid....** God hath not cast away his people which he foreknew.... But what saith the answer of God unto him? **I have reserved to myself** seven thousand men.... Even so then **at this present time also there is a remnant** according to the election of grace.

God did not cast away Israel in favor of the Church, but keeps a remnant in His grace (salvation) always. He would not cast off the Church either, and leave the earth without a manifestation of His grace.

2 Peter 2:9

The Lord knoweth how to deliver the godly out of temptations, and to reserve the unjust unto the day of judgment to be punished:

God knows how to keep His people from falling into apostasy, and He is certainly powerful enough to accomplish it. Throughout the Old Testament, God kept his chosen people Israel together. When they went astray, they were disciplined and corrected. For hundreds of years, God kept them from falling into complete apostasy. Why would Jesus take such care and trouble to form the New Testament Church, only to have it be completely lost again within 100 years? How likely is it that God would allow His only Son to die on the cross for sin, just to have that sacrifice be ineffectual for 1700 years? Why send His Son to earth to form the Church at all, only to have it completely corrupted so quickly after His departure? It makes no sense, and, if true, would show God to be virtually powerless against the forces of Satan.

Complete apostasy is not what these verses describe. After carefully examining the Bible verses Mormons cite, Christian writer Marvin Cowan concludes, "**But not a single one** of those verses **says that there will be a complete or total apostasy**, and some do not even apply to the church! The Bible teaches that apostasy had already begun in New Testament times.... But nowhere does it even infer that this will be a complete or total apostasy."[63] As Bill McKeever of Mormonism Research Ministry points out, "To say there was a total apostasy would be to credit Jesus Christ with a gross lie."[64] He continues, saying that it would be wrong "if Christ were to neglect the welfare of His church. Accusing Him of letting His church fall into a total apostasy would be blasphemous."[65]

By reviewing several Mormon doctrines, James Holding shows that there could not have been a total apostasy as Mormons claim. If that were so, then their teachings in a number of different areas would of necessity also be false.[66] He concludes, "Mormonism survives only if the egregious error that it presumes must have happened—the apostasy of the early church—actually did happen.

If, as we have shown, there was no apostasy, then Mormonism is an anachronism."[67]

The Falling Away and Restoration ...

In the 1950s, the Missionary Department of the Mormon Church issued a pamphlet entitled *The Falling Away and Restoration of the Gospel of Jesus Christ Foretold*. For many years this was given away freely at LDS Visitor Centers.[68] The pamphlet claims that "confirming this loss of truth [a complete apostasy] are many voices of history's great Christian reformers."[69]

After the caption CHRISTIANITY HAS CEASED TO EXIST, Martin Luther is quoted:

> I have sought nothing beyond reforming the Church in conformity with the Holy Scriptures.... I simply say that Christianity has ceased to exist among those who should have preserved it.[70]

After the caption GIFTS OF THE HOLY GHOST NO LONGER FOUND, an excerpt from a sermon by John Wesley is also quoted:

> It does not appear that these extraordinary gifts of the Holy Ghost were common in the Church for more than two or three centuries. We seldom hear of them after that fatal period when the Emperor Constantine called himself a Christian.... From this time they almost totally ceased.... The Christians had no more of the Spirit of Christ than the other heathens.... This was the real cause why the extraordinary gifts of the Holy Ghost were no longer found in the Christian Church; because the Christians were turned Heathen again, and had only a dead form left.[71]

In addition, two early American leaders are cited in support of the LDS claim. Following the caption WAITING FOR NEW APOSTLES, Roger Williams is quoted as concluding:

There is no regularly constituted church on earth, nor any person qualified to administer any church ordinances; nor can there be until new apostles are sent by the Great Head of the Church for whose coming I am seeking.[72]

Below the caption SEES A RESTORATION OF CHRISTIANITY, Thomas Jefferson is quoted:

The religion builders have so distorted and deformed the doctrines of Jesus, so muffled them in mysticisms, fancies and falsehoods, have caricatured them into forms so inconceivable, as to shock reasonable thinkers.... Happy in the prospect of a restoration of primitive Christianity, I must leave to younger persons to encounter and lop off the false branches which have been engrafted into it by the mythologists of the middle and modern ages.[73]

These statements would seem to support the LDS claim of a complete apostasy. These same quotes have also been used in several Conference Addresses by LDS Apostles and other leaders[74] and printed in their books.[75] They were reprinted again in 1984 in the *Missionary Scripture Guide*,[76] and included in the *GospelLink 2001* CD-Rom.[77]

In brief, an examination of these statements and the views of those being quoted, shows that they were being misused in the pamphlet, in LDS materials, and by Church leaders.

Martin Luther (1483-1546)

The Luther quotation is taken from two sources. The first sentence of the statement says nothing about a universal apostasy. The key words are "**reforming** the Church," not **restoring** the Church, which Mormon doctrine requires. Luther's stated position was that "I have sought nothing beyond **reforming the Church** in conformity with the Holy Scriptures."[78] What no longer exists cannot be reformed. The LDS pamphlet has edited Luther's remarks (without ellipsis points), concealing the meaning of his statement. When complete it reads, "I simply say that [true] Christianity has ceased to exist among those who should have preserved it—**the bishops and scholars.**" He then states plainly, "**But I have no doubt that the truth has always continued to live in some,** if only in the souls of children in the cradle. I do not repudiate the Church Fathers. But like all men, they, too, have erred at times."[79]

Luther's doctrine of the Church is easily established by consulting *Luther's Works*. Here are some brief examples: "For the Church is ruled by the Spirit of God and the saints are led by the Spirit of God (Rom. 8[:14]). And **Christ remains with his Church even to the end of the world** [Matt. 28:20]; and the Church of God is the pillar and ground of the truth [1 Tim. 3:15]."[80] "Who, then, even at the present time **would venture to deny** that ... **God has preserved for himself a Church among the common people.** ..."[81] "But **it is impossible that there has been no church for fourteen hundred years.**"[82]

John Wesley (1703-1788)

In the sermon quoted ("The More Excellent Way"), Wesley is dealing with the disappearance of the "extraordinary gifts of the Holy Ghost." He had just explained them as referring to such gifts as "healing the sick, prophesying ... speaking with strange tongues ... and the miraculous interpretation of tongues." He then went on to explain that **these were not essential for Christianity to continue,** and that there was "a more excellent way," quoting 1 Corinthians 12:31. One should read Wesley's entire sermon.[83]

Is there other evidence that Wesley's sermon was misused— that **he did not believe in a total apostasy?** There is. Second Thessalonians 2:2-3 is often cited as a proof text by Mormons as it is in the LDS brochure (p. 2). While recognizing apostasy in the Church, Wesley specifically comments on this passage:

> Is not this the *falling away* or *apostasy* from God, foretold by St. Paul in his second epistle to the Thessalonians, chap. ii, 3? Indeed, **I would not dare to say,** with George Fox, **that**

> **this apostasy was universal**; that there never were any real Christians in the world, from the days of the apostles till this time.... **there are now and have always been individuals who were real Christians....**[84]

In another sermon, Wesley acknowledged a falling away by the church (excepting Smyrna and Philadelphia) from God's standards beginning in the first century, saying, "and from this time, for fourteen hundred years, it was corrupted more and more, as all history shows, till scarce any, either of the power or form of religion was left." He then concluded, "**Nevertheless it is certain, that the gates of hell did never totally prevail against it [the Church]. God always reserved a seed for himself; a few that worshipped him in spirit and in truth.**"[85]

Finally, Wesley viewed the 18th Century as one that God had specially blessed:

> For whoever makes a fair and candid inquiry, will easily perceive that true religion has in no wise decreased, but greatly increased in the present century.... Shall we now say, "The former days were better than these?" ... No "former time," since the apostles left the earth, has been better than the present. None has been comparable to it in several respects. We are not born out of due time, but in the day of his power; a day of glorious salvation....[86]

It should be pointed out that Wesley did not give up his membership or ordination in the Anglican Church,[87] which he most likely would have done had he truly believed the church had ceased to exist on the earth.

Roger Williams (ca. 1603-1683)

Because of his view of the necessity of apostolic succession, Roger Williams came to believe that "no apostolic or pastoral ministry and hence no true church of Christ existed or was possible," but "he did not conclude that all preaching of the gospel and all assemblies of worship must cease during the reign of Antichrist. Throughout this period, he thought God had raised up 'prophets in sackcloth' to lead His people through the wilderness. Such men needed no commission or any calling by a church; they acted from the Holy Spirit...."[88] Williams aspired to be one of those prophets, himself.[89]

In his biography of Williams, Edmund Morgan states,

> When his opponents accused him of denying the church altogether, he compared himself to one who suffers the night or an eclipse of the sun without denying the sun's existence. He never urged men to stop worshipping God altogether; he kept discussing the proper form for the church as though it still existed; he even seemed to suggest that men should continue to search for a pure church and go through the motions of church worship while awaiting the return of Christ. But he could not conscientiously join with any group of worshippers who took upon themselves the name of a church.
>
> Williams longed to think that this problem would shortly be solved by Christ Himself.[90]

In what way did Williams believe that the "problem would shortly be solved by Christ Himself"? Certainly not by the Mormon's claimed restoration of the Church in 1830, but **by the Second Coming** and millennial rule of Jesus Christ[91]—which even the Mormons teach is still future.[92]

Finally, as Morgan concludes, "But though Williams' arguments often provide the logic for the conclusion, none of his voluminous publications and none of his surviving private letters were written for the purpose of persuading others that the church was dead."[93]

Thomas Jefferson (1743-1826)

It is surprising that anyone claiming to be informed would quote Thomas Jefferson in support of a complete apostasy of the Christian Church and a needed restoration. Jefferson was not a Christian. He has been identified by various terms, however. According to Adrienne Koch, his biographer, "Jefferson has at times been called atheist, deist, freethinker, Unitarian, Episcopalian, Socinian,"[94] and "at least toward the end of his life, was content to call himself a Unitarian."[95] After further examination of Jefferson's philosophy, Koch concludes, "Jefferson was thus a conservative materialist."[96]

In Jefferson's thinking a **departure from the teachings of Jesus were to be found in the writings of His disciples found in the Bible.** By editing "the Gospels by selecting only the 'genuine' statements of Jesus and rejecting the **'spurious' ones written by his misguided or dishonest disciples**, Jefferson trusted to disclose a new picture of Christianity."[97] "**Jefferson ... rejected miracles, inspiration, and revelation without compromise**; he was **acridly critical of the ignorance and fallibility of the apostles**, particularly denouncing St. Paul as the principal corrupter of the doctrines of Christ."[98]

Jefferson **rejected any supernatural interpretation of Jesus' person or inspiration,** claiming **He was only a man.**[99] While Jefferson did believe in "a Fabricator of all things ... a Superintending power"—he also wrote that "of the nature of this Being we know nothing."[100] In his humanistic interpretation of Christianity, what Jefferson meant by a "restoration of primitive Christianity," certainly was not the restoration of the church, apostles, ordinances, etc.—the Mormon view of the restoration—but a restoration of "the genuine and simple religion of Jesus ... such as it was preached and practiced by himself."[101]

LDS Scriptures and Authorities Contradict Apostasy Claim

The LDS claim of total Christian apostasy is also contradicted by teachings in their own scriptures. In the *Pearl of Great Price*, we read,

> And thus the Gospel began to be preached, from the beginning, being declared by holy angels sent forth from the presence of God, and by his own voice, and by the gift of the Holy Ghost. And thus all things were confirmed unto Adam,

by an holy ordinance, and the Gospel preached, and **a decree sent forth, that it should be in the world, until the end thereof; and thus it was.** Amen.[102]

If the gospel to be preached was given to Adam and was decreed by God to continue until the end of the earth, then where is there room for the total apostasy? This would contradict the clear teaching of this Mormon scripture. And this is not the only place where this view is contradicted.

McKeever writes,

> The claim of a total apostasy **not only contradicts the message in the Bible**, but **also contradicts the *Book of Mormon*.** Third Nephi 28:1-8 tells us that Jesus Christ supposedly told three Nephite disciples that they would never taste of death but remain alive until the Lord's coming in the clouds. Three of Christ's own disciples were actually to remain alive on this earth until the second coming. Did they apostatize also? A total apostasy would mean that they had.[103]

The chapter summary for 3 Nephi 28 states, "*The Three Nephites desire and are given power over death so as* ***to remain on the earth until Jesus comes again*** *... and* ***they are now ministering*** *among men.*"[104] According to the *Book of Mormon* timeline, given at the bottom of each page, this occurred in "A.D. 34-35." This was long before the LDS claim that the New Testament Church had become completely apostate. Certainly with these Nephite Apostles on the earth until Christ returns, there could not have been a total apostasy. Even if the rest of the world had turned apostate, these men would remain.

In addition, Joseph Smith revealed that the Apostle John also remains alive on earth preaching the gospel.

> And the Lord said unto me: John, my beloved, what desirest thou? For if you shall ask what you will, it shall be granted unto you. And I said unto him: Lord, give unto me power

over death, that I may **live and bring souls unto thee.** And the Lord said unto me; Verily, verily, I say unto thee, because thou desirest this **thou shalt tarry until I come in my glory,** and shalt prophesy before nations, kindreds, tongues and people.[105]

According to this, there are now **four Apostles commissioned by Christ that remained alive** and "tarried" from then until now. If this is true, there could not have been a complete apostasy. As Joseph Fielding Smith informs us,

> ... if [the First Presidency, the Twelve Apostles and all Church leaders] ... were killed off, and yet there was one Elder, possessing the Melchisedec Priesthood, he would have authority to organize the Church, under the command of God and the guidance of His Holy Spirit, as Joseph did in the beginning; that it should be re-established in its perfect form.[106]

In reply, Mormon apologists point to Mormon 1:13 (dated AD 322), where it is written, "But wickedness did prevail upon the face of the whole land, insomuch that the Lord did take away his beloved disciples, and the work of miracles and of healing did cease because of the iniquity of the people." Here they claim that Jesus removed the Three Nephites from the earth, enabling the complete apostasy. But the *Doctrinal Commentary on the Book of Mormon* explains that the Three Nephites were **only removed from their work** among the wicked Nephites and Lamanites, **not from the earth.**[107] Even if they had been taken, **the Apostle John would still remain.**

If all four of them had been removed from the earth, then an even larger problem remains. It would mean that Jesus had lied. He had promised the Nephites that "ye shall never taste of death; but ye shall live to behold all the doings of the Father unto the children of men, even until all things shall be fulfilled according to the will of my Father, when I shall come in my glory with the powers of heaven."[108] Jesus' promise to John was essentially the same.[109] To promise them that they would live and work on earth until He returned, and then take them away nearly 300 years later, would constitute deception. Certainly, then, this cannot be the case.

Leaders Claim Apostles Remain on Earth

Over the years, LDS leaders have affirmed that these Apostles **did remain on earth:**

> ... in a little while you will find another prophecy will be fulfilled, and that is the prophecy that Jesus made to **the three Nephites who,** having power over death, **are still living upon this continent**.... You will find that many districts where the Elders of Israel cannot reach will be penetrated by these men who have power over death.... My testimony is that **these men are going abroad in the nations of the earth** before the face of your sons, and they are preparing the hearts of the children of men to receive the Gospel. **They are administering** to those who are heirs of salvation, and preparing their hearts to receive the truth, just as the farmer prepares the soil to receive the seed.[110]

> The first quorum of Apostles were all put to death, **except John,** and we are informed that **he still remains on the earth,** though his body has doubtless undergone some change. **Three of the Nephites,** chosen here by the Lord Jesus as his Apostles, **had the same promise**—that they should not taste death until Christ came, and **they still remain on the earth in the flesh.**[111]

> We know that **John the Revelator and the three Nephites** were granted the privilege of **remaining on the earth in the translated state, to "bring souls unto Christ."** ... It is reasonable to believe that **they were engaged in this work** as far as the Lord permitted them to go **during these years of spiritual darkness.** There are legends and stories which seem to be authentic, showing that these holy messengers

were busy among the nations of the earth, and men have been entertained by them unawares.[112]

John the Beloved and the Three Nephites were translated. They were allowed **to live on, to minister on earth, to continue their apostolic duties** among the children of men until their Lord returned in glory at the time of his second coming.[113]

With John and the Three Nephites performing their apostolic duties since Christ was here, there could not have been a complete apostasy. Cowan points out that "such restoration and re-establishment, with the modern bestowal of the Holy Priesthood, **would be unnecessary and indeed impossible** had the Church of Christ continued among men with unbroken succession of Priesthood and power since the 'meridian of time.'"[114] This being the case, either Joseph Smith was wrong in making this claim, or the scriptures he produced are wrong, leaving a serious stumbling block to accepting his prophetic claim.

Conclusion

Today the Mormon Church teaches that there was a complete apostasy of the Christian Church. But this was not always the case. In the beginning, Joseph Smith simply felt it needed reform. Eventually, however, he concluded that all of the true Church and its authority had been entirely lost. By twisting the context of some Bible passages and ignoring others, Mormons try to support their current claim. They have followed the same pattern by misusing quotations from Christian and early American leaders. However, the Mormon's own scriptures and doctrines contradict this teaching.

Chapter 4
The Book of Mormon— Text Research

Joseph Smith's Claim –
> The Book of Mormon is a record of the forefathers of our western tribes of Indians ... translated into our own language by the gift and power of God.... I told the brethren that the Book of Mormon was the most correct of any book on earth, and the keystone of our religion, and a man would get nearer to God by abiding by its precepts, than by any other book.
> – *Teachings of the Prophet Joseph Smith*, 17, 194

The Book of Mormon

In any examination of the Church of Jesus Christ of Latter-day Saints, attention must inevitably be focused on the *Book of Mormon*. This book is considered by Mormons to be scripture, more correct than the Bible. The most common name that has been used to identify the LDS Church—Mormon (and its doctrinal system, Mormonism)—is taken from its title.

What Is It?

The *Book of Mormon* claims to be the writings of ancient American inhabitants. According to the book itself, a family of Jews migrated from the Old World to the American continents around 600 BC. They kept records that were engraved upon golden plates in a language called "Reformed Egyptian." These records told much of the history of the people, but centered mainly upon their religious beliefs and practices.

The *Book of Mormon* Brief Explanation explains that "in or about the year A.D. 421," a man named Moroni buried the bound set of golden plates in a hill called Cumorah[1] — the same hill Cumorah that is so identified today in upstate New York. The plates were allegedly given to Joseph Smith, Jr. in 1827, along with a spectacle-like device that was said to be the Urim and Thummim of the Bible. With it, Joseph Smith then "translated" about one-third of the material on the plates into the *Book of Mormon*.[2]

What Do Mormons Say About the Book?

The leadership of the LDS Church has consistently claimed that the *Book of Mormon* is the very cornerstone on which the Church is built. Joseph Smith himself stated, "Take away the Book of Mormon and the revelations, and where is our religion? We have none...."[3] He wrote that Mormons "believe the Book of Mormon to be the word of God."[4] Smith said, "I told the brethren that the Book of Mormon was **the most correct of any book** on earth, and **the keystone of our religion**, and a man would get nearer to God by abiding by its precepts, **than by any other book**."[5]

The Mormon Church teaches that the *Book of Mormon* is a book of scripture superior to any other book on earth. Bruce McConkie writes:

> Almost all of the doctrines of the gospel are taught in the Book of Mormon **with much greater clarity and perfection than** those same doctrines are revealed **in the Bible**. Anyone who will place in parallel columns the teachings of these two great books ... will find conclusive proof of **the superiority of Book of Mormon teachings**.[6]

On another occasion, McConkie makes the following remarks about the superiority of the *Book of Mormon*:

> **Men can get nearer to the Lord**, can **have more of the spirit** of conversion and conformity in their hearts, can **have stronger testimonies**, and can **gain a better understanding of the doctrines of salvation through the Book of Mormon than** they can through **the Bible**.... There will be more

people saved in the kingdom of God—ten thousand times over—**because of the Book of Mormon than there will be because of the Bible.**[7]

Not only will more people be saved because of the book, but according to Orson Pratt,

> **when a person ... rejects the** message of heaven in the **Book of Mormon ... he is cursed of God, and will die and go to hell,** unless he repents, notwithstanding his apparent honesty. Therefore, **no man,** nor woman, nor child ... **can be justified,** for one moment, **in rejecting** God's revealed will, contained in **the Book of Mormon....**[8]

Pratt also asserts that

> this book [of Mormon] must be **either true or false.** If true, it is one of the most important messages ever sent from God to man.... **If false, it is one of the most cunning, wicked, bold, deep-laid impositions ever palmed upon the world, calculated to deceive and ruin millions** who will sincerely receive it as the word of God.[9]

He adds, "if true, no one can possibly be saved and reject it [the *Book of Mormon*]; if false, no one can possibly be saved and receive it."[10]

Mormon leaders have consistently declared that the *Book of Mormon* is true and that there need not be any other evidence than the personal feelings of the heart to verify it. Ezra Taft Benson writes: "We do not have to prove the Book of Mormon is true. The book is its own proof. All we need to do is read it and declare it!"[11]

Gordon B. Hinckley, adds:

> As has been demonstrated for a hundred and fifty years, **the truth of the book will not be determined by literary analysis or by scientific research**, although these are reassuring and most welcome. **The truth will be determined** today

and tomorrow, as it has been throughout the yesterdays, **by the reading of it in a spirit of reverence and respect and prayer**.... **The evidence for its truth**, for its validity in a world that is prone to demand evidence, **lies not in archaeology or anthropology**, though these may be helpful to some. It lies not **in word research or historical analysis**, though these may be confirmatory. The evidence for its truth and validity lies within the covers of the book itself. **The test of its truth lies in reading it.** It is a book of God. Reasonable men may sincerely question its origin; but those who have **read it prayerfully** have come to know by a power beyond their natural senses that it is true....[12]

This evidence from prayer is suggested by one of the statements found within the *Book of Mormon* itself. In a verse identified as Moroni 10:4, this subjective, self-verifying test is given:

And when ye shall receive these things, I would exhort you that ye would **ask God**, the Eternal Father, in the name of Christ, **if these things are not true**; and if ye shall ask with a sincere heart, with real intent, having faith in Christ, **he will manifest the truth of it unto you, by the power of the Holy Ghost.**

In spite of Gordon Hinckley's statement that the validity and truthfulness of the *Book of Mormon* cannot be "determined by literary analysis or by scientific research," taking a closer look at the book **will show** whether it is really a volume of scripture given by God. Truth will remain true no matter how much it is analyzed or researched. "Prayerful" verification of the *Book of Mormon* has been and will always be a subjective test that proves nothing.[13]

Other Mormon leaders have seen the need for careful scrutiny of the book. B. H. Roberts states,

The fact should be recognized by the Latter-day Saints that **the Book of Mormon of necessity must submit to every test**, to literary criticism, as well as to **every other class of criticism;**

for our age is above all things critical, and especially critical of sacred literature, and we may not hope that the Book of Mormon will escape closest scrutiny; neither, indeed, is it desirable that it should escape. It is given to the world as a revelation from God. It is a volume of American Scripture. **Men have a right to test it by the keenest criticism**, and to pass severest judgment upon it, and we who accept it as a revelation from God have every reason to believe that **it will endure every test; and the more thoroughly it is investigated, the greater shall be its ultimate triumph.**[14]

Orson Pratt agrees, adding that

if, after a rigid examination, it [the *Book of Mormon*] **be found an imposition, it should be extensively published to the world as such;** the evidences and arguments on which the imposture was detected, should be clearly and logically stated, that those who have been sincerely yet unfortunately deceived, may perceive the nature of the deception.[15]

Why did LDS leaders have such a change of heart? They turned completely around from desiring that men put it to the test to telling their people **not** to test it. The reason is because men **had** tested it, and found that **it did not pass** the closest scrutiny and the most careful testing as they had hoped.

The rest of this chapter will examine the text of the *Book of Mormon* to see whether it is a true historical record. Much of the following information has been presented in greater detail in other published works. This chapter simply summarizes much of the available information. For those who wish to investigate further, the endnotes cite and recommend more detailed examinations.

Changes in the Text

Mormonism claims that when Joseph Smith translated the *Book of Mormon*, he accomplished it in a miraculous manner. God Himself supposedly supplied the very words that were to be used. Afterward,

Smith claimed that an angel from heaven stated, "These plates have been **revealed by the power of God**, and they have been **translated by the power of God**. The translation of them which you have seen **is correct**, and I command you to bear record of what you now see and hear."[16]

Edward Stevenson, an Elder in the Mormon Church during its early years, shares some information provided to him by Martin Harris, one of the scribes for the *Book of Mormon*:

> Martin explained the translation as follows: By aid of the seer stone,[17] sentences would appear and were read by the prophet and written by Martin, and when finished he would say, "Written," and if correctly written that sentence would disappear and another appear in its place, but if not written correctly it remained until corrected, so that **the translation was just as it was engraven on the plates, precisely in the language then used.**[18]

Early LDS pioneer Oliver Huntington writes in his journal about the translation of the *Book of Mormon* as he heard it from Joseph F. Smith—the nephew of Joseph Smith, Jr.—who later became the sixth president of the LDS Church:

> Joseph did not render the writing on the gold plates into the English language in his own style of language as many believe, but **every word & every letter was given to him by the gift & power of God**—so it is the work of God & not of Joseph Smith.... The Lord caused each word spelled as it is in the Book to appear on the stones in short sentences or words, and when Joseph had uttered the sentence or word before him & the Scribe had written it properly, that sentence would disappear & another appear. **And if there was a word wrongly written or even a letter incorrect the writing on the stones would remain there.** Then Joseph would require the Scribe to spell the reading of the last spoken & thus find the mistake, & when corrected the sentence or word would disappear as usual.[19]

Mormons today understand that this was the way the *Book of Mormon* was "translated," though they believe it was accomplished through the Urim and Thummim rather than a seer stone. LDS writer Grant Palmer points out,

> In other words, neither Mosiah [a *Book of Mormon* "prophet"] nor Joseph Smith could read the ancient scripts as a scholar would; rather, **they read what they saw, provided for them in their own language**, when they looked into the [translator's] stones. Converts to Mormonism in the early days understood that when Joseph looked in the seer stone, he **was shown the English text; he was a reader rather than a translator**. Martin Harris clerked for Joseph in 1828 and informed classical scholar Charles Anthon and ... John A. Clark that Joseph saw the text in English. Joseph simply "read" the translation, Harris said. When Joseph looked "through his spectacles ... [he] would then write down or repeat what he saw, which, when repeated aloud, was written down by Harris."[20]

If this was the procedure they used, then God gave the words **exactly** as they were to be printed in the *Book of Mormon*. No changes should ever be made in such an instance. This is, in fact, what several Mormon leaders have claimed over the years. For example, Joseph Fielding Smith said, "During the past week or two I have received a number of letters ... that there have been one or two or more thousand changes in the Book of Mormon since the first edition was published. Well, of course, **there is no truth in that statement**."[21]

B. H. Roberts (a very well-respected Mormon historian) admits that the *Book of Mormon* did have some errors, but he claims that "**the errors are constitutional in their character**; they are of the web and woof of the style, and not such errors as may be classed as typographical. Indeed the first edition of the Book of Mormon **is singularly free from typographical errors**."[22]

Another early LDS leader, John Widtsoe, writes that the *Book of Mormon* had not been changed at all. He says, "**It would not be possible to change any part of it** without being discovered."[23]

Widtsoe was right; changes have been discovered. As early as 1898, changes made to the *Book of Mormon* were being exposed. That year Lamoni Call published a book entitled *2000 Changes in the Book of Mormon*.[24] Again in 1965, Jerald and Sandra Tanner published *3,913 Changes in the Book of Mormon*—a photo-reprint of the original 1830 *Book of Mormon* with all the changes marked.

Even LDS writers admit that many changes have been made to the text of the *Book of Mormon*. Roberts, quoted earlier, writes, "**Many errors**, verbal and grammatical, **have already been eliminated** in the later English editions...."[25] Dr. Sidney Sperry from BYU[26] also admits that changes have been made. He writes,

> The writer happens to know that Dr. [James E.] Talmage was a stickler for good English and a close student of the text of the Book of Mormon. He knew as well as anyone the imperfections of the literary dress of the First Edition of the Nephite record and took a prominent part **in correcting many of them in a later edition** of the work (1920).[27]

LDS apologist Hugh Nibley writes, "**Sometimes the editors** of later editions of the Book of Mormon **have made 'corrections'** that were better left unmade."[28] If the descriptions of the translation process are correct, and if Joseph Smith's comments about the book are correct, and if the voice from heaven truly revealed that the first edition text was correct, then **no change** should ever have been made to the text. Even LDS pamphlets admit that there should be no corrections to a divinely inspired document. For instance, one entitled *The Challenge* affirms that "you must have **no changes in the text**. The first edition as you dictate it to your secretary **must stand forever**."[29]

If God is the real translator of the *Book of Mormon*, then the words He gave Joseph Smith were correct. Any errors identified in the text would be His fault. Roberts understood this clearly. Concerning errors in the *Book of Mormon* text, he agrees that "this is to assign responsibility for errors in language to a divine instrumentality, **which amounts to assigning such errors to God**. But that is unthinkable."[30]

Nibley, as well as many other LDS apologists, claimed that the changes made to the *Book of Mormon* were simply corrections in punctuation, spelling and grammar. He writes, "If one examines the long list of changes in various editions of the Book of Mormon one will find **not a single one** that alters the meaning of any passage ... these are mere mechanical details, as are also punctuation, spelling, and even grammar—those matters about which the critics of the Book of Mormon have made such a to-do."[31] Looking at the evidence, however, one must conclude that either Nibley was ignorant of the changes, or he was not being truthful.

While it is not our intention to review all the thousands of changes made to the book, we point out that (contrary to Nibley's claim) these are not just mechanical changes (spelling, grammar or punctuation) that were made. Many of the alterations involved **changing the very meaning** of the text—in some places to the **exact opposite**. Large passages were added or deleted without indication. The following examples are taken from the Tanner's exhaustive examination of the changes to the *Book of Mormon* text.

In the current edition of the *Book of Mormon* we read, "... learning from the mouth of Ammon that **king Mosiah** had a gift from God, whereby he could interpret..."[32] But in the original edition,[33] this verse stated "that **king Benjamin** had a gift from God ..."[34]

The reason this change is important is that it shows a serious mistake in the continuity of the story. King Benjamin had died 15 chapters earlier in the book.[35] That makes this a very serious change, because it completely alters the identity of the king in question.

In the current edition of the *Book of Mormon*, we read, "... come forth out of the waters of Judah, **or out of the waters of baptism**, who swear by the name of the Lord..."[36] But the original edition reads as follows, "... come forth out of the waters of Judah, which swear by the name of the Lord..."[37]

In order to add a reference to the LDS requirement for baptism, seven words were added to the text of this verse.

In the current edition of the *Book of Mormon*, we read, "And the mean man boweth **not** down, and the great man..."[38] But in the original edition, it reads, "... and the mean man boweth down, and the great man..."[39]

Here a word was added to the text that creates the opposite meaning.

In the current edition of the *Book of Mormon*, we read, "... I know that he allotteth unto men, yea, decreeth unto them decrees which are unalterable, according to their wills..."[40]

This verse currently reads the same as the original text of the *Book of Mormon*.[41] But this was not always the case. At some point, the words **"yea, decreeth unto them decrees which are unalterable"** were completely removed from the text. The phrase is not found in the 1908 edition,[42] the 1920 edition[43] or the 1964 edition[44] of the *Book of Mormon*. By 1981, however, these deleted words were restored to the verse.

Again, this is only a very small sampling of the thousands of changes in the text since the "Lord" had delivered it to Joseph Smith. Some are serious changes, not just "mechanical" adjustments. This makes it clear that the leadership of the LDS Church does not think the text of the *Book of Mormon* represents the direct words of God, nor an accurate record of history. Otherwise, they should not have made any changes.

That the original text needed grammatical changes shows that it could not have been the divine translation Joseph claimed. The changes made since his death show that the record does not reflect the teachings of God, but of the LDS leaders who have altered it at will.

Use of the Bible and Apocrypha

One feature of the text that has convinced many people that the *Book of Mormon* is authentic Scripture is the character of the language used. It is patterned after the style of Elizabethan English; the language in use during the early seventeenth century when the

King James Version of the Bible (hereafter *KJV*) was translated. Thus, the new volume **sounded** like Scripture.

However, in addition to mimicking the language style of the *KJV*, the *Book of Mormon* plagiarizes from it in many places as well. Parallels and literary borrowing are found from the Old Testament, the New Testament and the Apocrypha throughout the "golden Bible." This shows that Smith drew very liberally from these sources when writing the *Book of Mormon*.

Jerald and Sandra Tanner examined in detail the parallels between the *Book of Mormon* and the Bible.[45] When they completed this project, they had listed hundreds of *Book of Mormon* passages that had been borrowed from the Bible. They state that they "have found well over a hundred quotations from the New Testament in the first two books of Nephi alone."[46]

Space does not allow for an exhaustive listing of the quotes, but the following shows that the parallels go beyond coincidental usage.

The Old Testament and Apocrypha

The Old Testament and Apocrypha have many parallels in the *Book of Mormon*. The most obvious, perhaps, are the quotations of chapter after chapter from the book of Isaiah.

- Isaiah 2 through 14 copied as 2 Nephi 12 through 24
- Isaiah 29 copied as 2 Nephi 27
- Isaiah 48-49 copied as 1 Nephi 20-21
- Isaiah 50-51 copied as 2 Nephi 7-8
- Isaiah 52:7-10 copied as Mosiah 13:12-24
- Isaiah 53 copied as Mosiah 14
- Isaiah 54 copied as 3 Nephi 22

These examples show a little over 20 chapters copied from the *KJV* in just four books of the *Book of Mormon*. Eighteen of those are found in 1 Nephi and 2 Nephi. The Mormon Church freely admits there are parallels between these passages. They even point them out in the chapter summaries. Nevertheless, it still shows that Smith borrowed the information from the *KJV*. It seems ironic that so many chapters were quoted from Isaiah, because 2 Nephi in the *Book of Mormon* states that "Isaiah spake many things which were hard for many of my people to understand."[47]

Someone might wonder how the use of these parallel passages demonstrates plagiarism. When the *King James* Bible was translated, there were some words that had been added by the translators for clarification and to make the text easier to read. These additional words did not appear in the original text. Wherever translators added a word, it was printed in italics to clearly indicate it was not part of the original text. Where these chapters from Isaiah appear in the *Book of Mormon*, **many of the italicized words from the *KJV* are included**. This is a clear indication that they were merely copied from the Bible.

The Tanners point out 16 parallels between a single story from the Apocrypha and the corresponding story in the *Book of Mormon* — more than a coincidental match.[48] There were several other plagiarisms as well, including two unique names (Nephi and Ezias).[49]

The Tanners also list 45 parallels between the Old Testament and the *Book of Mormon*.[50] The list includes several stories that are so similar as to leave little doubt they were directly related. In other words, they were lifted from the Bible, altered to fit the place and people found in the *Book of Mormon*, then printed there as if they were original ideas or separate events. More serious than that, the *Book of Mormon* paraphrases the book of Malachi in at least four places[51] about **100-150 years before** the Book of Malachi was even written!

The New Testament

The New Testament has the highest number of plagiarisms and parallels in the *Book of Mormon*. This is to be expected, because most people are far more familiar with the New Testament than they are with the Old Testament. It would likely have been the same for Joseph Smith. The Tanners show more than 400 related verses and sayings between the two books.[52]

One glaring error they listed was that in one passage the *Book of Mormon* quotes Moses, but the words used were actually the Apostle Peter's paraphrase of Moses' words.[53] Yet the ancient authors of the *Book of Mormon* were supposedly separated by thousands of miles from the Middle East, where the original Apostles lived and wrote. Even more remarkable, the *Book of Mormon* quotation is dated about AD 34, but Peter's paraphrase was not written until sometime after AD 63.

Some LDS writers have tried to explain these parallels by simply claiming that God was the inspiration behind both books of Scripture; therefore, it should be no surprise that such similarities exist.[54] If the parallels somehow proved that God was the author of each book, then the various books of the Bible would have the same types of correlations. Yet they do not. Why would they be conspicuously absent from the books of the Bible, but so evident throughout the *Book of Mormon*?

Other Problems in the Book of Mormon Text

As is true of other sections of this chapter, there is so much information available that it is difficult to decide what textual problems to include. All should be considered together in any thorough analysis of the *Book of Mormon*. **We strongly recommend that readers examine the material fully for themselves before making their own judgment about the book.** Nevertheless, we present at least some of the information for consideration here.

1 Nephi 1:2 – This verse states that the golden plates were inscribed in the language of Nephi's father (a Jew) stating that it "consists of the learning of the Jews and the language of the Egyptians." First Nephi 3:19 verifies that the records were kept in the language of their Jewish fathers. Mosiah 1:4 adds that it was the "language of the Egyptians." So was the writing in Hebrew or Egyptian? Mormon 9:32 finally identifies this writing as "reformed Egyptian." Yet no people group has ever been known to have used such a language. Because the Jews hated the Egyptians, they would never have written in Egyptian, even in an altered form. The language of the Jewish fathers was always Hebrew. If these 1 Nephi verses were really true, then the plates should have been written strictly in Hebrew.

1 Nephi 16 – In this chapter alone, the phrase "It came to pass" is found 31 times, and appears more than 2,000 times throughout the *Book of Mormon*. This is very puzzling, considering that Jacob 4:1 claims it was very difficult to engrave information on the plates. Why then engrave this nearly meaningless phrase so often? There are no four-word phrases repeated this often in the Bible.

2 Nephi 5:15-16 – This passage presents three difficulties.

First, it mentions the Nephites using steel, which had not yet been invented.[55]

Second, several materials are mentioned in verse 15 as being "in great abundance"; among them gold, brass, silver, wood and ores (stone). But in verse 16, the writer says the same materials were not available. Verse 16 states that the Nephites built a temple "after the manner of the temple of Solomon." The end of the verse states that the "precious things" used in Solomon's temple "were not to be found upon the land" of the Nephites. According to the Bible, the "precious things" used in Solomon's temple were gold,[56] silver,[57] brass,[58] fine wood and stone.[59] How could these materials be "in great abundance" in one verse, then "not to be found upon the land" in the next?

The third problem with this *Book of Mormon* passage is that these Nephites were somehow able to build a temple "like unto the temple of Solomon" in a short time with just a few men on a new, uninhabited continent. Yet Solomon needed 163,300 workmen and seven years to build his temple.[60] This whole Nephite project, then, seems highly improbable.

Jacob 7:27 – This verse ends the book of Jacob by using the phrase, "Brethren, adieu." It is inconceivable to find a Nephite on a new continent, speaking in reformed Egyptian rather than Hebrew, writing between 544 and 421 BC, and speaking French—a language which would not develop for many centuries.

Enos 1:8 – In verse 5 (dated between 544-421 BC), we find that Enos was forgiven of his sins. The reason he was forgiven is stated in verse 8: "because of thy faith in Christ, whom thou hast never before heard nor seen." How could these people be familiar with the "Christ," a Greek word, which was not introduced until centuries later? These Jews, who realistically should have been speaking Hebrew, were supposedly speaking a reformed Egyptian. Yet here Enos uses a Greek word before its time in a foreign land.

Jarom 1:8 – In this verse, the writer mentions the use of "machinery," "iron" and "steel" in 420 BC. How could such things exist before they were invented? The logical explanation is that the book was not written when it is purported to have been. Instead, it more closely fits an early nineteenth-century setting.

Omni 1:15 – This verse tells us that the king over the people, named Mosiah, discovered a new group of people who were called "the people of Zarahemla." King Mosiah is able to learn that they "came out from Jerusalem" just a few years after the Nephites supposedly came to the New World. Yet verse 17 tells us that "their language had become corrupted" and "they had brought no records with them" and "the people of Mosiah, could not understand them." How, then, was Mosiah able to learn where these people came from and when? No one could understand them, they spoke a corrupt language, and they had no records, so it is unbelievable that King Mosiah could discern this specific information.

Mosiah 21:27 – This verse informs us that a group of people had kept records that were "engraven on plates of ore." Just how "plates of ore" could be made is a mystery. Ore is a rocky mineral. After being mined, the contents must be melted and refined; then plates can be made from the derived metal. Plates could not have been made from the ore itself.

Alma 7:10 – This verse has two significant difficulties.
First, it gives a prophecy of the Christ to come, and says that "he shall be born of Mary, at Jerusalem…." This verse was supposedly

written "about 83 B.C." according to the *Book of Mormon* footnote. Why, then, is Mary's name mentioned? In all the Old Testament prophecies about Mary and the birth of Jesus, she is never named. While it is certainly true that God knew what her name would be, it seems unlikely that He would not reveal it to any prophet of the Old Testament, but then reveal it to someone in the *Book of Mormon*. Instead, it is far more likely that the person writing this chapter of the *Book of Mormon* was familiar with the New Testament.

Second, Jesus is prophesied to be born "at Jerusalem." The New Testament is very clear that Jesus was born in Bethlehem, not Jerusalem.[61] Even the Old Testament prophesied specifically that Jesus would be born in Bethlehem.[62]

LDS writers, seeking to explain away this obvious error, have put forth many far-reaching rationalizations. The most common explanation is that this verse is simply referring to the "land of Jerusalem," the "bigger city" of Jerusalem or even the "area of Jerusalem."[63] But each of these assertions has insurmountable problems. The Bible is clear that Bethlehem is in the land of "Judaea," not the land of "Jerusalem."[64] Bethlehem was also not part of the "bigger city" of Jerusalem. Though they are closer together now, in that day the towns were farther apart and distinct from each other. Bethlehem is even called the "city of David" in the Bible,[65] never the city of Jerusalem. Nor was Bethlehem ever known as being in the "area" of Jerusalem. It was always connected with the area of Judea. In fact, there was a second town by the name of Bethlehem about ten miles northwest of Nazareth. So to distinguish the two cities from each other, Bethlehem (the birthplace of Jesus) was either called Bethlehem Ephratah[66] or Bethlehem-judah.[67] Ephrathah has also been identified as "the region in which Bethlehem was located."[68]

The Alma 7:10 phrase "at Jerusalem" is found 19 times in the *Book of Mormon*. In all the other instances, it denotes the specific city of Jerusalem, not the land around it or any other city.[69] Surely the phrase would have the same meaning in this verse that it does in all the others. This is simply an error in the text, not a generalization.

Alma 30:2 – This verse informs us that "there began to be **continual peace** throughout all the land." Yet in Alma 35:13, which occurred just two years later, war again ensues among the people. Are we really to believe that two years constitutes "continual peace"? Even commentators on the *Book of Mormon* have stated that this period of peace was a "relatively short period of time."[70]

Alma 46:13, 15-16 – In these verses, members of the Church are being identified as "Christians."[71] These verses were supposedly written, according to the *Book of Mormon* footnotes, in 73 BC. But the Bible is very clear that "the disciples were called Christians first at Antioch."[72] That was not until somewhere between AD 35-40.[73] If the believers and disciples were not called "Christians" until after the death of Jesus, then the use of the term in 73 BC in the *Book of Mormon* would not be possible.

Helaman 12:24 – This verse tells us that God will grant "grace for grace," but then stipulates that the grace is given "according to their works." Grace, by very definition, is not grace if it has to be earned by works. The Apostle Paul explained, "And if by grace, then it is no longer by works; if it were, grace would no longer be grace" (Romans 11:6 NIV). If grace were given based on works, then it is a wage, not grace. This verse is in contradiction with itself and with the Bible on this topic.

3 Nephi 9:2-15 – This passage lists horrible events transpiring on the earth. Many cities are burned,[74] dropped into the sea,[75] and buried in the earth.[76] Many other destructive events occurred[77] because of the wickedness of the people. What caused all this death and destruction? Verses 12 and 15 state plainly that the one causing all this destruction was "Jesus Christ the Son of God."

Yet the Jesus of the Bible did not come to destroy, but "to seek and to save that which was lost."[78] In fact, Jesus said in John 10:10 that it is the thief who comes to destroy, while Jesus came to give life, not take it away. This verse also contradicts Moroni 7:22 in the *Book of Mormon*, which says that "in Christ there should come every good thing." Is mass death and destruction a good thing?

Mass destruction on such a grand scale never happened in the Old World, even at the crucifixion of Christ.[79] Surely wickedness was worse there. After all, those who actually murdered Jesus were living there. Yet, according to this account, they were allowed to go free while on the other side of the world people were killed by the thousands. This is inconceivable; it is far from the character of Jesus to do such a thing.

3 Nephi Chapters 11-28 – In these chapters, the "crowning event"[80] of the *Book of Mormon* takes place. Jesus personally appears on the American Continent and ministers to the Nephite people. In 3 Nephi 11:8, Jesus descends from heaven. Then in 3 Nephi 18:39, he ascends into heaven again. Then in 3 Nephi 19:15, Jesus comes back again and ministers to the Nephite disciples. Finally, in 3 Nephi 28:12, Jesus departs again into heaven.

The problem created here is that Jesus has now come to earth three times. Yet none of these appearances recorded in the *Book of Mormon* qualifies as the "Second Coming." If Jesus really visited the American lands after His ascension, then the Bible should have prophesied for Christians to look for Jesus' fourth coming. Instead, it prophesies that Messiah was to come to earth once to fulfill the law[81] and once to establish His kingdom finally and forever.[82] These chapters in 3 Nephi contradict the prophecies of the Bible by claiming Jesus came again and again without fulfilling them.

4 Nephi 1:6 – This verse is very tedious to read, since the writer uses 57 words just to say that 59 years had passed. This excess verbiage seems even more absurd when we consider Jacob 4:1 in the *Book of Mormon*, which says that very little could be engraved upon the plates of gold because the process was so difficult.

Mormon 7:8-9 – This passage asserts that anyone who believes the Bible will believe the *Book of Mormon* also. The chapter summary makes the same claim: "*All who believe the Bible will also believe the Book of Mormon.*" Clearly, this is not true of most Bible readers.

Ether 6:4-12 – These verses tell of a group of people traveling to the New World by sea. A "furious wind" blows their barges there, but the journey still took 344 days. Verses 10-11 make it clear that the ships were **continuously** propelled toward the new land. This is amazing, because even if the "furious wind" propelled the ships at a slow rate (by today's standards) of only 10 mph, in that amount of time they would have traveled 82,560 miles—more than three times around the earth at the equator. This passage could not have been divinely inspired.

Ether 15:29-31 – This passage tells a story so absurd that it requires little comment, and only a brief summary for those unfamiliar with the *Book of Mormon*. It tells the story of the last great battle of two people groups. All are destroyed but the two leaders, named Coriantumr and Shiz. After they battle, Shiz faints because of loss of blood. Coriantumr then cuts off his head. Verse 31 tells what happened next: "And it came to pass that after he had smitten off the head of Shiz, that Shiz raised up on his hands and fell; and after that he had struggled for breath, he died." How likely is this?

Here we have briefly presented some of the teachings and statements found in the *Book of Mormon*.[83] They demonstrate that the book is not infallible, and did not originate as a divinely inspired record of actual people. Instead, they show that a person with an impressively complex but inexperienced and unschooled mind created the story.

Missing LDS Doctrines

Joseph Smith received a revelation from God in April of 1830 that said in part, "the Book of Mormon ... contains a record of a fallen people, and **the fulness of the gospel of Jesus Christ** to the Gentiles and to the Jews also."[84] Concerning this passage, the *Doctrine and Covenants Commentary* states:

> *Fulness of the gospel*] The Book of Mormon contains the "fulness of the gospel of Jesus Christ to Gentiles and Jews." The word "fulness" means "abundance," "completeness." In the epistles of Paul (Eph. 1:23; Col. 1:19) it means, as

Lightfoot has shown, the completed condition, as when a rent is mended.[85]

Bruce McConkie adds that "the *fulness of the gospel* consists in those laws, doctrines, ordinances, powers, and authorities needed to enable men to gain the fulness of salvation."[86]

Ezra Taft Benson agrees, saying, "The Book of Mormon is a second witness to Jesus Christ because it contains the plain and precious truths of His gospel. Within this sacred record is the fulness of the gospel of Jesus Christ; in other words, the Lord's requirements for salvation."[87]

If, as these Mormon leaders say, the *Book of Mormon* contains the fullness of the Mormon gospel, then we would expect to find there all the essential teachings of Mormonism. In other words, all the "laws, doctrines, [and] ordinances" necessary for a fulness of salvation. Yet the surprising truth is that it does not contain many of these essential LDS beliefs. Among them are:

- That certain ordinances are required for salvation, such as baptism and confirmation as a member of the Church of Jesus Christ of Latter-day Saints.
- The necessity of Aaronic and Melchizedek Priesthoods.
- That the gift of the Holy Ghost can only be passed on through the laying on of hands by someone with "authority," and that one must have this gift to be fully saved.
- That temple ordinances are necessary for individual salvation, and what those temple ordinances are.
- That there is marriage for eternity, and that it is a requirement for full salvation.
- That there are three degrees of heavenly glory, and full salvation is only found in the highest kingdom.
- That full salvation means man can advance to become a God, but only through obedience to Mormon teachings.
- That paying an honest and full tithe is a requirement for full salvation.

- That obedience to the Word of Wisdom is necessary for full salvation.[88]

In addition, many other vital teachings of Mormonism are not found in the *Book of Mormon*. Among them are:

- That God was once a man, and has a glorified body of flesh and bones.
- That God is eternally progressing, and changed from a man into a God at some point in time.
- That polygamy is not an abomination, and is practiced in heaven.
- That Joseph Smith, Jr. will judge us along with Jesus at the judgment seat.
- That the spirits of men were pre-existing with God.
- That there are innumerable numbers of Gods in the heavens.
- That there is no eternal hell.
- That a vote from the Church is required to accept a revelation from God.
- That eternal truths can be changed as time goes on, so they reflect the times in which the people are living.
- That Jesus and Satan are brothers.
- That we are to search out our kindred dead and perform temple ordinance work for them.

These teachings are not taught anywhere in the *Book of Mormon*, but most are now essential parts of the LDS gospel. As Bill McKeever and Eric Johnson of Mormonism Research Ministry conclude:

> In all actuality, there is no evidence to suggest that the Nephites mentioned in the *Book of Mormon* believed or practiced what modern-day Mormons believe and practice.... Many people are under the impression that, by reading the *Book of Mormon*, they will get a better understanding of LDS Church doctrines. But this is not so....[89]

Conflicting LDS Doctrines

Not only does the *Book of Mormon* lack many Mormon doctrines, it also contradicts many LDS teachings. It should be very embarrassing to LDS leaders that the book, which serves as the very foundation for their Church, actually teaches conflicting doctrines.

2 Nephi 24:12-15 – This passage (which is actually copied from the Bible—Isaiah 14) teaches that Satan fell because he desired to become like God. The *Book of Mormon* footnotes indicate the passage refers primarily to the King of Babylon, but more specifically to Satan. But the LDS Church leaders teach something quite different. In the Mormon gospel, Satan had proposed to God a plan of salvation that was rejected. Satan then rebelled and fought against God and Jesus, the result being that he was cast out of heaven.[90]

Not only is this contradictory to LDS teachings, but it also serves as a warning to LDS members. Since they believe that Mormon men can eventually become Gods,[91] they are guilty of the same sin that the *Book of Mormon* teaches resulted in Satan's expulsion from heaven.

2 Nephi 25:20 – This passage teaches that there is no other name under heaven but Jesus Christ whereby man can be saved. This passage was obviously inspired by Acts 4:12. Yet this is not what many LDS leaders have taught over the years. Many have taught that if it were not for the name of Joseph Smith, Jr. no man could find salvation.[92]

Jacob 1:15 – This verse, along with Jacob 2:24-33, teaches that polygamy is "wicked," and an "abomination." Mosiah 11:2 speaks in the same terms about the practice. Specifically condemned are the many wives and concubines of David and Solomon.[93] Yet the Mormon Church leaders taught in the past that the practice of polygamy was required for salvation,[94] and that David and Solomon's polygamy was justified.[95] In fact, they taught that God Himself gave the wives and concubines to them.[96] Why would God give David and Solomon many wives, but then call it an abomination?

Mosiah 3:11 – This verse teaches that all mankind "have fallen by the transgression of Adam ... or who have ignorantly sinned." The Mormon gospel, however, teaches that mankind did not fall because of the sin of Adam.[97] It also teaches that people must reach an age of accountability (8 years old) before they are responsible for their own sins. Before age 8, it teaches, children cannot even commit sin in ignorance.[98]

Mosiah 16:11 – This verse teaches that there is an "endless damnation" for those who reject the gospel of Jesus Christ. Yet the Mormon Church today teaches that there is no such thing as "endless damnation," that hell is only temporary.[99]

Alma 18:2-5, 24-28 – This passage teaches emphatically that God is a spirit. Alma 31:15 is even more emphatic, that "thou art God, and we believe ... that thou wast a spirit, and that thou art a spirit, and that thou wilt be a spirit forever." Yet the Mormon Church teaches that God is not a spirit, but a glorified man with a body of flesh and bones.[100]

Alma 34:31-36 – This passage teaches that salvation must be obtained in "this life," for after death a person's eternal destiny is "sealed." It also states that there "can be no labor performed" after this life. Moroni 10:26 teaches the same thing. But the LDS gospel teaches that there is a second chance for salvation after this life. Temple work is done on behalf of those who have died in order to increase their personal merit and help them earn salvation.[101]

Helaman 6:25-30 – This passage (along with 3 Nephi 12:33-37 and Ether 8:16-19) condemns the use of "secret oaths and covenants," and states emphatically that they are put into man's heart by Satan. Yet the Mormon endowment ceremony, which is taught to be an absolute requirement for salvation, contains numerous secret oaths and covenants.[102]

3 Nephi 11:36 – This passage teaches that "the Father, and I [Jesus], and the Holy Ghost are one." This passage echoes the

Testimony of the Three Witnesses, which also states that the Father, the Son and the Holy Ghost "is one God." The Mormon gospel, however, teaches that these three constitute three separate Gods.[103] It also teaches that there are innumerable Gods in the heavens besides them.[104]

Mormon 9:9-10 – This passage teaches that God does not ever change, but is the same from all eternity to all eternity. Mormon 9:19 and Moroni 8:18 both verify this as truth. Yet the Mormon Church teaches that God was once a man, then progressed and advanced until he eventually became a God.[105] This, of necessity, involves change—thus contradicting what the *Book of Mormon* states.

Many additional examples could be given which show that the teachings of the *Book of Mormon*, "the most correct of any book on earth,"[106] contradict the official teachings of the LDS Church over and over again. Which are we to believe: the divinely inspired *Book of Mormon*; or the divinely inspired LDS leadership? The simple fact that these two conflict with each other at so many points shows that they are not both truly inspired by God. And since one is dependent upon the other, can either be considered inspired by the true God of the Bible?

Conclusion

After close examination, the inevitable conclusion is that the *Book of Mormon* is not the divine record it claims to be. Even if it had begun that way, there have been so many changes made that the current edition could no longer be considered the divine record transmitted to Joseph Smith. Since the *Book of Mormon* was and still is the foundation for the Mormon Church and its leaders, the book and their teachings should not conflict with each other. Yet they do. Further, some of the most important doctrines taught by LDS leaders are not even contained in it.

The evidence shows that the book is a work of man, not of God, and that if it does guide and direct the leadership of the Mormon Church, it only does so superficially.

Chapter 5
The Book of Mormon—Further Research

Joseph Smith's Claim –
> ... a personage appeared at my bedside ... he said there was a book deposited, written upon gold plates, giving an account of the former inhabitants of this continent, and the source from which they sprang.
> – *History of the Church*, 1:11-12

Historical and Scientific Research

Not only are there many irreconcilable textual problems with the *Book of Mormon*, but research into many historical and scientific aspects of the book reveals insurmountable problems as well.

Book of Mormon Geography

When reading the Bible, people are often interested to know where the locations mentioned in the text are found on a map. Knowing the location and geography is sometimes vital to understanding why something in the Bible happened as it did.[1] Archaeology also has provided sufficient evidence corroborating the text of the Bible. If portions of the *Book of Mormon* could be verified by archaeological findings, there would be evidence that it is an actual historical record like the Bible. And if the historical portions of the book were verified to be true, then the spiritual teachings of the book would be worthy of consideration as well. In fact, no such evidence exists.

If the book identified some of the exact locations it mentions, there would be a place to search for artifacts in earnest. However, the *Book of Mormon* is vague in defining its geography. It is left up to the leaders of the Mormon Church, then, to pinpoint these locations.

Yet there is much confusion among these "inspired" men in regard to the geography of the book. It appears that none of them have been able to definitively place most of the geographic references from the *Book of Mormon* on any map. One well-known exception is the Hill Cumorah, which Joseph Smith pinpointed as being in upstate New York.

Hemispheric Model

Joseph Smith, however, believed and taught that the *Book of Mormon* geography pertained to nearly all of the New World—North, Central and South America. His belief was based mainly on information revealed to him by God. Writers at FARMS (the Foundation for Ancient Research and Mormon Studies)[2] and others have labeled this theory as the "Hemispheric Model" of *Book of Mormon* geography.

Early LDS leaders also taught this "Hemispheric Model" as revealed truth. Anthony Ivins taught during an official Church Conference that

> the passages which I have quoted ... definitely establish the following facts: That the Hill Cumorah, and the Hill Ramah are identical; that it was around this hill that the armies of both the Jaredites and Nephites, fought their great last battles; that it was in this hill that Mormon deposited all of the sacred records.... **We know positively that it was in this hill that Moroni deposited the abridgment ... and that it was from this hill that Joseph Smith obtained possession** of them [the golden plates].[3]

Teachings given during a General Conference of the Church are said to be inspired teachings.[4] That means this was not just a personal opinion, but divinely revealed truth.

Orson Pratt was most specific when he described *Book of Mormon* geography as including all of North and South America. He taught from the pulpit a sermon including the following:

Let me here observe that the Book of Mormon ... gives an account of the first settlement of this country by these inhabitants.... Instead of landing on the north-west coast of north America, **they landed on the south-west coast of South America**.... The righteous portion of these families left the first settlement and traveled **several hundred miles to the north**, and formed settlements.... The Nephites, as the righteous portion was called, sent forth **numerous colonies into North America. Among these colonies there was one that came and settled on the southern borders of our great lakes**.... The Lamanites, who dwelt in the **southern portion of South America**, also apostatized.... They drove all the Nephites out of South America and followed with their armies up into the north country, and finally overpowered them. They were gathered together **south of the great lakes in the country which we term New York**.[5]

Even as late as 1990, Church leaders continue to teach these points. In a personal letter dated 16 October 1990, F. Michael Watson, Secretary to the First Presidency, wrote, "The Church has long maintained, as attested to by references in the writings of General Authorities, that the Hill Cumorah in Western New York state is the same as referenced in the Book of Mormon."[6]

The Hemispheric Model has been taught recently as well in some official Mormon circles, though not in others. For example, it was taught in the LDS Business College during the spring of 1988.[7] The 1981 *Book of Mormon Student Manual* used in BYU religion classes, on the other hand, taught that no geography could be pinpointed for the book. Nevertheless, a possible *Book of Mormon* map was presented there.[8] The manual stated specifically that Joseph Smith had revealed that the Nephites occupied the land "we know today as North America."[9]

Limited Geography Model

The latest trend in *Book of Mormon* academic circles is subscription to what they label the "Limited Geography Model," a theory that all *Book of Mormon* geography is limited to the area of Central America alone.[10] This new theory contradicts what LDS Church leaders have taught for many years.

Joseph Fielding Smith gives an authoritative statement concerning this trend of thinking:

> SPECULATION ABOUT BOOK OF MORMON GEOGRAPHY. Within recent years there has arisen among certain students of the *Book of Mormon* **a theory** to the effect that within the period covered by the *Book of Mormon*, the Nephites and Lamanites **were confined almost entirely within the borders of the territory comprising Central America and the southern portion of Mexico....**This *theory* is founded upon the assumption that it was impossible for the colony of Lehi's to multiply and fill the hemisphere within the limits of 1,000 years....This modernistic theory of necessity, in order to be consistent, must place the waters of Ripliancum and the Hill Cumorah some place within the restricted territory of Central America, **notwithstanding the teachings of the Church to the contrary for upwards of 100 years.** Because of this *theory* **some members of the Church have become confused and greatly disturbed** in their faith in the *Book of Mormon*. It is for this reason that evidence is here presented to show that **it is not only possible that these places could be located as the Church has held during the past century, but that in very deed** *such is the case....* In the face of this **evidence coming from the Prophet Joseph Smith**, Oliver Cowdery, and David Whitmer, **we cannot say that the Nephites and Lamanites did not possess the territory of the United States** and that the Hill Cumorah is in Central America. Neither can we say that the great struggle which resulted in the destruction of the Nephites took place in Central America.... from all the evidence in the *Book of Mormon*, augmented by **the testimony of the Prophet Joseph Smith,** *these final battles took place in the territory known as the United States and in the*

neighborhood of the Great Lakes and hills of Western New York.[11]

Yet concerning this view, LDS scholar John L. Sorenson,[12] writes:

> Now, it does little for our satisfaction in understanding the scripture to take **that simpleminded view. It simply is not true**. The reason I say it is not true is because when we examine the Book of Mormon, which, after all, is the authority on the Nephites when we examine the Book of Mormon text ... we find that the Nephites lived in **a very small land ... a few hundred miles in length and a hundred or two hundred miles across**. Not thousands of miles, **not the whole Western Hemisphere**.[13]

The problem that this creates, of course, is that by making such assertions, Sorenson and others who hold his view are indirectly claiming to know more, or at least know better, than the inspired leaders and prophets of their Church. Many LDS writers justify this by claiming that the prophets were merely giving their "personal opinions" about these matters, and not speaking with any inspired authority or personal knowledge.[14] It is no wonder the LDS people are so confused about the issue. And if Mormons are confused, then it is not surprising that non-Mormons who read the *Book of Mormon* and seek this information would also become confused. The best policy would be to allow the leadership of the Church to set the official doctrines, rather than the contradictory musings of the uninspired apologists.[15]

Leaders Support Smith's Teachings

There are no current official statements by LDS leaders regarding the location of sites referred to in the *Book of Mormon*. However, many LDS leaders in the past have justified the official view expressed by Joseph Fielding Smith. For instance, Joseph Smith, Jr. claimed that numerous places mentioned in the *Book of Mormon* were located within the boundaries of the continental United States.[16] In order for Sorenson's theory to be true, Joseph Smith deliberately deceived those whom he told about *Book of Mormon* locations. Smith was adamant that the locations he was pointing out were actual *Book of Mormon* locations, indicating a sure knowledge of these things. He did not imply in any way that he was giving a personal opinion. He spoke with authority and supposed knowledge when making his claims. On several occasions, he plainly said that his information came directly from God. Consider the following account, taken from the *History of the Church*:

> [June 1834] We encamped **on the bank of the [Illinois] river** until Tuesday the 3rd. During our travels we visited several of **the mounds which had been thrown up by the ancient inhabitants of this country—Nephites, Lamanites, etc.**, and this morning I went up on a high mound, near the river, accompanied by the brethren.... On the top of the mound were stones which presented the appearance of three altars.... The brethren procured a shovel and a hoe, and ... discovered the skeleton of a man, almost entire, and between his ribs the stone point of a Lamanitish arrow, which evidently produced his death.... **the visions of the past being opened to my understanding by the Spirit of the Almighty, I discovered that the person whose skeleton was before us was a white Lamanite**, a large, thick-set man, and a man of God. His name was Zelph. He was a warrior and a chieftan under the great prophet Onandagus, who was known from the Hill Cumorah, or eastern sea to the Rocky Mountains.... **He was killed in battle by the arrow found among his ribs, during the last great struggle of the Lamanites and Nephites.**[17]

Joseph Smith explained that in a vision, the Angel Moroni claimed that this continent was where the *Book of Mormon* people lived: "He [Moroni] said there was a book deposited, written upon gold plates, giving an account of **the former inhabitants of this continent**, and the source from whence they sprang."[18] Orson Pratt, giving an account of this vision as he heard it from Joseph, stated that this angel of God had said "that **this continent had been inhabited by** two dis=tinct races of people. The first was called **Jaredites**, and came directly from the Tower of Babel. The second was **called Ne=phites the descendants of Joseph**, who came to this land in the day of Zedekiah King of Judah, about six hundred years—(p. 31) Before Christ!"[19]

Apostle Franklin D. Richards wrote a book giving some "gems" from Joseph Smith's history. Among them is a revelation given to Joseph Smith that told of Lehi's travels.[20] This revelation contained the following information: "They [Lehi's family] traveled nearly a south, southeast direction until they came to the nineteenth degree of north latitude; then, nearly east to the Sea of Arabia, then sailed in a southeast direction, **and landed on the continent of South America, in Chile, thirty degrees south latitude.**"[21] This account has never been officially contradicted, and has always been generally accepted as correct by LDS members and leaders alike.[22]

These statements indicate that Joseph Smith, Jr. definitely believed in and taught the "Hemispheric Model" based upon visions and revelations that he claimed to have received. If Lehi's family really arrived in what is now Chile at 30 degrees south latitude, then this places the Nephite landing well south of Central America—far outside the boundaries of the "Limited Geography Model."

The *Book of Mormon* itself also suggests the "Hemispheric Model." For instance, it describes battles taking place near, and the golden plates being buried in, the Hill Cumorah.[23] This hill was obviously well enough known by all the *Book of Mormon* people that it was identifiable without question.[24] Joseph Smith then unearthed these same gold plates in the Hill Cumorah located in upstate New York,[25] definitely identifying at the very least this one location. The *Encyclopedia of Mormonism* agrees that the Hill Cumorah, near Palmyra, New York, was the location of the final Nephite battle from the *Book of Mormon* and also the depository of the golden plates.[26] According to the book itself, then, the people were not limited to the Central American region.

Still, there are many LDS people who do believe that *Book of Mormon* lands are in Central America. On 7 March 2004, the *Deseret News* reported that "for years, thousands of LDS Church faithful have flocked to poverty-stricken areas in Central America to visit what they consider to be sacred ground—the so-called 'Lands of the Book of Mormon.'"[27]

No Archaeological Evidence

Whether the *Book of Mormon* geography is limited or hemispheric, **not a single site** in North, Central or South America has been proven by archaeological findings to be a definite *Book of Mormon* location. No evidence has been found that incontrovertibly shows any statement on New World geography in the *Book of Mormon* to be a verified fact.

The *Deseret News* reported:

> The reality, however, is that **there is no way to verify the authenticity** of [Central American areas] as the sites described in the Book of Mormon.... **LDS tour guides ... admit no one knows for sure** if the events described in the Book of Mormon indeed occurred there.... Mainstream **academics don't acknowledge any correlation** between the Book of Mormon and the Mayans. They regard the Book of Mormon as a religious—**not a historic**—document. **The LDS Church, meanwhile, takes no position** on any proposed Book of Mormon sites.... FARMS devotes considerable resources to the study of Mesoamerica, though it, like the LDS Church, does not take any official position on proposed sites.[28]

To be sure, many books and papers have attempted to show the **possibility** of such locations, but none of the evidence put forth is incontrovertible proof. They are all listed as mere speculations.[29] In fact, LDS anthropologist and scholar Thomas Murphy informs us that "**there's never been any evidence** that would show us that there was an Israelite migration to the new world—**not in genetics, or, for that matter, in any other source—historical, archaeological or linguistic.**"[30]

The Smithsonian Institution verifies Murphy's conclusion. In a standard letter sent to any who ask whether *Book of Mormon* places have ever been located in their archaeological research, officials state, "Smithsonian archaeologists see **no direct connection** between the archaeology of the New World and the subject matter of the book."[31]

Professors from Brigham Young University agree. Stephen Houston, professor of anthropology, admitted "there is, of course, **no official LDS position** about these locations. There are only theories...." George Talbot, BYU Travel Studies director, added, "I become very nervous with the [Central American] native guides who are LDS.... **There's not an archaeologist or professor at BYU that would agree with what they say.**"[32]

Even Mormon scholar John Sorensen (cited above) claims there is no archaeological evidence at all for the *Book of Mormon*. In a personal letter written in 1982, Sorenson wrote, "**No cities** named in the Book of Mormon **have been identified**.... In fact I want more evidence myself."[33] Sorenson also conceded that

> after nearly 150 years since the Nephite record was first published by Joseph Smith, we Mormons **have seemed unable to pin down a single city, define one route** traversed, or sketch an accurate picture of any segment of the life lived in their American promised land.... **we have been incapable of placing it in its specific setting.**[34]

The Lamanite Doctrine and DNA

The article "Mormon Scientist, Church Clash Over DNA Test," in the 8 December 2002, *Los Angeles Times,* reported:

> Anthropologist Thomas W. Murphy set out to test a key principle of his Mormon faith with the latest technology. He wondered: Would DNA analysis show—as taught by the Book of Mormon—-that many American Indians are descended from ancient Israelites? His finding: negative.[35]

Lamanites—The American Indians

The story line of the *Book of Mormon* follows the history of two people groups—Nephites and Lamanites. By the end of the book, only one group remains: the Lamanites. Since the 1820s, Joseph Smith, the General Authorities of the LDS Church, and Mormon scholars alike have taught (and LDS Church members have believed) that the descendants of the Lamanites, the American Indians, were originally Israelites.

The question of the ancestry of the American Indians was a widely discussed topic in the nineteenth century. "The most popular notion at the time was that Native Americans descended from Israelites."[36] Is this interpretation of the ancestry of the American Indians really the established teaching of the LDS Church? And if so, what was its origin?

The Doctrine of the Lamanites

In one of Joseph Smith's accounts of angelic visitations, he explained that the angel Moroni, "a messenger sent from God," told him about the ancestry of the America Indians.

> When I was about 17 years old, I saw another vision of angels in the night season.... He said unto me, "I am a messenger sent from God. Be faithful and keep his commandments in all things." He told me of a sacred record which was written on plates of gold. I saw in the vision the place where they were deposited. **He said the Indians were the literal descendants of Abraham.**[37]

In a letter written by Oliver Cowdery to W. W. Phelps, Cowdery recounts what he was told by Joseph Smith. It was published in the February 1835 *Messenger and Advocate:*

> On the evening of the 21st of September, 1823 ... He [the angel] then proceeded and gave a general account of the promises made to the fathers, and also gave a history of the **aborigines of this county, and said they were literal**

descendants of Abraham. He represented them as once being an enlightened and intelligent people, possessing a correct knowledge of the gospel, and the plan of restoration and redemption.[38]

Writing in reply, W. W. Phelps said,

> My last letter was mainly confined to the book of Mormon, which rarely fails to bring to my mind something about **the Indians, whose history and doings, upon this western continent, it unfolds.**... The Indians occupy a large portion of **the land of America**, and, as they are a part of the creation of God, **and are a remnant of the children of Israel**, they must necessarily hear the gospel.... The Indians are the people of the Lord; they are of the tribes of Israel; the blood of Joseph, with a small mixture of the royal blood of Judah....[39]

The title page of *Book of Mormon* states that it is "written to the **Lamanites, who are a remnant of the house of Israel**; and also to Jew and Gentile." The Introduction states that "it is a record of God's dealings with the ancient inhabitants of the Americas.... After thousands of years, all were destroyed except the **Lamanites, and they are the principal ancestors of the American Indians.**" In *The Pearl of Great Price,* Joseph Smith reported that the angel "said there was a book deposited, written upon gold plates, giving an account of **the former inhabitants of this continent**, and the source from which they sprang...."[40] He later clarified that "they were **principally Israelites**, of the descendants of Joseph.... **The remnant are the Indians who now inhabit this country.**"[41]

The introduction to Section 32 of *Doctrine and Covenants* states:

> *Revelation given through Joseph Smith the Prophet to Parley P. Pratt and Ziba Peterson, October 1830. HC 1:118-120. Great interest and desires were felt by the elders respecting* **the Lamanites, *of whose predicted blessings the Church***

*had learned from the Book of Mormon. In consequence, supplication was made that the Lord would indicate his will as to whether elders should be sent at that time to the **Indian tribes in the West**.*

In another revelation, Joseph quotes the Lord as speaking of a "journey into the regions westward, unto the **land of Missouri, unto the borders of the Lamanites.**"[42] A footnote in *History of the Church* explains in some detail what became known as the "mission to the Lamanites." "As the 'mission to the Lamanites' is a very prominent event in early Church history, it is proper that the labors of the brethren engaged in it should be spoken of more fully than appears anywhere in the Prophet's narrative...."[43]

The footnote continues and reports on what the chief of the Delaware Indians said in response to Oliver Cowdery's address to them: "We feel truly thankful to our white friends who have come so far and been at such pains to tell us good news, and especially this new news concerning **the Book of our forefathers....**" Elder Parley P. Pratt concluded his report on the mission:

> Thus ended our first Indian mission, in which we had preached the Gospel in its fulness and distributed the **record of their forefathers** among three tribes, viz.: the Catteraugus Indians, near Buffalo, N.Y.; the Wyandots, of Ohio; and the Delawares, west of Missouri.[44]

The following comments in *History of the Church* were made in January 1836:

> Much has been said and done of late by the general government in relation to the **Indians (Lamanites)** within the territorial limits of the United States.[45]
>
> **The Book of Mormon has made known who Israel is, upon this continent.** And while we behold the government of the United States **gathering the Indians,** and locating

them upon lands to be their own, how sweet it is to think that they may one day be gathered by the Gospel![46]

In 1842, at the request of the Editor of the *Chicago Democrat*, John Wentworth, Joseph Smith explained:

> The second race [of people on the American Continent] came directly from the city of Jerusalem, about six hundred years before Christ. **They were principally Israelites**, of the descendents of Joseph. The Jaredites were destroyed about the time that the Israelites came from Jerusalem, who succeeded them in the inheritance of the country. The principal nation of the second race fell in battle towards the close of the fourth century. **The remnant are the Indians that now inhabit this country.**[47]

About five months after Joseph Smith's death, a letter that he had written to newspaper editor N. E. Seaton on 4 January 1833 was published in *Times and Seasons*, in which he stated,

> The Book of Mormon is a **record of the fore fathers of our western tribes of Indians**; having been found through the ministration of an holy angel, and translated into our own language by the gift and power of God, after having been hid up in the earth for the last fourteen hundred years, containing the word of God which was delivered unto them. By it we learn that our **western tribes of Indians are descendants from that of Joseph** that was sold into Egypt, and that **the land America is a promised land unto them**....[48]

The following was stated in an address by Brigham Young:

> Do you pray for Israel? You will no doubt answer in the affirmative. **These Indians are the seed of Israel**, through the loins of Joseph, who was sold into Egypt; they are the children of Abraham, and belong to the chosen seed; were it not so, you would never have seen them with dark, red skins.[49]

Orson Pratt explained:

> Here (holding the Book of Mormon in his hand) we present a record of **this American continent, a history of a branch of the tribe of Joseph**, for nearly 600 years before Christ, and until 420 years after Christ, a history of the Lord's dealings with them from the time they **left Jerusalem** until one of their principal nations fell in battle, because of their apostacy; and the **descendants of the remaining remnant are this degenerated people we call Indians**, who still exist.[50]

Several following statements by Mormon historians and General Authorities are representative of **many others** that could be cited. For example, in their book, *The Mormon Experience*, Mormon history professors Leonard J. Arrington and Davis Bitton explain:

> When Joseph Smith published the Book of Mormon in 1830, he had offered special reasons for concern over the welfare of American Indians. **The Book of Mormon**, as mentioned earlier, **purported to be a history and religious record of three groups of Middle Easterners** who traveled to the Western Hemisphere over a fifteen-hundred-year period.... **It was regarded as evidence that American Indians, like some of their Hebrew ancestors, were part of God's chosen people**, and that they had flourished **in North and South America** under his protecting care....[51]

Clearly the idea that the American Indians (a.k.a. Lamanites) are descendants of the Jews has been **a foundational belief in the LDS Church since the beginning**. Joseph Smith himself introduced this doctrinal teaching.

Richard L. Bushman, who was professor of history at the University of Delaware, explains:

> The **critics cannot be faulted for saying that the Book of Mormon was a history of the Indians. The book obviously was that, and early Mormons told the world it was.** Lucy

Smith wrote to her sister-in-law in January, 1829, over a year before publication of the Book of Mormon, and described it as a record "placed in the earth many hundred years ago **by the forefathers of our Indians.**"[52]

The Book of Mormon gave the missionaries ample reason for making the long trip to the Missouri. **The book's main purpose was to recover the lost remnant of ancient Israel.**[53]

Thomas G. Alexander, professor of history and former director of the Charles Redd Center for Western Studies at BYU, writes: **"Because of Book of Mormon teachings Mormons believed the Indians to be descendants of the Children of Israel."**[54]

Joseph Fielding Smith has been called "the leading gospel scholar and the greatest doctrinal teacher of this generation,"[55] and is "universally esteemed as the chief doctrinal authority of the Church."[56] He explains:

> Six hundred years before the birth of Christ another civilization supplanted that previously mentioned which was destroyed about that time. This second civilization flourished about 1,000 years. **The people multiplied and spread over the face of the entire continent**.... But, like their predecessors, they forgot the Lord; his Spirit was withdrawn, and the greater part of the people was destroyed. *Their civilization perished*.... **Their descendants, the American Indians**, were wandering in all their wild savagery when the Pilgrim Fathers made permanent settlement **in this land.**[57]

Bruce R. McConkie writes:

> **Thus the [American] Indians were Jews by nationality** (D. & C. 57:4), **their forefathers having come out from Jerusalem**, from the kingdom of Judah (2 Ne. 33:8-10.).... there has been further dilution of the pure Lamanitish blood. But with it all, for the great majority of the descendants of

the original inhabitants of the Western Hemisphere, **the dominant blood lineage is that of Israel. The Indians are repeatedly called Lamanites in the revelations to the Prophet,** and the promise is that in due course they "shall blossom as the rose" (D. & C. 49:24)....[58]

In the recent LDS publication *Gospel Principles,* the reader is told that "**great numbers of Lamanites** in North and South America and the South Pacific **are now receiving the blessings of the gospel.**"[59]

As the owner of Signature Press and "liberal activist" George D. Smith observes: "The **traditional view of American Indians as Book of Mormon descendants is continually reaffirmed in church statements and publications,** as exemplified by a 1984 article in the *Church News* section of the church-owned *Deseret News* ... (26 Feb. 1984)."[60] He admits: "There is **no ambiguity** about the claim that the Book of Mormon was **the record of the entire American Indian population.**"[61]

Why is the historical accuracy of the teaching that the *Book of Mormon* Lamanites are of Jewish origin, and ancestors of the American Indians so important, so crucial? In his book *New Witnesses for God* (1903), Brigham H. Roberts clearly states what is at stake:

> I next call attention to the evidences of **the Hebrew origin of the native Americans,** which origin, of course, if established beyond reasonable doubt, will be one more item of evidence—one, too, of very great weight in the volume of cumulative evidence here being compiled, **since the Hebrew origin of the native American races is fundamental as testimony to the truth of the Book of Mormon.** The Hebrew origin of those races in our book is so unequivocally stated and so emphasized that **if the said American races could be proven beyond doubt to be of other than Hebrew origin, the claims of the Book of Mormon would be shattered.**[62]

The American Indians and DNA

What Roberts did not know was that science eventually would show that the American Indians were **not** of Hebrew origin, as the *Book of Mormon* and LDS leaders for decades, clearly taught.
An article in the *Salt Lake Tribune* explains the problem:

> **Generations of Mormons grew up with the notion that American Indians are descended from a lost tribe from the House of Israel.... The problem is mainstream science has failed to back that story.** Instead, archaeologists, linguists and genetic experts outside Mormon culture say **all the evidence points to Asia** as the place from which American Indians originated....[63]

Thomas W. Murphy's conflict with the LDS Church, mentioned earlier, was given national attention when newspapers picked it up.[64] The *Los Angeles Times* article reported:

> His conclusion is that "the Book of Mormon is a piece of 19th century fiction," said Murphy, a lifelong Mormon who calls himself a Latter-day skeptic. "And that means that **we have to acknowledge sometimes Joseph Smith lied.**" At the same time, Murphy says, he and other like-minded Mormon skeptics agree that "the book might be fiction, but inspired as well."[65]

This article also mentioned Murphy's chapter published in the book *American Apocrypha*,[66] where he concludes:

> So far, **DNA has lent no support to the traditional Mormon beliefs about the origins of Native Americans.** Instead, genetic data have confirmed that migrations from Asia are the primary source of American Indian origins. This research has substantiated already-existing archaeological, cultural, linguistic, and biological evidence. While DNA shows that ultimately all human populations are closely related, **to date**

no intimate genetic link has been found between ancient Israelites and indigenous Americans, much less within the time frame suggested by the Book of Mormon.[67]

Murphy was not the only Mormon scientist to reach such a conclusion. Australian scientist Dr. Simon Southerton posted his experience, "DNA Genealogies of American Indians and the Book of Mormon," on a web site.[68] He explained why, after being a dedicated Mormon for 30 years, he and his family left the LDS Church toward the end of 1998. Here are some brief excerpts from his lengthy account.

I now have ample appreciation of the extent to which the LDS Church manipulates and conceals truth and controls the flow of information to members in order to maintain the faith of the saints....

I collected more and more research papers but failed to find anything that supported migration of Jewish people before Columbus. Enough is known about the DNA lineages of Jews to be very confident that they are clearly distinguishable from Asian lineages. They would also be easily identifiable if they were present in the Americas in significant numbers. I struggled with the complete discrepancy between the research and my understanding of the Book of Mormon and the doctrine of the Lamanites. The Book of Mormon describes the occurrence of Hebrew civilizations in the Americas numbering in the millions. It is clear that the victorious Lamanites would have numbered in the millions in about 400 AD. I could not understand how such large numbers of people could have escaped detection....

The Introduction to the book states that the principle ancestors of the American Indians are the Lamanites. The original founders of both major Book of Mormon civilisations fled to a Promised Land kept from the knowledge of other nations. Historical accounts of these civilisations only mention the presence of people in the New World whose Hebrew origin is accounted for in the text. People who migrated away from these civilisations appeared to be entering further unoccupied territories. There is not a single mention of non-Israelite people in the entire history. According to the Book of Mormon there was clear reason to consider it Mormon doctrine that the American Indians are predominantly the offspring of Hebrew ancestors....

The area leaders initially questioned the validity of the science and assumed that my interpretation was incorrect. They were of the view that the American Indians were Lamanites and if the science doesn't agree with that conclusion then the science is wrong. They suggested I speak to a BYU professor who was an expert in this field.... I corresponded with this BYU professor on about four occasions until I became even more convinced of the seriousness of the situation.... In the midst of his lengthy defences of the Church he acknowledged that greater than 98% of American Indians came from Asia and that this conflicts with current thinking in the church regarding the whereabouts of the Lamanites today. Not only did he confirm my conclusions, he strengthened them even further....

I was amazed at the way educated Latter-day Saints at BYU accommodated the contradictions between science and the Book of Mormon.... I was amazed at the lengths that FARMS went to in order to prop up faith in the Book of Mormon. I felt that the only way I could be satisfied with FARMS explanations was to stop thinking. On the other hand I was also surprised at how readily the declarations of the prophets, including Joseph Smith, could be overlooked in order to salvage the wreck.

The recently produced video, *DNA vs. The Book of Mormon* (2003) includes the statements of several other scientists, who add to and support the conclusions of Murphy and Southerton concerning DNA studies and their conflict with *Book of Mormon* claims.[69]

George D. Smith summarizes the extent of the overall problem: "Twentieth-century research in archeology, population genetics, anthropology, and linguistics **contradicts the theory that Native Americans are of Hebrew origin**.... The Book of Mormon tries to place an Old World Culture into a New World setting that does not fit."[70]

Mormon Responses

Now that the *Book of Mormon* and the LDS leaders have been proven to be wrong, how can this information and their claim of divine inspiration be reconciled? The newly adopted position of LDS writers is that the Lamanites of the *Book of Mormon* **were not** the principal ancestors of the American Indians, but only a small group who were restricted to a limited geographical location. Some suggest that the current gene pool has been "diluted" to the point that the Hebrew origins are obscured. But in order to claim these things, Mormon apologists must ignore or reject the testimony of Joseph Smith, the account of what the angel Moroni specifically told him, and statements in the *Book of Mormon, The Pearl of Great Price* and *Doctrine and Covenants* where the doctrine is affirmed. They also must flatly reject the numerous affirmations of the doctrine by the General Authorities of the Church, Church publications and many LDS scholars.

Specifically, how has the absence of the genetic link been explained by some Mormon scholars?

"The idea that America may have been overwhelmingly peopled by folks from northwestern Asia is **perfectly compatible**" with Mormon doctrine, said Daniel Peterson, a lifelong Mormon and professor of Asian and Near Eastern Languages at Brigham Young. Genetic evidence that some Native American ancestors came from the Middle East could easily be lost over thousands of years, he said. Murphy disagrees, pointing to examples of other groups of people where genetic evidence can be found of ancient influences by foreign populations.⁷¹

In response to Peterson's statement, Bill McKeever of Mormon Research Ministry writes: "'Perfectly compatible'? Not if you take into account the many comments by LDS leaders who insisted that the Lamanite and Nephite populations numbered **in the millions**! It is said that the armies numbered in the millions at the alleged battle at the Hill Cumorah alone."⁷² In agreement, Apostle Orson Pratt claimed that previous to this battle, the entire Nephite population was gathered "around the hill Cumorah" and the Lamanites "gathered by **millions** in the same region." After "four years in gathering their forces ... the fighting commenced, the Lamanites coming upon the Nephites, and **destroying all of them**, except a very few, who had previously deserted to the Lamanites."⁷³

The Deseret News for 26 February 1984 contained an article in the *LDS Church News* section entitled, "Father Lehi's Family Tree," by BYU Professor Owen C. Bennion. He explains:

> The term Lamanites has been used to encompass all Polynesians, North and South American native peoples and subsequent mixtures. A better term might be children of Lehi or even Western Israelites. Children of Lehi are usually considered any people descended from Lehi. Although many have been referred to as Lamanites and considered descendants of Laman and Lemuel, they are also descended from Lehi's other sons: Nephi, Sam, Jacob and Joseph, who were promised their seed would not be annihilated.... Today these people are scattered throughout the Western Hemisphere from Tierra del Fuego at the tip of South America to Canada, and to the islands of the Pacific.⁷⁴

Another tactic used by FARMS in defense of the *Book of Mormon* is to pretend that the DNA evidence is what they expected all along. Obviously, this is at odds with what the LDS scientists were clearly expecting. Daniel Peterson, of FARMS, recently stated that views expressed by geneticists such as Simon Southerton are "naïve" and oversimplified. Peterson said, "his [Southerton's] contention is that the DNA research thus far doesn't support the Book of Mormon. Our contention would be that we would be surprised if it did."[75] Southerton explains the FARMS position further:

> LDS scholars have come to the conclusion that the Jaredite and Nephite peoples comprised a very small part of the vastly larger, pre-existing populations and that those who still believe the whole hemisphere was the stage for Book of Mormon events ... are simply wrongheaded and have made "incorrect interpretation[s] of the text."[76]

As already shown, however, these "incorrect interpretations" came from the leaders of the LDS Church via inspired teachings and divine revelations. In order to accept the FARMS claims on this subject, Mormon members would have to cast off the teachings of their divinely ordained leaders in favor of the FARMS uninspired and contradictory conclusions.

In his chapter in *American Apocrypha,* Thomas Murphy explains the significance of the DNA results:

> New genetic evidence adds to an already impressive amount of **linguistic, archaeological, cultural, biological, anatomical, and psychoanalytic data that challenge the traditional Book of Mormon view**. That view includes the belief that the Lamanites described in the text are the "principal ancestors of the American Indians." Remarkably, most Latter-day Saints **are unaware** of the many reasons why the scientific community rejects that claim.[77]

What about Mormon revisionist efforts to counter the DNA problem? After looking at the shortcomings of some of these, Murphy concludes:

> In their welcome but unsatisfying attempts to provide plausible explanations for the lack of genetic evidence for

Israelites in the Americas, both authors and BYU's leading geneticist **implicitly reject the long-standing popular Mormon beliefs, including those held by Joseph Smith, about Lamanites being the ancestors of today's American Indians.** The shift in the foundations of Mormon beliefs about the Indians, termed a "Galileo event" by Brent Metcalfe, may prove to be the most important historical result of wrestling with genetic data.[78]

From a scientific perspective, the Book of Mormon's origin is best situated in early nineteenth-century America, and Lamanite genesis can only be traced historically to ca. 1828. The term Lamanite is a modern social and political designation that lacks a verifiable biological or historical underpinning linking it to ancient American Indians.[79]

... I believe that we should avoid a fruitless quest to tie Native American origins to the Middle East. **There is as much chance of finding genetic proof of a Lehite civilization in the Americas as there would be of finding the Book of Mormon gold plates.**[80]

In conclusion, the statement by B. H. Roberts, quoted earlier, should be applied to the *Book of Mormon* in the light of these findings.

The Hebrew origin of those races in our book is **so unequivocably stated** and **so emphasized** that **if the said American races could be proven beyond doubt to be of other than Hebrew origin, the claims of the Book of Mormon would be shattered.**[81]

The Testimonies of the Witnesses to the Book of Mormon

The Introduction to *The Book of Mormon* includes two statements: "The Testimony of Three Witnesses" (Oliver Cowdery, David Whitmer, Martin Harris), and "The Testimony of Eight Witnesses" (Christian Whitmer, Jacob Whitmer, Peter Whitmer, Jr., John Whitmer, Hiram Page, Joseph Smith, Sen., Hyrum Smith, Samuel H. Smith). Mormons often cite these testimonies as evidence that the *Book of Mormon* is genuine. Detailed articles, chapters and essays in books, as well as entire books, have been written on these witnesses. As with other examinations, space does not permit an exhaustive treatment here, but the interested reader can consult the materials in the endnotes for further details.[82]

Testimonies Never Denied

The following statement by Dr. Francis W. Kirkham in his book *A New Witness for Christ in America,* is typical of the Mormon defense of the witnesses:

> From the beginning of the Church invective has been directed at the reliability and competency of the witnesses to the Book of Mormon.... But **at no time has any one ever adduced any evidence that shows them dishonest men.** And so far as the careful research of the writer shows, **no such evidence can be found.** Beyond this it is known that all the **witnesses maintained to their death the truth of their testimonies** first published in the first edition of the Book of Mormon.[83]

But not mentioned by Kirkham, and many other Mormon apologists, is the witnesses' worldview that one must know to understand the nature of their claimed experiences. As LDS insider Grant Palmer writes: "We are told that the witnesses never disavowed their testimonies, but we have not come to know these men or investigated what else they said about their experiences."[84] Sharing the same worldview, the 11 witnesses "believed in what has been called second sight. Traditionally, this included the ability to see spirits and their dwelling places within the local hills and elsewhere."[85] "The Smiths ... shared freely with neighbors and relatives about their ability to see subterranean chambers in the local hills. They told of seeing the guardian spirits, or angels, and their caves contained books, tables, swords, and treasures."[86] "The fact that the Smiths organized and participated in treasure digging expeditions indicates their belief in the physical reality of what they saw by second sight."[87]

Even before claiming to find the golden plates in the Hill Cumorah, Joseph Smith, his father, and his brother Hiram, had dug for buried treasure there.[88] And as Dan Vogel explains: "Significantly, **each of the three witnesses had a history of visions before gathering to pray** in the wilderness near the Whitmer farm in late June 1829. Such testimony must be considered if we are to fully understand the men who signed the testimony."[89] As already stated, the rest of the witnesses also believed in second sight.[90] "After meeting Joseph Smith, Harris participated in his own treasure adventures and said that he could 'see things' in the Hill Cumorah."[91]

Both Martin Harris and Oliver Cowdery claimed to have seen the "plates in vision **before** Joseph prophesied that they would view them together."[92] In an interview, "Harris told Joel Tiffany that he received revelations about Mormonism before his vision of the plates."[93] And, as Palmer writes, "Far removed from our own modern empiricism, the world view of the witnesses is difficult for us to grasp. The gold plates they saw and handled disappeared when placed on Cumorah's ground."[94] There were similar treasure-hunting experiences of others at the time:

> Alan Taylor ... has observed that treasure-seeking groups of that era often encountered spectral apparitions and sinking treasure chests. With expectations high, a suggestion from one participant would trigger a group vision, according to his research. Taylor found that years later some of these groups, still believing their experiences were real, would not deny them and never had.[95]

In his introduction to the Martin Harris Collection in *Early Mormon Documents*, volume 2, Vogel writes that

> despite the apparent claim in the Testimony that the plates were seen with "our eyes," **Harris seems to have repeatedly admitted the internal, subjective nature of his visionary experience**. Pomeroy Tucker, foreman in Grandin's printing office, said Harris "used to practice a good deal of his characteristic jargon about 'seeing with the spiritual eye,' and the like." ... "Martin was in the office when I finished setting up the testimony of the three witnesses," John H. Gilbert recalled. "Martin, did you see those plates with your naked eyes?" Gilbert asked. "Martin looked down for an instant, raised his eyes up, and said, 'No, **I saw them with a spir[i]tual eye.**'"... Another Palmyra resident reportedly pressed Harris about his testimony and was told "**I saw them with the eye of faith.**"[96]

And as Vogel states, "Harris continued to affirm the visionary nature of his experience apparently throughout his life."[97]

In a 15 April 1838 letter to excommunicated Apostle Lyman E. Johnson, Stephen Burnett explains how he became disillusioned and left the Church.

> I have reflected long and deliberately upon the history of this church & weighed the evidence for & against it—loth to give it up—but when **I came to hear Martin Harris state in a public** congregation [25 March 1838] **that he never saw the plates with his natural eyes only in vision or imagination, neither Oliver** [Cowdery] **nor David** [Whitmer] **& also that the eight witnesses never saw them & hesitated to sign that instrument for that reason**, but were persuaded to do it, the last pedestal gave way, in my view our foundations was sapped & the entire superstructure fell a heap of ruins....[98]

Warren Parrish was Joseph Smith's private secretary. In his 11 August 1838 letter to E. Holmes he writes, "Martin Harris, one of the subscribing witnesses, has come out at last, and says **he never saw the plates**, from which the book [of Mormon] purports to have been translated, except in vision, and he further says that **any man who says he has seen them in any other way is a liar, Joseph** [Smith] **not excepted.**"[99]

It is quite significant that Wesley P. Lloyd, former dean of the Graduate School at BYU, recorded that the Mormon historian B. H. Roberts also had concluded "that **the plates with the Urim and Thummim were not objective.**"[100]

After quoting the testimony of the eight witnesses, Palmer concludes: "Although this collective declaration again seems to describe a literal event, **the supporting evidence points to a less physical incident.** If the three witnesses and others inspected the plates in a vision, perhaps the eight did so also. **Their statements indicate that this is likely the case.**"[101]

Is Their Word Trustworthy?

While the three witnesses to the *Book of Mormon* "have been venerated by believers in the Book of Mormon" and "their disaffection with the church and the subsequent return of Cowdery and Harris" is known by many Mormons, "few are aware how harshly their characters were assailed by Joseph and other church officials at Kirtland and in church publications after 1838"—before Cowdery and Harris returned.[102]

David Whitmer was excommunicated in 1838 and never returned to the LDS church. And, as Petersen notes, "while it is true [David] Whitmer never denied his testimony of the former [*Book of Mormon*], it is equally true he did not repudiate Hiram Page, the Kirtland seeress, or God's voice in 1838" (see the endnote for details).[103]

Oliver Cowdery was excommunicated from the church in April 1838. Of nine charges against him recorded in *History of the Church*

3:16-17, six were sustained as grounds for his dismissal. Some of these clearly questioned his honesty.[104] "After his excommunication Cowdery joined the Methodist Church at Tiffin, Ohio [as a charter member], and became a Sunday-school superintendent."[105] A poem in the 15 July 1841 *Times and Seasons* **would indicate that Cowdery had expressed doubts about his testimony**:

...Or prove that Christ was not the Lord
Because that Peter cursed and swore?
Or Book of Mormon not his word
Because denied, by Oliver? ...[106]

On 12 November 1848 Cowdery was baptized again into the LDS Church, "but according to his brother-in-law, David Whitmer, with whom he spent the year prior to his death in 1850, Oliver rejected the Doctrine and Covenants, the sacred book of God's revelations to Joseph."[107]

Martin Harris was excommunicated from the Church in December 1837 (reinstated 1841). LaMar Petersen writes: "Of all the figures in early Mormonism none was more thoroughly discredited by friend and foe than Martin Harris. Even the Lord pronounced him a 'wicked man' for losing the 116 pages of the translation (D&C 10:1,7)."[108]

After the Mormons left Kirtland, Ohio, in 1838, Harris remained there for a number of years. His former employer Christopher Crary was non-flattering in his description of him, writing: "His mind, always unbalanced on the subject of Mormonism, had become so demented that **he thought himself a bigger man than Smith, or even Christ**, and believed that most of the prophecies of the Old Testament referred directly to him."[109]

As Dan Vogel found, "Those who knew Harris to be honest in business also described him as **an unstable religious eccentric**." In this realm, he was characterized as "a great man for seeing spooks," "slightly demented," and "a visionary fanatic." Harris also claimed earlier in his life that he had met and talked with Jesus Christ and that "he saw the devil." As Vogel rightly comments, "Whether or not the specifics are accurate, Harris's propensity for visionary experience must be considered if we are to understand this Book of Mormon witness."[110]

It should also be remembered that "during the 1840s he became a follower of Ann Lee and the Shakers, then switched allegiance to James Jesse Strang, claimant to Joseph's mantle, and served as a missionary in England for Strangite Mormonism. Altogether he joined eight different groups."[111] He made his way to Utah and was rebaptized into the church in 1870 and died in 1875.[112] Was Harris a credible witness?

Non-Mormon writer David Persuitte observes:

> Mormon writers have made much of the fact that the three witnesses apparently never clearly disavowed their testimony concerning the gold plates during their period of disenfranchisement from the church. However, **one cannot place a very great importance on this seeming steadfastness of the witnesses.** If any one of them had outspokenly denied his testimony, he would have exposed himself to the world as a base perjurer, and he would have brought down upon himself the wrath of those who had been converted to Mormonism because of that testimony.[113]

Of the eight witnesses, Christian Whitmer (d. 1835), Jacob Whitmer (left the church in 1838), Peter Whitmer, Jr. (d. 1836) and Joseph Smith Sr., "left no commentary regarding their testimonies."[114] Hiram Page left the church in 1838, and John Whitmer was excommunicated the same year. Hyrum Smith (d. 1844) and Samuel H. Smith (d. 1844) were Joseph Smith's brothers.[115]

James J. Strang—A Parallel?

James J. Strang was baptized by Joseph Smith on 25 February 1844; on 27 June of that year, Smith was murdered. On 5 August, Strang claimed that by a revelation dated 18 June 1844 Smith had appointed him as his successor, producing a letter to support his claim. However, it was judged to be a forgery. Strang's insistence on his appointment resulted in his immediate excommunication from the Church—the first of three.[116]

Why is Strang relevant to the immediate subject? Palmer explains that Joseph Smith "was not alone in producing witnesses of ancient records. James J. Strang ... like Joseph, **produced eleven signatories who testified that they too had seen and inspected ancient metal plates.**"[117] There were many other parallels to the claims and experiences of Joseph Smith. A local newspaper editor stated that in his judgment Strang and the witnesses were honest people.[118] And although one of the eleven was excommunicated, "**there is no direct evidence that he or any of the other ten men ever denied their testimonies.**"[119] Should Strang's witnesses be believed?

In February 1846, Mormon Apostle Heber C. Kimball denigrated Strang and his movement, stating that "Strangism was not worth investigating," adding, "it is not worth the skin of a fart."[120] Yet this denigrated but charismatic leader would claim 2,000 followers—including Joseph Smith's mother (Lucy Mack Smith), Martin Harris, and other prominent early Mormon leaders.[121] And as Palmer writes,

> In conclusion, **all of the living signatories to the Book of Mormon, except possibly Cowdery, accepted Strang's leadership, angelic call, metal plates, and his translation of these plates as authentic.** This replication of an earlier pattern of belief confirms that it must have been relatively easy for the witnesses to accept Joseph Smith's golden plates as an ancient record. Appreciating their mindset helps us understand Mormon origins in their terms.[122]

What Others Have Concluded About the Witnesses

Joel B. Groat

In the introduction to Part 1 of his "Facts On the Book of Mormon Witnesses" article, Groat writes:

The Three Witnesses, Oliver Cowdery, Martin Harris and David Whitmer, all initially describe their experience with the angel and the plates **as subjective and visionary rather than objective** and concrete. Their elaborations on the encounter, their departure from the LDS Church, as well as other events in their lives, raise questions about their level of discernment **and their credibility** as witnesses.

The testimony of the Eight Witnesses is more objective but is plagued by its own set of problems. All eight had close personal ties to Joseph Smith's family—four were David Whitmer's brothers, a fifth was married to a Whitmer sister, and Joseph's father and two brothers made up the remaining three. These close ties to Joseph Smith, coupled with discrepancies between the witnesses' published Book of Mormon statement and their later personal statements, as well as the question of coercion on the part of Joseph Smith, **all raise questions of their credibility** as well.[123]

In Part 2 of his article, Groat concludes:

According to historical evidence, the Mormon church's customary portrayal of the witnesses as eleven men of rational and critical mindsets, unquestioned honesty and integrity and unwavering commitment to the Mormon church and the Book of Mormon **is far from true**. Joseph **Smith himself questioned their integrity**, and many of them left the church and did not return.[124]

The witnesses' testimonies as a whole are presented as objective, solid, and irrefutable, but upon close examination **are seen to be subjective, ambiguous and, at times, contradictory**. The traditional portrayal of a tightly woven story of Mormon origins is slowly being unraveled by the historical evidence, much of which is now being compiled and published within the Mormon community itself.[125]

Jerald and Sandra Tanner

After reviewing the evidence, the Tanners conclude:

Since a person who is investigating the *Book of Mormon* has only the testimony of eleven men to rely on, he should be certain that they were honorable men. If the *Book of Mormon* witnesses were honest, stable and not easily influenced by men, we would be impressed by their testimony. Unfortunately, however, we find that this is not the case. **The evidence shows that they were gullible, credulous, and their word cannot be relied upon.**[126]

Apostle John A. Widtsoe said that the *Book of Mormon* plates were seen and handled "by eleven competent men, of independent minds and spotless reputations." We feel, however, we have demonstrated that **these witnesses were easily influenced by men and therefore were not competent witnesses.** Contrary to Apostle Widtsoe's statement, **these witnesses were not men of "spotless reputation,"** but rather men whose word could not always be relied upon. **Some of them even gave false revelations in the name of the Lord.** Mormons ask us to accept David Whitmer's testimony to the *Book of Mormon*, but will they accept Whitmer's revelations which he gave when he was with the McLellin group? Certainly not. Neither will they accept his statement that "God spake to me again by His own voice from the heavens, and told me to 'separate myself from among the latter Day Saints.'"[127]

Richard Abanes

In an endnote, research journalist and author Richard Abanes briefly examines the testimonies of the witnesses in the *Book of Mormon*, and writes:

Mormons have assumed that these statements mean that the individuals named actually saw the golden plates with their own eyes. However, **numerous historical documents demonstrate that these men only saw through visionary experiences. None of them actually ever saw the plates with their natural sight** in the same way anyone would be able to see or pick up a book on a table. The Three Witnesses, as it turns out, had the plates shown to them by an angel who appeared to them while they were praying in the woods. The Eight Witnesses only "saw" the plates as long as they were covered with a cloth of some kind. **Martin Harris, one of the so-called "Three Witnesses," went so far as to admit that none of the eight witnesses ever saw the plates.**[128]

LaMar Petersen

Examination of the statements of the three Book of Mormon witnesses shows that while they bore firm testimony both in and out of the church, sometimes the nature of that testimony has been misunderstood. The most dramatic damage to the accepted image of the three witnesses is **the very real possibility that their testimony may have been based on a visionary or mental experience, and not a physical one.**[129]

Dan Vogel

In his essay, "The Validity of the Witnesses' Testimonies," in *American Apocrypha*, Dan Vogel makes the point:

The important question is not whether the witnesses were trustworthy or if they continued to maintain their belief in the Book of Mormon throughout their lives. **The central question**—the question explored in this essay—**concerns the nature of their experiences** and if their statements are distinguishable from those claiming similar religious testimonies.[130]

He concludes:

> Given the fact that **the three witnesses saw a vision and that the experience of the eight witnesses seems to have been similarly visionary, there is no compelling evidence that Joseph Smith actually possessed anciently constructed plates**.... The real question is not the trustworthiness of the witnesses but whether testimony resulting from visions or hallucinations is reliable. Indeed, does the testimony of the Book of Mormon witnesses merit greater attention than that of other similar religious testimony? Or rather, is the nature of the witnesses' experiences different from the multitude of religious testimony confronting historians? Indeed, by what criteria do we accept the Book of Mormon witnesses while at the same time rejecting non-Mormon testimony? In the final analysis, **nothing distinguishes the visions of the Book of Mormon witnesses from those of their contemporaries**.[131]

Conclusion on the Witnesses

Mormons claim that the testimonies of the witnesses are proof that the *Book of Mormon* is true. But it can be also be argued that if the *Book of Mormon* was the non-historical creation of Joseph Smith, as the foregoing and following material demonstrates, then the testimonies of the 11 witnesses prove nothing. In that case one of three possibilities remains—they deceived themselves; Smith deceived them; or they participated in the deception.

What Mormon and Ex-Mormon Scholars Have Stated Concerning the *Book of Mormon*

After years of research and study into various facets of the *Book of Mormon*, even some LDS scholars have had to conclude that it is not the divine, historical record it claims to be. While some of them ultimately left the LDS Church, they did study and research while still members of the faith. Following are several examples of their conclusions.

Brigham H. Roberts

In his biographical essay on Brigham H. Roberts (1857-1933) in *Studies of the Book of Mormon*, Professor Sterling M. McMurrin writes that Roberts was

> Mormonism's **most competent historian and leading theologian**, as well as the most aggressive exponent and capable disputant in its leadership, Roberts quite naturally, and certainly very effectively, filled the role of **chief defender of the faith**. This, of course, entailed the defense of the Book of Mormon, the claims of its origin, the historical reliability of its narrative, its sometimes strange theology, and the necessity of its coming forth in the "last dispensation."[132]

Others have identified Roberts as "the most distinguished intellectual in the Church's history,"[133] and as "one of the most important figures in twentieth-century Mormonism."[134] The *Encyclopedia of Mormonism* described him as "one of the most eloquent orators and penetrating writers in the Church's history. An inveterate seeker, he grappled with many historical and scriptural issues as a 'defender of the faith.'"[135] "In sheer volume his literary output exceeds anything produced by a Mormon Church leader before or since."[136] In 1909, as the Church's leading apologist on the defense of the *Book of Mormon*, he published his three-volume *New Witnesses for God*. He was an important member of the presidency in the First Council of Seventy from 1888 until his death in 1933.[137]

In a 22 August 1921 letter to Apostle James E. Talmage, Mormon William Riter was "asking for a response to five questions submitted to him by a Mr. Couch of Washington, D.C., who was investigating the claims of the Book of Mormon."[138] Talmage passed these questions on to B. H. Roberts for a reply:

1. How could the great diversity in primitive Indian languages have occurred in such a short period of time after about A.D. 400, when the Nephites, whose Hebrew language was so highly developed, disappeared?
2. The Book of Mormon reports that the followers of Lehi, upon their arrival in the New World, found horses, which were not in existence when the first Spanish explorers arrived.
3. Although the Jews had no knowledge of steel in 600 B.C., Nephi was reported to have had a bow of steel after he left Jerusalem.
4. The Book of Mormon speaks of "swords and scimeters," and yet the "scimeter" does not appear in early literature before the rise of Mohammedanism, which took place after Lehi departed from Jerusalem.
5. Even though silk was not known in America, the Nephites knew and used silk.[139]

In his investigation "Roberts returned to his earlier defense, *New Witnesses for God* (1909), but also began a major reexamination of the issue. Over the next six months, he prepared two lengthy studies: the 141-page 'Book of Mormon Difficulties' (1921) and the 291-page 'A Book of Mormon Study' (1922)." Then in 1927, Roberts's, "'A Parallel,' more concisely listed the similarities between the Book of Mormon and *A View of the Hebrews*."[140]

In a letter dated 29 December 1921, Roberts asked for a meeting with the General Authorities. He wrote: "I found the difficulties more serious than I had thought for; and the more I investigated the more difficult I found the formulation of the answer to Mr. Couch's inquires to be." Roberts hoped

> that from the greater learning of the individual members of the Quorum of Twelve, or from the collective wisdom of all the brethren addressed, **or from the inspiration of the Lord**

as it may be received through the appointed channels of the priesthood of his Church, **we might find such a solution of the problems presented** in the accompanying correspondence, as will maintain the reasonableness for the faith of all in the Nephite scriptures....[141]

In response to Roberts's request, meetings took place on the 4th, 5th and 26th of January 1922, but the first two meetings did not answer his questions. He expressed his disappointment to President Heber J. Grant in a letter on 9 January that year.[142] Even after three additional meetings, **no answer was available**.[143]

In his meeting with Wesley P. Lloyd, mentioned earlier, Roberts discussed the Riter letter, his investigation of the problems, and his meeting with the Church authorities. Roberts reveals:

> In answer, they merely one by one stood up and bore testimony to the truthfulness of the Book of Mormon.... Bro. Roberts could not criticize them for **not being able to answer** it or to assist him, but said that in a Church which claimed continuous revelation, a crisis had arisen where revelation was necessary.... There was however a committee appointed to study this problem, consisting of Bros. Talmage, Ballard, Roberts and one other Apostle. **They met and looked vacantly at one and other, but none seemed to know what to do about it.** Finally, Bro. Roberts mentioned that he had at least attempted an answer and had it in his drawer. That it was an answer that **would satisfy people that didn't think**, but [it was] a very inadequate answer to a thinking man. They asked him to read it and after hearing it, **they adopted it by vote** and said that was about the best they could do.[144]

Lloyd went on to record that in Roberts's *Book of Mormon* study he

> swings to a psychological explanation of the Book of Mormon and shows that **the plates were not objective but subjective** with Joseph Smith, that his exceptional imagination

qualified him psychologically for the experience which he had in presenting to the world the Book of Mormon and that **the plates with the Urim and Thummim were not objective**.[145]

Roberts's material—titled *Studies of the Book of Mormon*—was published in 1985 by the University of Illinois Press, with a second edition in 1992 by Signature Books.[146]

Here are some of Roberts's statements in *Studies of the Book of Mormon*.

> ... **did Ethan Smith's View of the Hebrews furnish structural material for Joseph Smith's Book of Mormon?** It has been pointed out in these pages that there are many things in the former book that might well have suggested many major things in the other. Not a few things merely, one or two, or a half dozen**, but many;** and it is this fact of many things of similarity and **the cumulative force of them that make them so serious a menace to Joseph Smith's story of Book of Mormon's origin.** (p. 240)

> In the light of this evidence, there can be no doubt as to the possession of a vividly strong, creative imagination by Joseph Smith, the Prophet, an imagination, it could with reason be urged, which, given the suggestions that are to be found in the "common knowledge" of accepted American antiquities of the times, supplemented by such a work as Ethan Smith's *View of the Hebrews*, **would make it possible for him to create a book such as the Book of Mormon is.** (250)

> If from all that has gone before in Part I, the view be taken that the Book of Mormon is merely of human origin; that a person of Joseph Smith's limitations in experience and in education, who was of the vicinage and of the period that produced the book—**if it be assumed that he is the author**

of it, then it could be said there is much internal evidence in the book itself to sustain such a view. (251)

After looking at the Anti-Christs—Sherem, Nehor and Korihor—in the *Book of Mormon*, Roberts concludes:

... they are all of one breed and brand; so nearly alike that one mind is the author of them, and that a young and undeveloped, but piously inclined mind. **The evidence I sorrowfully submit, points to Joseph Smith as their creator. It is difficult to believe that they are the product of history,** that they come upon the scene separated by long periods of time, and among a race which was the ancestral race of the red man of America. (271)

The whole treatment of war and battles, some will say, **bears evidence of having originated in one mind** and that mind pious but immature.... Beautiful story of faith! Beautiful story of mother-assurance! **Is it history? Or is it a wonder-tale of a pious but immature mind?** In some cases blundering expressions bordering on comedy are found in recounting war events. (272, 273)

The allusions here to absurdities of expressions and incidents in the Book of Mormon are not made for the purpose of ridiculing the book, or casting undue aspersions upon it; but they are made to indicate **what may be fairly regarded as just objects of criticism under the assumption that the Book of Mormon is of human origin, and that Joseph Smith is its author**.... these lapses of the main characters about conditions obtaining, are certainly just such absurdities and lapses as would be looked for if a person of such limitations as bounded Joseph Smith undertook to put forth a book dealing with the history and civilizations of ancient peoples. (277)

I think it cannot be questioned but where there is sufficient resemblance between the Book of Mormon instances of religious emotionalism and those cited in the foregoing quotations from the works of Edwards *et al.* **to justify the thought that the latter might well have suggested and indeed become the source of the former.** (308)

What, then, is Roberts's conclusion? His biographer, Truman G. Madsen, argued that Roberts was just playing "devil's advocate,"[147] when concluding the *Book of Mormon* was not an authentic historical document. But as one reviewer commented, "Anyone who tells you this either hasn't read the book, or they are less than honest."[148] Jerald and Sandra Tanner observe:

While there is no evidence that B. H. Roberts publicly repudiated the Book of Mormon, a careful reading of his manuscript, "A Book of Mormon Study," **leads one to believe that he was in the process of losing his faith in its divine origin**. Although he may have started out merely playing the part of the "Devil's Advocate," we feel that he played the role so well that **he developed grave doubts about the authenticity of the Book of Mormon**.[149]

Brigham D. Madsen, in his Introduction to *Studies of the Book of Mormon*, writes that "the document reveals a Roberts whose dogmatic assertions of his *New Witnesses for God* had been **replaced by pained and troubled doubts about the Book of Mormon**, which he challenged his colleagues in the hierarchy to resolve."[150] Later he asks: "During the last six years of his life is there any evidence that Roberts still retained his faith in the authenticity of the Book of Mormon, despite his critical examination of the origin of the book"? He concludes, "The record is mixed."[151] "Whether or not Roberts retained his belief in the Book of Mormon may never be determined."[152] It is true that shortly before his death he affirmed the *Book of Mormon*—

But in his "A Book of Mormon Study," Roberts presents an intense and probing evaluation of the possibility that Ethan Smith's *View of the Hebrews* furnished a partial framework for Joseph Smith's written composition, that **the Mormon prophet had the intellectual capacity and imagination necessary to conceive and write the Book of Mormon**, and that internal contradictions and other defects **added further evidence that it might not be of divine origin.**[153]

In Madsen's presentation to the Algie Ballif Society on 22 March 1986,

> The real question, he said, was whether Roberts had in fact wavered in his commitment to the Book of Mormon: did he believe it was a divinely inspired historical record **or Joseph Smith's personal creation? Madsen argued that the record clearly shows that Roberts believed the latter.** 'That is the charge by B. H. Roberts against Joseph Smith,' he said...."[154]

And in his article in the Fall 1997 issue of *Dialogue*, Madsen writes, "One can sympathize with Roberts and his sorrow that, after venerating and admiring Joseph Smith for a lifetime, **he now had concluded that his hero was less than a prophet.**"[155]

In his essay "B. H. Roberts: Book of Mormon Apologist and Skeptic," George D. Smith, concludes that there were two sides to Roberts:

> **While speaking to the church as a general authority, Roberts addressed the book as an ancient record; privately, however, he voiced doubts.** In the last twelve years of his life, he encountered questions about Book of Mormon language, archeology, and geography that he could not answer. As he reexamined his earlier writings on the subject, he turned to his colleagues with two critical treatises that asked whether the prophet had created a "wonder tale" which, "I sorrowfully submit, points to Joseph Smith" as its

author. **He expressed his public faith and private doubts to the end of his life.**[156]

In his article on Roberts and his manuscripts on the origin of the *Book of Mormon*, researcher Wesley P. Walters writes:

> Whether Mr. Roberts wrote these works to summarize some of the main objections to the *Book of Mormon's* divine origin, or whether he himself had come to doubt the book's divinity seems difficult to determine. The letters that accompany the manuscripts suggest the former, but **the manuscripts themselves give a decided impression that Mr. Roberts had come to doubt the book's divine origin.** One Mormon professor, after reading the manuscripts, remarked, "B. H. Roberts came about as near calling Joseph Smith, Jr. a fraud and deceit as the polite language of a religious man would permit." **Whatever the motive, the manuscripts deserve consideration on their own merit and present one of the strongest statements ever set forth by a recognized Mormon authority questioning the divine origin of the *Book of Mormon*.**[157]

Finally, if Roberts's "A Book of Mormon Study" material did not really question Joseph Smith and the origin of the *Book of Mormon*, how can the following be explained? "Having discovered this long-lost manuscript in October 1973 in the possession of one of Roberts's grandsons, H. Grant Ivins" wrote a letter in which he explained:

> When the Church people talked Ben Roberts out of publishing this material, **they told him that to publish would ruin his father's reputation as a historian and as a 'defender of the church.'** In my opinion, the reverse is true. This book would establish him as an **honest historian, really seeking the truth**, no matter what it did to his other works.[158]

Even this life-long, dedicated General Authority of the Church, after studying the *Book of Mormon* carefully, came away doubting its divine authenticity. He reached this conclusion in spite of the assurances from the book itself that the Holy Spirit would attest to its truthfulness.

Thomas Stuart Ferguson

Thomas Stuart Ferguson (1915-1983) was a respected defender of the LDS faith, and a popular and well-known speaker and writer on *Book of Mormon* archaeology from the 1940s through the late 1960s. An account of his search for truth is reviewed in Stan Larson's *Quest for the Golden Plates: Thomas Stuart Ferguson's Archaeological Search for The Book of Mormon*.[159]

Ferguson wrote a number of articles and authored or co-authored four books: *Cumorah—Where?* (1947), *Ancient America and the Book of Mormon*[160] (1950), *Great Message of Peace and Happiness* (1952), and *One Fold and One Shepherd* (1958).[161] As Stan Larson explains, "Ferguson felt that his work in life was to be an instrument in verifying the historical claims of the Book of Mormon through archaeological excavations in Mesoamerica."[162]

Certain that the *Book of Mormon* was true, Ferguson was confident that confirmation could be established by archaeological exploration. In 1951, his plan as to how this could be done, with a request for funding, was sent to the LDS General Authorities. Ferguson believed his request would be approved, but he was wrong—"the Church politely rejected the archaeological proposal and offered no financial assistance."[163] While disappointed, "Ferguson's deep faith in the Book of Mormon gave him the necessary drive to continue on his own, without LDS institutional support."[164] He raised funds from private parties and in October 1952 organized the New World Archaeological Foundation (NWAF), with himself as president, and in December work began in Huimanguillo, Tabasco, Mexico.[165]

He persisted in contacting Church leaders and his presentation to the First Presidency in 1955 finally resulted in a financial pledge of $200,000 from the Church.[166] In a 15 March 1958 letter to the First Presidency, expressing his faith, Ferguson wrote: "The

Book of Mormon is either fake or fact. If fake, the cities described in it are non-existent. If fact—as we know it to be—the cities will be there. If the cities exist, and they do, they constitute tangible, physical, enduring, unimpeachable evidence that Joseph Smith was a true prophet of God and that Jesus Christ lives."[167] In 1960 it was announced "that NWAF would be reorganized as part of a new and continued support by the LDS Church through BYU." In the new arrangement, Ferguson was no longer the president, but served in the minor capacity of secretary.[168]

Ferguson's faith that the *Book of Mormon* would be verified by archaeology was still strong through the mid-1960s.[169] What initiated a change in his thinking was the discovery of the lost Book of Abraham papyri. After the LDS Church acquired them, Ferguson was ready to "put these new discoveries to the test," and he wrote a letter (4 December 1967) to Professor Aziz S. Atiya.

> I am a Mormon and recognize immediately that your discovery has a strong bearing upon the validity of the foundations of the Mormon Church. Since today Egyptologists can read and translate the documents on which the "Book of Abraham" is based, **we can readily determine whether, as of July 3, 1835** (the date when Joseph Smith claimed the manuscripts included writings of Abraham and Joseph) **Joseph Smith was fabricating, lying, and conjuring up "scripture"** for the Church. **If the manuscript material which you found is nothing more nor less that a bit of one of the *Book of the Dead*, such would be the required deduction** as to Joseph Smith as of 1835.... The Book of Abraham has been "suspect" to me for some time.[170]

Ferguson asked two Egyptologists to translate the papyri and he also studied two translations that had already been published. In a letter he concludes: "Since four scholars, who have established that they can read Egyptian, say that the manuscripts deal with neither Abraham nor Joseph—and since the four reputable men tell us exactly what the manuscripts do say—**I must conclude that Joseph Smith had not the remotest skill in things Egyptian-hieroglyphics.**"[171]

And, as Stan Larson observes, "After many years of archaeological investigations, disappointed by not finding the long-hoped-for confirmation of the *Book of Mormon*, **Ferguson finally concluded that the book was 'fictional'**" and would never be confirmed by archaeology.[172] However, Ferguson saw Mormonism as "the best available brand of **man-made religion**,"[173] and he continued to attend the LDS Church.

In the words of Stan Larson, Ferguson became a "closet doubter" Mormon.

> He saw many beneficial things in the religions of mankind, and Mormonism was to him the most useful—**but not ultimately true**. Though Ferguson doubted that Joseph Smith could translate Egyptian texts, though he repudiated the antiquity of the Book of Abraham, though **he rejected the authenticity of the Book of Mormon**, though he questioned that Joseph Smith or anyone else was a true prophet of God—still he considered the LDS Church to be a wonderful fraternity....[174]

Charles Larson's book, *By His Own Hand Upon Papyrus,* contains photocopies of several letters written by Ferguson between 1971 and 1979.[175] In one dated 20 February 1976, Ferguson stated that he had enclosed a copy of his "paper on Book of Mormon matters."[176] He explained: "The real implication of the paper is that you can't set Book of Mormon geography down anywhere—-**because it is fictional** and will never meet the requirements of the dirt-archeology. I should say—**what is in the ground will never conform to what is in the book**."[177] And as LaMar Petersen comments,

> Ferguson's 1975 listing of problems remains unanswered twenty-three years later. Thus, **these points stand as serious obstacles to authenticating the Book of Mormon**. In his study Ferguson remarked that no one, "from Joseph Smith to the present day, has put a finger on a single point of terrain that was a Book of Mormon geographical place."[178]

In a 9 February 1976 letter, Ferguson even recommended reading *Mormonism—Shadow or Reality?* by Jerald and Sandra Tanner (two of the LDS Church's most maligned critics), and Fawn Brodie's *No Man Knows My History.*[179] In a 24 May 1977 letter, quoted by Stan Larson, Ferguson concluded that Joseph Smith, "**was a phony** with lots of meritorious ideas."[180]

Shortly before his death, Ferguson visited with Ronald O. Barney, Senior Archivist at the Mormon Church Historical Department, and "confided in him that he was working on a project which he felt would show that the Book of Mormon was in reality *a 19th century production.*"[181]

Ferguson's study of the *Book of Mormon*, though begun with the most biased attitude in favor of the book,[182] led to the conclusion that it was not a divine historical record, and that Joseph Smith was not a true prophet.[183]

Dee F. Green

Mormon scholar, Dr. Dee F. Green, was editor of the University Archaeological Society Newsletter at BYU from 1958-61. When he wrote the article "Book of Mormon Archaeology: The Myths and the Alternatives," quoted below, he was Assistant Professor of Anthropology at Weber State College. He concluded:

> **The first myth we need to eliminate is that Book of Mormon archeology exists.** Titles on books full of archeological half-truths, dilettanti on the peripheries of American archaeology calling themselves Book of Mormon archaeologists regardless of their education, and a Department of Archaeology at BYU devoted to the production of Book of Mormon archaeologists **do not insure that Book of Mormon archaeology really exists**.... The Book of Mormon is really there so one *can* have Book of Mormon studies, and archaeology is really there so one can study archaeology, but the two are not wed. *At least they are not wed in reality since no Book of Mormon location is known with reference to modern topography.*[184]

Edward H. Ashment

Edward H. Ashment, former coordinator for Translation Services for the LDS Church, studied Egyptology at the University of Chicago and became a doctoral candidate. In his essay, "Making the Scriptures 'Indeed One in Our Hands,'" Ashment gives some examples where the *Book of Mormon* records the erroneous translations from the King James Version. He concludes: "Such examples as these, as well as those presented by [Stan] Larson, are additional evidence that **the Book of Mormon was originally composed in the nineteenth century**, the most ancient text upon which any of its contents were based being the KJV."[185] In a second essay he confirms: "Unfortunately **there is no direct evidence to support the historical claims** of the Book of Mormon—**nothing archaeological, nothing philological**."[186]

John C. Kunich

John Kunich joined the Mormon Church at the age of 25. He converted as a result of the "burning in the bosom" experience—"I felt like I was being enveloped by love." Later, in his reading of the *Book of Mormon*, he states, "From my biological background I knew that something was wrong in what I was reading there"—a problem in its accounts of population sizes.[187]

In his essay, "Multiply Exceedingly: Book of Mormon Population Sizes," he claims, "I believe we have **overlooked a fundamental difficulty** in Book of Mormon population sizes."[188] How did Kunich describe this "difficulty"? "Perhaps Book of Mormon peoples 'multiplied exceedingly' at **a rate thirty to fifty times the world average**."[189] After examining various explanations, he concludes: "All these factors taken together tend to argue against the population sizes reported in the Book of Mormon."[190]

And finally, he writes:

> Given the evidence presented in this essay, it is reasonable to conclude that **some of the details of events in the Book of Mormon are not literally historical**. Whether this is

due to modern scribal error, misinterpretation, the nature of revelation, the mode of transmission of the Book of Mormon text, or the nature of the text itself is left to individual interpretation.[191]

H. Michael Marquardt

H. Michael Marquardt joined the Mormon Church in 1961. "As he began to look into his new-found faith more closely, he discovered a mass of **contradiction, confusion, and suppression** of information.... Finally in 1976 he resigned from the LDS Church."[192] His research continued after leaving and resulted in the publication of a number of articles and books.[193] In his article, "The Use of the Bible In the Book of Mormon," after reviewing many specific examples, he concludes:

> It is plain to see that both the Old and New Testaments of the King James Version of the Bible have been used extensively **in the production and composition of the Book of Mormon.** Passages from the New Testament were adapted to represent a different century, language, and culture, and attributed to the pre-Columbian people of America.... When one adds the other contemporary material reflected in the book and the personal material from Joseph Smith's own life ... **it is quite clear that the Book of Mormon contains its own proof of modern origin. The evidence shows that it is a nineteenth-century religious fictional book and has no historical value as a religious record of ancient America.**[194]

Dan Vogel

Scholar Dan Vogel was a former Mormon who became disaffected with the Church after his studies into various aspects of LDS history.[195] While he continues to study and write about his findings, he does not wish to be labeled either "pro" or "anti" Mormon.[196] In the conclusion to his book *Indian Origins and the Book of Mormon,* Vogel writes:

I am keenly aware of the controversial nature of the subject, especially as it pertains to the historicity of the Book of Mormon.... For various reasons an increasing number of faithful Mormons are suggesting that it may be possible **to question the Book of Mormon's historicity** and yet maintain a belief in its sacred and inspired nature. They have joined with non-Mormon scholars in a search for clues from Joseph Smith's environment which might help to better understand the origin of Mormonism and its founding scripture: the Book of Mormon.... That some of the major features of the Book of Mormon's history of ancient America originated centuries before in religiously motivated minds and subsequently proved to be inaccurate would seem **to argue in favor of the book's modern origin**. Those readers who continue **to maintain the Book of Mormon's ancient historicity must do so in the face of what I consider to be some rather clear indications to the contrary**.[197]

What Non-LDS Scholars Have Said Concerning the *Book of Mormon*

Non-LDS scholars have also looked into the claims of the *Book of Mormon* and found them to demonstrate that the book is not historical. Here are some of their findings.

Michael D. Coe

Dr. Michael D. Coe, emeritus curator at the Peabody Museum,[198] former professor of anthropology at Yale University and a leading expert on the archeology of Mesoamerica, wrote "Mormons & Archaeology: An Outside View."[199] In it, he stated:

> Mormon archeologists over the years have almost unanimously accepted the Book of Mormon as an accurate, historical account of the New World peoples between about 2,000 B.C. and A.D. 421. They believe that Smith could translate

hieroglyphs, whether "Reformed Egyptian" or ancient American, and that his translation of the Book of Abraham is authentic.... **Let me now state uncategorically that as far as I know there is not one professionally trained archaeologist, who is *not* a Mormon, who sees any scientific justification for believing the foregoing to be true,** and I would like to state that **there are quite a few Mormon archaeologists who join this group.**[200]

The bare facts of the matter are that **nothing, absolutely nothing, has ever shown up in any New World excavation which would suggest to a dispassionate observer that the Book of Mormon, as claimed by Joseph Smith, is a historical document relating to the history of early migrants to our hemisphere.**[201]

When Coe's statement was cited some years after it was published, some Mormons denied its impact, stating that it was outdated. Bill McKeever of Mormonism Research Ministry wrote Dr. Coe to ask if his position had changed. In his 17 August 1993 reply he wrote:

> **I haven't changed my views** about the Book of Mormon since my 1973 article. I have seen **no archeological evidence before or since that date** which would convince me that it is anything but a fanciful creation by an unusually gifted individual living in upstate New York in the early 19th century.[202]

Thomas J. Finley

Dr. Thomas J. Finley, with expertise in Near Eastern languages, makes the point that "anachronisms are more significant than parallels for determining the historical setting of a written work. If a story purports to come from the early 1960s, but one of the characters mentions the Internet, then it would be reasonable to assume that the story was actually written in the 1990s or later."[203] At the end of his essay, "Does the Book of Mormon Reflect an Ancient Near Eastern Background?" Finley concludes:

> **There is no solid evidence that the Book of Mormon was written by Semites in ancient times.** Contrary evidence makes it more likely that the book is a product of Joseph Smith's time, with the KJV strongly influencing it. Its linguistic features and supposed original form on brass or gold plates differentiate it from known ancient Near Eastern literature. The social, cultural, and geographic features within the Book of Mormon derive easily from the KJV. In fact, some features are anachronistic even for the KJV. **We have not discovered any features of the Book of Mormon that would make plausible the hypothesis that Joseph Smith translated it from ancient gold plates.**[204]

Thomas D. S. Key

In *A Biologist Examines the Book of Mormon*, Dr. Thomas Key reviews some of the scientific problems that he found in his study of the *Book of Mormon*—including anatomical, anthropological, archaeological, astronomical, botanical, chemical, ecological, economical, genetic, geographical, geological, linguistic, mathematical, microbiological, physical, physiological, psychological, technological, zoological and other problems.

In his conclusion he writes,

> It is hard to find even a single page in the Book of Mormon **that is not saturated with many errors**.... the Book of Mormon has **not the slightest shred of evidence** to prove its scientific, historical, or theological accuracy.[205]

Conclusion

The *Book of Mormon* does not measure up to the claims made by the LDS Church. Reviewing all the evidence confirms this conclusion. Some LDS scholars and non-LDS scholars concur, as well.

Ample evidence shows the book is nineteenth-century fiction, while **no evidence** supports the Mormon claim that it is a divinely inspired and translated historical account.

Chapter 6
Joseph Smith's Abilities as a Translator

Joseph Smith's Claim –
 I commenced to translate the Book of Mormon....
– History of the Church, 1:32-33

 I spent the day ... in my private office (so called because in that room I keep my sacred writings, translate ancient records, and receive revelations)....
– History of the Church, 5:1

Testing the Translations

Joseph Smith informs us that after he finished translating the *Book of Mormon* from the golden plates, they were returned to an angel[1] who would keep the records until God was ready for the sealed portion of them to be translated.[2] Because of this, the original plates are no longer available to be examined to determine their authenticity or to check the accuracy of the translation.

How Can He Be Tested?

There are, however, other original records Joseph Smith claimed to translate which are available to us. By ascertaining the accuracy of the translations of these records, we will have an idea of whether we can trust his translation of the *Book of Mormon*. One set is known as the "Kinderhook plates," and the other is the papyri Smith used to translate the Book of Abraham.

153

The Kinderhook Plates

In the spring of 1843, six bell-shaped metal plates with curious markings were brought to Joseph Smith for possible translation. The following account in the *History of the Church* tells of the discovery of the plates and what Joseph Smith did with them:[3]

> I insert fac-similes of the six brass plates [both sides] found near Kinderhook, in Pike county, Illinois, on April 23 [1843], by Mr. Robert Wiley and others, while excavating a large mound.... The plates were found on the breast of the skeleton and were covered on both sides with ancient characters. I **have translated a portion of them, and find they contain the history of the person with whom they were found. He was a descendant of a Ham, through the loins of Pharaoh, king of Egypt, and that he received his kingdom from the Ruler of heaven and earth.**[4]

Very few people had ever heard of the Kinderhook plates before an article about them was published in the September 1962 *Improvement Era*. Welby W. Ricks, then President of the University Archeological Society at Brigham Young University, wrote the article. He explained:

> A recent rediscovery of one of the Kinderhook plates which was examined by Joseph Smith, Jun., **reaffirms his prophetic calling** and reveals the false statements made by one of the finders. A few years ago, two non-LDS professional engravers, Stanley B. Hill and Edward Pwiiski walked into the Chicago Historical Society and asked to view a bell-shaped brass plate known as the Kinderhook plate. **Their purpose was to determine whether it had been engraved with a pointed instrument or etched with acid.** What they found solved a seventy-four-year-old controversy and **put the plates back into the category of "genuine" which Joseph Smith, Jun., had said they were in the first place.**[5]

Ricks stated that the story connected with the Kinderhook plates "should be of interest to every Latter-day Saint."[6] He confirmed that the plates were shown to the Prophet, and that "Joseph Smith, Jun., **pronounced them genuine and translated a part of them.**"[7]

The article concludes:

> **The plates are now back in their original category of *genuine*.** What scholars may learn from this ancient record in future years or what may be translated by divine power is an exciting thought to contemplate. **This much remains. Joseph Smith, Jun., stands as a true prophet and translator of ancient records by divine means** and all the world is invited to investigate the truth which has sprung out of the earth not only of the Kinderhook plates, but of the Book of Mormon as well.[8]

These Kinderhook plates were obviously viewed as important by the early LDS Church and its leaders. The 1 May 1843 *Times and Seasons* had initially reported on them under the headline "ANCIENT RECORDS,"[9] where it was stated: "Circumstances are daily transpiring which give additional testimony to the authenticity of the Book of Mormon."[10] The *History of the Church* (in over seven pages) reproduced all the material in this article, added illustrations of the plates and further announced their authenticity.[11]

After mentioning "that the genuineness of this discovery of the Kinderhook plates is questioned by some **anti-Mormon writers,**" a note in *History of the Church* again confidently affirmed their authenticity:

> For while the statement in the text of the Prophet's journal **to the effect that the find was genuine, and that he had translated some of the characters and learned certain historical facts concerning the person with whose remains the plates were found**, may not have been known at the time to the alleged conspirators to deceive him[,] still it is quite apparent that the editor of the *Times and Seasons*— John Taylor, the close personal friend of the Prophet—**took**

the find seriously, and expressed implicit confidence in his editorial that the Prophet could give a translation of the plates. And this attitude the Church continued to maintain; for in *The Prophet*, (a Mormon weekly periodical, published in New York) of the 15th of February, 1845, there was published a *fac-simile* of the Kinderhook plates, together with the *Times and Seasons* editorial and all the above matter of the text. How easy to have covered Joseph Smith and his followers with ridicule by proclaiming the hoax as **soon as they accepted the Kinderhook plates as genuine!** Why was it not done? The fact that Fugate's story[12] was not told until thirty-six years after the event, and that he alone of all those who were connected with the event gives that version of it, is rather strong evidence that **his story is the hoax, not the discovery of the plates, nor the engravings upon them.**[13]

Much of the material in *History of the Church* had also been published in a large handbill by *The Nauvoo Neighbor* on 24 June 1843, on which it was stated: "The contents of the Plates, together with a Fac-Simile of the same, will be published in the 'Times and Seasons,' **as soon as the translation is completed.**"[14] This announcement again verified the fact that Joseph Smith viewed the plates as authentic and that he intended to prepare a translation of them for publication. But since he died the next year, to our knowledge, the translation was never completed.

Genuine or a Hoax?

Author Fawn Brodie views the plates differently from the above affirmations, and concludes: "Perhaps the most **deliberate hoax ever played on Joseph Smith** was contrived by three men in the near-by town of Kinderhook."[15] A **hoax**? Can this conclusion be proven? There is sufficient evidence that this was definitely the case.

Two men originally involved in the unearthing of the plates admitted to knowing it was all a hoax. Dr. W. P. Harris, in a letter dated 25 April 1855, explained his presence at the Kinderhook site and how he was originally convinced that the plates were genuine. Later, however, **he was told how the plates were fabricated and who had perpetrated the hoax.** This was only 12 years after the event. Then on 30 June 1879, Wilbur Fugate wrote a letter to James T. Cobb (with a sworn affidavit) explaining how **he was one of those who had planned and participated in the hoax and how the plates were produced and buried.**[16]

In *Mormon Portraits*, Dr. W. Wyl wrote about a Mormon elder who in 1858 attended a meeting in the Endowment House. During the meeting, Apostle Orson Pratt explained how members of an archeological society had gone to Kinderhook to check out the account of the plates, but that the trip was "without result." After a time they made contact with some of those who had signed as witnesses to the discovery of the plates, and were told that they had been "*made by a blacksmith*; they were told so by the artist himself. [Orson] **Pratt told the 'class' that he was well convinced that the plates were a fraud.**"[17]

Jerald and Sandra Tanner explain: "At the time of the Civil War the Kinderhook plates were lost." One of them had been acquired in 1920 by the Chicago Historical Society Museum and was later discovered there by M. Wilford Poulson, who had taught at BYU and was a researcher of early Mormon history. "Mr. Poulson did a great deal of research concerning the Kinderhook plates and **was convinced that they were made in the 1840's** as W. Fugate claimed."[18]

In 1965 Mormon physicist George M. Lawrence was permitted to make "some non-destructive physical studies of the surviving plate." After his study he concluded "the dimensions, tolerances, composition and workmanship are **consistent with the facilities of an 1843 blacksmith shop and with the fraud stories of the original participants.**"[19]

After Mormon professor Stanley B. Kimball received permission from the Chicago Historical Society to conduct "destructive tests" on the Kinderhook plate, he had them done by D. Lynn Johnson of Northwestern University. In Kimball's article, "Kinderhook Plates Brought to Joseph Smith Appear to Be a Nineteenth-Century Hoax," in the August 1981 issue of *The Ensign*, he stated that the electronic and chemical analysis of a metal plate (one of the six original plates) ... appears to solve a previously unanswered question in Church history, helping to further evidence **that the plate is what its producers later said it was—a nineteenth-century attempt to lure Joseph Smith into making a translation of ancient-looking characters** that had been etched into the plates.... As a result of these tests, we concluded that the plate owned by the Chicago Historical Society is *not* of ancient origin.[20]

Another article by Kimball on the "Kinderhook Plates" in the LDS *Encyclopedia of Mormonism* (1992), acknowledges that scientific tests "proved conclusively that the plate was one of the Kinderhook six; that it had been engraved, not etched; and that it was of nineteenth-century manufacture. **There thus appears no reason to accept the Kinderhook plates as anything but a frontier hoax.**"[21]

Conclusion

Joseph Smith and the LDS Church for years defended the Kinderhook plates as being genuine. Smith claimed (as recorded in *History of the Church*) that he could translate the plates and even gave a brief translation as an example. Church publications affirmed that the plates were genuine, and those who questioned them were attacked as "anti-Mormon." This defense continued into the twentieth century.[22]

Subsequent investigation, even by Mormon scholars, has established what others had already claimed and concluded: that the Kinderhook plates were a nineteenth-century hoax. Joseph Smith's statements about them, and his brief example of translating them, seriously undermines his veracity and his claim to be able to identify and translate ancient records by the gift of God. This inability is further demonstrated in other verifiable sources, such as *The Pearl of Great Price*—specifically, the Book of Abraham.

The Book of Abraham

The Book of Abraham, first published in *Times and Seasons* in 1842, and later included in *The Pearl of Great Price*, is crucial to Joseph Smith's claim as a Prophet, Seer and Revelator. What have LDS authorities and defenders written?

Wilford Woodruff records the following in his diary (19 February 1842):

> The Lord is blessing Joseph with power to reveal the mysteries of the Kingdom of God; **to translate ancient records and hieroglyphics old as Abraham or Adam** which caused our hearts to burn within us while we beheld their glorious truths opened unto us. Joseph the Seer has presented us (the Twelve) some of **the Book of Abraham which was written by his own hand** but hid from the knowledge of man for the last four thousand years but has now come to light by the mercy of God.[23]

William E. Berrett claims: "No prophet ever gave to the world a stronger challenge of his divine calling than did Joseph Smith **in his publication of the Book of Abraham.**"[24] Prof. Arthur Wallace states: "The Book of Abraham **is an important piece of evidence that stamps Joseph Smith as a prophet of God.**"[25] And B. H. Roberts, who has been identified "as Mormonism's most competent historian and leading theologian,"[26] writes:

> If Joseph Smith's translation of the Egyptian parchment could be discredited, and proven false, then **doubt would be thrown also upon** the genuineness of **his translation of the Book of Mormon**; and thus **all his pretensions as a translator would be exposed and come to naught.**[27]

Critics of the Book of the Abraham were often countered with the argument that Smith's translation could not be proven wrong without comparing it with the original papyri, thought to have been destroyed in the Chicago fire in 1871. Currently, however, researchers are able to do just that. While their whereabouts were known as early as 1962, the papyri were eventually "rediscovered" in 1966,[28] and returned to the LDS Church in 1967.[29] In his book, *By His Own Hand Upon Papyrus*, non-Mormon Charles M. Larson explains the importance of this issue: "But more was at stake than Joseph Smith's reputation; more even than the validity of the Book of Abraham. **Hanging in the balance was the entire religious system established by Joseph Smith.** Mormonism could at last be proven to be either true or false."[30] Mormon historian Klaus Hanson comments: "To a professional historian, for example, the recent translation of the Joseph Smith papyri **may well represent the potentially most damaging case against Mormonism** since its foundation."[31]

While numerous web sites, articles and entire books deal with the Book of Abraham, the subject can only be briefly reviewed here.[32]

A Brief History

In early July of 1835, Irish immigrant Michael Chandler visited Kirtland, Ohio, then the headquarters of the Mormon Church, where he exhibited four Egyptian mummies and some papyri. When the papyri were shown to Joseph Smith, he claimed that he could translate them.[33]

The mummies and the papyri were purchased for $2,400 (a large amount at the time) and Joseph Smith began translating the documents. There are numerous references in LDS records mentioning Smith "translating" the papyri.[34] On 5 July 1835 Smith recorded that

> with W. W. Phelps and Oliver Cowdery as scribes, **I commenced the translation of some of the characters or hieroglyphics**, and much to our joy found that **one of the rolls contained the writings of Abraham, another the writings of Joseph of Egypt**, etc.—a more full account of which will appear in its place, as I proceed to examine or unfold them.[35]

And on 20 July 1835, in a letter to his wife, Smith's scribe William W. Phelps, writes:

> He [Joseph Smith] soon knew what they were and said that the rolls of papyrus contained a **sacred record kept by Joseph in Pharaoh's court in Egypt and the writings of Father Abraham**. God has so ordered it that these writings and mummies have been brought into the Church.... when we **translate** and print them in a book [it] will **make a good witness to the Book of Mormon**.[36]

As H. Michael Marquardt explains, it is important to understand that "the early LDS Church leaders repeatedly claimed that the Egyptian text contained the **actual writing of Abraham**"[37] and "that Joseph Smith and the early Mormons represented the Book of Abraham to have been **penned by the very hand of Abraham himself**."[38]

Events caused the Mormons to flee from Kirtland to Missouri, then on to Nauvoo, Illinois, in 1839. As editor of *Times and Seasons*, Joseph Smith finally published a partial translation of the Book of Abraham with the papyri facsimiles in the 1 March, 15 March, and 16 May 1842 issues. Additional installments were promised.

The Prophet's claim that he would produce a "correct translation" of the papyri could not be verified or challenged at the time, for there were no Egyptologists in America. In fact, "Egyptologist E. A. Wallis Budge claimed that in 1837 'scarcely a dozen people in the whole world had any real knowledge' of the language."[39] After Smith's death in 1844, the papyri and mummies were held by Emma Smith, his widow, who eventually sold them. The papyri were on display in a St. Louis museum and then they were acquired by the Museum of Chicago.[40]

On 10 October 1880, *The Pearl of Great Price*, one of the Standard Works (which included the Book of Abraham) was canonized (officially recognized as scripture) by the LDS Church.[41] This was confirmed again by the vote of the Church accepting a new edition on 6 October 1902. Marquardt explains, "The LDS Church by these actions locked themselves into having to defend the Book of

Abraham as an actual production of Abraham instead of an Egyptian funerary text."[42] Though believed to have been lost,

> they had in reality found their way to the Metropolitan Museum of Art in New York City where they resurfaced in 1967. Their rediscovery established for certain that Joseph Smith had authentic Egyptian documents on which he based his translation of the Abrahamic work now published in the Pearl of Great Price.[43]

Egyptologists Reject the Book of Abraham

Smith's Book of Abraham translation was exposed as a fabrication years before the publication of Franklin S. Spalding's pamphlet, *Joseph Smith, Jr. As a Translator* (1912). French Egyptologist, M. Theodule Deveria, who worked at the Louvre Museum in Paris in the late 1850s, concluded that the Book of Abraham facsimiles were from an Egyptian funeral text.[44] In 1903 Dr. Woodward and Dr. Budge, two English Egyptologists, also came to the same conclusion.[45]

In his pamphlet Spalding reasoned: "Joseph Smith's competency as a translator of ancient languages can be ascertained in but one way. The original texts, together with his interpretations, must be submitted to competent scholars, and if they declare his translation to be correct, then it must be accepted as true."[46] The Book of Abraham would be ideal for such a test because the translations of the papyri facsimiles were available. Spalding sent these to eight prominent Egyptologists and asked for their professional judgments on Smith's interpretations. Excerpts from their responses are quoted below.

Dr. A. H. Sayce (Oxford University, England):

> It is difficult to deal seriously with Joseph Smith's **impudent fraud**.[47]

Dr. W. M. Flinders Petrie (London University):

> It may be safely said that there is **not one single word** that is true in these explanations.... None but the ignorant could possibly be imposed on by such **ludicrous blunders.**[48]

Dr. James H. Breasted (Haskell Oriental Museum, University of Chicago):

> To sum up, then, these three fac-similes of Egyptian documents in the "Pearl of Great Price" depict the most common objects in the mortuary religion of Egypt. Joseph Smith's interpretation of them as part of a unique revelation through Abraham, therefore, very clearly demonstrates that he was **totally unacquainted with the significance of these documents and absolutely ignorant of the simplest facts of Egyptian writing and civilization.**[49]

Dr. Arthur C. Mace (Assistant Curator, Department of Egyptian Art, Metropolitan Museum of Art, New York):

> The "Book of Abraham," it is hardly necessary to say, is a **pure fabrication**.... Joseph Smith's interpretation of these cuts is **a farrago of nonsense from beginning to end.** Egyptian characters can now be read almost as easily as Greek, and five minutes' study in an Egyptian gallery of any museum should be enough to convince any educated man of the **clumsiness of the imposture.**[50]

Dr. John Peters (University of Pennsylvania; led an expedition to Babylonia, 1888-1895):

> The plates contained in the "Pearl of Great Price" are rather comical and a very poor imitation of Egyptian originals.... The text of this chapter, as also the interpretation of the plates, **displays an amusing ignorance.** Chaldeans and Egyptians are hopelessly mixed together, although as

dissimilar and remote in language, religion and locality as are today American and Chinese. In addition to which **the writer knows nothing of either of them.**[51]

Dr. Edward Meyer (University of Berlin):

The Egyptian papyrus which Smith declared to be the "Book of Abraham," and "translated" or explained in his **fantastical way**, and of which three specimens are published in the "Pearl of Great Price," **are parts of the well known "Book of the Dead."**[52]

Dr. Friedrich Freiheer Von Bissing (Professor of Egyptology, University of Munich):

A careful study has convinced me that Smith probably believed seriously to have deciphered the ancient hieroglyphics, but that **he utterly failed. What he calls the "Book of Abraham" is a funeral Egyptian text**, probably not older than the Greek ages.... I hope this will suffice to show that Jos. Smith certainly **never got a Divine revelation** in the meaning of the ancient Egyptian Script, and that **he never deciphered hieroglyphic texts at all.**[53]

Dr. Samuel A. B. Mercer (specialist in Egyptology, Custodian of the Hibbard Collection of Egyptian Reproductions, Western Theological Seminary):

That the author **knew neither the Egyptian language nor the meaning of the most commonplace Egyptian figures**; neither did any of those, whether human or Divine, who may have helped him in his interpretation, have any such knowledge.... In general, it may be remarked that his **explanations from a scientific and scholarly standpoint are absurd**.... A criticism in his explanations could be made, but the explanatory notes to his fac-similes cannot be taken seriously by any scholar, as they seem to be undoubtedly **the work of pure imagination.**[54]

An article entitled "Studies About the Book of Abraham" in the *Encyclopedia of Mormonism* (1992) explains that the Spalding pamphlet "contained letters from eight leading Egyptologists concerning the three book of Abraham facsimiles and commenting upon the 'accuracy' of their interpretation by the Prophet Joseph SMITH. **The scholars unanimously agreed that the Prophet was wrong.** At the time no Latter-day Saint scholar was capable of refuting their claims."[55]

Shortly after the publication of Spalding's pamphlet, the 29 December 1912 Magazine Section of *The New York Times* featured an article with the headline: "MUSEUM WALLS PROCLAIM FRAUD OF MORMON PROPHET: Sacred Books Claimed to Have Been Given Divinely to the First Prophet Are Shown to be Taken from Old Egyptian Originals, Their Translation Being a Work of the Imagination—What a Comparison with the Metropolitan Museum Treasures Shows."[56]

Spalding's booklet resulted in many responses by Mormons and others. Dr. Mercer, quoted above, published an article in the September 1913 issue of *The Utah Survey*, "Joseph Smith as an Interpreter and Translator of Egyptian," in which he states, "The time has, therefore, come for a review of the whole controversy, not from a partial, but from a purely scientific and scholarly standpoint."[57] His article examines Spalding's publication in the light of Mormon replies (all of which he had) and gives his response.

Mercer summarizes the scholars statements and concludes that

> the scholars did not condemn the Prophet's translations because of religious prejudices—for some of the same scholars have very little interest in religion or dogma anyway—they condemned it purely on linguistic grounds. **Their condemnation was unanimous and independent....**
>
> No one can fail to see that the eight scholars are unanimous in their conclusions. Joseph Smith **has been shown by an eminently competent jury** of scholars **to have failed**

completely in his attempt or pretense to interpret and translate Egyptian figures and hieroglyphics.⁵⁸

In his review of the critics of Spalding's pamphlet, and his answers to their claimed discrepancies, Mercer writes that their "replies have been now examined and found wanting.... The **failure of the Mormon replies** is explained by the fact that **the unanimous opinion of the scholars is unassailable**. In the judgment of the scholarly world, therefore, **Joseph Smith stands condemned of self-deception or imposition**."⁵⁹

The Book of Abraham Papyri Found

After 1913, "Except for a few articles or books mentioning this controversy, nothing of importance occurred until the 1960s."⁶⁰ In 1966 a reproduction of Joseph Smith's "Grammar and Alphabet of the Egyptian Language" was published,⁶¹ and the 27 November 1967 *Deseret News* reported that the Book of Abraham papyri were turned over to the LDS Church by the Metropolitan Museum of Art in New York City.

Former Mormon Jim Robertson remembers the excitement of that event:

> A large ceremony took place showing the parchment being officially given back to the Mormon church. Pictures of the presentation were on TV and in the newspapers. Judy [his wife] and I jumped up and down with joy because **now we were going to prove to the world that the LDS church was true**. However, as is the case with all Mormons, we were kept very busy with our church jobs and didn't have time to think about this great discovery.⁶²

After the Robertsons left the Church and did some research, they found the LDS claims for the Book of Abraham were false.

In the February 1913 *Improvement Era*, Mormon writer John Henry Evans had published an article in which he "argued that in order to give a fair test of Joseph's true ability to translate Egyptian, and before the scholars could get away with charges that the entire Book of Abraham was a false translation, 'they would have to examine the original papyrus, or a copy of it, from which the Book of Abraham was translated.'"[63] In 1967, this could finally be done.

As discussed in Chapter 5, well-known Mormon apologist Thomas S. Ferguson wrote a letter concerning the Book of Abraham to Professor Aziz S. Atiya, in which he expressed his doubts concerning Smith's translation.[64] He also asked two Egyptologists to translate the papyri and examined two translations that had already been published. After this, he concluded: "that **Joseph Smith had not the remotest skill" in translating.**[65] All the Egyptologists who were questioned agreed that Joseph Smith failed as a translator. Amazingly, when the Book of Abraham papyri are discussed by Michael D. Rhodes in the *Encyclopedia of Mormonism,* he claims that "the Prophet's explanations of each of the facsimiles **accord with present understanding of Egyptian religious practices**."[66]

Mormon Egyptologist Dr. Stephen E. Thompson cites Rhodes and writes:

> This is a remarkable statement in view of the fact that non-Mormon Egyptologists who have commented on Joseph Smith's interpretation of the facsimiles **uniformly agree that his interpretations are not correct from the perspective of the Egyptologist,** who attempts to interpret Egyptian religious literature and iconography as he or she believes the ancient Egyptians would have.[67]

Thompson's article explores the claim from the *Encyclopedia of Mormonism* in detail, discussing the problems in each of Smith's explanations of the facsimiles. He concludes:

> In the preceding I have argued that (1) Joseph Smith's interpretations of the facsimiles in the Book of Abraham are not in agreement with the meanings which these figures had in their original, funerary, context; (2) anachronisms in the text of the book make it impossible that it was translated from a text written by Abraham himself; and (3) what we know

about the relationship between Egypt and Asia renders the account of the attempted sacrifice of Abraham [in the Book of Abraham] extremely implausible.... I see no evidence that Joseph Smith had a correct conception of "Egyptian religious practices" or that a knowledge of such was essential to the production of the Book of Abraham.[68]

Commenting on Thompson's findings, former BYU professor Dr. David P. Wright states:

I agree with him that **the Book of Abraham does not derive from Abraham and is apparently not historical.** If I have any quibble with Thompson it is that I think that **we can be much more confident about these conclusions** and that **we can go further** and argue in fact that **the book is not ancient but specifically the composition of Joseph Smith.**[69]

Wright concludes:

These evidences coupled with Thompson's observations show that the Book of Abraham **is not the composition of Abraham, not historical, and, in fact, the product of Joseph Smith's creative—inspired, if you will—exegesis**. This auctorial conclusion can be made with confidence. It is far from a wild speculation. In contrast it must be noted that **much of the scholarship that has been written defending the antiquity of the book** (and Abrahamic authorship or its historicity), **most of it by Hugh Nibley, is weak and speculative if not essentially flawed by lack of precision** in reading texts and by methodological looseness.[70]

Edward H. Ashment, who had been coordinator of translation services for the LDS Church, studied Egyptology at the University of Chicago, and who is a respected LDS Egyptologist, concludes that there is no factual basis to the rationalizations which have been devised to explain away the dissonance caused to the Book of Abraham by the Joseph Smith Egyptian Papers and by the Joseph Smith Papyri. Moreover, **the attempt to demonstrate the historicity of the Book of Abraham** by means of searching far and wide for parallels **is suspect because of its complete disregard for the cultural, temporal, and special matrices** of the matrices it uses.

It is therefore suggested that such means of dealing with the dissonance concerning the Book of Abraham **be abandoned.**[71]

LDS Response

What has been the LDS response? Stan Larson makes this important observation:

> It is surely significant that previous to the discovery of the Joseph Smith Egyptian papyri at the Metropolitan Museum of Art **there was a consistent explanation in Mormonism that Joseph Smith—through the gift and power of God—translated Egyptian characters into the English language resulting in a modern-day restoration of Abraham's record.** Only after the 1967 announcement of the discovery of the papyri and their subsequent translation has **the traditional explanation been replaced by a variety of contradictory theories.**[72]

Even then, none of these theories is the official position of the Church. In his article, "The Book of Abraham Revisited," Marquardt writes,

> It is time for the LDS Church to realize that identification of the Egyptian materials as the Book of Abraham and the canonization of it as scripture **is an historical error** made in years past. It is time also to accept the documents for what they really are—strictly Egyptian funeral texts, rather than

authentic Abrahamic records recorded by the father of the faithful.[73]

This being the case, what is the true source of much of the Book of Abraham? In his study, *The Book of Abraham Papyrus Found*, Marquardt shows that it is the King James Version of the Bible. After comparing the two texts, he writes,

> The Book of Abraham as quoted and compared above **is based upon Genesis** of the Old Testament. **Nearly one half of the Book of Abraham text was derived from the Biblical text**.... It is evident that the Book of Abraham text was composed with the Bible at hand.... **The Book of Abraham is not a translation which fact is evident** because the story about Abraham was obviously taken from the King James Version of Genesis. That **Joseph Smith did not ever translate Egyptian correctly** can be seen throughout his Egyptian papers.[74]

Conclusion

Summing up the situation, Charles M. Larson writes:

> **Fact: Not a single word, thought, or concept** from Joseph Smith's Book of Abraham, including his explanations of his three facsimiles, is in any way related to the subject matter of the common Egyptian funeral texts from which they were supposedly translated. Furthermore, modern examination of the "Egyptian Alphabet and Grammar" papers that had once so greatly enhanced the Mormon Prophet's claim to be a true translator has **exposed them as a collection of gibberish, having no connection to genuine ancient Egyptian.**
>
> One by one, **virtually every Mormon belief about the Book of Abraham once considered essential to its support and regarded as faith promoting, has been shattered by the facts.**

Not one trace of reliable evidence has appeared that would support the LDS view of the Book of Abraham as an authentic scripture, while an enormous amount of evidence is available to show that it is **a man-made production of the nineteenth century**, created by Joseph Smith to support his claim among the people to be a "prophet, seer, and revelator."

The evidence against the Book of Abraham is so overwhelming ... that many consider it a God-given means to demonstrate the fraudulent nature of Joseph Smith's claim to be a prophet of God.

The Book of Abraham **cannot possibly be** what it is represented to be; and if it is not authentic, neither are the doctrines it teaches, nor the system to which it belongs. [75]

In both instances that can be verified—the Kinderhook plates and the Book of Abraham—Joseph Smith has been shown to be unable to correctly translate materials, even with his claimed assistance of divine inspiration. How, then, can his translation of the *Book of Mormon* be accepted?

Chapter 7
Prophetic Claims

Joseph Smith's Claim –
> I received the following commandment ... there shall be a record kept among you; and in it thou shall be called a seer, a translator, a prophet, and apostle of Jesus Christ....
> – *History of the Church*, 1:78

> False prophets always arise to oppose the true prophets and they will prophesy so very near the truth that they will deceive almost the very chosen ones.
> –*Teachings of the Prophet Joseph Smith*, 365

Prophecies of Joseph Smith and Other LDS Church Leaders

In the fall of 1831, there were several men who were turning against the Prophet Joseph Smith. Ezra Booth, who had apostatized from the Church, began publicly questioning Joseph's authority as well as his ability to give revelations. According to Fawn Brodie, Booth had claimed that Smith's revelations "sprang out of mundane crises rather than from the promptings of the Lord."[1]

Joseph was upset by such disloyalty. He often excommunicated Church leaders for what was essentially insubordination.[2] He had revelations condemning those who questioned him.[3] In most instances, either the revelation or Joseph's chastening was enough to correct the errant person and to bring him into submission. But occasionally these did not work, as in the case of Booth.

Historical evidence shows that Joseph demanded unquestioned faith in his prophecies and in the authority he claimed. A revelation came forth on 1 November that year condemning all that would question the authority of the leadership of the Mormon Church. Supposedly quoting God, Joseph revealed that everyone should search these commandments, for they are true and faithful, and **the prophecies** and promises which are in them **shall all be fulfilled.** What I the Lord have spoken, I have spoken, and I excuse not myself; and though the heavens and the earth pass away, my word shall not pass away, **but shall all be fulfilled,** whether by mine own voice or by the voice of my servants, it is the same.[4]

Most early LDS Saints believed every word of prophecy that Joseph Smith gave. George Q. Cannon wrote on one occasion that Joseph "uttered a remarkable prophecy which, **like every other prediction from his lips, has been literally fulfilled.**"[5] Most LDS Church members today believe this to be true as well. Their impression is that Joseph Smith never gave any prophecy that failed to come to pass.

One LDS writer, Nephi Morris, wrote an entire volume dedicated to proving the truthfulness of Joseph Smith's prophecies. In the preface, he stated,

> Joseph Smith accepted the title and assumed the office of Prophet.... he made numerous prophecies.... Time is the supreme test of a prophecy. He who undertakes to foretell events must know that Time in its merciless pursuit will find him out. Of all the pretenses of the false prophet, **prophesying is the most hazardous.**[6]

John A. Widtsoe wrote,

> So far, **no prophecy of Joseph Smith has failed.** They speak unitedly of a prophetic vision second to none in sacred or profane history. Joseph Smith is fully entitled to be called a Prophet of God.... **The fulfilment of these prophecies alone** fully justifies the title *Prophet,* by which Joseph Smith is ordinarily known.[7]

Joseph Fielding Smith, who became the tenth prophet of the LDS Church, wrote about Joseph Smith, that

he was either a prophet of God, divinely called, properly appointed and commissioned, **or he was one of the biggest frauds this world has ever seen.** *There is no middle ground.... The doctrines of false teachers will not stand the test when tried by the accepted standards of measurement, the scriptures.*[8]

The early LDS publication, *The Evening and the Morning Star*, once published an article on false prophets, in which it was plainly stated,

> The only way of ascertaining a true prophet, is to compare his prophecies with the ancient word of God, and see if they agree, and if they do **and come to pass**, then certainly he is a true prophet: For it is not possible that the Lord will suffer FALSE prophets, to bring forth the truth, moved upon by the Holy Ghost, for it is written that the Holy Ghost dwelleth not in unholy temples. By their fruits shall they be known.
> **When, therefore any man, no matter who, or how high his standing may be, utters, or publishes, any thing that afterwards proves to be untrue, he is a false prophet.**[9]

What is the Bible's test for a true prophet?

> But the prophet, which shall presume to speak a word in my name, which I have not commanded him to speak ... that prophet shall die.... When a prophet speaketh in the name of the LORD, if the thing follow not, nor come to pass, that is the thing which the LORD hath not spoken, but the prophet hath spoken it presumptuously.... (Deuteronomy 18:20-22)

> Then the LORD said unto me, The prophets prophesy lies in my name: I sent them not, neither have I commanded them, neither spake unto them: they prophesy unto you a false vision ... and the deceit of their heart. Therefore thus saith the LORD concerning the prophets that prophesy in my name,

and I sent them not.... By sword and famine shall those prophets be consumed. (Jeremiah 14:14-15)

Beware of false prophets, which come to you in sheep's clothing, but inwardly they are ravening wolves. Ye shall know them by their fruits.... (Matthew 7:15-16)

For there shall arise false Christs, and false prophets, and shall shew great signs and wonders; insomuch that, if it were possible, they shall deceive the very elect. Behold, I have told you before. (Matthew 24:24-25)

We are able to discern whether or not someone who claims to be a prophet is a true one. By their "fruits" we will know them. If they utter prophecies (predictions) that do not come to pass, they are false prophets.

What is a prophecy, though? It is a **prediction of the future** under the influence of divine guidance.[10] To **predict** something means to foretell a future event.[11] A revelation is a communication by a divine agency, a disclosing of something previously unknown.[12] These authoritative definitions tell us that a declaration is a prophecy if it is said to be communicated through a divine source, and if it **foretells or predicts** future unknown events. One LDS apologist defined prophecy as "1. the **foretelling or prediction** of what is to come. 2. something that is declared by a prophet, esp. **a divinely inspired prediction**, instruction, or exhortation. 3. **any prediction or forecast**. 4. the action, function or faculty of a prophet."[13] By examining Joseph Smith's **predictive prophecies**, and putting them to the test, we will be able to know whether he was a true prophet.

Is it right to put him to the test? Does Scripture approve testing of those who claim to be prophets? Absolutely.

Prove all things; hold fast that which is good. (1 Thessalonians 5:21)

Beloved, believe not every spirit, but **try the spirits whether they are of God**: because **many false prophets are gone out** into the world. (1 John 4:1)

I know thy works, and thy labour, and thy patience, and how thou canst not bear them which are evil: and thou hast tried them **which say they are apostles, and are not, and hast found them liars**. (Revelation 2:2)

Here, 26 of Joseph Smith's prophecies are examined—at least one for each year from the completion of the *Book of Mormon* until his death. In addition, further examples of prophecies made by successors to Smith are reviewed.

Joseph Smith's Prophecies

June 1829—*Book of Mormon* Copyright

David Whitmer, one of the Three Witnesses to the *Book of Mormon*, tells us of a prophecy that Joseph Smith gave in 1829.

In June 1829, the translation of the Book of Mormon was finished.... When the Book of Mormon was in the hands of the printer, more money was needed to finish the printing of it. We were waiting on Martin Harris who was doing his best to sell a part of his farm, in order to raise the necessary funds. After a time Hyrum Smith and others began to get impatient.... Brother Hyrum said it had been suggested to him that some of the brethren might go to Toronto, Canada, and sell the copy-right of the Book of Mormon for considerable money: and **he persuaded Joseph to inquire of the Lord about it.** Joseph concluded to do so ... and **received a revelation that some of the brethren should go to Toronto, Canada, and that they would sell the copy-right of the Book of Mormon.**[14]

This revelation is not mentioned in the official *History of the Church*. It was not included in the revelations published in either the 1833 *Book of Commandments* or any edition of the *Doctrine and Covenants*. Some are skeptical of the revelation since the information about it comes from Whitmer, who apostatized from the Church. However, LDS historian B. H. Roberts writes, "In the text of this chapter, attention is called to the fact that our knowledge of the 'Toronto Journey Incident' rests chiefly upon the testimony of David Whitmer.... the **incident must be considered as it is presented by him, since his testimony may not be set aside.**"[15]

H. Michael Marquardt looked into the matter further and found additional proof that this revelation was authentic. In a letter Hiram Page wrote to William McLellin in 1848, Page said,

> Joseph [Smith, Jr.] he[a]rd that there was a **chance to Sell a copyright in canada** for any useful book that was used in the States Joseph thought this would be a good opertunity to get a handsom[e] Sum of money.... it was told me **we were to go by revilation** but when we assembled at father Smiths; there was no revilation for us to go but we were all anctious [anxious] to get a revilation to go; **and when it came we were to go to kingston where we were to Sell** if they would not harden their hearts; but **when we got their [there]; there was no purcheser**....[16]

Former Apostle William McLellin also verified that there was a revelation on the subject:

> But again, **Joseph [Smith, Jr.] had a revelation** for Oliver [Cowdery] and friends **to go to Canada to get a copyright secured** in that Dominion to the Book of Mormon. **It proved so false that he never would have it recorded, printed or published, I have seen and read a copy of it, so that I know it existed.** So do all those connected with him at the time.[17]

On another occasion, McLellin again verified that "**J.[oseph] Smith's revelation for Cowdery to go to Canada was never printed.** M.[artin] Harris had **the copy that I read** in Manuscript."[18]

Both McLellin and Whitmer admitted that the prophecy did not come true. Whitmer explains, "Hiram Page and Oliver Cowdery went to Toronto on this mission, but **they failed entirely** to sell the copy-right, returning without any money."[19]

B. H. Roberts writes,

> In that view of the case **we have here an alleged revelation** received by the Prophet, through the "Seer Stone," directing or allowing men to go on a mission to Canada, **which fails of its purpose**; namely, the sale of the copyright of the *Book of Mormon* in Canada.... **The revelation respecting the Toronto journey was not of God**, surely; else it would not have failed.... in **this instance of the Toronto journey, Joseph was evidently not directed by the inspiration of the Lord.**[20]

What did Joseph have to say about this revelation having failed? Whitmer tells us,

> we asked Joseph how it was that he had received a revelation from the Lord for some brethren to go to Toronto and sell the copy-right, and the brethren had utterly failed in their undertaking. **Joseph did not know how it was, so he enquired of the Lord about it, and behold the following revelation came through the stone:** "*Some revelations are of God: some revelations are of man: and some revelations are of the devil.*"[21]

Roberts accepts this account as fact, saying, "Then in explanation of the failure of that revelation, **the Prophet's announcement that all revelations are not of God**; some are of men and some even from evil sources."[22]

Here is the most obvious case of a prophecy given by Joseph Smith that did not come true. Why trust **any** revelation of Joseph

Smith after this? Not only did he prove himself to be a false prophet, but he even admitted that he did not know whether his revelations were from God or Satan.

Roberts suggests,

> The question presented by this state of facts is: May this Toronto incident and the Prophet's explanation be accepted and **faith still be maintained in him as an inspired man,** a Prophet of God? I answer unhesitatingly in the affirmative. The revelation respecting the Toronto journey was not of God, surely; else it would not have failed; but the Prophet ... saw reflected in the "Seer Stone" his own thought, or that suggested to him by his brother Hyrum, rather than the thought of God.[23]

This false prophecy should serve as a warning about Smith's prophetic abilities. His explanation of why it failed makes it even more disconcerting to accept subsequent revelations he claimed to have.

Whitmer added, "I will say here, that **I could tell you other false revelations** that came through Brother Joseph as mouthpiece, (not through the stone) but this will suffice. Many of Brother Joseph's revelations were never printed. The revelation to go to Canada was written down on paper, but was never printed."[24] This failed prophecy was so embarrassing to him that he refused to have it published.[25] The current leadership of the LDS Church also continues to suppress it.

September 1830—The Gathering

The following revelation was given to Joseph Smith in Fayette, New York, prior to a Church conference. After stating that the words given are "the voice of Jesus Christ," the revelation states,

> Wherefore **the decree hath gone forth from the Father** that **they shall be gathered in unto one place** upon the face of this land, to prepare their hearts and be prepared in all things against the day when tribulation and desolation are

sent forth upon the wicked. For **the hour is nigh and the day soon at hand** when the earth is ripe; and **all the proud and they that do wickedly shall be as stubble**; and I will burn them up, saith the Lord of Hosts, that **wickedness shall not be upon the earth**; For the hour is nigh, and that which was spoken by mine apostles must be fulfilled; for as they spoke so shall it come to pass....[26]

Did the gathering take place as decreed? Before we can ascertain that, we must know where, exactly, that gathering place was located. *The Doctrine and Covenants Commentary* for this revelation tells us.

> 8 ... *Gathered in unto one place*] **Jackson County, Mo., is the central gathering place of the Saints**. On this subject the Prophet Joseph, in a letter to the Elders of the Church, dated September 1st, 1835, and published in the *Messenger and Advocate,* said, in part: —"I received, by a heavenly vision, a commandment in June following [1831] to take my journey to **the Western boundaries of the State of Missouri**, and there designate the very spot which **was to be the central place for the commencement of the gathering together** of those who embrace the fulness of the everlasting gospel."[27]

The LDS Saints did move to Missouri, but encountered difficulties that led to the expulsion of the Mormons from the state. They never did gather together afterward in Missouri.

7 March 1831—Zion (New Jerusalem)

Owing to "many false reports" being spread about Mormonism, Joseph went to the Lord in prayer. He then received a revelation that is currently published as *Doctrine and Covenants,* Section 45. Near the end of the revelation, the following prophecy appears:

> Wherefore **I, the Lord, have said** ... assemble ye yourselves together ... gather up your riches that ye may purchase an

inheritance which shall hereafter be appointed unto you. And **it shall be called the New Jerusalem**, a land of peace, a city of refuge, a place of safety for the saints of the Most High God; **And the glory of the Lord shall be there, and the terror of the Lord also shall be there**, insomuch that **the wicked will not come unto it**, and **it shall be called Zion**. And it shall come to pass among the wicked, that every man that will not take his sword against his neighbor must needs flee unto Zion for safety. And **there shall be gathered unto it out of every nation under heaven; and it shall be the only people that shall not be at war one with another**. And it shall be said among the wicked: Let us not go up to battle against Zion, for the inhabitants of Zion are terrible; wherefore we cannot stand. And it shall come to pass that **the righteous shall be gathered out from among all nations, and shall come to Zion**, singing with songs of everlasting joy.... And **all nations shall be afraid because of the terror of the Lord**, and the power of his might. Even so. Amen.[28]

Zion, or New Jerusalem, was to be built in Jackson County, Missouri.[29] Before it was built, however, the Mormons were driven from the state. To this day, the city has not been built. It is not a refuge for the Saints, it is not the gathering place from all nations, and it is not the only place on earth where there is no war. The nations do not fear it.

Some might claim that this was a command, not a prophecy; therefore, it does not matter that it did not come true. Yet in the section just quoted, "the Lord" gave 11 specifics that He said "shall" happen—not might happen, or that would happen "if" something else was done first. When the Lord says something shall happen, it does—regardless of man's actions.[30]

22, 23 September 1832—Temple Lot and Promised Desolation

Joseph Smith gave a prophecy while in Kirtland, Ohio, that states,

> A revelation of Jesus Christ unto his servant Joseph Smith, Jun ... Yea, the word of the Lord concerning his church ... for the gathering of his saints to stand upon Mount Zion, which shall be the city of New Jerusalem. Which city shall be built, beginning at the temple lot, which is appointed by the finger of the Lord, in the western boundaries of the State of Missouri, and dedicated by the hand of Joseph Smith, Jun., and others with whom the Lord was well pleased. Verily this is the word of the Lord, that the city New Jerusalem shall be built by the gathering of the saints, beginning at this place, even the place of the temple, which temple shall be reared in this generation. For verily this generation shall not all pass away until an house shall be built unto the Lord.... Therefore, as I said concerning the sons of Moses—for the sons of Moses and also the sons of Aaron shall offer an acceptable offering and sacrifice in the house of the Lord, which house shall be built unto the Lord in this generation, upon the consecrated spot as I have appointed—[31]

As already mentioned, the Mormons were forced out of Missouri and had to abandon their property there. As a result, the temple was never built. The revelation specifically stated that "this generation" would not pass away before it would be; three times it mentioned specifically "this generation." More than 170 years later, that generation is gone.

But did Joseph Smith literally mean the generation then living, or did he mean some future generation? His contemporary leaders were told that the generation mentioned was the one living at the time that Smith gave the revelation.

For example, George A. Smith said that

> here we ... prepare ourselves for a day when we shall go to the place that has been appointed for the building up of the city of Zion and for the building of the house which shall be a great and glorious temple, on which the glory of the Lord shall rest—a temple that will excel all others in magnificence

that have ever been built upon the earth.... And let me remind you that it is predicted that **this generation shall not pass away till a temple shall be built**, and the glory of the Lord rest upon it, according to the promises.[32]

George Q. Cannon said in 1864, "The day is near when a Temple shall be reared in the Center Stake of Zion, and the Lord has said his glory shall rest on that House in this generation, **that is in the generation in which the revelation was given, which is upwards of thirty years ago**. How much are we prepared for this?"[33]

Orson Pratt also verified this in 1870,

> God has been with us from the time that we came to this land, and I hope that the days of our tribulation are past. I hope this, because God promised in the year 1832 that we should, **before the generation then living had passed away**, return and build up the City of Zion in Jackson County; that we should return and build up the temple of the Most High where we formerly laid the corner stone.... The Latter-day Saints just as much expect to receive a fulfillment of that promise **during the generation that was in existence in 1832** as they expect that the sun will rise and set to-morrow. Why? Because **God cannot lie**. He will fulfil all His promises. **He has spoken, it must come to pass**.[34]

In spite of the undaunted faith of these early LDS Saints and leaders,[35] the prophecy failed. All of the generation living when the prophecy was given—even the ones born that same year—have passed away. This is not an outsider's interpretation of the prophecy, but the interpretation of those who heard the prophecy and who must have discussed its details with Joseph Smith at the time. They were also LDS Church leaders, who, we are told, are led by divine inspiration in such matters.

Later on in the same prophecy, there is another interesting revelation. Near the end, we are told,

> Nevertheless, let the bishop go unto **the city of New York**, also to the city of **Albany**, and also to the city of **Boston**, and warn the people of those cities with the sound of the gospel, with a loud voice, **of the desolation and utter abolishment which await them if they do reject these things. For if they do reject these things the hour of their judgment is nigh, and their house shall be left unto them desolate.**[36]

The mission was not the success that they had hoped for, and the gospel message was rejected in each city. In fact, Joseph Smith wrote a three-page letter to his wife, Emma, while in New York City. In the letter, he shares with Emma his disappointment at the wickedness of the people and their unwillingness to hear the gospel message. He also reminds Emma that the Lord will surely destroy these cities because of their actions.[37]

In spite of their wickedness and rejection, the cities mentioned in the revelation were not destroyed. The *Doctrine and Covenants Commentary* mentions the following concerning this mission:

> Shortly after this Revelation was given, the Prophet Joseph, accompanied by Bishop Whitney, took a hurried journey to Albany, New York, and Boston. In the *Millennial Star*, Vol. X., p. 286, there is an extract from an article from the *Albany Express,* in which a conflagration is described, by which buildings and property to the value of $2,000,000 was destroyed at Albany. Several lives were lost and many business men were utterly ruined.[38]

Obviously, the authors of that volume view this tragic fire as partial fulfillment of the prophecy given. However, this is not the case. The fire was real and caused significant damage and loss, but the city of Albany was not left desolate and survives to this day. The city of New York suffered a significant fire, as well, on 16 December 1835. Joseph Smith even visited the "burnt district" in the summer of 1836.[39] And yet, in spite of the fire, this city was also not destroyed as prophesied.

27 December 1832—Judgment of God

Joseph received a lengthy revelation from God while in Kirtland, Ohio. The revelation was apparently given to him in portions, some on 27 December, some on 28 December, and the rest not until 3 January 1833. The revelation begins with, "Verily, **thus saith the Lord**...." Right in the middle of the revelation, we read the following prophecy:

> Abide ye in the liberty wherewith ye are made free; entangle not yourselves in sin, but let your hands be clean, until the Lord comes. **For not many days hence and the earth shall tremble and reel to and fro as a drunken man; and the sun shall hide his face, and shall refuse to give light; and the moon shall be bathed in blood; and the stars shall become exceedingly angry, and shall cast themselves down as a fig that falleth from off a fig-tree.** And after your testimony cometh **wrath and indignation upon the people**.... the testimony of **earthquakes**, that shall cause groanings in the midst of her, and men shall fall upon the ground and shall not be able to stand ... the voice of **thunderings**, and the voice of **lightnings**, and the voice of **tempests**, and the voice of the **waves of the sea heaving themselves beyond their bounds**. And **all things shall be in commotion**; and surely, **men's hearts shall fail them**; for fear shall come upon all people. And angels shall fly through the midst of heaven, crying with a loud voice, sounding the trump of God, saying: Prepare ye, prepare ye, O inhabitants of the earth; for the judgment of our God is come. Behold, and lo, the Bridegroom cometh; go ye out to meet him. **And immediately there shall appear a great sign in heaven, and all people shall see it together.**[40]

It has certainly been "many days" since this prophecy was given. From the last day of the revelation until the first day of 2006 amounted to 63,187 days,[41] yet **none** of these prophesied events have occurred.

Some might claim that 63,187 days is "not many" considering the overall age of the earth, and that is true. They might claim that some of these things have happened, and that the prophecy may yet still come true. Any who would make such claims are not taking into account Joseph's other prophecies connected with this revelation—prophecies about the return of Christ to the earth.

This was given at a time when Joseph Smith was often prophesying about events surrounding the return of Christ, as the next prophecy, given just one day later, shows. Joseph expected the people living at that time to see these things fulfilled. When all of his comments on this matter are taken together, it becomes clear that he literally believed it would not be "many days" before these things were fulfilled.

4 January 1833—Scene of Bloodshed

Joseph Smith wrote a letter to the editor of a newspaper in Rochester, New York, in which he gave the following prophecy:

> *Mr. Editor:*—Sir ... **I am prepared to say by the authority of Jesus Christ, that not many years shall pass away before the United States shall present such a scene of** *bloodshed* **as has not a parallel in the history of our nation; pestilence, hail, famine, and earthquake will sweep the wicked of this generation from off the face of the land, to open and prepare the way for the return of the lost tribes of Israel from the north country.** The people of the Lord, those who have complied with the requirements of the new covenant, have already commenced gathering together to Zion, which is in the state of Missouri; therefore I declare unto you the warning which the Lord has commanded to declare unto this generation ... **there are those now living upon the earth whose eyes shall not be closed in death until they see all these things, which I have spoken, fulfilled....** [Signed] **Joseph Smith, Jun.**[42]

A footnote in the *History of the Church*[43] makes reference to the "Asiatic Cholera" that rapidly spread through the United States in the later half of 1832, implying that this plague partially fulfills the prophecy. Yet there were only 3,731 cases in New York City, and about 40 percent of those afflicted died.[44] While the disease did spread through the Midwest, this still does not meet the specific requirements of the prophecy. There was no significant bloodshed, pestilence, hail, famine or earthquake that destroyed the wicked of that generation. The ten tribes did not "return ... from the north," and, of course, the generation that was then living has passed away.

2 August 1833—Zion (Cannot Be Moved)

The *History of the Church* records the following prophecy of Joseph Smith:

> Verily I say unto you my friends, **I speak unto you with my voice, even the voice of my Spirit, that I may show unto you my will** concerning your brethren in the land of Zion, many of whom are truly humble and are seeking diligently to learn wisdom and to find truth.... And, now, behold, if **Zion do these things she shall prosper, and spread herself and become very glorious, very great, and very terrible. And the nations of the earth shall honor her, and shall say: Surely Zion is the city of our God, and surely Zion cannot fall, neither be moved out of her place, for God is there, and the hand of the Lord is there; And he hath sworn by the power of his might to be her salvation and her high tower.**[45]

The city of Zion was "moved out of her place," because the Mormons were driven from Missouri before it could be established, and to this day the Saints have not returned.

Some might claim this prophecy was dependent upon Zion doing "these things"; therefore, the failure of the prophecy rests with those men and not God. But within the prophecy is an unconditional promise from God: "God ... hath sworn ... to be her salvation." There was no condition placed upon this promise. Yet God was clearly not "her salvation."

18 December 1833—Joseph Smith, Sr.'s Patriarchal Blessing

On this day, Joseph Smith gave a Patriarchal Blessing to his father, Joseph Smith, Sr., in which we find the following:

> The following blessings **by the spirit of prophecy**, were pronounced **by Joseph Smith, Jr.**... Blessed of the Lord is **my father**, for he shall stand in the midst of his posterity and shall be comforted by their blessings **when he is old and bowed down with years**, and **shall be called a prince over them**, and shall be numbered among those who hold the right of patriarchal priesthood, even the keys of that ministry.... And again, blessed is my father, for the hand of the Lord shall be over him and **he shall be full of the Holy Ghost; for he shall predict whatsoever shall befall his posterity unto the latest generation**, and shall see the affliction of his children pass away, and their enemies under their feet: And **when his head is fully ripe** he shall behold himself as an olive tree whose branches are bowed down with much fruit.... And **his days shall yet be lengthened out**: and **when he shall go hence he shall go in peace**, and his rest shall be glorious, and his name shall be had in remembrance to the end. Amen.[46]

According to the *Encyclopedia of Mormonism*,[47] Joseph Smith, Sr. died on 14 September 1840 at age 69. This may seem like a fulfillment of the prophecy, since 69 is considered by some to have been quite an old age in those days. But the fact is that the revelation was given just six years prior to his death. Six years does not seem to be a "lengthening out" of a life, unless that person were on his deathbed. Smith's father was not.

In addition, Smith, Sr. did not predict "whatsoever shall befall his posterity." If he had, he would have known that his own son, who gave the blessing, would be killed during a mob attack in about

10 years. He was never called a "prince over" his family. He saw the "affliction of his children" for the rest of his life; those afflictions never did "pass away." He never saw the enemies of his children put "under their feet." Lastly, when he died, he did not "go in peace." Instead, he died after succumbing to a horrible, lengthy illness (consumption).[48]

21 April 1834—Church Destroyed if Zion Not Delivered

Joseph Smith presided over a conference on this day. The clerk, Oliver Cowdery, recorded the following:

> **President Joseph Smith, Jun., prophesied.** "If Zion is not delivered, the time is near when all of this Church, wherever they may be found, **will be persecuted and destroyed in like manner.**"[49]

As already mentioned, "Zion" (Jackson County, Missouri) was never "delivered," nor was the rest of the Church "destroyed." Instead, it has grown over the years. While many Mormon members see this growth as proof that the Church is true, in this case it continues to show that Joseph Smith was a false prophet.

22 June 1834—Destruction of Enemies

More than 200 Mormon men, called "Zion's Camp," traveled to Clay County, Missouri, in the hopes of redeeming LDS lands in the area. After they arrived, the Camp was infected with cholera and had to disband. In an effort to placate the men and continue their hopes, Joseph Smith gave a public address. Part of the address was a prophecy, which quoted God.

> Therefore it is expedient in me that mine elders **should wait for a little season, for the redemption of Zion.** For behold, I do not require at their hands to fight the battles of Zion; for, as I said in a former commandment, even so will I fulfil—**I will fight your battles.** Behold, **the destroyer I**

have sent forth to destroy and lay waste mine enemies; and not many years hence they shall not be left to pollute mine heritage, and to blaspheme my name **upon the lands which I have consecrated for the gathering together** of my saints.⁵⁰

One of the men of the Camp, Reed Peck, recorded more of what was said: "**Joseph Smith**, before he returned from the campaign **prophesied publicly** to them, that '**within three years they should march to Jackson County and there should not be a dog to open his mouth against them.**'"⁵¹

The Mormon lands in Jackson County never were redeemed, not in 1837 nor to the present day. In fact, "Zion's Camp" never marched again. The "enemies" of the Mormon Church actually prevailed in this instance, and never were destroyed.

16 August 1834—Redemption of Zion

In a letter to several members of the High Council of Zion, Joseph Smith, among other things, wrote the following prophecy:

> **I shall now proceed to give you such counsel as the Spirit of the Lord may dictate.** You will recollect that your business must be done by your High Council. You will recollect that the first Elders are to receive their endowment in Kirtland, **before the redemption of Zion.**... This petition is to be sent to the governor of Missouri, to solicit him to call on the President of the United States for a guard to protect our brethren in Jackson county ... and in case that they proceed to endeavor to take life ... gather up the little army, and **be set over immediately into Jackson county.**... use every effort to prevail on the churches to **gather to those regions and locate themselves, to be in readiness to move into Jackson county in two years from the eleventh of September next, which is the appointed time for the redemption of Zion.**⁵²

The "appointed time" indicated by the "counsel" of the "Spirit of the Lord" came and went without Zion being redeemed.

14 February 1835—Return of Christ (56-Year Prophecy)

At a special meeting on this day, Joseph Smith selected, ordained and instructed Twelve Apostles for the Church. During the meeting, the following was recorded:

> **President Joseph Smith, Jun.**, presiding ... then stated that the meeting had been called, because God had commanded it; and **it was made known to him by vision and by the Holy Spirit**. He then gave a relation of some of the circumstances attending us while journeying to Zion—our trials, sufferings; and said God had not designed all this for nothing, but He had it in remembrance yet; and **it was the will of God that those who went to Zion, with a determination to lay down their lives, if necessary, should be ordained to the ministry, and go forth to prune the vineyard for the last time, or the coming of the Lord, which was nigh—even fifty-six years should wind up the scene.**[53]

Fifty-six years after this prophecy was given would have been the year 1891. Did any of the early LDS Mormons who heard Joseph give this prediction believe that 1891 would mark the return of Christ? Absolutely. Many of them were counting on it.

Oliver B. Huntington recorded the prophecy in his journal:

> On the 14th of Feb. 1835, Joseph Smith said that God had revealed to him that the comeing of Christ would be **within 56 years, which being added to 1835 shows that before 1891** and the 14th of Feb. **the Saviour of the world would make his appearance** again upon the earth and the winding up scene take place.[54]

In 1887, the LDS Juvenile Instructor Office printed and distributed a book by Elder Robert Smith of Payson, Utah. In this book, he went to great lengths to show from different calculations that the year 1891 would mark the return of Jesus Christ to the earth. He wrote,

> Now, we will prove by the prophet Joseph Smith that the same year, **1891, is the commencement of the reign of righteousness**. In Section 130, Doctrine and Covenants, Joseph was told that if he lived to be 85 years old he would live to see the scene wound up or the Redeemer on the earth. He was born December 23rd, 1805, and if we give him the 85 years, we would not count the year 1805, we should have to count 1806, as the year 1805 was mostly gone ... therefore, **we have 1806 and 85, making 1891; again in the year 1835 Joseph was told positively that 56 years would wind up the scene ... 56 and 1835 are 1891**. Thus we have abundant proof that **that year will begin the reign of righteousness**....[55]

Some leaders in the Church were uncomfortable with what most LDS members were expecting would happen in 1891. Many members of the Church were so sure of the return of Christ that year that they were neglecting their daily lives in favor of speculation regarding Christ's return. Heber J. Grant, a young and fairly new Apostle, during the Church Conference of October 1890, felt compelled to warn the church by saying,

> I have been gratified with the remarks that have been made **about events, which some have imagined will take place in 1891**. Some spend nearly the whole of their time in hunting mysteries, while neglecting important duties as they come along. The best course to pursue is to fulfil daily the duties required as they present themselves.[56]

Another Apostle, John W. Taylor, the son of the third President of the Mormon Church, made similar remarks as well that day, commenting on what some LDS members "expected" to transpire in 1891.[57] Nevertheless, 1891 came and went without the return of Christ.

Some might claim this was not really a prophecy, that Joseph Smith was only giving his **opinion** on the matter. They might say that Joseph only claimed that 56 years "**should**" wind up the scene, and not that they definitely **would**. To do so, they must overlook the fact that Joseph gave many other prophecies and statements which also pointed to the year 1891.[58] They also have to ignore the fact that Smith's contemporaries all regarded this as a definite prophecy. All of the evidence shows that Joseph's intent was to definitely fix the date of Christ's return.

6 August 1836 — Salem, Massachusetts Prophecy

While on a mission through the New England area in the summer of 1836, Joseph Smith received the following revelation:

> **I, the Lord your God**, am not displeased with your coming [on] this journey, notwithstanding your follies. **I have much treasure in this city** [Salem, Massachusetts] **for you,** for the benefit of Zion, **and many people in this city, whom I will gather out in due time for the benefit of Zion, through your instrumentality**. Therefore, it is expedient that you should form acquaintance with men in this city, as you shall be led, and as it shall be given you. And it shall come to pass in due time that **I will give this city into your hands, that you shall have power over it**, insomuch that they shall not discover your secret parts; **and its wealth pertaining to gold and silver shall be yours.... For there are more treasures than one for you in this city**.[59]

In spite of the direct quotation from the Lord, the prophecy proved to be false. They returned from the mission with very few converts and no treasure. The *History of the Church* records that they had "baptized **a good number** into the Church."[60] Where this information came from, though, has not been ascertained. The original diary of Joseph Smith after 3 April 1836 has either been lost or suppressed by the LDS Church. Joseph's Journal manuscript, meanwhile, does not begin until April of 1838.

The notation in the *History* does go on to add, however, that they remained in Boston for two or three weeks and baptized 17 people.[61] Why this number is specifically cited, but the number of baptisms in Salem was not, is very curious.

Brigham Young verified this exact number of baptisms in Boston during that trip in his *Manuscript History*. He writes, "I returned to Boston, where I found my brother Joseph, who had been doing a good work. **We baptized 17 in Boston.**"[62] Perhaps this is the number baptized in Boston and Salem, combined. If so, 17 converts are not "many" nor "a good number" of baptisms and would not fulfill the prophecy.

Again, some may point to the fact that the prophecy says all this will happen "in due time," leaving room to be fulfilled at a later date. If that is the case, then the overall number of baptisms over the years could fulfill the prophecy. But the Mormon Church is still no closer to having power over that city or its "treasure" of gold and silver.

6 April 1837—Kirtland Built Up

During a Solemn Assembly held in the Kirtland Temple, Joseph Smith spoke about building up the city of Kirtland, Ohio. The meeting was reported in the *Messenger and Advocate*.[63] At the end of his remarks, we find the following:

> He [Joseph Smith] then closed at about 4 (P. M.) by **uttering a prophesy** saying **this place** must be built up, and **would be built up, and that every brother that would** take hold and **help secure and discharge those contracts** that had been made, **should be rich.**[64]

The city of Kirtland, Ohio, was never built up. To this day it remains a small community.[65] Those Mormons at the time who did invest in the land lost their money. When this information was transferred into the official *History of the Church*, the statement that Joseph had uttered these comments as "a prophecy" was deleted without indication.⁶⁶ Apparently, those who compiled the official *History* recognized that it was a failed prophecy.

17 April 1838—David Patten Prophecy

Joseph Smith gave this prophecy while in Far West, Missouri:

> Verily **thus saith the Lord**: It is wisdom in my servant **David W. Patten**, that he settle up all his business as soon as he possibly can, and make a disposition of his merchandise, **that he may perform a mission unto me next spring**, in company with others, even twelve including himself, **to testify of my name** and bear glad tidings **unto all the world**.⁶⁷

In spite of the fact that it was God's will for Patten to serve a mission in the spring of 1839, he was killed during the Battle of Crooked River on 25 October 1838.⁶⁸

8 July 1838—Oliver Granger Prophecy

In Far West, Missouri, Joseph Smith gave the following revelation:

> Verily **thus saith the Lord** ... I say unto you, I remember my servant **Oliver Granger**; behold, **verily I say unto him that his name shall be had in sacred remembrance from generation to generation, forever and ever, saith the Lord.** Therefore, let him contend earnestly for the redemption of the First Presidency of my Church, saith the Lord; and when he falls he shall rise again, for **his sacrifice shall be more sacred unto me** than his increase, saith the Lord. Therefore, let him come up hither speedily, unto the land of Zion; and **in the due time he shall be made a merchant unto my name**, saith the Lord, for the benefit of my people. Therefore let no man despise **my servant Oliver Granger, but let the blessings of my people be on him forever and ever**.⁶⁹

Granger's name does not appear at all in the *Deseret News 2001-2002 Church Almanac*, though all those who are considered of importance in Church history have their names and biographies found there. His name appears only twice in the *Encyclopedia of Mormonism*[70] — both times as a brief mention with no significant comments about him. In the *LDS Biographical Encyclopedia*, his name also appears only twice[71] — both times merely stating that he was the father of Sarah Kimball. Sarah is far more prominently remembered in Church history than her father Oliver.

In a search of more than 3,000 LDS works on CD-Rom,[72] Granger was mentioned fewer than 100 times. Twenty-five of those were footnote remarks listing him as the recipient of a letter. More than half of the remainder were casual mentions of him in a list with other people. The only LDS books found that mention him in detail were the *Doctrine and Covenants Encyclopedia*, which devoted only 10 sentences to his life;[73] and *Who's Who in the Doctrine and Covenants*, which printed 25 sentences about him.[74]

LDS speaker Byron Merril once made the statement that "**almost forgotten by the modern Saint are** the names of David Fullmer, **Oliver Granger**, William Huntington, and Algernon Sidney Gilbert."[75] LDS writer Robert Millet refers to Granger two times in his writings, once as "**a little-known character** in Church history";[76] and then a second time as "**a little-known man.**"[77] Oliver Granger remains a virtual unknown among LDS people.

20 March 1839—Joseph Will Triumph Over Foes

While a prisoner at Liberty Jail in Missouri, Joseph Smith prayed to God, begging for assistance and deliverance from his troubles. He received an answer, including a prophecy. Part of that prophecy reads as follows:

> My son, peace be unto thy soul; **thine adversity and thine afflictions shall be but a small moment**; And then, if thou endure it well, God shall exalt thee on high; **thou shalt triumph over all thy foes**.... And **they who do charge thee with transgression, their hope shall be blasted, and**

their prospects shall melt away.... God hath set his hand and seal to change the times and seasons, and **to blind their minds**, that they may not understand his marvelous workings; that he may prove them also **and take them in their own craftiness**; Also because their hearts are corrupted.... And **not many years hence, that they and their posterity shall be swept from under heaven, saith God**, that **not one of them is left** to stand by the wall.⁷⁸

None of those events came to pass. Instead, Joseph Smith himself was "swept from under heaven" just five years later.

5 October 1840 — Blood Sacrifices to Be Restored

During a General Conference of the Church, Robert Thompson read an article on the Priesthood. The article had been composed by Joseph Smith, and included a lengthy discourse on Old Testament sacrifices. Joseph wrote,

The offering of sacrifice has ever been connected and **forms a part of the duties of the Priesthood**.... **These sacrifices**, as well as every other ordinance belonging to the Priesthood, **will, when the Temple of the Lord shall be built**, and the sons of Levi be purified, **be fully restored and attended to in all their powers, ramifications, and blessings.**⁷⁹

The Nauvoo Temple was not completed until 1846, nearly two years after the death of Joseph Smith. The sacrifices which he described, and which he claimed would be "fully restored" once the temple was completed, were never reintroduced. Joseph Fielding Smith explained that "the law of sacrifice will have to be restored, or *all things* which were decreed by the Lord would not be restored.... Sacrifice by the shedding of blood was instituted in the days of Adam and of necessity will have to be restored."⁸⁰ These sacrifices had not yet been restored as late as 1956, when this was first published. According to Smith, even then they were not expected to be restored for quite some time.⁸¹

Latter-day Saints might claim that this does not qualify as a "prophecy" since it does not have "thus saith the Lord" in it. However, many of Joseph Smith's prophecies did not contain these words. Some might claim it was just an article Joseph wrote, and therefore not inspired. But the writing was prepared for the General Conference of the Church. Words given in General Conference are considered to be "divinely inspired,"[82] an extension of the *Doctrine and Covenants*,[83] and have also been called "scripture."[84] This article qualifies, then, having been read from the conference pulpit.

19 January 1841 — George Miller Prophecy

After the Mormons had been forced to leave the state of Missouri, Joseph Smith received a revelation directing what these Saints should do next. In that revelation, he received the following information about George Miller.

> Verily, **thus saith the Lord** unto you ... my servant **George Miller is without guile; he may be trusted because of the integrity of his heart; and for the love which he has to my testimony I, the Lord, love him**. I therefore say unto you, **I seal upon his head the office of a bishopric.... Let no man despise my servant George, for he shall honor me**.[85]

According to this prophecy, the Lord apparently was well pleased with Miller. Having a blessing sealed on a person in Mormonism means that it is given to him for all time,[86] and even more so in this case, since God is the one claiming to seal the blessing on Miller.

Yet the *Church Chronology* records the following under the date of 3 December 1848: "At a meeting held in the G. S. L. City fort, **fellowship was withdrawn** from Apostle Lyman Wight **and Bishop Geo. Miller.**"[87] The reason for his disfellowship is unknown, but obviously the leaders of the Church at that time did not feel he could be trusted. They "despised" him to the point of taking this action, and withdrew the office that God had sealed upon him.

Some claim that blessings from God are contingent upon man's faithfulness. But, as illustrated by the Apostle Peter's denial and restoration, the Bible tells us that God is faithful to His promises even when men are not.[88]

28 April 1842—Zion (Kings and Queens to Pay Respect)

In the afternoon on 28 April 1842, Joseph Smith met with the newly organized Female Relief Society and gave them instruction and counsel regarding what their duties would be. During his remarks, he proclaimed,

> **I now deliver it as a prophecy**, if the inhabitants of this state, with the people of the surrounding country, will turn unto the Lord with all their hearts, **ten years will not roll round before the kings and queens of the earth will come unto Zion, and pay their respects** to the leaders of this people; they shall come **with their millions, and shall contribute of their abundance** for the relief of the poor, and the building up and beautifying of Zion.[89]

No kings or queens have ever made it a point to visit the Female Relief Society and "contribute of their abundance" to them, and certainly not within "ten years." Some might point out that this prophecy was contingent upon the inhabitants of the state and surrounding country turning to the Lord. Since God knows the hearts of the people as well as the future, why would He give prophecies that he knows will not come to pass? As mentioned, God is faithful, even when man is not.[90] He does not give prophecies that are completely dependent on the inconsistent heart of man.

1 September 1842—Joseph Will Triumph Over Enemies (again)

In a letter that Joseph Smith wrote to the members of his Church who were in Nauvoo, Illinois, we find the following prophecy:

> Forasmuch as **the Lord has revealed unto me** that my enemies, both in Missouri and this State, were again in the

pursuit of me ... as for the perils which I am called to pass through, they seem but a small thing to me ... for to **this day has the God of my fathers delivered me** out of them all, and will deliver me from henceforth; for behold, and lo, **I shall triumph over all my enemies, for the Lord God hath spoken it.**[91]

Joseph did not triumph over all his enemies, for a mob murdered him less than two years later in Carthage, Illinois.

20 January 1843—Joseph to Drink Wine in Jerusalem

Joseph met with his leadership council on 20 January 1843. During the evening, Elder Orson Hyde, who had just returned from a mission trip to Palestine, told the men about "the excellent white wine" he had while he was there. According to Joseph Smith's Journal,

Joseph prophesied in the name of the Lord that he would drink wine with him in that country.[92]

Yet Joseph Smith was killed in June 1844, having never been to Palestine.

Another interesting point is that this prophecy was given nearly ten years after Joseph "revealed" the Word of Wisdom.[93] In that revelation, the drinking of wine was prohibited unless it was homemade and for sacramental purposes. This shows that Smith had little or no regard for his own Word of Wisdom revelation.[94]

6 April 1843—Return of Christ (When Joseph Would Be 85)

Joseph Smith spoke during the afternoon session of the Church conference and again predicted Christ's return. He said:

Were I going to prophesy, I would **say the end [of the world] would not come in 1844, 5, or 6, or in forty years. There are those of the rising generation who shall not taste**

death till Christ comes. I was once praying earnestly upon this subject, and a voice said unto me, "My son, if thou livest until thou **art eighty-five years of age, thou shalt see the face of the Son of Man.**" I was left to draw my own conclusions concerning this; and I took the liberty to conclude that if I did live to that time, He would make His appearance. But I do not say whether He will make his appearance or I shall go where He is.[95]

Joseph spoke very ambiguously here, not pinning down whether or not he would live to see the Lord return to earth. But he definitely said that some of the "rising generation" would not taste death until Christ comes. That generation has died and Christ has still not returned. Some would say that Smith was not actually giving a prophecy here, just his own opinion.

But the very next line of Smith's remarks definitely is prophecy. He said,

I prophesy in the name of the Lord God, and let it be written—the Son of Man will not come in the clouds of heaven **till I am eighty-five years old.**[96]

Smith did not live to be 85 years old. He died at age 39. That makes this prophecy an impossibility. Furthermore, for the prophecy to be true, the Lord can **never** return since Joseph never reached that age. If the prophecy meant Christ would return when Joseph turned 85, then the Lord should have returned no later than 1891.[97]

18 May 1843—US Government Overthrow (Potsherd Prophecy)

On this date, Joseph Smith had dinner with Illinois Judge Stephen A. Douglas. During the conversation the troubles of the Mormon Saints came up, along with the fact that the President of the United States, Martin Van Buren, would not do anything to help them. Smith then said,

I prophesy in the name of the Lord God of Israel, unless the United States redress the wrongs committed upon the Saints in the state of Missouri and punish the crimes committed by her officers that in a few years the government will be utterly overthrown and wasted, and there will not be so much as a potsherd [a fragment of broken pottery] **left**, for their wickedness in permitting the murder of men, women and children, and the wholesale plunder and extermination of thousands of her citizens to go unpunished.... **Judge, you will aspire to the presidency of the United States**; and if ever you turn your hand against me or the Latter-day Saints, you will feel the weight of the hand of the Almighty upon you; and you will live to see and know that I have testified the truth to you; for the conversation of this day will stick to you through life.[98]

The United States Government never did "redress the wrongs" against the Mormon Church, and yet they were not "utterly overthrown and wasted." There is certainly more than a "potsherd left" of them.

Yet, many Mormons turn to this prophecy as evidence that Joseph Smith was a true prophet. How? By ignoring the primary remarks about the government and singling out the last line of Joseph's comments—that Judge Douglas would aspire to the Presidency of the United States, and that if he ever turned against the Mormons he would "feel the weight of the hand of the Almighty." (We will examine this portion of the prophecy in greater detail in Chapter 8.)

Judge Douglas did run for Presidency, but lost after turning against the Mormons. Nephi Morris believes this is "incontrovertible evidence" that the prophecy was true.[99] But in order to conclude this, he has to ignore the main message of that prophecy—that the US Government would be destroyed "in a few years"—which certainly did not come to pass. In his book, *Prophecies of Joseph Smith and Their Fulfillment*, Morris even resorted to physically cutting out Joseph Smith's remarks about the government from the photograph of the *Millenial Star* issue for 26 February 1859, where the story had originally been printed.[100] Why? Because the main portion of the revelation had proven false, and he needed to hide that fact.

Even if Joseph is given the benefit of the doubt regarding Judge Douglas,[101] there is still the fact that, contrary to his prophecy, the US Government was not destroyed.

16 December 1843—US Government Overthrow (Grease Spot Prophecy)

During a Nauvoo City Council meeting held in his own house, Joseph Smith said,

> **I prophesied**, by virtue of the holy Priesthood vested in **me, and in the name of the Lord Jesus Christ**, that, **if Congress will not hear our petition and grant us protection, they shall be broken up as a government**, and God shall damn them, and **there shall nothing be left of them—not even a grease spot**.[102]

Congress did not hear their petition nor grant them protection, yet they were not "broken up as a government." Instead, the US government has grown to enormous size, power, and wealth.

Interestingly enough, when this information was transferred into the official *History of the Church*, **the last half of Joseph Smith's comments were left out.**[103] By that time, it was obvious that the prophecy had not come true. By eliminating the last half of his statement, LDS authorities mislead those who read the *History*.

This is clearly demonstrated by a footnote that was inserted which implied that the prophecy had come true. It reads in part,

> This prediction doubtless has reference to the party in power; to the "government" considered as the administration; not to the "government" considered as the country; but the administration party, the Democratic Party, which had controlled the destiny of the country for forty years. It is matter of history that a few years later the party then in power lost control of the national government....[104]

This is a futile attempt to try to make the prophecy appear to be true. However, since the Democratic Party is still very much in existence, the prophecy remains unfulfilled.

6 February 1844—Termination of Cooking

This evening, Joseph Smith attended a dinner party at John Taylor's home. In company with him were his younger brother Hyrum, Sidney Rigdon, the Twelve Apostles and their wives. During the meal, he

> **prophesied at the table that 5 years would not roll round before the company would all be able to live without cooking.**[105]

This is a very silly thing to say; yet Joseph gave it as a prophecy. Some might claim that it is possible now, or even in 1849, to live without actually cooking. The only way to do this is to live off the land by eating nuts, berries, fruits and raw vegetables. That was possible at the time Smith gave these remarks, so that cannot be what he was referring to.

The writers of the *History of the Church* apparently saw the absurdity of this remark as well, because **this prophecy was deliberately deleted** when this event was transferred into the official *History*.[106]

How Many False Prophesies?

The exact number of false prophesies Joseph Smith uttered may never be fully known. Estimates vary among those who have studied LDS history. *The Evangel* ran a series in which 53 false prophecies given by Joseph Smith were briefly reviewed.[107] *The Inner Circle* mentioned 58.[108] Robert Morey, after a great deal of research into the subject, wrote "there are over sixty false prophecies of Joseph Smith which have been documented...."[109]

Whatever the actual number may be, the fact remains that, according to the Bible, **just one false prophecy** is enough to disqualify a person as a true prophet. Joseph Smith's brother Hyrum held a different view, however. He once said about prophesying that "if you hit once in 10 times that is alright."[110]

The latest interpretive trend is that if a prophecy fails or if a doctrinal teaching later proves to be untrue, Mormon apologists claim that it was just the prophet's uninspired **opinion**, and not a prophecy from God. But of the 26 prophecies listed above that did not come to pass, 13 of them are officially identified by the LDS Church as "revelations"; 11 of them are specifically called "prophecies" by either Joseph Smith himself or other LDS members who heard them declared; and 15 of them are either direct quotes attributed to God or Jesus, or begin with the phrase "thus saith the Lord." Many of the cited examples contain a combination of these claims. There is no getting around the fact, then, that Joseph Smith solemnly proclaimed more than a few prophecies that did not come to pass. The only credible explanation for this is that he was a false and untrustworthy prophet.

Following Joseph's Example

If Joseph Smith was a false prophet, then those leaders who followed in his authority after him might also be false prophets. As such, they would be liable to give false predictions as well. A brief research reveals that this is exactly the case. Here are a few examples:

President Brigham Young[111]

On several occasions, Young prophesied that those of African descent would never receive the Mormon Priesthood until all others had first been redeemed and resurrected (*Journal of Discourses* [hereafter *JD*] 2:143; 7:290-91; 11:272). This proved false when Spencer Kimball changed Church policy in 1978 and gave the priesthood to all worthy males (*Doctrine and Covenants*, Declaration 2). Young prophesied that all Mormons are literally Jews, and that no Gentiles would come into the Church (*JD* 2:268-69). He later contradicted this statement by saying that when a Gentile comes into the Church, and receives the Holy Ghost, he will have fits and convulsions while the Holy Ghost changes his blood (*JD* 12:270). Young prophesied that the Church Elders would be thought of as kings on their thrones before 1882 (*JD* 4:40). He prophesied that the Civil War would fail to free the slaves (*JD* 10:250), and that the slaves would remain enslaved forever (*JD* 7:290-91). He prophesied that Joseph Smith's sons would eventually come to take over the Mormon Church and none would resist them (*JD* 8:69). He prophesied that the US Government was about to be completely destroyed, and the only ones who could save it were the Mormons (*JD* 12:119-20). He prophesied that God would make the Latter-day Saints the wealthiest people on earth (*JD* 17:120). He also proclaimed that the sun and the moon were inhabited (*JD* 13:271).

Apostle Heber C. Kimball

Though not a prophet, Kimball also gave many false prophecies. As an Apostle in the Church, he was supposedly led by divine inspiration. His favorite prediction was of a famine soon to hit the United States and the world, unlike any ever seen, which he said would come upon the earth before 1861 (*JD* 5:21, 174). It would be so great that the US would run out of sugar while the Mormons had plenty (*JD* 5:94), and millions from all nations would flee to them for bread (*JD* 3:228, 253). He prophesied that those hearing him would live to see no grain raised outside of Salt Lake City, Utah (*JD* 3:253). He prophesied that the Mormons would have power over all people. He predicted that all Utah governors, judges and officials would be LDS from that day on (*JD* 5:173), that Brigham Young would be President of the United States with himself (Kimball) as Vice-President and Daniel Wells as Secretary of the Interior (*JD* 5:219). He predicted that the US President would bow to the Mormons, along with all of their enemies (*JD* 5:93), and that Mormons would soon control all nations and kingdoms (*JD* 3:228). He prophesied that Utah would forever be separated from the United States very soon (*JD* 5:10), and that their state would forever be known as Deseret, and no longer as Utah (*JD* 5:161). He promised that if people would put a Bowie knife under their pillows at night, they would never have any more nightmares, since Satan was afraid of weapons (*JD* 5:164). He prophesied twice that Brigham Young would be Governor over Utah as long as he lived—once on 30 August 1857 (*JD* 5:164) and again on 27 September 1857 (*JD* 5:274-75). In spite of this, President Buchanan turned the Governorship of the territory over to non-Mormon Alfred Cumming before that year ended. Kimball prophesied in December 1857 that he would live to return to Jackson County, Missouri, along with Brigham Young and "thousands and millions of others" to built the temple as Joseph Smith prophesied (*JD* 6:190). He died about 10 years later without ever returning to Missouri.

Apostle Orson Pratt

Also not an official prophet, Pratt seldom prophesied. But when he did, he was wrong. This was because his prophecies were all based upon his faith in Joseph Smith's false prophecies. Pratt predicted that the Lord would return the Saints to Jackson County, Missouri, that it would be the headquarters for the Mormon Church, and that the prophets and apostles would all live there and direct the church from that place (*JD* 13:138). Instead, Salt Lake City, Utah, has been the Church headquarters and the dwelling place of the prophets and apostles. Pratt reiterated this prophesy on other occasions, as well (*JD* 13:362; 17:111).

President Wilford Woodruff

Woodruff prophesied that "the hour is at the door when my [the Lord's] wrath and indignation shall be poured out upon the wicked of this nation." God would pour out his wrath upon "this nation and upon all the nations of the earth...." The revelation continues, "Their murders, blasphemies, lyings, whoredoms and abominations have come up before my face and before the heavens, and the wrath of mine indignation is full. I have decreed plagues to go forth and lay waste mine enemies, and not many years hence they shall not be left to pollute mine heritage." God promised that he would "spare none," but would "burn them up."[112]

President Lorenzo Snow

Snow, like many of his contemporaries, prophesied that some then living and hearing his voice would return to Jackson County and build the temple there—which still has not happened.[113]

President John Taylor

In 1886, Taylor prophesied that the law of Celestial Marriage (polygamy) could not be revoked and would never be, and that all Mormons were required to live by it.[114] This proved false when Wilford Woodruff had a revelation and issued the Manifesto just four years later in 1890, which withdrew the original command.

Conclusion

We have seen examples of false prophecies, predictions and statements given by those succeeding Joseph. Most of them were given from the Church pulpit, which means they are to be considered "inspired."[115] According to the test in Deuteronomy 18:22, there is no place for error in prophecy: "if the thing follow not, nor come to pass, that is the thing which the LORD hath not spoken...." If a man gives false prophecies, he is a false prophet.

Chapter 8
Amazing Predictions?

Joseph Smith's Claim –
> I received the following commandment.... Wherefore, meaning the church, thou shalt give heed unto all his [Joseph Smith's] words and commandments which he shall give unto you.... For his word ye shall receive, as if from mine [God's] own mouth....
> – *History of the Church*, 1:78

> My enemies say that I *have* been a true prophet. Why, I had rather be a fallen true prophet than a false prophet.
> – *Teachings of the Prophet Joseph Smith*, 365

Joseph Smith's True Prophecies?

Over the years, certain of Joseph Smith's predictions have been cited as proof of his divine calling, since Mormons accept them as prophecies that came true. The four most often cited examples are his (1) Word of Wisdom Prophecy,[1] (2) Stephen Douglas Prophecy,[2] (3) Civil War Prophecy,[3] and (4) Rocky Mountain Prophecy.[4]

Word of Wisdom Prophecy

After pondering the subject of tobacco use in their meetings, Joseph Smith inquired of the Lord on the matter and received a revelation known as the Word of Wisdom. It is currently printed as *Doctrine and Covenants*, Section 89. The *Doctrine and Covenants Commentary* says the following about this revelation:

> There is, possibly, no Revelation in this volume [the *Doctrine and Covenants*] that has been more frequently commented upon by the Elders in their discourses, or more

fully explained. There certainly is **none that has received stronger confirmation by scientists.**... the rules given, far in advance of anything suggested by scientists, have been **amply sanctioned.**... the Prophet deals with a subject that belongs properly to the domain of science, and scientists, therefore, without intention on their part, become witnesses to the fact that **Joseph Smith spoke by divine inspiration,** when **they confirm the truths set forth.**[5]

What does the revelation say? Most Mormon members, when asked, will reply that it forbids the use of coffee, tea, alcohol and tobacco. Actually, the revelation contains much more.

Coffee and tea are not specifically forbidden; that became a later interpretation of the revelation. What are specifically forbidden are all hot drinks,[6] though most Mormons have no compunction about drinking hot chocolate or hot ciders in the winter. Hot soup could be placed into that category, as well. Some wine is allowed by the revelation,[7] as is beer,[8] but otherwise the use of alcohol as a beverage is forbidden.[9] Meat is to be eaten very sparingly and only in times of winter and famine.[10] While all grains are said to be good for food, men are cautioned to consume only wheat.[11]

In practice, however, most LDS families either ignore or are unaware of these very specific commands, but they do abstain from all tobacco and alcohol. They hold steadfastly to the coffee and tea abstention, as well.[12] The leaders of the Church apparently do the same thing.[13]

The claim is often made that the principles set forth in this revelation were new and in advance of any medical knowledge on the subject at the time. If this information were new and unheard of in Joseph Smith's day, then there would be some credibility to this claim. If not, then Joseph was just repeating information from other sources.

What was the real inspiration behind the prophecy? Was Joseph truly just pondering the matter, or was there some other reason for the revelation? Concerning how he came to receive this prophecy, Brigham Young gives us this revealing information:

I think I am as well acquainted with the circumstances which led to the giving of the Word of Wisdom as any man in the Church.... The first school of the prophets was held in a small room situated over the Prophet Joseph's kitchen.... When they assembled together in this room after breakfast, **the first they did was to light their pipes**, and, while smoking, talk about the great things of the **kingdom, and spit all over the room**, and as soon as the pipe was out of their mouths **a large chew of tobacco would then be taken**. Often when the Prophet entered the room to give the school instructions **he would find himself in a cloud of tobacco smoke**. This, **and the complaints of his wife at having to clean so filthy a floor**, made the Prophet think upon the matter, and he inquired of the Lord relating to the conduct of the Elders in using tobacco, and the revelation known as the Word of Wisdom was the result of his inquiry.[14]

Book of Mormon witness David Whitmer verified Young's account, telling us that Emma Smith, Joseph's wife, remarked, "It would be a good thing if a revelation could be had declaring the use of tobacco a sin, and commanding its suppression." The Elders joked about it, and in reply they said that "the revelation should also provide for a total abstinence from tea and coffee drinking...." Whitmer then informs us that the matter was soon thought about in a more serious manner, and "the 'Word of Wisdom' was the result."[15]

It was apparently **not** a matter of Smith arbitrarily pondering the subject of tobacco use and receiving the revelation. According to those who knew the facts, he just did not like teaching in a cloud of smoke. Added to this, his wife had suggested that a revelation might be had to stop the tobacco use altogether by the Elders. In return, the Elders wanted to expand the prohibitions to include those refreshments the women delighted in. The sudden "inspiration" of the revelation is not as miraculous as it seems.

What information was available on these matters at the time? Jerald and Sandra Tanner's research provides the following information. LDS writer Leonard Arrington reports that the Philadelphia *Journal of Health,* prior to Joseph receiving this revelation, **strongly** condemned the use of **alcohol, tobacco and meat-eating**. The *Millennial Harbinger* printed this report in June of 1830,[16] three years before the "revelation" received by Smith. Arrington also showed that there was actually a Kirtland Temperence Society with 239 members that had been organized on 6 October 1830—more than two years in advance of the revelation.[17] Tanners also cited Whitney R. Cross, who reports that **abstaining from alcohol, coffee, tea and tobacco was widely discussed** in the early 1830s.[18]

Actually, these prohibitions were nothing new in the area where Joseph Smith lived and at the time he received his "revelation" on the subject. **They were the popular topic of conversation for the day**. He received the revelation mainly to placate his wife, who had to clean up after the Elders. Then he gave additional provisions in the revelation, so that the men were not the only ones having to give up their common habits. To be sure, the information in the revelation was, for the most part, good advice with excellent health benefits. But it was not as miraculous as claimed.

Still, there is more about this prophecy to consider. At the end of the revelation is this remarkable statement:

> Behold, verily, **thus saith the Lord unto you**: In consequence of evils and designs which do and will exist in the hearts of conspiring men in the last days, I have warned you, and forewarn you, by giving unto you this word of wisdom by revelation.... And **all saints who remember to keep and do these sayings**, walking in obedience to the commandments, shall receive health in their navel and marrow to their bones; And shall find wisdom and great treasures of knowledge, even hidden treasures; And shall run and not be weary, and shall walk and not faint. **And I, the Lord, give unto them a promise, that the destroying angel shall pass by them**, as the children of Israel, **and not slay them**. Amen.[19]

This portion qualifies as prophecy, because it is given as a promise directly from the Lord. Yet who of the Mormon members, from the time of this prophecy until today, has had the "destroying angel pass by them"? Even the most faithful, spiritual and steadfast Mormons of the past have obviously died. While compliance with the Word of Wisdom will certainly benefit anyone physically, it cannot guard against all sicknesses or medical maladies. It also does not automatically result in "wisdom" and "great treasures of knowledge." Yet these are exactly what the revelation promises.

When all is taken together, this prophecy is not proof of a divine calling on Joseph Smith's part. It only shows that he was able to reiterate the popular opinions of his day.

Stephen A. Douglas Prophecy

This prophecy was briefly discussed in Chapter 7 under the date of 18 May 1843. The main point of the prophecy—the destruction of the US Government—was shown to be false. Just after that prophecy, in the same discourse, Joseph made comments concerning Stephen A. Douglas aspiring to the US Presidency, and warned him never to turn his back on the Mormon people. Mormons like to point to these comments as proof of Joseph Smith's divine prophetic calling. Nephi Morris writes, "The divine inspiration of this great manifestation is proven at the hands of time. Its genuineness is equally well established. Its publication long prior to the culminating events it foreshadowed are also proven beyond a doubt."[20]

How could Joseph possibly know (17 years before the fact) that this man would run for President? Morris tells us that "an intimate and friendly relationship existed"[21] between Judge Douglas and Joseph Smith. Obviously Douglas had great political aspirations. According to a footnote by Morris, he was "a masterful politician." He was elected to the Illinois State Legislature in 1836, and rose quickly to become a Judge in the Illinois Supreme Court by age 28. He was elected to the House of Representatives in 1843, the same year that Joseph had this interview with him.[22]

It is not difficult to see that Judge Douglas would likely have shared with his friend his ambition to run for Congress that fall. The two "intimate" friends probably discussed the possibility of Douglas eventually running for the US Presidency.[23] On the occasion Joseph gave his "prophecy," Morris tells us that they spent "fully three hours" together.[24] Political ambition would have been a natural subject in their discussion, and one can reasonably assume that Judge Douglas was seeking the support of the Mormon leader and his Church for his upcoming congressional campaign.[25] It is not so miraculous, then, that Joseph Smith would "foresee" his friends' political ambition culminating in an eventual run for the Presidency of the United States.[26]

But Mormons also point to the fact that once Judge Douglas turned against the Mormons, he lost the election and his political career, which, some believe, fulfills what Joseph prophesied. In reality, this is not what happened.[27]

After being elected to the House in 1843, Congressman Douglas went on to become a US Senator in 1846 and a leader of the Democratic Party. In 1856 (the same year that *The Deseret News* first printed Joseph Smith's "prophecy" about him) Douglas was seeking the nomination of the Democratic Party for the presidential election of that year. **At that time he was still very friendly toward the Mormons.** Nevertheless, **he was passed over** for the Democratic nomination that year in favor of James Buchanan.

The following year a very strained relationship developed between the Mormons and the US Government. Brigham Young was in a constant state of agitation towards the United States, and stirred up the Mormon people to open rebellion against federal authority. On 12 June 1857, Senator Douglas finally spoke out against the Mormon establishment on three points: (1) They would not recognize the US Government's authority, (2) They took terrible oaths in the temple which were subversive towards the US Government, and (3) They were inciting the American Indians to hostility against the United States. The Senator also opposed the practice of polygamy, as did most people in the Eastern states (and throughout the country) at that time. All of the Senator's charges against Mormonism were true.

Was it wrong for Senator Douglas to take this position? Absolutely not. It was required of him as a United States Senator to uphold the government against all that were hostile and subversive towards it. His oath of office required him to take this stand. It was not personal hatred of Mormonism that fueled this political stand, but the actions of Brigham Young against the government that caused the division.

It was only **after** he stood against the Mormon insurrection that Senator Douglas was nominated by the Democratic Party for the presidential bid of 1860. He lost that election by a landslide to the Republican candidate—Abraham Lincoln.

According to Joseph's prophecy, if Judge Douglas were ever to turn against the Mormons, he would "feel the weight of the hand of the Almighty." Yet when he was friendly towards the Mormons, he lost the nomination of the party for President. After speaking against the anti-US Mormon teachings, he won the nomination of his party.

Following the election, Morris writes, "Scarcely anything remains to be said of Mr. Douglas after that unhappy, fateful political contest."[28] But there is a reason for that—Senator Douglas died seven months later. Morris claims that Douglas died a "disappointed" and "broken-hearted man." On the contrary, he remained a proud and committed Senator until his death.

After losing the election, he valiantly volunteered his services to President Lincoln after the outbreak of the Civil War to tour the Southern states and rally support for the Union cause. This is not the act of a disappointed or broken-hearted man, but of a proud American and an expert statesman who loved the country he served so well. While on this tour, he unfortunately contracted typhoid fever, which caused his death on 3 June 1861.

Were the loss of the election and the contraction of typhoid the chastening "hand of the Almighty"? If so, then Joseph Smith's own loss of the US Presidency he sought because of his sudden terrible death in 1844 could be used as evidence of the chastening hand of God as well. Were the Mormons who died of illness and exposure while crossing the plains en route to the Salt Lake Valley being chastened? No one would claim such a thing. To say this was the case for Senator Douglas, but not for these others, would be highly biased and selective reasoning. In all, the facts about Douglas's political career and life do not fit the specifics of Smith's prophecy.

Civil War Prophecy

On Christmas Day 1832, Joseph said he was pondering the subject of war when a revelation came to him from God. The revelation is found today in the *Doctrine and Covenants* as Section 87. Specifically, it is about

> the wars that will shortly come to pass, **beginning at the rebellion of South Carolina**, which will eventually terminate in **the death and misery of many souls**....[29]

The United States Civil War began on 12 April 1861, 28 years after this prophecy was given. It did, indeed, begin in South Carolina. For these reasons, many Mormons argue, Joseph Smith must have been a true prophet.

Morris calls this "one of the most outstanding prophecies made by Joseph Smith.... It was most specific with respect to the Civil War...."[30] He goes on to write, "To appreciate the magnitude of this 'miracle of knowledge' let any living person undertake to describe or foretell events thirty, or even ten years distant. It is *humanly impossible*."[31]

The facts point to the conclusion that it was **not** so remarkable. Problems between the northern and southern states had begun as far back as 1826 and escalated when South Carolina declared the tariffs of 1828 and 1832 null and void and would not enforce them.[32] The rebellious acts of South Carolina and the civil unrest in the southern states were widely printed in the newspapers of the time.[33] Even foreign writers such as Charles Dickens[34] and Alexis DeTocqueville[35] had given just as accurate a "prophecy" that there would be an inevitable struggle between the northern and southern states that would include bloodshed and war.

In fact, Morris even admits in his book that "a state of rebellion actually existed in South Carolina at the very time the prophecy was made."[36] Alice Smith McKay researched the subject in great detail for her Master's thesis in 1930. She concluded that this prophecy was "the natural result of the stirring conditions of that particular period of history."[37] She went on to correctly state that "the conditions at

South Carolina pointed directly to war. Joseph Smith ... accurately interpreted the facts and information known.... The prediction was given at a period of actual preparation for war in South Carolina."[38]

Joseph Smith obviously expected the war to begin very soon, which explains why he said in the prediction that war "**will shortly come to pass.**"[39] But since that current state of affairs did not develop into war at the time expected, Smith refused to have the revelation published during his lifetime. Some of Joseph's revelations were printed as the *Book of Commandments* in July of 1833, but this "most outstanding" one **was not among them**. That book was expanded and republished as the *Doctrine and Covenants* in 1835, but again, **the prediction on war was left out**. LDS writers have suggested that the prophecy was written down and circulated privately among the LDS members,[40] as if to show that it was authentic and that Joseph Smith believed in it. There is no question that the prophecy is authentic at this point, and obviously Smith expected the prophecy to be fulfilled. But the fact is that the prophecy was deliberately left out of Church publications at the time. This implies that Smith viewed the prophecy as unfulfilled and did not want that fact published.

While the prophecy was inscribed in the handwritten *History of the Church*, it was not printed in either the *Times and Seasons*[41] or the *Millenial Star*[42] when they published that portion of the Church's history. That means Smith deliberately left this "miracle of knowledge" out of those printings. Since he regularly printed his prophecies for the Church to see, **it is very suspicious that this one was left out of all the Church publications.**

In fact, it did not appear at all in print until July of 1851[43]— seven years after Joseph Smith had died. Why then? Because once again difficulties were arising between the northern and southern states; and once more South Carolina was at the center of the heated debate. These new developments were even printed in *The Deseret News* in the months leading up to the publication of the revelation.[44] Even then, the difficulties still did not escalate into war for **another ten years.**

To accept this prophecy as true, the focus has to be on the fact that South Carolina was listed as the starting place for the war. The rest of the prophecy must be ignored. For example, verse 2 of the revelation states that "war **will be poured out upon all nations, beginning at** this place [South Carolina]." That never came to pass. Many Mormons also interpret those words to be a prophecy about World Wars I and II. But the verse specifically states that the world wars spoken of would **begin in South Carolina,** again tying them directly to the Civil War. Once again, that never happened. As Bill McKeever, Director of Mormonism Research Ministry, points out, "To say these world wars [WW I & WW II] had any connection whatsoever with the rebellion at South Carolina defies reasoning."[45] Verse 6 states that because of this conflict, "**famine, and plague, and earthquake**" would befall the earth "until the consumption decreed **hath made a full end of all nations**." None of that happened. So not only was this an unremarkable prophecy based on the current events of Joseph Smith's time, but most of it failed.

Joseph felt the war he prophesied would "shortly come to pass." Since it did not, he refused to openly publish the revelation. Only years later, when the war once again seemed inevitable, did the leadership of the Church publish the prophecy.

Rocky Mountain Prophecy

The *History of the Church* records that Joseph Smith wrote the following on 6 August 1842:

> **I prophesied** that the Saints **would continue to suffer much affliction** and would **be driven to the Rocky Mountains**, **many would apostatize**, others would be **put to death** by our persecutors or **lose their lives in consequence of exposure or disease**, and **some** of you will live to go and **assist in making settlements** and build cities and see **the Saints become a mighty people in the midst of the Rocky Mountains**.[46]

If this prophecy could be verified, then it would be impressive that Smith could predict this, for these events are exactly what befell the early Mormons. They left Illinois after the death of Joseph Smith.[47] They proceeded, after a stay in Winter Quarters, Nebraska, to the "west of the Rocky Mountains" and settled there in July of 1847.[48] Many left the Church after the death of Joseph Smith.[49] As they trekked across the plains toward the Rocky Mountains, a great many tragically lost their lives to exposure and illness brought on by the journey.[50] They made many settlements along the way, and even beyond Great Salt Lake City.[51] Salt Lake City has become a massive city, and few would argue that the Mormon settlers there did become a "mighty people in the midst of the Rocky Mountains."

Morris writes, "It was humanly impossible for him [Joseph Smith] to foretell the possibilities of a country so vaguely conceived and of which there was such meagre knowledge."[52] T. B. H. Stenhouse adds,

> As early as 1842, he prophesied that the Saints would remove to the Rocky Mountains, and in the spring of 1844, while troubles were increasing upon him, he selected a company of men to explore that unknown region, prophesying at the same time that within five years from that date, the Saints should be located there beyond the influence of mobs.[53]

Stenhouse accepts one of Smith's diary entries as proof of his prophetic mantle in this case. Yet the entry cited does not mention the Rocky Mountains. Instead, it records that Smith sent out men to scout throughout "the localities, California and Oregon"[54] to find a suitable settling place.

Morris published his book in 1920, and about this prophecy he wrote, "**The earliest printed publication of this prophecy**, known to the writer, **is to be found in the *Deseret News*, in 1852**. It was published in its regular order as the History of the Church appeared in that paper. **We have not had access to the original record** as kept by the Prophet, containing this remarkable prophecy."[55] Why did Church leaders wait so long to publish the prophecy? And since Morris was preparing a volume in defense of Joseph Smith's prophetic ability, it seems odd that he would not be granted access to the original document. Clearly he attempted to see it, or he would not have made this comment in his book.

In their research, Jerald and Sandra Tanner discovered the probable reason why Morris's request was denied. They write, "We are now happy to announce that a photograph of the portion of the original handwritten manuscript containing this 'prophecy' has been located at the Visitor Center in Nauvoo, Illinois.... Now that we have a photograph of the page containing this 'prophecy,' we can see why it was suppressed for all these years." The reason, they explain, is that "the part concerning the Mormons becoming 'a mighty people in the midst of the Rocky Mountains' **has been crammed in at the bottom** in a smaller handwriting. This would seem to indicate that **it was added sometime after the page had originally been written.**"[56]

Examination of the original shows their conclusion is correct. The page in question is found in the *Documentary History of the Church*.[57] It is obvious that information was added—squeezed between the lines for the dates of Thursday 4 August, Friday 5 August, and Saturday 6 August. The entire portion given as "prophecy" by Joseph Smith is part of this information added later. The handwriting on the page, according to the Tanners, appears to be the writing of Thomas Bullock, who was the scribe who recorded the original information on the page. But **when** he added the extra material cannot be definitely determined. Bullock, as the Tanners point out, worked in the Historian's Office in Salt Lake while this portion of the *History of the Church* was being worked on in 1854. And as they show in great detail, more than 60 percent of the *History of the Church* was written after the death of Joseph Smith.[58]

In fact, LDS Historian Dean C. Jessee researched this prophecy in detail, and showed that the prophecy portion could not have been written on the manuscript until more than a year after Joseph Smith had died. In fact, he proved that the page containing the prophecy had not even been written until July of 1845.[59] Smith died in June 1844.

Morris claims that the prophecy was printed in the *Deseret News* in 1852,[60] but the photograph of the prophecy from that paper which he includes was from the 7 November 1855[61] issue—more than **eight years after the Mormons had already settled there.** Morris's 1852 date was apparently an error. The LDS history books had been packed up in Nauvoo, Illinois, on 4 February 1846, and were not unpacked in Salt Lake City until 7 June 1853.[62] The work on compiling and finalizing the *History of the Church* did not begin in earnest until 10 April 1854, under the direction of the new Church Historian, George A. Smith.[63] The prophecy was printed for the first time in the 7 November 1855 issue of the *Deseret News* in its regular order as that paper printed the history of Joseph Smith.[64]

The very earliest that the prophecy could have been added to the manuscript was July 1845. It is more likely that it was added to the manuscript page after 1853 or 1854. If so, that was well after the Mormons had already settled in the Salt Lake Valley. It is easy to make an accurate prophecy several years after the events have happened. It must be proven beyond question that the specifics of the prophecy were uttered well before the events they foretold in order to accept the predictions as genuine. This means that the Rocky Mountain Prophecy, unless found recorded and published elsewhere (prior to the *Deseret News* article in 1855 and prior to the settling of the Mormons in the Great Salt Lake Valley in 1847) cannot be considered authentic. As the Tanners rightly state,

> From this it is evident that the prophecy concerning the Rocky Mountains **could have been added years after** the Mormons were in Utah.... Unless the Mormon leaders can establish that the entry in the Manuscript History was taken from another source written during Joseph Smith's lifetime, **the prophecy** as found in the *History of the Church* **becomes of no historical value.**[65]

Morris suggests that several people had early knowledge of this "prophecy," thus making it authentic. **Did LDS leaders really know** about it? If, as he and other LDS writers claim, the membership of the Church was well aware of the prophecy before moving West, and if the leaders of the Church were indeed circulating handwritten copies of the prophecy, then we can expect to see verification of this in their contemporary writings. Is this the case? **No.**

In a circular letter to the Church, printed in October of 1845, Brigham Young stated that the leadership intended to move the

Church to a "far distant region of the west." He closed the circular by stating, "there are said to be many good locations for settlements on the Pacific, especially at Vancouver's Island, near the mouth of the Columbia."[66] This indicates that when he was planning to leave Nauvoo, Young had the Pacific coast in mind for a settlement, not "the midst of the Rocky Mountains."

Morris cites, among other things, an entry from the journal of Heber C. Kimball on 31 December 1845, concerning the move of the Saints to the west.[67] Examination of that journal entry, however, does not show knowledge of the prophecy. In fact, he did not even know where the Saints would settle. According to the journal entry, Young was "examining maps with reference to **selecting a location** for the Saints **west of the Rocky Mountains**...."[68] This indicates they had no knowledge of Smith's prediction that they would settle "in the midst of the Rocky Mountains." They were instead looking for a place to live on the **western side** of them.

Brigham Young had written a letter just 13 days before this journal entry, definitely indicating that he was planning to have the Saints "settle **on Vancouver's Island**."[69] Vancouver Island is in Canada, northwest of the current state of Washington. That is well outside the "midst of the Rocky Mountains." J. H. Beadle informs us that "at a conference held before they left Nauvoo, **to determine their destination**, Lyman Wight had strongly urged Texas, John Taylor proposed Vancouver's Island, many were in favor of Oregon and Brigham Young insisted upon California."[70]

The same day the Saints (LDS members) left Nauvoo for the West, 238 additional members departed from New York on the ship *Brooklyn* to sail around Cape Horn for the Pacific Coast of California. At the time, they planned to meet Brigham Young and the Mormons traveling with him there.[71] This is verified by the fact that when several Mormon men were enlisted in the Mormon Battalion to fight for America in the Mexican War, they expected to be discharged in California, where the rest of the Mormon pioneers intended to settle.[72]

M. R. Werner writes, "Finally, in 1846 they began their trek to the West, which they believed to be inhabited by God.... **Just where** in the West **they were going, the Mormons did not know,** but **Oregon and California** were in the mind of Brigham Young."[73] Major Howard Egan was in the first company of Mormon pioneers to travel West with Brigham Young. In his diary, it is noted that "the family moved with the general exodus of the Saints about the 1st of March, 1846.... **At that time there was no definite plan as to the future destination of the people.** There had been vague ideas afloat of **Oregon, Vancouver and Upper California** as probable places of refuge."[74]

Beadle agreed that "they then thought of taking Oregon and establishing an independent government there...."[75]

Many of the Saints were under the impression they were headed for the northern Pacific Coast, as was indicated by a hymn John Taylor wrote. The Mormons sang it often on their journey across the plains and Rocky Mountains.[76] Also remembering this hymn, Elder W. Riter, who had traveled with Brigham Young and followed him into the Salt Lake Valley, states, "You will remember that when our people started from Nauvoo they only followed the setting sun. **They did not know where they were going.** There was **an indefinite idea** that they were going to California; for you may remember that in some of the old editions of our hymn book there is a hymn: 'In Upper California—Oh, that's the land for me!'"[77]

While many Mormons had already left Nauvoo on their way to the West, other leaders of the Church had been discharged to England. An idea of where the main body of the Church would be going was sent along with them. Oliver B. Huntington was one of the missionaries who went to England. He records in his journal on 16 October 1846:

> A council meeting was appointed at the office in Stanley Buildings Bath St.... the Twelve did not get there until four.... this much was talked over. **It was the intention of the Twelve**, here, or the authorities of the Church in England to petition the [English] government, to cede to us as her subjects **a part or the whole of the Island of Vancouver**, on the western coast of America; and also ship us there. **This was given as the intended course to be taken by the Church.**[78]

It was along the wagon trail that Young heard more about the Great Salt Lake Valley.[79] But even after receiving several reports favorable to settling there, he was not sure that this was where the Mormon pioneers would settle. Clearly, Young was not aware of any prophecy Smith had given about settling in the Rocky Mountains, or he would have followed the revelation to the letter, and settling there would have been his intent all along. As Jon Krakauer observed, "… it was commonly understood by the [LDS] faithful that it was a Saint's sacred duty to assist in the fulfilling of prophecies when the opportunity arose."[80]

As late as 6 June 1847, Young was still unsure where they would locate. That day, he wrote a letter to Samuel Brannan that said they **might** settle in the Great Basin, but that **his mind was not yet made up** on a specific location.[81] Brannan argued against it, and tried to persuade Young to go with their original plan of settling on the California coast.[82] But as the wagon journey progressed, Young finally decided the matter in his mind,[83] and upon seeing the Great Salt Lake Valley decided that this was where they would stop.

The strongest evidence Morris gives in support of Smith's prophecy is from the diary of Anson Call. The entry appears under the date of 14 July 1843. But nothing that Call recorded from Smith's comments verifies the prophecy as authentic. Call writes that Smith had said the water he was drinking at the time "tastes much like the crystal streams that are running in the Rocky Mountains which **some of you** will participate of. There are **some of those** standing here that will perform a great work in that land." Smith went on to say that Call would "assist in building cities **from one end of the country to the other**." At the end of the entry, he says that "multitudes will die, many will apostatize."[84]

Call's record indicates that Smith never gave a prophecy. It contains no prophetic elements. The entry indicates nothing of the Saints settling "in the midst of the Rocky Mountains," nor of them becoming a great people there. Instead, it seems to indicate that Smith had no intention of the Church relocating. He had in mind that some of the Saints would perform missionary work or create new settlements in that area. The most this entry indicates is that

Smith said some of the Saints would assist in building cities there and "from one end of the country to the other."

LDS apologist Michael Fordham claims that a blessing Joseph Smith gave to Paulina Eliza Phelps qualifies as proof for the authenticity of this prophecy.[85] But examination of the blessing shows that all Smith said was that this young lady would eventually "go to the Rocky Mountains."[86] It does not mention the whole Church being forced to migrate there. Fordham also lists a reference from the *Mosiah Hancock Autobiography*, in which Hancock tells of Smith prophesying they would live in "the valley of the Great Salt Lake."[87] Once again, this entry says nothing of the whole Church moving there.

Fordham additionally points to a discourse given by Wilford Woodruff, wherein he claims that Joseph Smith prophesied about the Church filling "the Rocky Mountains" where they would "build temples to the Most High."[88] But again, Woodruff never claimed that Smith prophesied of the whole Church settling there, but only that "tens of thousands of Latter-day Saints" would gather in the Rocky Mountains. In fact, Joseph Smith made this claim right after prophesying that the Mormon Church would fill "North and South America—it will fill the world."[89] This shows that Smith's remarks were never meant to be a prophecy about the Mormon Church specifically settling in the Rocky Mountains.

Davis Bitton sums the situation up well, stating, "there is no such prophecy in the handwriting of Joseph Smith, or published during the prophet's lifetime, but it was referred to in general terms during the trek west. After the arrival in the Salt Lake Valley the prophecy became more specific as time went on."[90] The only definite conclusion that can be reached is that this prophecy cannot be shown to be authentic.

Conclusion

After examining 26 prophecies of Joseph Smith in the last chapter (as well as mentioning many from other LDS leaders), and taking a close look at four prophecies in this chapter, we have seen that all have proven false except for the Rocky Mountain prophecy.

Even that prophecy cannot be verified as fully authentic, and the available evidence shows that Joseph Smith never made a very clear prediction.

According to the Bible, it takes only one false prophecy to show a man to be a false prophet.[91] Joseph Smith fails the test. He even admitted that he could not distinguish between prophecies from God or from the devil.[92] The startling fact that he said such a thing should make any person wary of his claims.

> Thou shalt not hearken unto the words of that prophet, or that dreamer of dreams: for the LORD your God proveth [tests] you, to know whether ye love the LORD your God with all your heart and with all your soul. Ye shall walk after the LORD your God, and fear him, and keep his commandments, and obey his voice, and ye shall serve him, and cleave unto him. (Deuteronomy 13:3-4)

> Son of man, prophesy against the prophets of Israel that prophesy, and say thou unto them that prophecy out of their own hearts, Hear ye the word of the LORD: Thus saith the Lord GOD; Woe unto the foolish prophets, that follow their own spirit, and have seen nothing! ... They have seen vanity and lying divination, saying, The LORD saith: and the LORD hath not sent them: and they have made others to hope that they would confirm the word.... And mine hand shall be upon the prophets that see vanity, and that divine lies: they shall not be in the assembly of my people, neither shall they be written in the writing of the house of Israel, neither shall they enter into the land of Israel; and ye shall know that I am the Lord GOD. (Ezekiel 13:2-3, 6, 9)

Chapter 9
Changing Mormon Truths

Joseph Smith's Claim –
Water, fire, truth and God are all realities. Truth is "Mormonism." God is the author of it. He is our shield. It is by Him we received our birth. It was by His voice that we were called to a dispensation of His Gospel in the beginning of the fullness of times. It was by Him we received the Book of Mormon; and it is by Him that we remain unto this day....
– *Teachings of the Prophet Joseph Smith*, 139

Changing LDS Doctrines

One of the reasons many Mormons believe theirs is the only true Church of Jesus Christ is that their leaders are given "on-going revelations."[1] Since, as they claim, they have a living prophet who speaks directly to God and reveals His will to the people, they have a direct link to the truth. Other churches that do not make this claim, they believe, are apostate.

Yet an examination of several doctrines shows that the same God could not possibly be revealing His will to each of the Mormon prophets and apostles. The reason this is clear is that their leaders have found it necessary over the years to change a number of "eternal truths." In many cases, they changed them to the **exact opposite** of what they claim God had revealed previously. Since the God of the Bible never changes,[2] if He were revealing His will to both earlier and later LDS leaders, then the teachings revealed should be exactly the same.

Even the leaders of the Mormon Church agree that God's word and His Gospel should never change. In a 1965 editorial, the First Presidency of the Mormon Church wrote,

One of the most important things we may learn about our religion is that **God is unchangeable**, the same yesterday, today and forever. By this we may know that **the principles of salvation will always remain the same** ... the saving principles **must ever be the same. They can never change** ... the Lord and His Gospel **remain the same**—always.[3]

The facts show, however, that the God of Mormonism constantly changes His mind. Doctrines of the Church that are true one day are said to be untrue later. Here are just a few examples.

Polygamy

Joseph Smith claimed that the command to practice polygamy came to him as a revelation from God.[4] Joseph then revealed the principle secretly to his most trusted leaders in Nauvoo, Illinois. He practiced the teaching himself while vigorously denying it publicly (a fact which is undisputed by the Mormon Church today), trying to keep it secret from the world and even from most of his own Church.[5] After Smith's death, Brigham Young proclaimed the doctrine publicly and encouraged all Mormon males to practice it. He and his contemporaries declared that living this principle of God was to continue. Those who sought the abolition of polygamy were strongly and publicly reprimanded, for the principle was to be in force among God's people forever.

Speaking of the practice of plural marriage, John Widtsoe proclaimed:

> **It came to the Church by revelation and commandment from the Lord** to Joseph Smith shortly before his death.... It was admittedly an honorable relationship, which did not in any way violate the high marriage and family ideals of the Church.[6]

Brigham Young declared:

> **Monogamy,** or restrictions by law to one wife, **is no part of the economy of heaven** among men.... **this monogamic order of marriage**, so esteemed by modern Christians as a holy sacrament and divine institution, **is nothing but a system established by a set of robbers**.... Why do we believe in and practise polygamy? Because **the Lord introduced it** to his servants **in a revelation given to Joseph Smith**, and the Lord's servants have always practised it.[7]

> Since the founding of the Roman empire monogamy has prevailed more extensively than in times previous to that ... **hence this monogamic system** which now prevails throughout all Christendom, and which had been so fruitful a source of prostitution and whoredom throughout all the Christian monogamic cities of the Old and New World, until **rottenness and decay** are at the root of their institutions both national and religious.[8]

> **The only men who become Gods**, even the Sons of God, **are those who enter into polygamy**. Others attain unto a glory and may even be permitted to come into the presence of the Father and the Son; but they cannot reign as kings in glory, because they had blessings offered unto them, and they refused to accept them.[9]

Joseph F. Smith proclaimed,

> Some people have supposed that **the doctrine of plural marriage** was a sort of superfluity, or **non-essential to the salvation or exaltation of mankind**. In other words, some of the Saints have said, and believe, that a man with one wife, sealed to him by the authority of the Priesthood for time and eternity, will receive an exaltation as great and glorious, if he is faithful, as he possibly could with more than one. **I want here to enter my solemn protest against this idea, for I**

know it is false.... **The marriage of one woman to a man for time and eternity ... is only the beginning of the law, not the whole of it.** Therefore, whoever has imagined that he could obtain the fullness of the blessings pertaining to this celestial law, by complying with only a portion of its conditions, has deceived himself. **He cannot do it ... he cannot receive the fullness of the blessings unless he fulfills the law....** I understand **the law of celestial marriage** to mean that every man in this Church, who has the ability to obey and practice it in righteousness and will not, shall be damned, I say **I understand it to mean this and nothing less, and I testify in the name of Jesus that it does mean that.**[10]

Early Mormon Heber C. Kimball was once told by Joseph Smith that if he did not practice polygamy he would lose his Apostleship and be damned.[11]

Even when the US Government declared polygamy illegal, LDS leaders would not abandon the practice. The Government then went further and threatened to take action against any who engaged in it. But Mormons firmly believed that God had revealed the doctrine and commanded them to live it. Polygamist John Taylor feared the possible action of the Government, and had to go into hiding to avoid arrest and imprisonment. He was not able to live with his wives or family, and wanted to end the exercise of polygamy in the Church so that he and other Church members could live openly. Finally, he asked God if Mormons could officially discontinue the practice. In reply, he was given another revelation proclaiming the doctrine to be eternal, and was answered that even God Himself could not repeal it.

My son John: You have asked me concerning the New and Everlasting Covenant and how far it is binding upon my people. **Thus saith the Lord All commandments that I give must be obeyed** by those calling themselves by my name unless they are revoked by me or by my authority and **how can I revoke an everlasting covenant [?]** For I the Lord am everlasting and **my everlasting covenants cannot** be abrogated nor done away with; but they stand forever. Have I not given my word in great plainness on this subject? ... Nevertheless **I the Lord do not change and my word and my commandments and my law do not.** And as I have heretofore said by my servant Joseph **all those who would enter into my glory must** and shall obey my law.... **I have not revoked this law nor will I for it is everlasting** and those who will enter into my glory must obey the conditions thereof, even so, Amen.[12]

In this revelation, God is very forceful and clear with John Taylor that both the doctrine and the practice of polygamy would never be repealed. Once again, it was clearly stated that living the law of Celestial Marriage (polygamy) was required for salvation in the highest level of the hereafter.

After realizing that the Mormon Church, even under threat of imprisonment would not voluntarily abandon polygamy, the US Government was forced to take even harsher action. It threatened seizure of all LDS Church-owned property, unless its leaders complied with federal law. The result was nothing short of amazing: God repealed the practice of polygamy in the Church.

Wilford Woodruff issued the "Manifesto," in which he said,

> Inasmuch as laws have been enacted by Congress forbidding plural marriages, which laws have been pronounced constitutional by the court of last resort, **I hereby declare my intention to submit to those laws, and to use my influence with the members of the Church over which I preside to have them do likewise.**... And I now publicly declare that my advice to the Latter-day Saints is to **refrain from contracting any marriage forbidden by the law of the land.**[13]

Apparently, a great number of Church members questioned this "Manifesto." They felt God did not inspire it. It had certainly not been given as a "revelation" and the Manifesto did not include the words "Thus Saith the Lord." Yet Woodruff made it very clear publicly that the command had come directly from God.

I say to Israel, **the Lord will never permit me** nor any other man who stands as the President of this Church, **to lead you astray**. It is not in the programme. **It is not in the mind of God.** If I were to attempt that, the Lord would remove me out of my place, and so He will any other man who attempts to lead the children of men astray from the oracles of God and from their duty.[14]

The Lord showed me by vision and revelation exactly what would take place **if we did not stop this practice.** If we had not stopped it, you would have had no use for ... any of the men in this temple at Logan; for all ordinances would be stopped throughout the land of Zion.... I saw exactly what would come to pass if there was not something done. **I have had this spirit upon me for a long time.... the God of heaven commanded me to do what I did do**; and when the hour came that I was commanded to do that, it was all clear to me. **I went before the Lord, and I wrote what the Lord told me to write.**[15]

It was no longer just a matter of Woodruff encouraging the Saints to avoid polygamy. Now it became a command from God forbidding it. Did God change His mind? Other leaders of the Mormon Church clearly understood that the reversal of the doctrine on polygamy had come by revelation. John Widtsoe wrote:

In 1890, under revelation from the Lord to the then Prophet, Wilford Woodruff, **the practice of plural marriage was suspended.**[16]

The recent *Encyclopedia of Mormonism* (1992) clearly states that the change came about by revelation:

Under direction of the Prophet Joseph Smith, some members of the Church of Jesus Christ of Latter-day Saints began to practice **plural marriage.... this was viewed as a divine commandment....** The **revelation of God** concerning eternal marriage **is D&C 132**.... The Church of Jesus Christ of Latter-day Saints officially discontinued the practice of plural marriage in 1890.... Some schismatic groups have not accepted **the revelation of God to Wilford Woodruff, fourth President of the Church, ending Church-sanctioned plural marriage**....[17]

In order to come to terms with this obvious contradiction, some LDS writers claim that, while the **practice** of polygamy is forbidden, the **principle** remains true. In this way, they reason, God is not contradicting Himself. LDS author John J. Stewart writes:

The Church has never, and certainly will never, renounce this doctrine. The revelation on plural marriage is **still an integral part** of LDS scripture, and **always will be.** If a woman, sealed to her husband for time and eternity, precedes her husband in death, it is his privilege to marry another also for time and eternity, providing that he is worthy of doing so.[18]

Bruce McConkie explains that

plural marriage was openly taught and practiced until the year 1890. At that time conditions were such **that the Lord by revelation withdrew the command to continue the practice**.... Obviously **the holy practice will commence again after the second coming** of the Son of Man....[19]

While this may seem like a plausible argument, it ignores the facts. Over and over Brigham Young and other early leaders repeatedly taught that obedience to the principle of polygamy (which was interpreted as practicing the plural marriage system here on earth) **was a requirement for salvation.** Even when President John Taylor earnestly sought to suspend the practice of polygamy, he was forbidden to do so by God, who claimed that not even He could revoke that law.

Currently, however, the Mormon Church teaches that plural marriage is **not** a requirement for salvation. This directly contradicts the teachings of early Mormon prophets and apostles, who had said that salvation could never be obtained without it. Today, they teach that "plural marriage **is not essential to salvation or exaltation**."[20]

As proof that God does occasionally change His mind, some LDS writers have pointed to the fact that He commanded blood sacrifices in the Old Testament,[21] but forbids them in the New Testament.[22] This overlooks the original significance of the practice. The blood sacrifices of the temple[23] were meant to be a sign and reminder of the death of the Messiah that was to come.[24] Once that sacrifice was made, there would be no reason for a sign pointing forward to it. Therefore, Jesus instituted the sacrament of bread and wine as a symbolic **reminder** of His own impending sacrifice.[25]

Another practice some LDS writers point to is God commanding His people in the Old Testament to kill,[26] though earlier He had given the commandment not to kill.[27] Again, the purpose for this command is different. God was punishing the foreign nations for their sins, and the instrument He used in their destruction was Israel. God was giving Israel those lands, and He did not want the sinful inhabitants to remain and tempt His people to sin. The command to kill, then, was intended to provide punishment to the guilty and to preserve the righteousness of His people. This instruction did not violate the commandment in Genesis 9:4-6 because in that passage, man is making the decision to kill on his own. In the battles under Joshua and other military leaders, God was the one determining who should die. Since God is the giver of life, He is the only one with the right to take it away. Nevertheless, in neither case (blood sacrifices nor the command to kill) did God say the practice was an everlasting commandment that would never be changed or revoked. That makes them substantially different from the LDS revelation on polygamy.

The command to practice plural marriage was not given to be either a sign or a punishment. In fact, the only reason for the revelation on polygamy was apparently to "multiply and replenish the earth."[28] It seems incredible that God would command it for this purpose when the earth was heavily populated already. Adam himself had only one wife with whom to originally populate the earth, and Noah and his family repopulated it, each man again with only one wife. Why would God consider it so important to populate the Mormon Church, but not the whole world?

Finally, since the principle and doctrine of polygamy was never repealed, only the current practice of it, it does not fall into the category of either of the Old Testament examples that were given. Basically, the LDS God has only "temporarily" suspended the practice of a principle. The Biblical God never did that. The punishment for disobedience has also apparently been removed by the Mormon deity. When they practiced polygamy, it was an absolute requirement for salvation, never to change. Now that it has been suspended, monogamous Mormon couples, they teach, can still advance to exaltation.

In the Bible, God has always communicated that in marriage, His plan is one man with one woman for life.

> Therefore shall **a man** leave his father and his mother, and shall cleave unto his **wife:** and **they shall be one flesh.** (Genesis 2:24)

It is clear that it is one man and one woman only, and when they unite in marriage, they form "one flesh."

> When thou art come unto the land which the LORD thy God giveth thee ... and shalt say, I will set a king over me ... **neither shall he multiply wives to himself, that his heart turn not away....** (Deuteronomy 17:14, 17)

> And he [Jesus] answered and said unto them, Have ye not read, that he which made them at the beginning made them male and female, And said, For this cause shall **a man** leave father and mother, and shall cleave to his **wife:** and **they twain shall be one flesh?** Wherefore **they are no more twain, but one flesh.** What therefore God hath joined together, let not man put asunder. (Matthew 19:4-6)

A bishop then must be blameless, **the husband of one wife**.... Let the deacons be the **husbands of one wife**.... (1 Timothy 3:2, 12)

[A bishop must] be blameless, **the husband of one wife**.... (Titus 1:6)

Blood Atonement

Times were very turbulent for members of the Mormon Church during the early leadership of Brigham Young. Having lost their prophet—Joseph Smith—to a mob of attackers, they were then encouraged to leave their city of Nauvoo and trek into the wilderness in search of a new place to live and worship. After enduring unbelievable hardships, sicknesses and personal losses along the way, they finally decided to settle in the valley of the Great Salt Lake and build their lives there, far outside the territory of the United States. After settling there 24 July 1847, they started to build their new city and spread out to create settlements to the north and south of this location.

Conditions proved very difficult for the Mormons. Establishing so many settlements, fighting with Indians, experiencing famine and battling the frontier—all this was very discouraging. Many started to grumble and some apostatized from the LDS Church. Many wanted to leave what would become Utah for what is now California. Others refused to obey the prophet. Thievery and adultery started to become a problem. Attendance at services on Sundays dropped dramatically as the Saints began to think of Sunday as just another day to work at survival.[29]

These deteriorating conditions and attitudes were unacceptable to Brigham Young. Something had to be done to keep the people under control and in line with his leadership. He demanded complete obedience to his law and his directives; nothing less would do. Young devised a course of action, headed by himself and by one of his counselors, Jedediah M. Grant.[30] This became known as the Mormon Reformation.

The Reformation began 14 September 1856.³¹ The most severe part of this period in Mormon history involves the means Young employed to deal with those who would not submit to the Church and repent of their sins. Punishment for such things was the doctrine known as blood atonement—that an individual must have his or her own blood shed in order to atone for various sins. Brigham Young warned:

> I feel to call upon this congregation to know whether any of them, or whether all of them wish salvation. If they do, I have the Gospel of salvation for them.... As **I told you last Sabbath,** if I was not mistaken, my feelings were that this people were preparing themselves, many of them, for apostacy; were preparing themselves for the apostacy of their neighbors and their families; their children and their friends were all leading the way of the sinner.... **if the people are disposed to awake out of their lethargy and walk up to their religion, to their duty** ... then we will be brethren. And **if not, the thread must be severed**, for I cannot hold men and women in fellowship that serve the devil and themselves, and give no heed to the Almighty; I cannot do it.... the people are full of idolatry, the spirit of contention and the spirit of the world are in them, and they are full of the things of the world. Well, I just say, my brethren and sisters, it cannot be suffered any longer, a separation must take place; you must part with your sins, or the righteous must be separated from the ungodly.³²

> **We need a reformation** in the midst of this people; **we need a thorough reform**, for I know that very many are in a dozy condition with regard to their religion.... You are losing the spirit of the Gospel, is there any cause for it? No, only that which there is in the world.... I want all the people to say what they will do, and I know that God wishes all His servants, all His faithful sons and daughters, the men and the women that inhabit this city, to repent of their wickedness, **or we will cut them off**.... There are sins that men commit

for which they cannot receive forgiveness in this world, or in that which is to come, and if they had their eyes open to see their true condition, they would be perfectly willing **to have their blood spilt upon the ground**, that the smoke thereof might ascend to heaven as an offering for their sins; and **the smoking incense would atone for their sins.**... I know, when you hear my brethren telling about cutting people off from the earth, that you consider it is strong doctrine; but it is to save them, not to destroy them.... I do know that there are sins committed, of such a nature that if the people did understand the doctrine of salvation, they would tremble because of their situation. And furthermore, I know that there are transgressors, who, if they knew themselves, and **the only condition upon which they can obtain forgiveness**, would beg of their brethren **to shed their blood.**... I will say further; **I have had men come to me and offer their lives to atone for their sins.** It is true that the blood of the Son of God was shed for sins through the fall and those committed by men, **yet men can commit sins which it can never remit.**... there are sins that the blood of a lamb, of a calf, or of turtle doves, cannot remit, but **they must be atoned for by the blood of the man.**[33]

Mormon members who were complacent suddenly found themselves fearing for their lives. Mormon leaders called for the Saints to repent immediately, be re-baptized to wash away their sins and devote themselves anew to the Church and its leaders. All were in fear of being "cut off" by the leadership of the Church.

Some LDS writers think that the doctrine of blood atonement was intended only as a scare tactic, and that Brigham Young never really meant any of these teachings to be taken literally.[34] But in fact, the practice was actually carried out on many occasions. His 19th wife, Ann Eliza Young, informs us,

The "Reformation" was productive of nothing but evil. The most revolting and blasphemous doctrines were taught, and between **Blood-Atonement,** Massacres of the Gentiles, and the worst phases of Polygamous Marriage, there was nothing good in the Territory.... The very thought of it brings a shudder. The most horrible things were taught from the pulpit, and decency was outraged every time a Mormon leader opened his mouth to speak.... **No one dared to neglect the counsel of the priesthood.** Whoever ventured to do so was charged at once with apostasy. Men and women alike were ruled by the arbitrary will of one man. There is no despotic monarchy in the world where the word of the sovereign is so absolute as in Utah. And never, in the whole history of Mormonism, has the despotic rule been so arbitrary as it was during the period of, and for a short time after, the Reformation.[35]

Bill Hickman served as one of the "Destroying Angels" employed by Brigham Young to carry out some of these blood atonement murders. He ultimately confessed to either knowing personally of, or participating in, more than a dozen murders in Utah during that period, many of them carried out by direct orders from Brigham Young.[36] R. N. Baskin, who later became the Chief Justice of the Supreme Court in Utah, writes,

> In the excavations made within the limits of Salt Lake City during the time I have resided there, **many human skeletons have been exhumed** in various parts of the city.... it is evident that the death of the persons to whom they once belonged **did not result from natural causes**, but from the use of **criminal means**....[37]

The blood atonement doctrine could actually be practiced at that time in Utah because of the Mormon isolation from the rest of the country. The only law enforcement in Utah was almost entirely LDS. Most government officials, judges and lawmen were LDS and under Brigham Young's control; therefore, none questioned it. They simply watched their own behavior and minded their own business.

The inevitable result of such a doctrine was the death and misery of many people, some of whom were entirely innocent. Blood atonement teachings from the pulpit and in the temple ceremony led some

Mormon members to excessive zeal. In one case, more than 120 men, women and children were murdered by Mormons in southern Utah in early September 1857, partly because they were rumored to have the gun that had killed Joseph Smith. This brutal crime is known as the Mountain Meadows Massacre.[38] It could have been the outrage of the country and the US Government over this affair that eventually brought the blood atonement teachings to an end.

Young was teaching this violent form of punishment from the pulpit as doctrine. Blood atonement was even a part of the LDS temple ceremony for over 100 years, and therefore qualifies as having been revealed directly from God. On both counts, the teaching can be classified as official revealed Church doctrine. The leaders of the Church certainly felt that way. Though speaking specifically about the punishment for adultery, Orson Pratt called the blood-atonement doctrine "the law of God." He wrote that the people of Salt Lake City "know, that if they have any [adulterous] connections out of the marriage covenant, **they not only forfeit their lives by the law of God,** but they forfeit their salvation also."[39]

During the temple ceremony, the temple official used to tell temple patrons the following in reference to the First Token of the Aaronic Priesthood:

> You, and each of you, covenant and promise that you will not reveal this, the first token of the Aaronic Priesthood, with its accompanying name, sign and penalty: Should you do so, **you agree that your throat be cut from ear to ear and your tongue torn out by the roots from your mouth.** All bow your heads and say, Yes.[40]

This was immediately followed by participants drawing their thumbs across their throats from ear to ear, bowing their heads, and saying "Yes." There were two more penalties given during the ceremony that were just as graphic. For the Second Token of the Aaronic Priesthood, the penalty was that they "**agree to have your breast cut open** and your **heart and vitals torn from your body** and fed to the fowls of the air and beasts of the field."[41] The First Token of the Melchizedek Priesthood had them "**agree to have your bodies**

cut asunder in the midst and all **your bowels gush out** upon the ground and the entrails fed to the swine."[42]

In later years, the language was toned down, but the representation of the penalty remained the same. During the 1900s, temple Mormons accepted these penalties under the following language:

> I, _____ (think of the new name) do covenant and promise that I will never reveal the First Token of the Aaronic Priesthood, together with its accompanying name, sign and penalty. Rather than do so I would suffer my life to be taken.[43]

This pledge was accompanied by drawing his or her thumb across the throat.[44] The same was done for the other two penalties.[45] This shows that the doctrine was still being taught to LDS temple patrons throughout most of the twentieth century.

Though evidence shows that this doctrine was actually practiced in the nineteenth century in Utah, the historical fact is actually a secondary point. The primary point is that the practice **was officially taught as a doctrine** of the Mormon Church, **but later changed**. Currently, the LDS Church does not teach it. Joseph Fielding Smith[46] writes:

> ...were you not aware that it [the blood atonement doctrine] was but the repetition of the *ravings of the enemies of the Church,* **without one grain of truth?**[47]

> He [Christ] carried that load [sin] for us if we will only accept him as our Redeemer and keep his commandments.... So I say **there never was a sin committed that was not atoned for.**[48]

The *Encyclopedia of Mormonism* has this to say about the blood atonement doctrine:

> Several early Church leaders, most notably Brigham Young, taught ... **the voluntary shedding of a murderer's blood—**

presumably by capital punishment—as **part of the process of atonement** for such grievous sin. This was referred to as "blood atonement." ... **This view is not a doctrine of the Church and has never been practiced by the Church at any time.**[49]

This change in doctrine also resulted in another change: the executions of the penalties were removed from the temple ceremony completely on 10 April 1990.[50] Once taught as doctrine revealed from heaven as the "law of God," blood atonement was later discontinued. Now, official sources specifically state that the teaching is not a doctrine of the Church. Does God really change His mind like that?

What does the New Testament say about atonement? It states specifically that the only blood that can atone for any sin is the blood of Jesus Christ. That blood was shed to atone for all the sins of mankind—none are excluded for any reason.

> For all have sinned, and come short of the glory of God; **Being justified freely** by his grace through **the redemption that is in Christ Jesus**. Whom God hath set forth **to be a propitiation** through faith in **his blood**.... (Romans 3:23-25)

> Therefore as by the offence of one judgment came upon all men to condemnation; even so **by the righteousness of one the free gift came** upon all men unto justification of life. (Romans 5:18)

> **There is therefore now no condemnation** to them which are in Christ Jesus, who walk not after the flesh, but after the Spirit. For the law of the Spirit of life in Christ Jesus hath made me free from the law of sin and death. (Romans 8:1-2)

> By the which will **we are sanctified through the offering of the body of Jesus Christ** once for all. (Hebrews 10:10)

> But this man, after he had offered **one sacrifice for sins for ever**, sat down on the right hand of God. (Hebrews 10:12)
>
> For **by one offering** he hath **perfected for ever them** that are sanctified. (Hebrews 10:14)
>
> But if we walk in the light, as he is in the light, we have fellowship one with another, and **the blood of Jesus Christ** his Son **cleanseth us from all sin**. (1 John 1:7)
>
> If we confess our sins, he is faithful and just to **forgive us our sins**, and to cleanse us **from all unrighteousness**. (1 John 1:9)

God never changed His mind about this doctrine; it has always remained the same. Salvation comes through the atonement of the blood of Jesus Christ alone. It cannot be purchased by a man's own blood no matter what the crime. The fact that Brigham Young and other LDS leaders taught that a man could (or must) atone for his own sin shows that the God of the Bible was not inspiring them.

The Creation of Adam

Brigham Young's revelations occasionally were very controversial in the LDS Church. His inspired utterances from the pulpit at times caused quite a stir among the lay members and the leadership as well. One such revelation shared with the Mormon congregation concerned Adam's creation. Young taught that "when our father Adam came into the Garden of Eden, he came into it with a *celestial body*, and brought Eve, *one of his wives*, with him."[51]

It was not until a year and a half later that he expounded just exactly what he meant by that. "You believe Adam was made of the dust of this earth. This I do not believe, though it is supposed that it is so written in the Bible; but it is not, to my understanding."[52] If Adam were not made from the dust of this earth, then from what dust was he made? According to Young, Adam was not created on this particular earth, as the Bible proclaims in Genesis 2:7. Instead,

Adam was born to parents **on another earth** in the same way our children are born to parents on this earth. Adam and Eve were then brought to this earth. They were intergalactic transplants in an effort to propagate life on this planet. In 1856, he declared this truth in exact detail to the congregation:

> Though we have it in history that our father Adam was made of the dust of this earth, and that he knew nothing about his God previous to being made here, **yet it is not so**.... You may read and believe what you please as to what is found written in the Bible. **Adam was made from the dust of an earth, but not from the dust of this earth.**[53]

Three years later, Young continued to teach this as doctrine:

> Here let me state to all philosophers of every class upon the earth. When you tell me that father Adam was made as we make adobes from the earth, you tell me what I deem an **idle tale**. When you tell me that the beasts of the field were produced in that manner, you are speaking **idle words devoid of meaning. There is no such thing** in all the eternities where the Gods dwell. Mankind are here because they are the offspring of **parents who were first brought here from another planet**, and power was given them to propagate their species, and they were commanded to multiply and replenish the earth.[54]

This was very much in line with his views about life throughout the universe. Young did not believe earth humans were alone. He taught that other people lived in outer space, fully believing it to be true.

> Who can tell us of the inhabitants of this little planet that shines of an evening, called **the moon**? When we view its face we may see what is termed "the man in the moon," and what some philosophers declare are the shadows of mountains. But these sayings are very vague, and amount to nothing; and when you inquire about **the inhabitants of**

that sphere you find that the most learned are as ignorant in regard to them as the most ignorant of their fellows. So it is with regard to **the inhabitants of the sun**. Do you think it is **inhabited? I rather think it is.** Do you think there **is any life there? No question of it**; it was not made in vain. It was made to give light to **those who dwell upon it**, and to other planets; and so will this earth when it is celestialized.[55]

This belief was even represented in the temple ceremony under Brigham Young's direction. The following are from early exposés of the ceremony.

It is stated by Elohim (person representing Elohim, or God) that man was not made of dust, as other sects believe, but was born of woman, and that "the creation of Adam was done figuratively just to impress on you how man was made."[56]

In speaking of the creation, he (the lecturer) is sure to say that **Adam was not made out of the dust of the earth** but begotten the same as other men; that the creation of Adam was done by a figure just to show you how man was made; and that **when he came here** [to earth] **he brought one of his wives with him**. On days when there are few who are going through the temple for the first time, this lecture before the veil is very much shortened, only the essential part which refers to the creation of Adam being recited or read.[57]

Yet somewhere along the way, Young's God must have changed His mind about how Adam originated, for He revealed the complete opposite "truth" to leaders in the Church years later. Joseph Fielding Smith teaches:

He [Adam] received his tabernacle of flesh **from the dust of *this* earth**. He belongs to it.... *The Book of Mormon*, the *Doctrine and Covenants*, and the *Pearl of Great Price* all declare that **Adam's body was created** from the dust of the ground, that is, **from the dust of *this* ground, this earth**.[58]

No longer was Adam "brought here from another planet," nor was he created "from the dust of an earth," but not this earth. Instead, he was created from "the dust of *this ground, this earth.*" Opposing doctrines cannot both be true. The unchanging God of the Bible could not possibly be the one giving these revelations to LDS leaders.

Priesthood to the Sons of Cain

Mormonism has taught since the time of Joseph Smith that people of African heritage have dark colored skin because they are cursed by God. This curse was originally given to Cain for having killed Abel, and all who are born with dark skin are his descendants. At the time of the Great Flood of Noah, this curse is said to have been preserved through the wife of Ham,[59] who was also a descendant of Cain.

The reason some are born under this curse, Joseph Smith revealed, was that they did not fight valiantly during a war in heaven prior to this life. They are, therefore, given less privilege when they come to earth, and must live with the "curse." In addition, they were forbidden to receive the LDS priesthood.

> **As a result of his rebellion, Cain was cursed with a dark skin**; he became the father of the negroes, and **those spirits who are not worthy** to receive the priesthood **are born through his lineage.**[60]

> Negroes in this life are denied the priesthood; **under no circumstances can they hold this** delegation of **authority** from the Almighty.[61]

How long was this ban to last? According to Brigham Young, "any man having one drop"[62] of cursed blood in him would be forbidden from receiving the LDS priesthood until all white males had received it first. Young explained:

When all the other children of Adam have had the privilege of receiving the Priesthood, and of coming into the kingdom of God, and of being redeemed from the four quarters of the earth, and have received their resurrection from the dead, **then it will be time enough to remove the curse** from Cain and his posterity. He deprived his brother of the privilege of pursuing his journey through life, and of extending his kingdom by multiplying upon the earth; and because he did this, **he is the last to share** the joys of the kingdom of God.[63]

You see **some classes of the human family that are black**, uncouth, uncomely, disagreeable and low in their habits, wild, and seemingly deprived of nearly all the blessings of the intelligence that is generally bestowed upon mankind.... **How long is that race to endure the dreadful curse** that is upon them? That curse will remain upon them, and **they never can hold the Priesthood or share in it until all the other descendants of Adam have received the promises** and enjoyed the blessings of the Priesthood and the keys thereof. **Until the last ones of the residue of Adam's children are brought up** to that favourable position, the children of Cain cannot receive the first ordinances of the Priesthood. They were the first that were cursed, and **they will be the last from whom the curse will be removed.** When the residue of the family of Adam come up and receive their blessings, then the curse will be removed from the seed of Cain, and they will receive blessings in like proportion.[64]

Why are so many of the inhabitants of the earth **cursed with a sin of blackness?** It comes in consequence of their fathers rejecting the power of the Holy Priesthood, and the law of God. They will go down to death. And **when all the rest of the children have received their blessings in the Holy Priesthood, then that curse will be removed** from the seed of Cain, and they will then come up and possess the priesthood, and receive all the blessings which we now are entitled to.⁶⁵

Brigham Young was obviously very adamant about this teaching and remained so during his entire tenure as president of the Church. LDS writers always affirmed that this doctrinal position was revealed by God and could never be changed. In his book, *The Way to Perfection*, Joseph Fielding Smith wrote under the heading "The Curse Upon Cain and His Descendants":

> Not only was Cain called upon to suffer, but because of his wickedness he became the father of an inferior race. **A curse was placed upon him** and that curse has been continued through his lineage and must do so while time endures. Millions of souls have come into this world **cursed with a black skin** and have been **denied the privilege of Priesthood and the fulness of the blessings of the Gospel.** These are the descendants of Cain. Moreover, they have been made to feel their inferiority and have been separated from the rest of mankind from the beginning.⁶⁶

Smith also informs us that

> **this doctrine did not originate with President Brigham Young but was taught by the Prophet Joseph Smith.** At a meeting of the general authorities of the Church, held August 22, 1895, the question of the status of the negro in relation to the Priesthood was asked and the minutes of that meeting say: "President George Q. Cannon remarked that **the Prophet taught this doctrine: That the seed of Cain could not receive the Priesthood** nor act in any of the offices of the Priesthood **until the seed of Abel should come forward and take precedence** over Cain's offspring."⁶⁷

Several LDS writers on the subject have interpreted this teaching the same way. For example, in 1967 John L. Lund writes:

Brigham Young revealed that **the Negroes will not receive the Priesthood until a great while after the second advent of Jesus Christ**, whose coming will usher in a millenium of peace.... Social pressure and even government sanctions cannot be expected to bring forth a new revelation.[68]

Lund emphasized that "it would be foolish indeed to give anyone **the false idea that a new revelation** is immediately forthcoming on the issue of the Negroes receiving the Priesthood."[69]

John Stewart verifies that God revealed this doctrine given by Joseph Smith:

> Now, in view of historical facts, can the apologizer reasonably believe that **the LDS doctrine enunciated by Joseph Smith on the Negroes' not holding the Priesthood**—that this was actuated by his desire to please the public or to satisfy some personal prejudice? If this was not the reason, then what was? The fact is that **every doctrine the Prophet Joseph announced** for the organization and direction of the LDS Church **was revealed to him by the Lord**. Many were his teachings and practices which displeased the world, but he held fast to them because the doctrines were of divine origin.[70]

It could be claimed that the statements of these men are only their personal opinions. If that is the case, then the LDS teachings on this subject might not have been revelation as much as policy. But the First Presidency of the LDS Church has verified what these men wrote: that the LDS position, which originally denied the Priesthood to those of African heritage, **was a direct revelation from God**.

In 1947, a prominent Mormon sociologist, Dr. Lowry Nelson, questioned this doctrine. He believed that all were equal in the sight of God and deserved equal treatment with regard to the Priesthood. The First Presidency wrote him a letter in return that said, in part:

> Your position seems to lose sight of **the revelations of the Lord** touching the pre-existence of our spirits, the rebellion

in heaven, and the doctrine of our birth into this life and the advantages under which we may be born.... **From the days of the Prophet Joseph even until now, it has been the doctrine of the Church, never questioned by any of the Church leaders, that the Negroes are not entitled to the full blessings of the Gospel.**[71]

In 1951, the First Presidency again reiterated that **God had revealed this truth.** In a statement issued 17 August 1951, they write:

The attitude of the Church with reference to negroes remains as it has always stood. It is **not a matter of the declaration of a policy but of direct commandment from the Lord**, on which is founded the doctrine of the Church from the days of its organization, to the effect that **negroes may become members of the church but that they are not entitled to the priesthood** at the present time.... Under this principle there is no injustice whatsoever involved in this deprivation as to the holding of the priesthood by the negroes.[72]

Whether this LDS doctrine is legal, moral or socially acceptable is not the issue. The issue is that it was claimed to be a direct revelation from God, and the duration of the deprivation was to be until after the Second Coming of Christ. It is quite startling, then, that in 1978 a new revelation was received by President Spencer Kimball—one that completely contradicts the teachings of Joseph Smith, Brigham Young and the Church leaders for more than 100 years.

In early June of this year, the First Presidency announced that **a revelation had been received** by President Spencer W. Kimball **extending priesthood and temple blessings to all worthy male members** of the Church.[73]

Dear Brethren: As we have witnessed the expansion of the work of the Lord ... we have pleaded long and earnestly in behalf of these, our faithful brethren.... [God] has heard our prayers, and **by revelation has confirmed that the long-promised day has come when every faithful, worthy man in the Church may receive the Holy Priesthood**....[74]

God revealed to Brigham Young that the "long-promised day" would not occur until all non-African LDS men had a chance to hold the priesthood. It would not happen until the resurrection day. It would not take effect until after the Second Coming of Christ. None of these days have come, and yet the Mormon God gave this revelation, completely contradicting His earlier revealed promises.

The Temple Ceremony

Concerning the LDS Temple Ceremony, we are told that "Joseph Smith received the temple endowment and its ritual, as all else he promulgated, by revelation from God."[75] Brigham Young tells us,

> Your endowment is, to receive all those ordinances in the House of the Lord, which are necessary for you, after you have departed this life, to enable you to walk back to the presence of the Father, passing the angels who stand as sentinels, being enabled to give them the key words, the signs and tokens, pertaining to the Holy Priesthood, and gain your eternal exaltation in spite of earth and hell.[76]

Ezra Taft Benson adds:

> The endowment was revealed by revelation and can be understood only by revelation.... The laws and ordinances which cause men and women to come out of the world and become sanctified ... were given by revelation and are comprehended by revelation.[77]

Here two leaders of the Mormon Church confirm that the endowment ceremony was given by revelation from God. The teachings of the endowment are necessary, they claim, for full salvation through the Mormon gospel. Were they supposed to remain the same forever? They certainly should be if they were truly revealed by God and essential for salvation. LDS writers agree:

> The Gospel **can not possibly be changed** ... the saving principles **must ever be the same. They can never change** ... the Gospel **must always be the same** in all its parts.[78]

As temple work progresses, some members wonder if the ordinances can be changed or adjusted. **These ordinances have been provided by revelation**, and are in the hands of the First Presidency. Thus, the temple is **protected from tampering**.[79]

Now the purpose in Himself in the winding up scene of the last dispensation is that all things pertaining to that dispensation should be conducted precisely in accordance with the preceding dispensations ... therefore **He set the ordinances to be the same forever and ever**, and set Adam to watch over them, to reveal them from heaven to man, or to send angels to reveal them.[80]

Perhaps it is not so surprising to see that even the temple ceremony has been changed. In addition to several minor changes over the years, on 10 April 1990, a completely revised endowment ceremony was implemented in all LDS temples worldwide.

> The Mormon Church **has changed some of its most sacred rituals**, eliminating parts of the largely secret ceremonies.... Church officials have confirmed that **changes went into effect in mid-April**, but the ceremonies are considered to be too sacred, they say, for them to comment further.... Bruce L. Olsen, managing director of the church's communications office in Salt Lake City, denied that the changes were made in response to criticism or social pressure. The Mormon Church believes "in continued and modern revelation," Mr.

Olson said, so that practices might be changed when "the Lord clarified" church teaching.[81]

The changes were not announced to the membership at large, but temple attendees are being read a statement from the governing First Presidency which says the revisions, following long and prayerful review, were unanimously approved by that three-member body and the advisory Quorum of the Twelve Apostles.[82]

This was not the first time that changes were made to the ceremony. The first LDS temple rites in Kirtland, Ohio, consisted of little more than a foot washing, followed by a service that closely resembles a charismatic outpouring.[83] The bulk of the endowment ritual was not instituted until the Nauvoo Temple was nearly completed, after Joseph Smith had been initiated into the first three degrees of Freemasonry.[84] The newly expanded Mormon temple ceremony incorporated many details from the Freemason ritual. In fact, a great deal of the LDS endowment was virtually identical to the counterparts in the Masonic temple rites.

Although said to have been revealed by God, changes to it continued over the years. Mormons attending temple services during the time immediately following the 1990 changes were read a statement by the First Presidency, which said in part, "Since the temple Endowment was first administered in this dispensation, minor **changes have been made** from time to time by the First Presidency and Council of the Twelve, acting unitedly in their capacity as Prophets, Seers and Revelators."[85]

Changes were again made to the ceremony on 18 January 2005. This time, the ceremonies and clothing pertaining to the "Washing and Anointing" were altered so as to be less offensive to the Church membership.[86]

LDS apologists try to explain the changes by claiming that a separation exists between the "ordinances" of the temple, and the "ceremony."[87] They contend that the "ordinances" revealed by God have always remained the same while the "ceremony" surrounding the ordinances has changed whenever deemed necessary. Further investigation however, shows that this is not true.

Brigham Young claimed that the "ordinances" of the temple included, "key-words, signs, tokens and penalties."[88] The temple ceremony prior to 10 April 1990 also connected these items together as essential ordinances.[89] Yet the penalties associated with the required tokens were completely removed from the ceremony in April 1990.[90] Some of the covenants that temple patrons were required to bind themselves to have also been removed, while others were substantially changed. Many items of the endowment that one prophet said were "required" for full salvation were completely removed from the ceremony by another. How can this be? Only if the "revelations" regarding the endowment were of human origin, not divine.

Conclusion

These are just a few of many changes made to LDS doctrine over the years.[91] The Bible teaches that God is always the same. He does not change. His truths do not change. He does not ever contradict Himself.

> But **thou art the same**, and thy years shall have no end. (Psalm 102:27)

> For I am the LORD, **I change not**; therefore ye sons of Jacob are not consumed. (Malachi 3:6)

> For **God is not the author of confusion**, but of peace, as in all churches of the saints. (1 Corinthians 14:33)

> Jesus Christ **the same yesterday, and to day, and for ever**. (Hebrews 13:8)

> Every good gift and every perfect gift is from above, and cometh down from the Father of lights, **with whom is no variableness, neither shadow of turning**. (James 1:17)

Even LDS leaders have claimed the same about God. The LDS First Presidency once wrote that

> **God is unchangeable, the same yesterday, today and forever.**... It is obvious therefore that **no one can change the Gospel, and that if they attempt to do so, they only set up a man-made system** which is not the Gospel, but is merely a reflection of their own views. And since only God can save, only His Gospel can save, and if we substitute "any other Gospel," there is no salvation in it.[92]

Speaking of those inside the Mormon Church who point out contradictions in the revelations, Boyd K. Packer says,

> There are those within the Church who are disturbed when changes are made with which they disagree or when changes proposed are not made. They point to them as evidence that the leaders are not inspired. They write and speak to convince others that the doctrines and decisions of the Brethren are not given through inspiration.... **Changes in organization or procedures are a testimony that revelation is ongoing.** While doctrines remain fixed, the methods or procedures do not.... The Lord established that process when He gave revelations relating to temple ordinances.... **There will be changes made in the future as in the past.** Whether the Brethren make changes or resist them depends entirely upon the instructions they receive through the channels of revelation which were established in the beginning. The doctrines will remain fixed, eternal; the organization, programs, and procedures will be altered as directed by Him whose church this is.[93]

If the changes were made in simple procedures only, it would be possible to agree with this assessment. But as we have seen, the changes are made to direct revelations, to doctrines and to essential ordinances of the Mormon Church. What was said to be absolutely necessary for salvation in one generation is removed entirely by another. What one LDS prophet preached as absolute truth is called false doctrine by a later prophet. Even some Mormon leaders realize this fact, and have had to warn their members not to probe Church history with too fine a comb.[94]

For those who choose to follow the teachings of the Bible, such distinctions and warnings are unnecessary. The truth of the gospel of Jesus Christ always remains the same.

The Apostle Paul wrote,

> But I fear, lest by any means, as the serpent beguiled Eve through his subtlety, so your minds should be corrupted from the simplicity that is in Christ. For if he that cometh preacheth another Jesus, whom we have not preached, or if ye receive another spirit, which ye have not received, or another gospel, which ye have not accepted, ye might well bear with him. (2 Corinthians 11:3-4)

> I marvel that ye are so soon removed from him that called you into the grace of Christ unto another gospel: Which is not another; but there be some that trouble you, and would pervert the gospel of Christ. But though we, or an angel from heaven, preach any other gospel unto you than that which we have preached unto you, let him be accursed. (Galatians 1:6-8)

Far from being proof of "ongoing revelation," changes such as the ones examined in this chapter show conclusively that the God of the Bible is not inspiring the men who are leading the Mormon Church. Christians are admonished not to be

> tossed to and fro, and carried about with every wind of doctrine, by the sleight of men, and cunning craftiness, whereby they lie in wait to deceive. (Ephesians 4:14)

Changing LDS Publications

One of the practices that LDS critics have continuously pointed out is that Mormon leaders alter their published texts whenever they deem it necessary. They certainly have the right to change materials they have created. But they have also changed their official *History of the Church* and their books that are considered scripture.[95] In addition, they have frequently ignored the standard and accepted practice of indicating those changes in the text so that readers know they have been made.[96] This demonstrates their intent to hide the truth from those who read their materials.

The *History of the Church*

The whole purpose for an official history is to document accurately what has happened in the development of an institution or a person by systematically listing recorded events of the past. In order for the work to be of any value as an actual history, the events recorded must be as factual and truthful as possible. Anything deliberately changed or altered from the actual facts would compromise any value it has as a history.

When the *History of the Church* was commissioned, the Mormon Church leaders stated that their goal in providing it was to compile an actual and factual record of the events in their Church history. The Preface to Volume 1 states:

> The events which make up the history of the Church in this age are the most important that history can chronicle. It is due therefore both to the Saints themselves and to the world that **a faithful and complete history of the facts** in which the Church of Jesus Christ of Latter-day Saints had its origin ... be made known to mankind.... there is placed on record at the same time the highest order of historical evidence **of the truth** of what is stated.[97]

Though started under Joseph Smith's leadership, George A. Smith and Wilford Woodruff compiled the *History of the Church* for publication after the Church had relocated into the Great Salt Lake Valley in the mid-1800s. When they had completed the publication, they wrote:

> The *History of Joseph Smith* is now before the world, and we are satisfied that a history **more correct in its details** than this was never published. To have it **strictly correct**, the greatest possible pains have been taken by historians and clerks engaged in the work.... We, therefore, hereby bear our testimony to all the world, unto whom these words shall come, that the *History of Joseph Smith* is true, and is **one of the most authentic histories ever written.**[98]

In spite of their "greatest possible pains" to list the facts, later leaders of the church decided that some of the information was too factual to share with the public. Therefore the work was revised and changed. However, no attempt was made to identify any changes in the text. Instead, they merely commented that, due to their revision, "the work has been brought to a still higher state of perfection."[99] While complete perfection is not expected from the work, altering it without indication as to where or how creates serious doubt as to which parts of the work, if any, are actually reliable.

Joseph Fielding Smith asserted, "*The most important history in the world is the history of our Church, and* **it is the most accurate history in all the world.** It must be so."[100] Speaking of the multi-volume *History of the Church*, LDS Apostle John A. Widtsoe claims:

> The *History of the Church* and the utterances therein contain, if read properly, a continued evidence that Joseph Smith told the truth about the coming forth of the restoration. It is a precious production that will be counted as a blessing throughout the years.... **There is in them no attempt to "cover up" any act of his life.** The story of each event is told as it happened. Mormon history and doctrine have been **carefully preserved** in the published records of the Church—and **all has been published.**[101]

Widtsoe went on to add that "the *History of Joseph Smith*, published by the Church, as to events and dates, **may be accepted as an unusually accurate** historical document ... and become more and more a proof of the honest sincerity of the founders of the Church in this dispensation. **The history is trustworthy. No flaws have been found in it.**"[102]

Jerald and Sandra Tanner of Utah Lighthouse Ministry looked into the accuracy of these claims, and published extensive documentation that proves beyond question that the *History of the Church* has, in fact, been deliberately altered. In their book, *Changes in Joseph Smith's History*, they write that

> the Mormon Historians **have broken almost all the rules of honesty**. It is a well known fact that when an omission is made in a document **it must be indicated** by ellipses signs. The Mormon Historians have almost completely ignored this rule; in many cases they have **deleted thousands of words without any indication**. They have also added thousands of words without any indication. They have changed the spelling, grammar, punctuation and rearranged the words. There can be no doubt that **the changes were deliberate**....[103]

They go on to state, "When we say that there have been more than 62,000 words added or omitted in the History of the Church, it should be understood that we did not read many of the revelations, affidavits, etc. A more thorough study would, no doubt, reveal many other changes."[104]

The Tanners were not the first to recognize that the *History* was seriously flawed. J. Reuben Clark, a member of the First Presidency of the Church at the time, met with the Twelve Apostles and the First Presidency in 1943 and frankly told them:

> The Documentary History of the Church[105] unfortunately as printed **does not contain all of the documentary history** as it was written. Brother Roberts **made some changes** in it. We do not know always what the changes were or what they are, so that, as an absolute historical source, **the printed**

Documentary History is not one that we can invariably rely upon.... Frequently, he [Roberts] started out apparently to establish a certain thesis ... and if some facts got in the way it was too bad, and **they were omitted**.[106]

Even LDS Scholars have discovered this disturbing truth for themselves. Writing in *Dialogue: A Journal of Mormon Thought*, LDS scholar Davis Bitton writes,

> In discussing his [B. H. Roberts's] use of primary sources we must here say something about his edition of Joseph Smith's documentary *History of the Church* (the DHC).... When we compare the DHC with the earlier published versions, in fact, we discover that **hundreds of changes have been made**. These include **deletions, additions, and simple changes of wording**.... And he [Roberts] would not, I think, be proud of the fact that for researchers in early Mormon history Rule Number One is "**Do not rely on the DHC**; never use a quotation from it without comparing the earlier versions."[107]

LDS writer Samuel Taylor also commented on the *History*, saying,

> Also, this work **has been "corrected" by many hands**, making corroboration from original sources necessary. Jerald and Sandra Tanner, in their *Changes in Joseph Smith's History*, detail "More than 62,000 words added or deleted" in the first six volumes. Even so, the **Tanners overlooked some changes**, a notable example being alteration of the conference minutes of October, 1843.... A comparison of the minutes as originally published in the *Times and Seasons* (4:330), and as revised in the DHC (6:47), will reveal **exactly opposite accounts** of what happened.[108]

For example, Joseph Smith wrote of his early childhood, claiming that "I frequently fell into many foolish errors and displayed the weakness of youth and **the corruption of human nature**, which I am sorry to say led me into **divers temptations, to the gratification of many appetites offensive in the sight of God.**"[109] When this account was reprinted in the *History of the Church*, the word "corruption" was changed to "foibles," and the phrase "to the gratification of many appetites" was entirely omitted with no indication of change. In addition, 82 words were added as if Joseph Smith had written them, making it appear that he had been guilty of nothing more than "levity."[110]

Another example would be the "prophecy" of the Saints becoming a great people in the Rocky Mountains.[111] A copy of the handwritten account for this entry was located (see Chapter 8), and it was found that the "prophecy" had been written in sometime after the rest of the page was written. And the rest of the page was not even started until July of 1845, more than a year after Joseph Smith's death.[112]

The original history openly published that Joseph Smith admitted to breaking the "Word of Wisdom" by drinking beer, and that he suggested the use of whiskey and tobacco to others. This was deleted from the *History* in later publications. The name of the angel who first visited Joseph Smith was changed from "Nephi" to "Moroni." Several portions of prophecies that never came to pass were deleted. Swearing and cursing were removed from the text. There was also a deletion of 307 words from the account of the murder of Joseph Smith, words conveying a story that the editor of the *History* personally believed was a myth.[113] There are many other examples of text altering that could be cited.

In 1982, Dean C. Jessee wrote an article in which he attempted to justify the extreme altering of the *History*. He claimed that at the time the work was compiled, there was "a much less critical standard of accuracy than exists today." Without those accepted standards, liberties with the text were fully acceptable, he claims. Therefore, he concludes "even with its textual flaws ... the sequence of events and the purposes of most readers it served quite adequately."[114] However, this does not answer the many claims made about the *History* (already cited). For instance, George A. Smith and Wilford Woodruff's claim that the "greatest possible pains" had been made to document accurately and completely the Church history; the Preface, which claims that the "highest order of historical evidence of the truth" has been recorded; or John Widtsoe's claim that "Mormon history and doctrine have been carefully preserved" in its pages. If Jessee's justification applies to the *History of the Church*, then all of these statements are disingenuous.

Joseph Fielding Smith wrote about this very kind of deception, saying, "In regard to the recording of history, **the thing that is most important is accuracy**. *If history is not accurate, it is harmful.*"[115] Despite this assertion, the LDS *History of the Church* is anything but accurate.

D. Michael Quinn agrees, saying,

> The Accommodation History ... actually **practiced by some LDS writers** is intended to protect the Saints, but **actually disillusions them**.... Ezra Taft Benson reports with obvious irritation the fact that LDS Seminary and Institute teachers ask him, "**When and where can we begin to tell them our *real* story?**" and Elder Benson observes, "Inferred in that question is the accusation that the Church has not been telling the truth."[116] The tragic **reality is that there have been occasions when Church leaders**, teachers, and writers **have not told the truth** they knew about difficulties of the Mormon past, but have offered to the Saints instead a mixture of **platitudes, half-truths, omissions, and plausible denials**.... A so-called "faith-promoting" Church history which conceals controversies and difficulties of the Mormon past actually undermines the faith of Latter-day Saints who eventually learn about the problems from other sources.[117]

LDS writer Klaus Hansen writes, " ... the Church like almost any other institution has attempted to create **a deliberately propagandistic version** of its own past, a version that can be sustained more easily by **keeping evidence secret or by 'editing'** — in conformity with the 'official' version — those sources made available to the public."[118]

Most Mormons believe that the *History of the Church* is a factual and accurate record. Although they have intentionally made changes, LDS leaders do not discourage this belief in any way. Instead, they continue to encourage the *History's* use as the only true version of events concerning the earliest years of the Church.

The deception of the LDS leaders is not restricted to the thousands of changes, additions and deletions in the text. The *History* is purported to be written or dictated by Joseph Smith himself, and the first six volumes read as if they were from the personal diaries of Joseph Smith. In fact, the title page of the first volume introduces the work as the "History of Joseph Smith, the Prophet **BY HIMSELF**."[119] But in fact, more than half of the history was written and compiled after his death, making it impossible that the majority of the *History* was ever written or dictated by him.

While some might consider this matter of authorship trivial, it seriously underscores that a great deal of the work was plagiarized. The information written in the last half of the *History*, while still written in the first person as if it were Joseph telling the story, actually came from many other journals and manuscripts. For one example, an entire paragraph was copied directly out of Heber C. Kimball's personal journal.[120] The personal and reflexive pronouns he used were then changed so that the entry read as if Joseph Smith had written the account, when in fact it originally reflected Kimball's experiences.[121] The footnote in the *History of the Church* for this entry ignores the fact that it was taken from Kimball, and instead claims that his journal merely "corroborates" the account.[122]

In the Summer 1971 issue of *Brigham Young University Studies*, Dean C. Jessee published an article he had written while a member of the LDS Church Historian's Office. What he wrote verified what the Tanners had claimed all along: Joseph Smith had not written the majority of the *History*. Jessee wrote, "At the time he [Willard Richards] began writing, not more than 157 pages [of the *History*] had been completed, covering events up to November 1, 1831. By May 8, 1843, he had written 114 pages beyond.... At the time of Joseph Smith's death, the narrative was written to August 5, 1838...."[123] As the Tanners point out, "Since there were almost 2,200 pages, this would mean that **over 60% of Joseph Smith's *History* was not completed during his lifetime!**"[124]

The *History of the Church*, then, is not what it claims to be. It was mostly written by men other than Joseph Smith, who altered the manuscript, plagiarized from other journals, suppressed original manuscripts to conceal the truth, and then claimed that the work was the most accurate and reliable history ever published.

Jerald and Sandra Tanner concluded that it was far from reliable. They wrote that most LDS historians are "men who follow the philosophy of Ezra Taft Benson, [at that time] President of the Council of the Twelve Apostles. Benson is a man who believes **that it is wrong to tell the whole truth about Mormon history.**[125] He believes, in other words, **that there should be a cover-up** with regard to certain things that have occurred in the past."[126] They go on to say, "The Mormon Historians evidently feel that more converts can be won to the church with a bogus history than with a true factual one. It is apparently felt that **the truth will not bear its own weight** and that **a little forgery here and there is not wrong** as long as it helps win converts to the Church."[127]

LDS researchers have come to the same conclusion. Klaus Hansen tells us why: "…the fact is that **an unvarnished version** of the history of the Church **that lets the chips fall where they may is potential dynamite.**"[128] Evidently, the leadership of the Church does not want its members to know the whole truth about its early history. They only want a sanitized and censored version to be published.

T. Edgar Lyon, Associate Director of the LDS Institute of Religion, writes,

> But why should Latter-day Saints concern themselves with **authentic history**? What difference does it make to the tourist if he is told **fact or fiction**? Personally, I do not appreciate being victimized by someone who **while posing as an authority disseminates error**, however trivial it may seem…. We should be certain that the interpretation we offer … **is as accurate as research can make it**. If we do not do this, **our unreliable presentation will reflect on the integrity of the Church.**[129]

The *Book of Mormon*

The altering of publications by Mormon leaders is not limited to their official Church *History*. They have changed their volumes of scripture as well. Though supposedly translated by the power of God and then verified to be true and correct by angelic visitation, the *Book of Mormon* has undergone thousands of changes in its text over the years. In numerous cases, the changes altered or even reversed the meaning of the passage. In every case, the changes have been made with no indication in the text itself.[130]

Of the few Mormons aware of the changes, many assume that they were merely grammatical or punctuational. Those that make such claims have either not checked out the allegations for themselves (therefore make claims they cannot support), or they have seen the changes and are not being truthful about them. Confrontation with the truth can sometimes be futile, however. In one instance, a couple named Jerry and Dianna Benson asked Mormon missionaries about the changes. The missionaries "insisted that any changes were only misspellings and not serious...." They were adamant "that no changes had occurred and when shown from copies of the originals that not only changes had occurred, but they were serious doctrinal changes [they] insisted their church was still true.... it seemed not to really matter at all."[131]

In Chapter 4, we made note of the fact that God supposedly gave the very words and even the spelling of those words to Joseph Smith. It was supposedly a miraculous work of God and not of Joseph Smith. The text, then, is not open to adjustment by later LDS leaders. Yet that has not stopped them from making thousands of changes anyway.

Those who read a current edition of the *Book of Mormon* have no idea that it has been altered from the original "translation." Only by comparison with the original edition would they see the many changes—a practice that the leadership of the Church has often discouraged.[132] Joel Groat of the Institute for Religious Research makes the following point:

Today the Mormon Church gives potential converts a copy of **a corrected and grammatically sanitized** Book of Mormon but still points to Joseph Smith's lack of education as evidence for its divine origin. What is implied is that Joseph could not have produced such a book without divine aid. What they do not say is that Joseph's poor grammar, so evident in the first edition, **is now masked by thousands of changes and corrections** made by later LDS leaders. As a result, today **we do not have** the Book of Mormon as it came from the hand of Joseph Smith, but rather **a heavily edited version** as it has come through the hands of LDS church leaders.[133]

The changes are not restricted to early LDS Church leaders. When the 1981 Edition of the *Book of Mormon* went to press, 35 words had been added to Alma 32:30 that had never been there before. Yet just three chapters earlier in Alma, we are told that man cannot alter God's words.[134]

The *Doctrine and Covenants*

The *Doctrine and Covenants*, another book regarded by Mormons as scripture, is a collection of revelations from God to the leaders of the Mormon Church over the years. Most of them were revelations to Joseph Smith as he was establishing and organizing the Mormon Church. Certainly the text of these revelations should be regarded as sufficiently sacred to escape alteration. In fact, when Oliver Cowdery wanted some words deleted from a particular revelation, Smith said, "I immediately wrote to him in reply, in which I asked him, **by what authority** he took upon him to command me **to alter or erase, to add or diminish to or from a revelation or commandment from the Almighty God.**"[135] Smith also had written to W. W. Phelps on 31 July 1832, saying, "I will exhort you to be careful **not to alter the sense of any of them [revelations] for he that adds or diminishes to the prop[h]ecies must come under the condemnation** writ[t]en therein[.]"[136] In spite of his objections, Smith and Cowdery both were later involved in heavily editing the revelations.

Unlike the *Book of Mormon*, Church leaders admit to having made changes in the *Doctrine and Covenants*. The introduction to the 1981 edition states that "some errors have been perpetuated in past editions, particularly in the historical portions of the section headings. Consequently this edition contains corrections of dates and place names and also a few other minor corrections when it seemed appropriate...."[137] But this explanation is deliberately deceptive. While some corrections were made in section headings, the bulk of the changes were made to the texts of the revelations themselves; in fact, many were not "minor corrections," but major doctrinal changes.

Changes were made to the revelations even before they originally went to press. But since that first edition, numerous additional changes have been made.[138] Joseph Smith began this practice of altering the text, according to B. H. Roberts. After quoting a statement by Parley P. Pratt, which claimed the revelations had not had any revisions or corrections made to them, he informs us that

> this statement of Elder Pratt's is true in a general way ... [but] needs modifying only to the extent of saying that some of the early revelations first published in the "Book of Commandments," in 1833, **were revised** by the Prophet himself in the way of **correcting errors** made by the scribes and publishers; and some **additional clauses were inserted** to throw increased light upon the subjects treated in the revelations, **and paragraphs added, to make the principles or instructions apply to officers not in the Church at the time** some of the earlier revelations were given. The **addition of verses, 65, 66 and 67** in sec. xx of the Doctrine and Covenants, is an example.[139]

There were hundreds of changes made between the 1833 *Book of Commandments* and the same revelations when printed in the 1835 *Doctrine and Covenants*. H. Michael Marquardt writes,

> The most **drastic alterations were made** in 1835, when the **texts were amended, added to, excised, and in some**

cases assigned different historical settings. About a third of the texts from July 1828 to 23 April 1834 were revised. Among other emendations, the changes softened language, reinterpreted economic matters, added offices existing at the time of revision, and **inserted references to priesthood restoration**.[140]

In many cases, several revelations were combined and presented as a single one. Marquardt, along with Wesley Walters, notes that "in the 1835 Doctrine and Covenants **the texts of five** of the six revelations received on 6 April 1830 and originally published in the 1833 Book of Commandments **were amalgamated into a single revelation** and the references to the location were deleted."[141]

The changes did not go unnoticed at the time they were made. Richard Van Wagoner writes, "Upgrading revelations and retrospectively editing the past **are hallmarks** of early Mormonism. **Thousands of substantive alterations were made**...."[142] In fact, they were so common that in 1842 Jonathan Turner wrote:

> It would have been well for the world if Smith's divinity, instead of giving him a pair of stone spectacles, had given him a divine printer, and a divine press, and such types that he might have been enabled **to fix the meaning of his inspired revelations**, so that it would be possible to let them stand, at *least two years*, **without abstracting, interpolating, altering, or garbling, to suit the times**.[143]

If the book comprised only instructions thought up and dictated by Joseph Smith, and they needed additions or revisions as the Church grew and developed, this could be understood and condoned. But these were purported to be **direct revelations from God**, many of them supposedly quoting Him or Jesus Christ. To add clauses or paragraphs, especially without any indication in the text, yet still present them as the direct words of God or Jesus, is duplicitous.

Some early members of the Church, such as *Book of Mormon* witness David Whitmer, recognized that changes had been made. Whitmer writes, "Some of the revelations as they now appear in the

Book of Doctrine and Covenants **have been changed and added to**. Some of the changes being of the *greatest importance* as **the meaning** is *entirely changed* on some very important matters.... The revelations were printed in the Book of Commandments *correctly!*"[144]

While LDS leaders do admit that they have made these "minor corrections," they claim they were made only "to bring the material into conformity with the historical documents."[145] But this is not true. LDS scholars have documented and catalogued the changes. BYU student Peter Crawley commented that "all of the chapters in the Book of Commandments are reprinted in the 1835 Doctrine and Covenants, but **with substantial changes**."[146] John W. Fitzgerald wrote his Master's thesis in 1940 on the subject while studying at BYU.[147] Fifteen years later, another BYU scholar, Melvin J. Petersen, wrote his thesis on the same subject.[148] Petersen informs us that there have been **703 words changed, 1,656 words added and 453 words deleted** from the revelations since they were first published.[149] The scope of these changes is very significant, and encompasses far more than simple errors made by scribes or printers.

For example, Chapter IV of the *Book of Commandments* was changed so significantly that it barely resembles the *Doctrine and Covenants* Section 5 that it became. This is because 280 words were added, and 194 of the original words were deleted. They can scarcely be called the same revelation. Chapter VI from the *Book of Commandments* went from three short verses to eight when it became Section 7 of the *Doctrine and Covenants*. It **nearly doubled** in size because of **the addition of 112 words**. Perhaps the most significant addition is to Chapter XXVIII of the *Book of Commandments*. When republished as Section 27 of the *Doctrine and Covenants*, this revelation **had grown by 455 words**.

Even later additions to the *Doctrine and Covenants* have not been free from alterations. In 1976, Mormon leaders decided to canonize a revelation concerning heaven that Joseph Smith had received in 1836. The original revelation is from Joseph Smith's diary.[150] Yet when published as *Doctrine and Covenants* Section 137, more than half of the revelation was omitted. Why? The omissions cover up errors that show Smith was not a true prophet.

For example, in the introduction of the revelation, Joseph Smith said, "I saw Father Adam, Abraham, and Michael and my father and mother...." In *Doctrine and Covenants* 137:5, the words "and Michael" have been deleted, because Smith later revealed that "Adam" and "Michael" were the same person.[151] Therefore, the second part had to be removed to conceal the contradiction. Later in the vision, Joseph prophesied that William McLellen would preach in the south and heal a lame man. But Joseph Smith had not foreseen that McLellen would later be excommunicated from the church and become a persecutor, never fulfilling the prophecy. Near the end of the revelation, Joseph Smith prophesied seeing his Twelve Apostles in the Celestial Kingdom together. But more than half of them ended up leaving the church either by choice or by excommunication. In order to keep the current membership from seeing that Smith was not a true prophet, the altered revelation was published instead of the original one. Yet there is no indication in the current text that any changes have been made.

Two specific examples examined below demonstrate clearly that the *Doctrine and Covenants* is not a divine record. The first is the deliberate falsification of a revelation relating to Oliver Cowdery's use of a divining rod (8:6-7). The other is the book's teachings regarding the location of the Garden of Eden (107:53-55; 116; 117:8).

Divining Rod or Gift of Aaron? Because the foundation of the Mormon Church is steeped in stories of divine intervention and revelation, one possible reason LDS leaders alter their scriptures is to conceal information that could cause current Mormon members to question their Church's history. For example, since Joseph Smith was supposed to be a prophet of God, it might make his testimony suspect if members learned that he was heavily involved in the occult. A true prophet would not be practicing those things that God has always condemned. This is exactly what one specific change was intended to hide.

In Section 8 of *Doctrine and Covenants*, mention is made of "the gift of Aaron."[152] It seems very mysterious, and no explanation of what is meant is found in the text as currently published. When the *Doctrine and Covenants Commentary* is consulted, this information is provided:

> *This is thy gift*] It was Oliver Cowdery's special gift to understand the "still, small voice" of the Spirit, and if he would follow it, he would be delivered from the hand of the enemy.... *The gift of Aaron*] Oliver Cowdery also had the "gift of Aaron." Aaron was the elder brother of Moses.... He was his spokesman before Pharaoh, and he assisted him in opening up the dispensation which Moses was commissioned to proclaim (Exodus 4:27-31). This was the gift of Aaron. In some respects Oliver Cowdery was the Aaron of the new and last dispensation.[153]

Was the "gift of Aaron" really just the gift of being a spokesman, or of understanding the Spirit? Other LDS commentaries on this subject teach the same thing. For instance, we are told that, "Oliver Cowdery's gift was the spirit of revelation (Section 8:3, 4), by which he could obtain knowledge of things divine. He also had the gift of Aaron. Aaron was the spokesman of Moses, and Oliver Cowdery became the first spokesman of the Prophet...."[154]

It is clear that this is what Church leaders want people to believe about Oliver Cowdery. But the truth is far different. The phrase "gift of Aaron" **was never a part of the original revelation**. It has been inserted, and the original wording was deleted.

When this revelation was originally published, it was Chapter VII in the *Book of Commandments*. But in that edition, these verses read:

> Now this is not all, for you [Oliver Cowdery] have another gift, which is the *gift of working with* **the** *rod:* behold it has told you things: behold there is no other power save God, that can cause this *rod of* nature, to work in your hands, for it is the work of God; and therefore whatsoever you shall ask me to tell you by that means, that will I grant unto you, that you shall know.[155]

This revelation was received in April 1829, when Joseph Smith was supposedly translating the *Book of Mormon* with Cowdery as his scribe. If it were known that Oliver Cowdery was engaging in dowsing (using a divining rod) during this period, and that God approved of this practice in the revelation, then it creates an irreconcilable contradiction. After all, seeking answers by divination rather than by consulting God is condemned in the Bible.[156]

The fact is that Joseph Smith, Jr. and Oliver Cowdery both believed in divining rods, and thought that God would communicate through such a device. But after the *Book of Commandments* was published, Joseph Smith drew some sharp criticism because of his ties to the magical arts.[157] For this reason, he obscured the true wording of the original revelation when it was published again a few years later.

Were Joseph Smith and his contemporaries really engaging in forbidden occult practices? Historian D. Michael Quinn provides the following information:

> According to Vermont neighbors, five years before the birth of Joseph Smith, Jr. [1805], **his father participated with William Cowdery** in a religious group **using divining rods** "mostly as a medium of revelation." Almost thirty years later Jesse Smith wrote in a family letter that his brother **Joseph Sr.** had "**a wand or rod**" for obtaining obscure knowledge. That same year William's son **Oliver Cowdery introduced himself to the Smith family as a divining "rodsman."**[158]

"Rodsman" Oliver Cowdery became Joseph Smith's scribe as he dictated the *Book of Mormon*, and as already cited, "Joseph Jr. later announced a revelation commending Cowdery's 'gift of working with the rod.'"[159] Quinn also provides the following interesting information on the men selected for the Quorum of Twelve Apostles—the highest governing body of the Church after the First Presidency—which was organized in 1835:

> [It] includes **astrologer** John F. Boynton, **rodsman** Heber C. Kimball ... **amulet-wearer** [Brigham] Young, and **treasure-**

quest enthusiasts Luke S. Johnson and Orson Hyde. They are ordained apostles by the *Book of Mormon*'s three witnesses, **rodsman** Oliver Cowdery, **seer stone enthusiast** David Whitmer, and **treasure-quest participant** Martin Harris.[160]

In Quinn's *Early Mormonism and the Magic World View*, he writes that "after the organization of the church in 1830 ... **early Mormons continued using divining rods**" and he gives specific examples (Apostle Heber C. Kimball, Apostle Orson Hyde, President Brigham Young).[161] LDS writer Marvin S. Hill informs us that "some of the **rodsmen or money diggers** who moved into Mormonism were Oliver Cowdery, Martin Harris, Orrin P. Rockwell, Joseph and Newel Knight, and Josiah Stowell."[162]

In his "Selected Chronology of the Church of Jesus Christ of Latter-day Saints, 1830-47," Quinn provides the following information. The entry for 20 March 1843 reads:

> James C. Brewster publishes his claim that as part of an 1836 Ohio treasure-quest, Presiding Patriarch Joseph Smith, Sr., "**anointed the mineral rods** and seeing stones with consecrated oil, **and prayed over them in the house of the Lord** in Kirtland."[163]

The entry for 6 June 1844 records:

> [Heber C.] Kimball clothes himself in endowment robes, prays in the "true order," **while holding a divining "rod,"** and asks yes-no questions. Movement of the rod means "yes" and no movement means "no." **This is the first verified use of the divining rod** in Mormonism since an 1829 revelation commended Cowdery's use of his "**rod of nature ... behold it has told you things.**"[164]

The entry for 28 July 1847 states that

> [Brigham] Young **selects the site of the Salt Lake temple by using** Oliver Cowdery's **divining rod**.[165]

The biographical sketch on Heber C. Kimball states that the "last recorded prayer '**by the rod**'" took place in 1862.[166] Quinn concludes that "there is no evidence that they were used in divination after the death of Heber C. Kimball in 1868."[167] When Quinn revised his book for publication in 1998, he had revised this statement to say that since that time, "LDS leaders ignored divining rods," but he lists several examples of LDS members continuing to use the rods into the twentieth century.[168]

While it was Joseph Smith who originally tried to conceal the use of dowsing among members of his early Church leadership, later LDS leaders have chosen to keep the information hidden as well. They not only allow publication of books which explain the "gift of Aaron" in *Doctrine and Covenants* 8 incorrectly, but they also deleted references to receiving information "by the rod" from Heber C. Kimball's published diary.[169]

Mormon scholar Stanley B. Kimball, however, was more honest in his publication on the life of Heber C. Kimball. He writes:

> Heber also told of **an unusual rod** he had **received from Joseph Smith**.... **Joseph did give him and Brigham Young real rods**, because "they were the only ones of the original twelve who had not lifted up their hearts against the Prophet."[170]

The Garden of Eden: Near East or Midwest? Revelations in *Doctrine and Covenants*,[171] as well as present LDS teachings, place the Garden of Eden on the North American continent in the area of Jackson and Daviess Counties, Missouri. According to Joseph Smith, this is the area where Adam and Eve lived after their expulsion from the garden. Smith claimed that the name of the area in Adam's own language was Adam-ondi-Ahman. Joseph Fielding Smith explains:

> In accord with the revelations given to the Prophet Joseph Smith, we teach that *the Garden of Eden was on the American continent located where the City of Zion, or the New Jerusalem, will be built.* When Adam and Eve were

driven out of the Garden, they eventually dwelt at a place called *Adam-ondi-Ahman,* situated in what is now Daviess County, Missouri."[172]

Ivan J. Barrett recounts what Joseph Smith told those who were with him as they looked for settlement locations in Missouri:

He also told them that Jackson County was once the Garden of Eden from which Adam was driven. After Adam had traveled northeast seventy miles he had built the altar on which they were then standing and there offered sacrifice unto the Lord. One of the number later wrote: "I thought it a great privilege to be at that time with the Prophet, and to hear his words regarding the mound and pile of rocks laid up at so early a period in the world's history."[173]

On 15 March 1857 in his conversation with Orson Hyde, Brigham Young stated:

Now it is a pleasant thing to think of and to know where the Garden of Eden was. Did you ever think of it? I do not think many do, for **in Jackson County was the Garden of Eden. Joseph has declared this**, and I am as much bound to believe that as to believe that Joseph was a prophet of God.[174]

In his discourse on 27 June 1863, Heber C. Kimball explained that "the spot chosen for **the garden of Eden was** Jackson County, **in the State of Missouri**, where Independence now stands...."[175]

In contradiction to these statements, the Bible and *The Pearl of Great Price* (Book of Moses) place the locale of the Garden of Eden and the expulsion of Adam and Eve in the Middle East. These teachings cannot both be true. That Eden was in the Middle East is established by the naming of the rivers that flow from it in Genesis 2:14: "And the name of the third river is **Hiddekel** [the Hebrew name of the Tigris]: that is it which **goeth toward the east of Assyria**. And the **fourth river is Euphrates**." Moses 3:14, is almost identical: "And the name of the third river was Hiddekel; that **which** goeth toward the east of Assyria. And the **fourth river was the Euphrates.**"

Joseph Fielding Smith explained the contradiction in this way:

> The rivers spoken of in Genesis and in the Book of Moses are **rivers that existed when *all* the waters of the earth were in one place.** If all the waters were in one place, then obviously all the land was in one place.... Noah and his family in the Ark sailed during the time of the flood from some place evidently in what is known now as America, and landed at Ararat thousands of miles away.... during the flood great changes were made on the face of the earth. The land surface was **in the process of division into continents**.... not too many centuries after Noah landed at Ararat, the entire land surface of the earth was changed and divided, and what had previously been one grand continent, was broken up into many continents and islands. So it is impossible for us today to know exactly what changes were made in that world catastrophe.... Of course we rely definitely on the word of the Lord to the Prophet Joseph Smith.... **while these rivers carry the same names, they are not the same rivers** which were in the Garden of Eden.[176]

While this seems like a plausible explanation on the surface, it is not when we consider the authorship of the book of Genesis. Genesis, Exodus, Leviticus, Numbers and Deuteronomy were all written by Moses, most likely during the 40 years of Israel's wandering in the wilderness.[177] This is undisputed by Mormons today.[178] The *Book of Mormon* even speaks of the "five books of Moses."[179] This means that these books were written somewhere between 1446 and 1406 BC, **well after** the flood of Noah and the division of the continents.

That being the case, the names of places and rivers both before and after the flood were all supplied by Moses. They were not documented by Adam and later added to by Moses. When Moses identified the rivers that flowed from the Garden of Eden, he did so **according to his knowledge of the rivers at that time**[180] as well as according to the revelation of the information God had given him on the subject.

When Moses identified the rivers of Tigris and Euphrates and the area of Assyria, then, it was according to the rivers and places known at the time of writing, not at the time of the Garden of Eden. This is clearly seen by the wording of Genesis 2:10-14. As Moses named the rivers that branched off from the Garden of Eden, he tells where each of them "flows around"[181] — not where they once flowed. And since Assyria was not a pre-flood location, but a locale at the time of Moses, we have further proof that the locations identified referred to post-flood-era topography. That way Moses was clearly explaining where the location of the Garden had been according to the knowledge current at the time of writing.

While the precise location of Eden has not been established, the mention of the Tigris and Euphrates rivers and of the land of Assyria can not be construed to mean that Eden was located on the American continent. Only by ignoring the context and grammar of the Genesis account, by receiving a false revelation or by sheer imagination could Joseph Smith have arrived at his erroneous teaching regarding the location of the Garden of Eden.

The *Pearl of Great Price*

The *Pearl of Great Price* is a collection of Joseph Smith's writings that were formerly printed in Church publications. These include the Book of Moses; the Book of Abraham; Joseph Smith's translation of a section from the Gospel of Matthew; a portion of Joseph Smith's History; and The Articles of Faith for the Church. These were first published in 1851 in booklet form (with some additional material) for the benefit of the members of the Church living in England. It was canonized as scripture in October 1880.

As already discussed in Chapter 6, the Book of Abraham was examined by qualified Egyptologists who concluded that Joseph Smith's "translation" was a total failure. Even this book has not been free from textual changes over the years. The Church leadership admits that "several revisions have been made in the contents as the needs of the Church have required."[182] They go on to suggest that the changes were minor—merely rearrangement, removal of duplicated material, and arrangement into chapters and verses. But again, it is easily demonstrated that many of the changes are major, and that they completely alter doctrines taught in the book.

The other sections of the *Pearl of Great Price* have also not escaped alteration. Particularly obvious are changes made in the Book of Moses. LDS scholar James Harris informs us that "from the standpoint of **omissions and additions of words**, the American Edition [of the Book of Moses] is the most spectacular rendition.... Some of **the words added** to the American Edition **had impressive doctrinal implications**.... [this] edition **was more drastically changed** than any previous publication by a member of the Church."[183]

In the current edition, Moses 4:19-22 has been completely changed from the original edition. Three words were deleted and 76 words added. In Moses 5:22-31, more than 200 words have been added to the text from how it was originally published. Overall, in the first eight chapters of Moses more than 1,000 words have been added to the original text as printed in 1851. Again, not a single indication of change has been provided in the current text. Changes were also made to Joseph Smith—History and The Articles of Faith with no indication.

How can anyone realistically view these LDS scriptures (the *Book of Mormon*, the *Doctrine and Covenants*, and the *Pearl of Great Price*) as inspired when Mormon leaders have taken such liberties with the texts?

Conclusion

These problems call into question the veracity of the Mormon leaders. The information they publish about Joseph Smith and the restoration of the Church has been finely polished in order to be faith promoting. The revelations and scriptures themselves have been altered to produce the same effect. But the actual history of the Church is far different than the miraculous stories imply. If Mormon members are basing their faith on these manufactured scriptures and histories, then their faith is without foundation.

Chapter 10
The Mormon Godhead

Joseph Smith's Claim –
> Men say there is one God; the Father, the Son and the Holy Ghost are only one God! I say that is a strange God anyhow ... he would be a giant or a monster.
> – *History of the Church*, 6:476

Unity, Not Trinity

No examination of the claims of Joseph Smith would be complete without a look at his doctrines regarding the Godhead. He taught that there were many Gods, but three in particular are of concern to this earth. He taught that these three Gods were individual Gods acting in unity, and that the Christian teaching about the "Trinity"[1] was heresy. Here we will examine LDS teachings regarding God the Father, Jesus Christ and the Holy Ghost.[2]

God the Father

At first glance, LDS teachings about God the Father seem orthodox. Apostle Bruce McConkie writes, "By definition, God (generally meaning the Father) is the one supreme and absolute Being; the ultimate source of the universe; the all-powerful, all-knowing, all-good Creator, Ruler, and Preserver of all things."[3] Mormon missionaries proclaim that "God is perfect, all-wise, and all-powerful. He is also merciful, kind, and just.... We are children of our Father in Heaven. We are created in his image."[4] It takes a deeper look into LDS teachings to see how the Mormon doctrines about God differ significantly from the Biblical teachings.

For example, the Mormon Church teaches that God was not always God.[5] He was once a man on another planet like Earth.[6] He was a sinner trying to earn salvation and learn obedience to his God there.[7] He has a glorified, physical body of flesh and bones.[8] Because of this, He is able to be in only one place at one time.[9] By obedience and progression, he finally became God over his own Earth.[10]

Milton Hunter explains the God of Mormonism this way:

> How He Became God ... we must accept the fact that there was a time when Deity was much less powerful than He is today. Then how did He become glorified and exalted and attain His present status of Godhood? ... **God** undoubtedly took advantage of every opportunity **to learn the laws of truth** and as He became acquainted with each new verity He righteously obeyed it.... As **He gained more knowledge through persistent effort** and continuous industry, as well as through absolute obedience, His understanding of the universal laws **continued to become more complete.** Thus **He grew in experience and continued to grow** until **He attained the status of Godhood.** In other words, **He became God** by absolute obedience to all the eternal laws of the Gospel....[11]

One of the requirements for becoming a God was that He have a wife.[12] LDS leaders have gone further and taught that He is, in fact, a polygamist.[13] Although they teach that God is all-powerful, they also teach that He is bound by and subject to the laws of nature and physics.[14] He was not able to create anything from nothing, but had to organize existing materials into an earth.[15] He also is helpless to interfere with the free will of man.[16]

These teachings contradict the teachings of the Bible. The Bible is clear that God has been God from all eternity.[17] He was never a man.[18] He is a Spirit,[19] and omnipresent.[20] God has always been and will always be sinless and perfect.[21] He is all-powerful, creating everything from nothing, merely speaking them into existence.[22] He is fully in control of all events.[23] In fact, it was God who decreed the laws of nature, and since He created them, He is able to transcend them at will.[24]

When the facts are known, it is evident that the LDS God is nothing at all like the God of the Bible (see the chart contrasting the Mormon God and the Biblical God at the end of this chapter). But there are still more problems with the LDS concept of God. As with other LDS doctrines,[25] their teachings about God have changed over the years, and He is not always defined consistently from one Church leader to the next.

God, or Gods?

When Joseph Smith began his prophetic career, God supposedly revealed to him truths that had been lost to the Christian world. One of the earliest revelations Smith claimed he received was of the golden plates, which he allegedly translated into the *Book of Mormon*.[26] He claimed it contained the "fulness of the everlasting Gospel."[27] However, many teachings in the book contradict Smith's later doctrines about God.

For example, this "divinely translated" *Book of Mormon* teaches a clear and definite monotheistic doctrine:

> JESUS is the CHRIST, the ETERNAL GOD, manifesting himself unto all nations.[28]

> And the honor be to the Father, and to the Son, and to the Holy Ghost, **which is one God.**[29]

> And now, behold, my beloved brethren, this is the way; and there is none other way nor name given under heaven whereby man can be saved in the kingdom of God. And now, behold, this is the doctrine of Christ, and the only and true doctrine **of the Father, and of the Son, and of the Holy Ghost, which is one God,** without end. Amen.[30]

> And Zeezrom said unto him: Thou sayest there is a true and living God?
> And Amulek said: Yea, there is a true and living God.
> **Now Zeezrom said: Is there more than one God?**
> **And he answered, No.**

> Now Zeezrom said unto him again: How knowest thou these things? And he said: **An angel hath made them known unto me.** And Zeezrom said again: Who is he that shall come? Is it the Son of God? And he said unto him, Yea. And Zeezrom said again: Shall he save his people in their sins? And Amulek answered and said unto him: I say unto you he shall not, for it is impossible for him to deny his word. Now Zeezrom said unto the people: See that ye remember these things; for **he said there is but one God**; yet he saith that the Son of God shall come, but he shall not save his people—as though he had authority to command God.[31]
>
> Now, this restoration shall come to all, both old and young, both bond and free, both male and female, both the wicked and the righteous; and even there shall not so much as a hair of their heads be lost; but every thing shall be restored to its perfect frame, as it is now, or in the body, and shall be brought and be arraigned before the bar of **Christ the Son, and God the Father, and the Holy Spirit, which is one Eternal God**, to be judged according to their works, whether they be good or whether they be evil.[32]

The doctrine of monotheism (that there is only one God) in the *Book of Mormon* was so strong that it actually taught modalism—the belief that Jesus Christ and God the Father are the very same Being:

> And because he said unto them that **Christ was the God, the Father of all things,** and said that he should take upon him the image of man, and it should be the image after which man was created in the beginning; or in other words, he said that man was created after the image of God, and **that God should come down among the children of men, and take upon him flesh and blood,** and go forth upon the face of the earth—[33]

And now Abinadi said unto them: I would that ye should understand that **God himself shall come down among the children of men, and shall redeem his people.** And because he dwelleth in flesh **he shall be called the Son of God**, and having subjected the flesh to the will of the Father, **being the Father and the Son**—The Father, because he was conceived by the power of God; and the Son, because of the flesh; **thus becoming the Father and Son—And they are one God, yea, the very Eternal Father** of heaven and of earth. And thus the flesh becoming subject to the Spirit, **or the Son to the Father, being one God**, suffereth temptation, and yieldeth not to the temptation, but suffereth himself to be mocked, and scourged, and cast out, and disowned by his people.[34]

Teach them that redemption cometh through **Christ the Lord, who is the very Eternal Father.** Amen.[35]

Now Zeezrom saith again unto him: **Is the Son of God the very Eternal Father?**
And Amulek said unto him: **Yea, he is the very Eternal Father of heaven and of earth**, and all things which in them are; he is the beginning and the end, the first and the last; And he shall come into the world to redeem his people; and he shall take upon him the transgressions of those who believe on his name; and these are they that shall have eternal life, and salvation cometh to none else.[36]

Behold, I am he who was prepared from the foundation of the world to redeem my people. **Behold, I am Jesus Christ. I am the Father and the Son.** In me shall all mankind have life, and that eternally, even they who shall believe on my name; and they shall become my sons and my daughters.[37]

After writing the *Book of Mormon*, Smith continued having revelations declaring that there was only one God. For example, a revelation given to him in April of 1830 states:

And gave unto them commandments that they should love and serve him, **the only living and true God**, and that he should be the only being whom they should worship.[38]

Which **Father, Son, and Holy Ghost are one God**, infinite and eternal, without end, Amen.[39]

Monotheism was also clearly taught in the Book of Moses, which Joseph Smith "translated" between June 1830 and February 1831.

...but **there is no God beside me**, and all things are present with me, and I know them all.[40]

...Nevertheless, calling upon God, he received strength, and he commanded, saying: Depart from me, Satan, for **this one God only** will I worship, which **is the God of glory**.[41]

And I, God, said: Let there be light;...**And I, God**, divided the light from the darkness. And **I, God**, called the light Day;...And again**, I, God**, said:...[42]

When Smith dictated his "Inspired Version" of the New Testament, which he completed on 2 February 1833,[43] he was still teaching the concept of a single God.

And the scribe said unto him, Well, Master, thou has said the truth; **for there is one God, and there is none other but him**.[44]

For there is one God, and one mediator between God and men, the man Christ Jesus.[45]

During the later 1830s, when the Saints were located in Nauvoo, Illinois, Smith's doctrine about God changed, reflecting a new belief in a plurality of Gods. This change in doctrine is most obvious in the Book of Abraham. He had been "translating" the document since

1835. After a brief amount of translation work in July 1835,[46] he took a long break before working on it again in early 1842.[47]

A significant shift from one God to many Gods is found in the book between Chapters 3 and 4—Chapter 3 being largely monotheistic in teaching and Chapter 4 being obviously polytheistic. Since this portion of the book was published in the *Times and Seasons* on 16 March 1842, Smith had definitely changed his teachings on God at least by the early part of that year.[48]

Even so, Smith must have been grappling with the concept, because in September 1842, he was still teaching publicly that there was only one God. In an editorial for the *Times and Seasons*, he wrote

> that as there was **but *one* Lord, *one* faith, *one* baptism, and *one* God** and father of us all, even so there was but *one* door to the mansions of bliss. *Amen*.[49]

He eventually settled the matter in his own mind, because by April 1844 there is no doubt that Smith was openly teaching the plurality of Gods doctrine. In the famous "King Follett Discourse," we find the following statements:

> God himself was once as we are now, and is an exalted Man, and sits enthroned in yonder heavens. That is the great secret ... God himself, the Father of us all, dwelt on an earth the same as Jesus Christ himself did.... Here, then, is eternal life—to know the only wise and true God; and **you have got to learn how to be Gods yourselves**, and to be kings and priests to God, **the same as all Gods have done** before you.... Thus, **the head God brought forth the Gods** in the grand counsel.... The **head God called together the Gods** and sat in grand council to bring forth the world.... In the beginning, the **head of the Gods called a council of the Gods; and they came together and concocted a plan** to create the world and people it.[50]

By mid-June of that year, Smith was elaborating even further:

> I will preach on **the plurality of Gods**. I have selected this text for that express purpose. I wish to declare **I have always and in all congregations** when I have preached on **the subject of the Deity, it has been the plurality of Gods**. It has been preached by the Elders for fifteen years. I have always declared God to be a distinct personage, Jesus Christ a separate and distinct personage from God the Father, and that the Holy Ghost was a distinct personage and a Spirit: and **these three constitute three distinct personages and three Gods**.... **Many men say there is one God**; the Father, the Son and the Holy Ghost are only one God! **I say that is a strange God anyhow ... he would be a giant or a monster**.... Where was there ever a son without a father? And where did a tree or anything spring into existence without a progenitor? And **everything comes in this way**. Paul says that which is earthly is in the likeness of that which is heavenly, Hence if Jesus had a Father, **can we not believe that *He* had a Father also?**[51]

This change from his original teaching is the complete opposite of what Smith had previously taught about God. Either there is only one God, or there are many. Both teachings cannot be true. It is inconceivable that God would have "overlooked" all other Gods when giving the inspiration for the Bible and needed to correct Himself later on. Since God does not contradict Himself, this new teaching had to have originated in the mind of Smith.

According to the Bible, there is only one God, and no others.

> Unto thee it was shewed [shown], that thou mightest know that the LORD he is God; **there is none else beside him**. (Deuteronomy 4:35)

> Ye are my witnesses, saith the LORD, and my servant whom I have chosen: that ye may know and believe me, and understand that I am he: **before me there was no God formed, neither shall there be after me**. (Isaiah 43:10)

Thus saith the L ORD the King of Israel, and his redeemer the L ORD of hosts; I am the first, and I am the last; and **beside me there is no God**. (Isaiah 44:6)

... ye are even my witnesses. **Is there a God beside me?** yea, **there is no God; I know not any**. (Isaiah 44:8)

Look unto me, and be ye saved, all the ends of the earth: for **I am God, and there is none else**. (Isaiah 45:22)

And this is life eternal, that they might know thee **the only true God**, and Jesus Christ, whom thou hast sent. (John 17:3)

Adam-God Doctrine

Brigham Young is most well known for teaching that the God of this earth was the first man, Adam. Young proclaimed that God revealed this doctrine to him. But he was not unique in teaching this doctrine; Joseph Smith had also taught it. Smith said,

Daniel in his seventh chapter speaks of **the Ancient of Days**; he means **the oldest man, our Father Adam**.... The Son of Man stands before him, and there is given him glory and dominion.[52]

... it is the place where **Adam shall come** to visit his people, or **the Ancient of Days shall sit,** as spoken of by Daniel the Prophet.[53]

In vision Daniel witnessed the enactment of a drama of magnificent splendor as **the Mighty God, to whom the title of the Ancient of Days is given**, presents to his son, Jesus Christ, a Kingdom so that all people, nations and languages may serve Him.[54]

Whereas Smith merely taught two truths that must be connected (that Adam was the Ancient of Days, and also that the Ancient of Days was God), Young was clearer and more precise in his revelation on this subject:

> When our **Father Adam** came into the garden of Eden, he came into it with a *celestial body*, and brought Eve, *one of his wives*, with him. He helped to make and organize this world. He is MICHAEL, *the Archangel*, the ANCIENT OF DAYS! about whom holy men have written and spoken—HE *is our* FATHER *and our* GOD, *and the only God with whom* WE *have to do.*[55]

Mormons clearly understood what Young was teaching, and it was reiterated in a number of writings at the time.

> Then **Adam is really God!** And why not? If there are Lords many and Gods many, as the Scriptures inform us, **why should not our Father Adam be one of them**? ... He is the first, **the Father of all the human family**, and his glory will be above all, for **he will be God over all**. It is upon this foundation that **the throne of Michael is established as Father, Patriarch, God**....[56]

> ... every knee shall bow, and every tongue confess that **he is the God of the whole earth**. Then will the words of the Prophet Brigham, **when speaking of Adam**, be fully realized—"**He is our Father and our God**, *and the only God with whom* WE *have to do.*"[57]

This view proved to be troubling to many Church members, and some would not accept it. When they spoke out against it, they were reprimanded. Elder James Caffall, a member of the Church Special General Council, said,

> ... some of the officers have not met in council for three years. They are lacking in faith on one principle—the last

"cat that was let out of the bag." ... **they are troubled about Adam being our Father and God.**[58]

Another member of that council, Elder James Little, remarked,

> ... I believe in the principle of obedience; and **if I am told that Adam is our Father and our God, I just believe it.**[59]

Young addressed these dissenters himself on the matter:

> Some have grumbled because I believe **our God to be so near to us as Father Adam**. There are many who know **that doctrine to be true.**[60]

> Some years ago, I advanced a doctrine with regard to **Adam, being our Father and God**, that will be a curse to many of the Elders of Israel because of their folly. With regard to it they yet grovel in darkness and will. **It is one of the most glorious revealments** of the economy of Heaven, yet the world hold it in (derision).... But they are ignorant and stupid like the dumb ass.[61]

> How much unbelief exists in the minds of the Latter-day Saints in regard to **one particular doctrine which I revealed to them, and which God revealed to me**—namely that **Adam is our Father and God**—I do not know, I do not inquire, I care nothing about it.[62]

Christian writers have discussed this early LDS doctrine for years, and the usual Mormon response is that Young never actually taught this, or else was misunderstood. Nevertheless, it is clear that he did emphatically teach this doctrine. Other LDS writers claim that Young was just giving his opinion, not a revelation. But the last quotation above shows that Young said it was clearly a revelation from God, not his own opinion.

After much study, Bruce R. McConkie had to admit that Young actually did teach this concept as LDS doctrine.

I said: 'There are those who believe or say they believe that **Adam is our father and our God**.... I, of course, indicated the **utter absurdity of this doctrine** and said **it was totally false**. Since then I have received violent reactions from Ogden Kraut and other cultists in which they have expounded upon the views of Brigham Young.... **they have plain and clear quotations saying all of the things about Adam** which I say are false. The quotations are in our literature.... Yes, **President Young did teach that Adam was the father of our spirits, and all the related things that the cultists ascribe to him. This, however, is not true. He expressed views that are out of harmony with the gospel.**[63]

Spencer W. Kimball, twelfth president of the Mormon Church, also rejected Young's view, saying the following in a Church conference on 2 October 1976:

We warn you against the dissemination of doctrines which are not according to the scriptures and which are alleged to have been taught by some of the General Authorities of past generations. Such, for instance, is **the Adam-God theory. We denounce that theory** and hope that everyone will be cautioned against **this and other kinds of false doctrine.**[64]

Which revelation is the truth, then? Did God really reveal the Adam-God doctrine to Brigham Young, as he claimed? If so, why does the current church leadership call it a "false doctrine"? Either Brigham Young was a false prophet for teaching this doctrine, or Spencer Kimball was in error for calling it a false doctrine. How can the Mormon Church claim to be led by a true prophet when its leaders contradict each other?

God's Progression

Another doctrine heavily promulgated by Brigham Young in the mid-1800s was that God continually progresses in knowledge and power. This doctrine is closely tied to the teachings of Joseph

Smith, who revealed that Mormon men would progress in knowledge and power until they eventually become Gods themselves. This, Smith revealed, was exactly what God Himself had done. He was once a man on an earth who had to learn obedience to his God. He progressed in knowledge and power throughout the ages until he eventually became the God of this earth.

> ... I am going to tell you how **God came to be God.** We have imagined and supposed that God was God from all eternity. **I will refute that idea.... He was once a man** like us; yea, that **God himself, the Father of us all, dwelt on an earth,** the same as Jesus Christ Himself did....[65]

Brigham Young took this doctrine further, revealing that God continues to progress in wisdom and knowledge and power throughout all eternity.

> To this end has He ordained all things to increase and multiply. The Lord God Almighty has decreed this principle to be the great, governing law of existence.... We are now, or may be, as perfect in *our sphere* as God and Angels are in theirs, **but the greatest intelligence in existence can continually ascend to greater heights of perfection.** We are created for the express purpose of increase. There are none, correctly organized, but can increase from birth to old age.... The Deity within us is the great principle that causes us to increase, and to grow in grace and truth.... **So it has been, beginning with Father Adam, and so it will continue** to be the duty of his posterity who will be sanctified, and enter into the celestial kingdom.[66]

Some men seem as if they could learn so much and no more. They appear to be bounded in their capacity for acquiring knowledge, as **Brother Orson Pratt, has in theory, bounded the capacity of God.** According to his theory, God can progress no further in knowledge and power; but **the God that I**

serve is progressing eternally, and so are his children: **they will increase to all eternity**, if they are faithful.⁶⁷

As evidenced here, at least one LDS leader, Orson Pratt, did not believe Young's teaching that God continues to progress. He spoke out publicly against the doctrine, saying that

> **the Father and the Son do not progress** in knowledge and wisdom, because they already know all things.... Now we wish to be distinctly understood that each of these personal Gods [Father, Son and Holy Ghost] has equal knowledge with all the rest; there are none among them that are in advance of the others in knowledge.... They are all equal in knowledge, and in wisdom, and in the possession of all truth. **None of these Gods are progressing in knowledge: neither can they progress** in the acquirement of any truth.⁶⁸

Pratt presented a logical argument. If God did not have all power and knowledge, then what would happen if He learned a new truth tomorrow that contradicted what He knew to be true today? What if some other God with more power appeared and wanted to usurp the creation of our God? Such thoughts are unthinkable and logically absurd. Yet this doctrine was still taught openly from the pulpit by Young.

Other early leaders sided with Brigham Young's revelation on the subject.

> The Lord has given revelations according to the capacity of the children of men. If there was a point where man in his progression could not proceed any further, the very idea would throw a gloom over every intelligent and reflecting mind. **God himself is increasing and progressing in knowledge, power, and dominion, and will do so, worlds without end.** It is just so with us.⁶⁹

Men have to be rewarded according to their works; if a man ceases to work, there is no more blessings for him. He is lariatted out, as **Orson Pratt lariatted out the Gods in his theory**; his circle is as far as the string extends. **My God is not lariatted out.** I do not want the old men to grow dull.... No. I do not want the old men to think that they have done enough, but to exert themselves to the last, and not to **believe in a God that is lariatted out**, nor be lariatted out themselves....[70]

This doctrine was not only forcefully taught, but dissenters were publicly ridiculed and corrected by the prophet himself as well as other leaders. If this was a revealed truth from God, then God must continue to progress in knowledge and wisdom forever, never attaining to a fullness of all things.

As mentioned, McConkie verified that Young did, in fact, teach this very thing. He wrote,

> **Yes, Brigham Young did say some things about God progressing in knowledge and understanding**, but again ... Young taught, emphatically and plainly, that God knows all things.... the issue is, **which Brigham Young shall we believe** and the answer is: We will take the one whose statements accord with what God has revealed in the Standard Works.[71]

How is it possible to reconcile that this "prophet" of God not only taught incorrect doctrine, but also contradicted himself? What do LDS leaders say about this conflict? McConkie informs us, "President Joseph Fielding Smith said that Brigham Young will have to make his own explanations on the point there involved.... that is something he will have to account for."[72]

As McConkie intimates, Young's doctrine is no longer what the Mormon Church teaches today. Consider these later statements made by LDS leaders on the subject:

There are those who say that God is progressing in knowledge and is learning new truths. **This is false—utterly, totally, and completely.** There is **not one sliver of truth in it.** It grows out of **a wholly twisted and incorrect view** of the King Follet Sermon and of what is meant by eternal progression.[73]

It seems very strange to me that members of the Church will hold to the doctrine, "God increases in knowledge as time goes on." ... **Where has the Lord ever revealed to us that he is lacking in knowledge?** That he is still learning new truth; discovering new laws that are unknown to him? ... I don't know where the Lord has ever declared such a thing. **It is not contained in any revelation that I have read.**[74]

Our Father in heaven is infinite; He is perfect; ***he possesses all knowledge and wisdom.***[75]

One of the most important things we may learn about our religion is that **God is unchangeable, the same yesterday, today and forever.** By this we may know that the principles of salvation will always remain the same, and that we need not be disturbed by "new ideas" or "modern innovations" in the Gospel which may come our way.... the saving principles must ever be the same. They can never change ... **the Lord and His Gospel remain the same—always.**[76]

Not only does this teaching conflict with what Young taught, but it also creates another problem with current Mormon doctrine. If God became God by progressing and advancing in knowledge and power, then how can it possibly be said that he is "the same yesterday and today and forever"? Perhaps by the reckoning of the beginning of this earth until now, this progressive Mormon God could be considered the same yesterday and today. But the Bible teaches clearly that God has forever been the same; that He has **never** changed.

> But **thou art the same**, and thy years shall have no end. (Psalm 102:27)

> **For I am the LORD, I change not;** therefore ye sons of Jacob are not consumed. (Malachi 3:6)

> Every good gift and every perfect gift is from above, and cometh down from **the Father** of lights, **with whom is no variableness, neither shadow of turning.** (James 1:17)

God does not change. But the revelations coming from the LDS prophets do. A person can never tell when something taught as an eternal truth today will later be identified as a false doctrine.

Jesus Christ

Like the LDS teachings about God the Father, their teachings about Jesus Christ appear orthodox on the surface, but research shows that the Mormon Jesus is not the Jesus of the Bible. A comprehensive examination of the differences would require a major volume, but a look at several key points will reveal the vast differences between them.

The Mormon Jesus

The Mormon Church teaches that all humans, angels and demons are essentially of the same race—spirit children of God. Jesus was the firstborn spirit.[77] Satan was another spirit born early in the preexistence.[78] Therefore, in Mormon doctrine, Jesus and Satan are literally brothers.[79] In fact, they are also literally brothers with all of mankind. The deeper implication of this teaching is that Jesus was a creation of God.[80] A war broke out in heaven over whether Jesus or Satan had better plans for the redemption of mankind.[81] Satan and those who sided with him were cast out of heaven, left to become demons.[82] Jesus and those who followed Him in heaven were all sent to earth to become human.

One of the most controversial of Mormon doctrines has always been that of how Jesus' physical body on earth was sired. LDS teachings on the subject are abundantly clear that Jesus was borne of a physical, sexual union between God the Father and the virgin Mary.[83] Otherwise, LDS leaders assert, Jesus would have been illegitimate.[84] Mormon writers have taught that here on earth Jesus was contaminated with a fallen nature,[85] was married, was a polygamist,[86] and fathered children.[87]

Regarding salvation, LDS leaders have consistently taught that Jesus did not pay for sin on the cross, but did so in the Garden of Gethsemane.[88] His atonement did not pay for all the sins of mankind,[89] but actually only provided for the resurrection of all. This is what they mean by "saved by grace"[90]—that resurrection is a gift, but salvation beyond that must be earned. Because of this interpretation, they teach that Jesus Christ did not do the greatest work for mankind. This was done by Joseph Smith, instead.[91]

The Biblical Jesus

The Bible's clear teachings about Jesus are very different (see the chart contrasting the Mormon Jesus and the Biblical Jesus at the end of this chapter). The Jesus of the Bible was never created, but was always God—eternal and uncreated.[92] Jesus and Satan were not brothers, but Satan was, in fact, an angelic being created by Jesus.[93]

Here on earth, Jesus' body was created by the overshadowing of the Holy Ghost,[94] not by a sexual union between Mary and God the Father. Jesus was sinless.[95] He was never married[96] and never fathered children.[97]

The blood of Jesus shed on the cross accomplished salvation.[98] It was not by any suffering in Gethsemane. And while His blood was sufficient to pay for all the sins of mankind,[99] it is efficacious only for those who believe in Him,[100] and no man ever has done, nor ever will do, anything for mankind that even comes close to the work that Jesus accomplished.[101]

The Holy Ghost

The third member of the Godhead in LDS theology is the Holy Ghost. Not much is known about Him in the Mormon Church, for the simple fact that, according to the leadership, it has not been revealed to them.[102] They do believe that He is a Personage of Spirit,[103] but also that He can be in only one place at one time.[104] His influence, however, can be felt everywhere.[105] His main mission is to testify about Christ, and to be the Father's messenger.[106] LDS leaders are emphatic that the Holy Ghost had no part in the physical birth of Jesus,[107] even though the *Book of Mormon* clearly teaches that "he [Jesus] shall be born of Mary ... she being a virgin ... who shall be overshadowed and **conceive by the power of the Holy Ghost**, and bring forth a son, yea, even the Son of God."[108]

The Gift of the Holy Ghost

The gift of the Holy Ghost is given to Mormons only through the laying on of hands. This gift means nothing more to them than that a person has the right to fellowship with the Holy Ghost—He does not always dwell with a person continually.[109] While people outside the Mormon Church can have moments of inspiration given by the Holy Ghost, only Mormon members have the right to regular instruction from this Personage.[110]

Mormonism has taught that in order to become a God, a person must have a body of flesh and bone.[111] This leads to the inevitable question, how did the Holy Ghost get to be a God without a physical body? When this question is asked, Mormon members are usually rebuked and told to keep their minds on matters of their own salvation and avoid fruitless speculation.[112] Basically, they are not given an answer, but are made to feel guilty for having posed a contradictory question.

Holy Ghost vs. Holy Spirit

In the Mormon Church, a distinction is made between the Holy Ghost and the Holy Spirit. This separation of the two is probably a result of the LDS Church using the *King James Version* of the Bible, which employs both terms.[113] This has apparently led their leadership to conclude that the Holy Ghost is a Personage and the Holy Spirit is a force of action.

While the Holy Ghost is a Personage of Spirit and a third member of the LDS Godhead,[114] the Holy Spirit is an impersonal, spirit-like influence that proceeds forth from the Father and the Son,[115] to be the "agency by means of which God governs and controls in all things...."[116] The Holy Spirit fills the immensity of space, thereby giving the impression that God is omnipresent, though, in fact, they believe that God is actually limited to one place at one time.[117]

Early Mormon Parley P. Pratt once described the Holy Spirit not as an actual spirit entity, but as some form of fluid material:

> The purest, most refined and subtle of all these substances, and **the one least understood, or even recognized,** by the less informed among mankind, **is that substance called the Holy Spirit**.... There is **a divine substance, fluid or essence, called Spirit**, widely diffused among these eternal elements.... This divine element, or Spirit, is **the immediate, active or controlling agent** in all holy miraculous powers.[118]

To complicate matters further, Bruce McConkie identified the "Spirit of the Lord" as meaning **three different things:** (1) the spirit body of Jesus Christ before He came to earth as a human, (2) the Spirit of Christ and God, which is the impersonal influence by which God controls everything, and (3) a synonym for the Holy Ghost, the third member of the Godhead.[119] It is no wonder, then, that no LDS authority has been able to define specifically and completely what is meant by these terms.

The Biblical Holy Ghost

In the Bible, the Holy Ghost (referred to as the Holy Spirit in newer translations) is fully God along with the Father and the Son. He is a personal spirit entity, but is no less God than the Father or

Jesus Christ. Unlike the LDS concept of the Holy Spirit, the Bible teaches that He is omnipresent,[120] omniscient,[121] omnipotent,[122] and eternal.[123] He even assisted in the work of creation.[124]

In the work of redemption, the Holy Spirit is greatly involved. It was the Holy Spirit who overshadowed Mary before the birth of Jesus.[125] He also anointed Jesus at His baptism and bestowed power on Him to prepare for His earthly ministry.[126] He was sent from God to be a teacher and a comforter to men,[127] though not necessarily through the laying on of hands.[128] The Holy Spirit inspired Scripture, thus bringing the special revelation of God and the message of redemption to mankind.[129]

The Holy Spirit testifies of Christ and forms and increases the Church. He regenerates, sanctifies, and dwells inside believers as the principle of new life.[130] He gives gifts of ministry to believers,[131] and brings forth obvious fruits of His presence in them.[132] He teaches and guides the Church, protects it from error and prepares it for its eternal destiny.[133]

Conclusion

On all three Persons of the Godhead (God the Father, Jesus Christ and the Holy Spirit), it is evident that the Mormon teachings are in conflict with those of the Bible. As shown, there are many places where the LDS teachings conflict even with each other. Such is not the case with the Biblical teachings. All Scriptures about God are in perfect harmony, revealing awesome and consistent truths about our God, our Savior, our Comforter.

The Mormon God and the Biblical God Contrasted

While all of these stated LDS teachings are historically accurate, later Church leaders have contradicted some of them. Teachings that are currently different have been indicated.

The Mormon God	The Biblical God
1. There is a plurality of Gods.	1. There is only one God.
2. God the Father is one of three Gods who deal primarily with this earth – the other two Gods being Jesus Christ and the Holy Ghost.	2. The Godhead is a unity of three beings–God the Father, Jesus Christ and the Holy Spirit—but still only one God.
3. God was not always God, but worked his way up to that position.	3. God was God from all eternity
4. God was once a man who lived on another planet.	4. God was never a man. He has life in Himself, not from any other source.
5. God lived on an earth, was a sinner, and had to earn salvation from his God.	5. God has always been sinless and perfect.
6. God has a glorified, physical body of flesh and bones.	6. God is a Spirit.
7. God is married, and is a polygamist.	7. There is no mention of God being married.
8. God has both physical children (from his former human life) and spiritual children (who he used to populate our earth).	8. Those who believe in Jesus Christ are called the children (or sons) of God.
9. God could not create everything from nothing, but could only organize existing matter into a universe.	9. God created everything from nothing, merely speaking the earth into existence.

10. God is helpless to interfere with the free will of man.	10. God is fully in control of all events.
11. God is subject to the laws and principles of nature, and is unable to contradict them.	11. God set the laws of nature, and is able to contradict them at will.
12. God is limited in knowledge, and continues to learn new truths as time goes on. **The current teaching is that God is omniscient.**	12. God is omniscient.
13. God changes how he deals with man as the times on earth change.	13. God saves all men the same way in all eras, providing salvation by grace through faith.
14. Adam, the first man on this earth, was God. ** **The current teaching is that Adam is a type of god to us, but not our God.**	14. Adam was a creation of God.
15. One of God's wives is his own daughter – Mary - and their union brought about the earthly body of Jesus Christ.	15. God did not commit incest. The Holy Spirit overshadowed Mary to create the earthly body of Jesus Christ.
16. God is only able to be in one place at one time.	16. God is omnipresent.
17. God has shown himself to certain mortal men whenever He has seen fit.	17. God has never been seen by man at any time.
18. God's entire purpose is to make more Gods out of human beings.	18. God's purpose in redemption is to demonstrate His grace to man.

References for the above:

From LDS Authorized Materials	From the Bible
1. *History of the Church*, 6:306, 474-76; *Discourses of Brigham Young*, 51, 388; *Abraham* 4:1; *The Seer*, 1:37; *Mormon Doctrine*, 321, 576-77; *Key to the Science of Theology*, 41.	1. Deuteronomy 4:35, 39; 6:4; Nehemiah 9:6; Psalm 86:10; Isaiah 43:10; 45:5-6; 46:9; John 17:3; Ephesians 4:4-6; 1 Timothy 2:5.
2. *History of the Church*, 6:474; *Mormon Doctrine*, 317, 319.	2. John 10:27-30; Romans 9:5; 2 Corinthians 13:14; Ephesians 4:1-6; 1 Timothy 3:16.
3. *History of the Church*, 6:305; *The Gospel Through the Ages*, 114-15; *Journal of Discourses*, 1:123; 6:3.	3. Genesis 21:33; Psalm 90:2; 93:2; Isaiah 41:4; Habakkuk 1:12; Romans 16:26.
4. *The Gospel Through the Ages*, 104-7; *Journal of Discourses*, 1:123; 6:3; *The Articles of Faith*, 430.	4. Numbers 23:19; Deuteronomy 30:20; Job 9:32; 10:12; 33:4; Psalm 36:9; Isaiah 40:18; John 5:26.
5. *Journal of Discourses*, 1:123; 6:3; *The Articles of Faith*, 430.	5. 1 Samuel 2:2; Isaiah 40:18; Matthew 5:48; 1 Timothy 1:17; 1 John 1:5.
6. *Doctrine and Covenants* 130:22; *Key to the Science of Theology*, 44; *The Articles of Faith*, 42; *Mormon Doctrine*, 319; *Journal of Discourses*, 6:3.	6. Genesis 1:2; 1 Kings 8:27; John 4:24; Colossians 1:15; 1 Timothy 1:17; 6:16; 1 John 4:12.

7. *Joseph Smith: the Mormon Prophet*, 69; *The Seer*, 38-39, 172; *Mormon Doctrine*, 516-17; *Gospel Principles*, 11.

8. *The Seer*, 38-39; *Mormon Doctrine*, 742, 745, 751.

9. *Doctrine and Covenants* 93:33; *History of the Church*, 3:387; 6:308-9; *Encyclopedia of Mormonism*, 2:868-69; *Teachings of the Prophet Joseph Smith*, 350-52.

10. *Doctrine and Covenants* 93:30-31; 98:8; *Mormon Doctrine*, 26-28; 2 Nephi 2:27; 10:23; Helaman 14:31.

11. *Journal of Discourses*, 13:140-41; *Jesus the Christ*, 148; *Doctrine and Covenants* 88:36-39; *Mormon Doctrine*, 433; *Key to the Science of Theology*, 45.

12. *Journal of Discourses*, 1:93; 6:120; 11:286. **Current contradictory teachings**: *Doctrines of Salvation*, 1:7-8; 2:35.

7. The Bible says nothing of God being married. Biblical human marriage is to be monogamy: Genesis 2:24; Matthew 19:5-6; 1 Timothy 3:2; Titus 1:6.

8. John 1:12-13; Romans 8:14-17; 9:8; Galatians 3:26; Hebrews 2:11-13; 1 John 3:1.

9. Genesis 1:1-25; Job Chs. 38-39; Psalm 33:6, 9; 148:5-6; Acts 17:24-28; Romans 4:17; Hebrews 11:3.

10. Psalm 115:3; Jeremiah 32:17, 27; Matthew 3:9; 19:26; Luke 1:37; Romans 1:20; 8:28-39; 9:16-18; Ephesians 1:11.

11. Genesis 18:14; Exodus Ch. 14; 1 Kings Ch. 17; Job 42:2; Psalm 104; Isaiah 38:5-8; Jeremiah 32:17; Matthew Ch. 14; Luke 1:37.

12. 1 Samuel 23:10-13; Psalm 139:1-4; 147:5; Isaiah 29:15-16; 40:27-28; 42:9; Matthew 10:29-30; Hebrews 4:13.

13. Ensign (November 1989), 15-16; *Conference Report* (October 1921), 17; *Mormon Doctrine*, 200-2; 577-78.

14. *History of the Church*, 3:386-87; *Journal of Discourses*, 1:50-51; 4:1; *Millenial Star*, 17:195. **Current contradictory teachings**: *Mormon Doctrine*, 18; *Deseret News – Church Section* (9 October 1976).

15. *Journal of Discourses*, 1:50; 4:218; 8:115; 11:268; *Doctrines of Salvation*, 1:18; *The Seer*, 158; *Mormon Doctrine*, 547.

16. *Evidences and Reconciliations*, 76-77; *Journal of Discourses*, 6:345; *The Articles of Faith*, 42-43; *Mormon Doctrine*, 359.

17. *Doctrinal New Testament Commentary*, 3:399; Joseph Smith – History 1:17-19; *Answers to Gospel Questions*, 2:161-63; *Doctrine and Covenants* 88:68; 93:1; *Inspired Version* of 1 John 1:19; 4:12.

13. Genesis 15:6; Habakkuk 2:4; Romans 1:17; 2:1-16; 3:21-22; 4:4-5, 13, 22-25; 5:1; 10:9-13; Galatians 3:6-9; Hebrews Ch. 11.

14. Genesis 1:26-27; 2:7; 5:1-2; Luke 3:38; Romans 5:14; 1 Timothy 2:13.

15. Leviticus 18:6; Isaiah 7:14; Matthew 1:18, 20; Luke 1:35.

16. 1 Kings 8:27; Psalm 139:7-10; Isaiah 66:1; Jeremiah 23:23-24; Acts 7:48-50; 17:27-28; Revelation 3:20.

17. Exodus 33:20-23; John 1:18; 6:46; 1 Timothy 1:17; 6:16; 1 John 4:12.

18. Moses 1:38-39; *Journal of Discourses*, 3:93; *Teachings of Spencer W. Kimball*, 25; *The Miracle of Forgiveness*, 2.	18. Romans 9:22-24; 2 Corinthians 4:13-15; Ephesians 1:4-14; 2:4-10.

The Mormon Jesus and the Biblical Jesus Contrasted

While all of these stated LDS teachings are historically accurate, some later Church leaders may have contradicted some of them on occasion.

The Mormon Jesus	The Biblical Jesus
1. Jesus was the first-born spirit child of God the Father and God the Mother. He is, thus, a creation of God.	1. Jesus was not a creation of God, but was instead God from all eternity, uncreated. Rather than being a creation of God, He was the very Creator of all things.
2. Jesus and Satan are literal brothers to each other, and to the rest of mankind.	2. Jesus created the angel who became Satan and the rest of us. We are not brothers and sisters literally with Jesus or Satan.
3. Jesus was chosen to be savior of the world because of His birthright as the first child in the family of God.	3. Jesus freely gave Himself up as a ransom for our sins.
4. Jesus only **helped** create the earth under God's direction. Adam and others helped Him to do this.	4. In the Bible, creation is attributed to all three Persons of the Godhead: Father, Son and Holy Spirit. The New Testament emphasizes Christ's priority and His key role as creator and sustainer.

5. Jesus did not create everything out of nothing. He only organized the available materials into an earth and universe.	5. Jesus created all there is from nothing.
6. Jesus was not God before His earth life. He is only called the God of the Old Testament because He was acting under the direction of God.	6. Jesus was always God, even while on earth. Jesus took references to God, His attributes and works from the Old Testament and applied them to Himself.
7. Jesus was born in Jerusalem.	7. Jesus was born in Bethlehem.
8. Jesus was born out of a physical sexual relationship between God the Father and Mary. As such, it was not a miraculous birth.	8. Jesus was conceived by the Holy Spirit overshadowing Mary and causing her to conceive supernaturally.
9. There was no difference between Jesus Christ and all other men.	9. Jesus Christ was completely different from other men because of Who He is.
10. Jesus was contaminated with a fallen nature.	10. Jesus had a sinless nature.
11. Jesus did not always know He was the Son of God. He had to learn a little at a time and eventually came to this knowledge.	11. Jesus was fully aware of who He was even while a young child.
12. Jesus did no miracles on the earth.	12. Jesus performed many miracles as proof that He was God.
13. Jesus was married, and also a polygamist.	13. Jesus was never married.

14. Jesus had children while on the earth.	14. Jesus did not have any children.
15. Jesus atoned for sin in the Garden of Gethsemane, **not** on the cross.	15. Jesus atoned for sin on the cross.
16. In addition to working out the salvation of mankind on God's behalf, Jesus was working to attain His own salvation.	16. Jesus atoned for the sins of men, but had no sins of His own. Therefore He did not need salvation for Himself.
17. Jesus' atonement did not pay for all sins.	17. Jesus' atonement was fully sufficient for all sins.
18. Jesus was crucified because He was a polygamist.	18. Jesus was crucified as it was prophesied, because He performed miracles on the Sabbath, and because He claimed to be the Messiah and the Son of God—making Himself equal with God.
19. Jesus did not receive the "fullness" of God until after the resurrection.	19. Jesus always possessed the "fullness" of God, even while He was on earth in a physical body.
20. Jesus will not be alone in judging men. He will have help from Joseph Smith, Jr.	20. Jesus will judge all inhabitants of the earth.
21. Jesus did not do the greatest work for mankind. John the Baptist and Joseph Smith, Jr. both did greater works.	21. Jesus has done more for man than anyone else. **No other human** has or can contribute to man's salvation.

References for the above:

From LDS Authorized Materials	From the Bible
1. *Journal of Discourses*, 18:290; *Doctrine and Covenants* 76:23-24; 93:21-23; *Gospel Principles*, 11.	1. John 1:1-3, 14; 8:58; 1 Corinthians 8:6; Ephesians 3:9; Colossians 1:16-18; Hebrews 1:2.
2. *Journal of Discourses*, 13:282; *Joseph Smith – An American Prophet*, 308, 341; *Mormon Doctrine*, 750-51.	2. Job 1:6; Psalm 148; Isaiah 14:12-23; Ezekiel 28:11-19; John 1:1-3; Colossians 1:16-18; Revelation 12:9.
3. *Journal of Discourses*, 18:290.	3. Matthew 20:28; John 1:4; 3:14-17; 10:11, 15-18; Galatians 1:3-4; 2:20; Ephesians 5:2; Hebrews 1:1-3; 12:1-2; 1 Peter 2:21-24; 1 John 3:16.
4. *Doctrines of Salvation*, 1:74; *Pearl of Great Price*, Abraham 4:1; LDS Temple Ceremony (creation of the first day).	4. God (Genesis 1:1); Son (John 1:1); Holy Spirit (Genesis 1:2). New Testament references to Jesus (John 1:1-3; 1 Corinthians 8:6; Colossians 1:16-17; Hebrews 1:1-3).
5. *Doctrine and Covenants* 93:33; *Doctrines of Salvation*, 1:74; *Mormon Doctrine*, 169; *Journal of Discourses*, 6:5.	5. John 1:3; Hebrews 1:1-3; 11:3.

6. *Doctrines of Salvation*, 1:30; *Doctrine and Covenants* 76; *Gospel Principles*, 27-28; *Jesus the Christ*, 33.

6. Isaiah 7:14; 9:6; John 1:1-3; 10:30-33; Colossians 1:19, 2:9. Attributes: Exodus 3:14 (cf. John 8:58); Matthew 21:15-16 (cf. Psalm 8:1-2); Mark 13:31; Luke 21:33 (cf. Psalm 119:89; Isaiah 40:8); Luke 10:19 (cf. Psalm 91:13); Luke 19:10 (cf. Ezekiel 34:11-12, 16); John 10:11, 14 (cf. Genesis 48:15; Psalm 23).

7. *Book of Mormon*, Alma 7:9-10

7. Micah 5:2; Matthew 2:1, 5, 6, 8, 16; Luke 2:4, 15; John 7:42.

8. *Journal of Discourses*, 1:50; 3:319; 8:115, 211; *Doctrines of Salvation*, 1:18; *Mormon Doctrine*, 547; *Jesus the Christ*, 81.

8. Isaiah 7:14; Matthew 1:18-25; Luke 1:27, 34-35.

9. *Journal of Discourses*, 4:218; *Mormon Doctrine*, 257.

9. Man: Genesis 6:5; 1 Kings 8:46; Romans 3:23; 1 John 1:8. Contrast these with Jesus: 2 Corinthians 5:21; Philippians 2:5-12; Hebrews Chs.1-2; 4:15; 7:24-28; 1 Peter 2:22; 1 John 3:5.

10. *Journal of Discourses*, 6:95-96; *Doctrinal New Testament Commentary*, 3:238; *Mormon Doctrine*, 257. **Elsewhere, McConkie contradicts this**: *Mormon Doctrine*, 736.

10. 2 Corinthians 5:21; Hebrews 4:15; 7:26; 1 Peter 2:22; 1 John 3:5.

11. *Doctrines of Salvation*, 1:32; *Doctrine and Covenants* 93:11-14.	11. Luke 2:40, 47, 49.
12. *Journal of Discourses*, 13:140-41; *Jesus the Christ*, 80, 148.	12. John 3:1-2. See these examples: Matthew 8:23-27; 9:27-35; 12:9-13, 22; 14:22-33; Mark 1:40-45; 4:35-41; 5:35-42; 8:22-26; Luke 5:4-7; 7:11-17; 8:22-25; 17:11-19; 18:35-43; John 2:1-11; 5:1-9; 9:1-41; 11:1-46; 21:5-6, 10-11.
13. *Journal of Discourses*, 1:345-46; 2:82, 210; 4:259-60; *The Seer*, 172.	13. There is no Biblical record or inference that Jesus ever married. There is only a reference about the future marriage of Christ to His Church.
14. *Journal of Discourses*, 2:80-82, 210; *The Seer*, 172.	14. There is no Biblical record of Jesus having fathered children.
15. *Jesus the Christ*, 613-14; *Doctrine and Covenants* 19:16-18; *Gospel Principles* (1992), 73; *Conference Report* (Oct. 1947), 147-48; *Come Unto Christ* (1988), 66.	15. Isaiah Ch. 53; 1 Corinthians 1:18; Ephesians 2:14-16; Colossians 1:19-22; Hebrews 9:28; 10:10; 1 Peter 2:24.
16. *Mormon Doctrine*, 257; *Doctrines of Salvation*, 1:32; *Doctrinal New Testament Commentary*, 3:238.	16. 2 Corinthians 5:21; 1 Thessalonians 5:9-10; Titus 2:14; Hebrews 2:10; 4:15; 7:24-27; 1 Peter 2:21-24; 3:18; 1 John 3:5.

17. *Doctrines of Salvation*, 1:133-35; *Mormon Doctrine*, 520; *Journal of Discourses*, 3:247; 4:219-20; *LDS Bible Dictionary* - Atonement.	17. Mark 3:28-29; 1 Corinthians 6:9-11; Titus 2:14; Hebrews 9:24-28; 1 John 1:7-9; 2:1-2.
18. *Journal of Discourses*, 1:346.	18. Matthew 26:63-64, 68; 27:11, 17, 22, 37; Mark 14:61-64; John 5:16-18; 8:52-58; Acts 2:22-24.
19. *Doctrines of Salvation*, 1:33.	19. Matthew 11:27; John 1:14-16; Colossians 1:19-20; 2:3, 9-10.
20. *Journal of Discourses*, 7:289; 9:312; *Gospel Truth*, 1:255; *Come Unto Christ* (1988), 142.	20. Isaiah 33:22; John 5:21-23; Acts 10:42; 17:30-31; Romans 2:16; 14:10; 2 Corinthians 5:10-11; 2 Timothy 4:1; Revelation Ch. 5; 22:12-13.
21. *History of the Church*, 5:258, (see also HC Index, 63, 182), 6:408-09. An unauthorized source also shows this to be the case: *Salt Lake Tribune* (2 September 1989—Dr. Lee Letter to the First Presidency of the LDS Church).	21. John 3:14-18, 36; 14:6; Acts 4:12; 10:43; Romans 5:12-21; 6:23; Philippians 2:5-12; 1 Timothy 2:5-6; 1 John 5:11-12; Revelation Ch. 5.

Chapter 11
The Mormon Priesthood

Joseph Smith's Claim –
All men are liars who say they are of the true Church without the revelations of Jesus Christ and the Priesthood of Melchizedek, which is after the order of the Son of God.... they do it on their own responsibility, without authority from God....
– *Teachings of the Prophet Joseph Smith*, 375-76

Priesthood Restored, or Usurped?

Another Mormon claim that must be examined for its validity is that only those who hold the priesthood in their Church have the authority to act on behalf of God. LDS Apostle John Widtsoe writes, "An **authoritative Priesthood forms the foundation** of the Church of Christ. This is made clear in ancient and modern revelation."[1] Gordon Hinckley asserts, "**Without the priesthood** there might be the form of a church, but **not the true substance**."[2] Ezra Taft Benson adds, "The greatest power in this world is the power presented **in this priesthood**. That is the power that brought this earth into existence. No greater honor or blessing can come to man than the authority to act in the name of God."[3]

Aaronic and Melchizedek Priesthood

Mormons are certainly familiar with the concept and history of the LDS priesthood, but for those who are not, we give a brief review. On 15 May 1829, John the Baptist is said to have appeared and conferred the Aaronic priesthood on Joseph Smith and Oliver Cowdery by the laying on of hands, thus giving them authority to administer certain ordinances of the gospel among men. Later, the

Apostles Peter, James and John appeared and conferred on them a higher priesthood—the Melchizedek priesthood.[4] With both of these priesthoods restored to the earth, those who held them would be able to officiate the affairs of God's kingdom among men with full authority. Mormons believe that this restoration of the priesthood is one of the most significant events of history.

Before its restoration, Mormons believe that no one on earth had the authority to act on behalf of God, or to administer ordinances such as baptism, communion and even marriage. On 16 May 2004, a special Church broadcast commemorated the 175th anniversary of the restoration of the priesthood, and all male members over the age of 12 were encouraged to watch.[5]

Joseph Smith taught that the Melchizedek priesthood includes the Aaronic. In fact, he taught that there is really only one priesthood (the Melchizedek) which is divided into two levels. He states, "All Priesthood is Melchizedek, but there are different portions or degrees of it."[6] *Doctrine and Covenants* 107:5 teaches that "all other authorities or offices in the church are appendages to this [Melchizedek] priesthood." Bruce McConkie explains, "As there is only one God and one power of God, it follows that there is only one priesthood, the eternal priesthood.... It is, however, proper and common to speak of the two great orders of priesthood as priesthoods; hence, the revealed statement, 'There are, in the church, two priesthoods, namely, the Melchizedek and Aaronic....'"[7] Mormons believe that this priesthood is God's authority that empowers one properly ordained to validly administer the ordinances of the gospel. Without this LDS priesthood, nothing done in the name of the Lord is effectual.

No Other Church Has Authority

Spencer Kimball has stated, "The priesthood is the power and authority of God delegated to man on earth to act in all things pertaining to the salvation of men. It is the means whereby the Lord acts through men to save souls. Without this priesthood power, men are lost.... **There is no priesthood anywhere else today than in this restored [LDS] Church.**"[8] James Talmage writes, "**We claim** that the authority to administer in the name of God **is operative in The Church of Jesus Christ of Latter-day Saints** today; and that this power or commission was conferred upon the first officers of the Church by ordination under the hands of those who had held the same power in earlier dispensations."[9]

Mormonism teaches that the presence or absence of this priesthood determines whether a church is of God or not. Ezra Taft Benson writes, "One of the distinguishing features and **a very important feature of the true Church of Christ is its priesthood**, the authority of God."[10] Where is this priesthood? Only in the Mormon Church, according to Gordon Hinckley, who said, "The priesthood is **here**. It has been conferred upon **us**. We act in that authority. We speak as sons of God in the name of Jesus Christ and as holders of this divinely given endowment."[11] Based on this requirement, the LDS Church teaches that it is the only true Church while all other churches are false.[12]

Mormonism teaches that to function without this priesthood authority is a grievous sin in God's sight. Kimball remarks, "**Presumptuous and blasphemous are they** who purport to baptize, bless, marry, or perform other sacraments in the name of the Lord while in fact lacking his specific authorization."[13] In support of their position, Mormons often quote Hebrews 5:4, "And no man taketh this honour unto himself, but he that is called of God, as was Aaron." Aaron, they explain, received this priesthood from Moses by the laying on of hands—a Mormon requirement for transmission of the priesthood.[14]

Obviously, the doctrine of the restored priesthood is an important one. Refutation of Mormon claims regarding it **would undercut the entire basis of authority in their Church**. Indeed, a close look at these claims reveals some very serious problems with their restored priesthood doctrine.

Apostasy Not Complete

As discussed in Chapter 3, the Mormon Church teaches that because of the **complete apostasy** of the primitive church, **the true priesthood was lost from the earth**. In order to establish the true

Church again, it became necessary for God to restore His priesthood first. However, as already demonstrated, there was not a complete apostasy, making this claim without foundation. That leads, then, to questioning the origin of the LDS priesthood.

Origin of LDS Priesthood

As mentioned, Mormons believe that there cannot be a true Church of Jesus Christ without the priesthood. Widtsoe writes, "The Church itself **is a product of the Priesthood.** Therefore, whenever the Church of Christ is upon earth the Priesthood is a part of it. The Church is the instrument through which Priesthood operates."[15] The Mormon priesthood, then, had to have been restored **first** in order for the true Church to be organized. Since the LDS Church was officially organized on 6 April 1830, the priesthood restoration **must** pre-date this event.

Unknown Priesthood and Angelic Ordinations

Significantly, no Mormons seem to have known about the priesthood until several years **after** the Church had already been established. David Whitmer was one of the three witnesses to the *Book of Mormon,* and one of the first converts to Joseph Smith's teachings. He gave an interview in 1885 in which he said, "**I never heard** that an Angel had ordained Joseph and Oliver to the Aaronic Priesthood **until the year 1834[,] [183]5. or [183]6—in Ohio**.... I do not believe that John the Baptist ever ordained Joseph and Oliver as stated and believed by some."[16]

Another early LDS convert, William E. McLellin explained, "I joined the church in 1831. For years **I never heard of John the Baptist ordaining** Joseph and Oliver. **I heard not of James, Peter, and John** doing so."[17] In 1870, he added, "I heard Joseph tell his experience of his ordination and the organization of the church, probably, more than twenty times, to persons who, near the rise of the church, wished to know and hear about it. **I never heard of** Moroni, **John, or Peter, James and John**."[18] Again in 1872 he repeated that "as to the story of John, the Baptist ordaining Joseph and Oliver on the day they were baptized; **I never heard of it in the church for years, altho I carefully noticed things that were said.**"[19]

In 1887, Whitmer published *An Address To All Believers In Christ*, which often is cited by Mormons to prove that he never denied his testimony of the *Book of Mormon*. In this publication, Whitmer states that the "matter of the **two orders of priesthood** in the Church of Christ,[20] and lineal priesthood of the old law being in the church, **all originated in the mind of Sydney Rigdon.**"[21] He further stated that the teachings concerning high priests and priesthood were first introduced into the church "almost **two years**" after its beginning—after about two thousand people had become members.[22] This information is verified by many early LDS writings.[23] In fact, LDS writer Grant Palmer admits, "**In none of these** scriptural writings[24] do we find other-worldly beings laying hands upon mortals to bestow priesthood authority.... Accounts of **angelic ordinations from John the Baptist and Peter, James, and John are in none** of the journals, diaries, letters, or printed matter **until the mid-1830s.**"[25]

In October 1834, Oliver Cowdery, with Joseph Smith's assistance, began a series of articles on the rise of the Church that was published in the *Messenger and Advocate*. This series promised accuracy and detailed coverage concerning the early history of the Church. But it left out many important details of the restoration, **including these angelic ordinations to the priesthood,** as though they were not even known at the time. In "A Revelation on Church Government" that Smith received in April 1830, there was no mention of either the Aaronic or Melchizedek priesthoods.[26] Some time later, Smith went back and added three verses to the revelation, one of which mentions a "high priesthood."[27] LaMar Petersen concludes, "There seems to be **no support** for the historicity of the Restoration of the Priesthood in journals, diaries, letters, nor printed matter **prior to October, 1834.**"[28]

Historian D. Michael Quinn informs us that

> according to current tradition, both the Aaronic and Melchizedek priesthoods functioned in the church after the spring of 1829.... A closer look at contemporary records

indicates that men were first ordained to the higher priesthood **over a year after the church's founding. No mention of angelic ordinations can be found** in original documents **until 1834-35.**[29]

When the *Book of Commandments* was printed in 1833, there was no mention of these angelic ordinations. No mention was made of John the Baptist ordaining either man to the Aaronic priesthood, and no mention of Peter, James and John ordaining them to the Melchizedek priesthood. Petersen writes, "The important details that are missing from the 'full history' of 1834 are likewise missing from the *Book of Commandments* in 1833. The student would expect to find all the particulars of the [priesthood] Restoration in this first treasured set of 65 revelations ... but **they are conspicuously absent.**"[30] Dan Vogel agrees that mention of these angelic visitations did not begin until well after Joseph Smith organized the Church in 1830. He writes, "**In 1834 Smith and Cowdery began** making public announcements that angelic ordination to the "Aaronic priesthood" had preceded their baptisms.... **In the mid-1830s Smith and Cowdery also began claiming** that the ancient apostles Peter, James, and John had appeared soon after their baptisms and ordained them to the Melchizedek priesthood."[31]

The first time that any mention of angelic messengers is made was on 12 February 1834 at a meeting of the Kirtland High Council. The "Minute Book" records the following information: "Bro. Joseph then rose and said: I shall now endeavor to set forth before this council, the dignity of the office **which has been conferred upon me by the ministering of the Angel of God**, by his own will and by the voice of this Church."[32] It was not long before Oliver Cowdery, who was present at the "restoration" of the priesthoods, also started telling about angels. In 1835, he said:

> [Joseph Smith] **was ordained by the angel** John, unto the lesser or Aaronic priesthood, in company with myself.... we repaired to the woods ... and called upon the name of the Lord, and he answered us out of the heavens, and while we were in the heavenly vision **the angel came down** and

bestowed upon us this priesthood;... **After this we received the high and holy priesthood**, but an account of this will be given elsewhere, or in another place.[33]

In spite of the mention of angelic visitations, Cowdery never named all three of the visitors in his ordination to the Melchizedek priesthood until 1849.[34]

Whitmer charged that the revelations concerning the priesthood and other Church matters had been added to or changed after their original publication in the *Book of Commandments* in 1833.[35] He was right, as a comparison of these revelations with those published subsequently in the 1835 *Doctrine and Covenants* reveals.[36] Not only was the information (found in *Doctrine and Covenants* Section 27) referring to John the Baptist and Peter, James and John **missing** from the *Book of Commandments*, **but it was also missing** from the same revelation published in 1833 in *The Evening and Morning Star*.[37] Additionally, **the only known manuscript copy of the revelation makes no reference to either LDS priesthood**.[38]

John the Baptist

John the Baptist is mentioned in two revelations as having ordained Joseph Smith and Oliver Cowdery to the Aaronic priesthood. Currently they are published as Sections 13 and 27 in the *Doctrine and Covenants*. But Section 13 was never originally part of the *Book of Commandments*. It was added in 1876—32 years after Joseph Smith's death. Section 27 was originally Chapter XXVIII when published in the *Book of Commandments*, and contained only seven verses, comprising 193 words. Currently, this same revelation contains 18 verses, comprising 650 words. More than 450 words have been added. The **references to John the Baptist ordaining Joseph and Oliver are among the added words**.

Additionally, Oliver Cowdery had written a paper in 1829 entitled "A commandment from God" (or "Articles of the Church"), in which he states that his authority for baptism was given to him by "Jesus Christ." There was not a single mention or allusion to John the Baptist.[39] Based upon this evidence, Vogel concludes,

"This suggests that the event [John the Baptist's visitation on 15 May 1829] was either **a later invention or a reinterpretation** of an earlier vision."[40]

Peter, James and John

The *History of the Church* records that Joseph Smith and Oliver Cowdery were anxious to receive the high priesthood, and prayed to receive it. Smith writes that "the word of the Lord came unto us in the chamber, commanding us that I should ordain Oliver Cowdery to be an Elder in the Church of Jesus Christ; and that he also should ordain me to the same office...."[41] They were told to delay the ordination, however, until a vote could be had among the Church approving the decision. No mention is made of any kind of angelic ordinations. It was not even required that they receive the priesthood from anyone else; they were just to ordain each other.

Peter, James and John are mentioned ordaining Joseph and Oliver to the Melchizedek priesthood in only one place—*Doctrine and Covenants* 27:12, the same revelation that had more than 450 words added to it. The reference to Peter, James and John **was among the added words**. This is a clear indication of **"retrospective changes** made in the public record to create a story of logical and progressive development."[42]

Another significant problem is that there is apparently no original account of the restoration of the Melchizedek priesthood. LDS scholar Brian Q. Cannon writes,

> The written record regarding the restoration of the Melchizedek Priesthood is less complete. Although repeatedly testifying that Peter, James and John had appeared to them and restored this high priesthood authority ... neither Joseph Smith nor Oliver Cowdery specified the date of that restoration or reported the words used by Peter in ordaining them to this priesthood....[43]

Mormon writer Larry C. Porter agrees, stating that "the day, month, and year designation ... is absent in the case of the

Melchizedek Priesthood. Similarly, knowledge of the attendant circumstances of that restoration is limited."[44]

The original account of the Melchizedek restoration is not just incomplete or limited, but **it is entirely missing**. B. H. Roberts writes that "**there is no definite account of the event** in the history of the Prophet Joseph, **or, for matter of that, in any of our annals**...."[45] John Widtsoe confirms that "**we have not**, unfortunately, **any account** so definite, of the reception by Joseph and Oliver of the Melchizedek Priesthood, as we have the confirmation of the Aaronic Priesthood."[46] Palmer confirms that "**no contemporary narrative exists** for a visitation to Joseph and Oliver by Peter, James and John. In fact, the date, location, ordination prayer, and any other circumstances surrounding this experience **are unknown**."[47]

About 1833, Joseph Knight wrote a history of Mormonism's most important events up to that time. D. Michael Quinn informs us that "Knight's history made **no reference** to either John the Baptist or to Peter, James, and John. **This omission is significant** because Knight was eager to discuss angelic ministrations."[48]

Even Joseph Smith's own family did not know about the restoration of the Melchizedek priesthood. Quinn writes, "Smith's own mother made **no reference** to angelic restoration of authority in an 1831 letter she wrote to her brother about the new church."[49] Joseph Smith III, the son of the founder of Mormonism, admits that

> **there is no historical evidence of such an event. Nor is there any evidence** that Peter, James, and John were present, either when the instruction was given to ordain or when the ordination actually took place.... It is not safe then to write historically that Joseph Smith and Oliver Cowdery **were ever ordained literally** under the hands of Peter, James, and John. He who does so writes recklessly and **without sufficient evidence** upon which to base his conclusion.[50]

Irreconcilable Differences

Many LDS scholars who have studied the event place the ordination within a few weeks of the Aaronic priesthood ordination date.[51]

Probably the closest documented date is found in a brief mention of the event in Oliver B. Huntington's journal. This entry places the Melchizedek ordination on a night after Joseph and Oliver had been on trial in Colesville, New York, defended by attorney John Reid.[52] Joseph Smith places the date of this incarceration in mid-to-late June of 1830.[53] Wesley Walters located the court bill for this trial, which was dated "July 1st 1830."[54] Quinn goes to great lengths to show that this event happened early in July of 1830. If this is really when Joseph and Oliver received this priesthood, then "this would have been the morning of 6 July 1830, exactly three months after the church's organization."[55] This conclusion is corroborated by Franklin D. Richards, who told the Quorum of Twelve Apostles that Peter, James and John gave the Melchizedek priesthood to Joseph Smith at "about the time of his [Smith's] June-July 1830 trials."[56]

That date is several weeks after the Church was organized. But according to LDS sources, Smith could not have legally organized the Church unless he had received this Melchizedek priesthood first. **That creates an irreconcilable problem for the LDS claim of authority.**[57]

Brian Cannon informs us that "**in 1835** the original edition of the Doctrine and Covenants gave **the first precise published account** of the appearance of Peter, James and John to Joseph and Oliver. This edition indicates that the three ancient apostles had 'ordained' and 'confirmed' Joseph and Oliver as 'apostles' and granted them 'the keys of your ministry.'"[58] As pointed out earlier, however, this reference was **added to the original revelation** from the *Book of Commandments*. This later modification gives the entire account the appearance of being sheer invention. These events cannot be considered authentic and reliable when the account of them was deliberately added years afterward. Alterations are also found in revelations concerning the LDS priesthood currently found in *Doctrine and Covenants* Sections 20, 42 and 68.

As already mentioned, Whitmer claimed that Sidney Rigdon had invented the "matter of the two orders of priesthood in the Church of Christ," saying he "explained these things to Brother Joseph...."[59] Other evidence shows that this is highly probable. For instance, the *History of the Church* records that "on the 3rd of June [1831], the Elders from the various parts of the country where they were laboring, came in; and the conference before appointed, convened in Kirtland.... **the authority of the Melchizedek Priesthood was manifested** and conferred **for the first time** upon several of the Elders."[60] George Smith corroborates this account, stating that it was during this meeting that "**the Elders first received** the ordination of the High Priesthood."[61] LDS Elder John Corrill verifies that at this meeting "the Malchisedec [Melchizedek] priesthood was then **for the first time introduced**...."[62] And LaMar Petersen confirms that "historical research in early Mormon documents shows that **the term 'priesthood' was not used until 1831.**"[63]

It is very suspicious that the priesthood was never mentioned or introduced to the leading elders of the Church for so long.

Retrofit Priesthood

Grant Palmer recognizes that

> thus, by degrees, the accounts [of priesthood restoration in Mormonism] became more detailed and more miraculous.... **Details usually become blurred over time; in this case, they multiplied and sharpened**.... The most plausible explanation is that **they were retrofitted** to an 1829-30 time period **to give the impression** that an impressive and unique authority **had existed in the church from the beginning**.[64]

The evidence supports David Whitmer's claim that the LDS teachings about a restored priesthood authority originated well after the founding of the Church, and that they were subsequently added to the early revelations and history. This is certainly a dubious foundation for such sweeping claims to be God's infallible, and only, authority on earth.

Priesthood and the Bible

An understanding of the Bible's teachings regarding this subject gives a decisive answer to the Mormon claim of having a restored

Levitical (or Aaronic) priesthood, and a restored Melchizedek priesthood. A thorough study of Hebrews 7 is vital to correctly interpreting the New Testament teachings regarding them.

Levitical (Aaronic) Priesthood

The Bible records that the Levitical priesthood was given to the tribe of Levi (hence the name) and that only Aaron and his descendants held positions as anointed priests.[65] Numbers 18:7 makes this abundantly clear. Speaking to Aaron,[66] the Lord said, "But only you and your sons may serve as priests in connection with everything at the altar and inside the curtain. I am giving you the service of the priesthood as a gift. **Anyone else who comes near the sanctuary must be put to death**" (*NIV*). No one else can hold the Aaronic priesthood but Aaron and his descendants. All of them were of the tribe of Levi.[67] In the Mormon Church, however, most of the Aaronic priesthood holders are said to be descendants of Ephraim,[68] so on that basis alone they do not qualify to hold this priesthood.

Melchizedek Priesthood

The Aaronic priesthood was also meant to be provisional and temporary. It could not truly accomplish the required cleansing, forgiveness and sanctification of men. It was only a shadow of the cleansing to be done by the Great High Priest—Jesus Christ. Therefore, it was abolished when Christ died on the cross since its purpose had been fulfilled.[69] Consider Hebrews 7:11-16:

> If therefore perfection were by the Levitical Priesthood[70] ... **what further need was there that another priest** [of a different priesthood order] **should arise after the order of Melchisedec**, and not be called after the order of Aaron? For the priesthood [of Aaron] being changed [replaced by Melchizedek], there is made of necessity a change [replacement] also of the law. For he [Christ] of whom these things are spoken pertaineth to another tribe, **of which no man gave attendance at the altar**. For it is evident that our Lord sprang

out of Juda; of which tribe Moses spake nothing concerning priesthood. And it is yet far more evident: for that after the similitude of Melchisedec there ariseth another priest [Christ, of a different priesthood order], **Who is made, not after the law ... but after the power of an endless life.**

The new situation is clear. Jesus Christ, "a priest for ever after the order of Melchisedec,"[71] has by His sacrifice on the cross, "changed" (which means "replaced"[72]) the Aaronic priesthood, establishing in its place His own priesthood "after the order of Melchisedec." No one today can be in the possession of the Aaronic priesthood. Proof of this is found in the fact that there are no examples of Aaronic priests in the New Testament Church. That is a difficult fact to explain away if such a position actually existed. Instead of an order of priests who keep dying off, and who practice an imperfect priesthood, we have Jesus, Who lives forever and has the perfect and permanent priesthood.

Hebrews 7:23-24 reiterates clearly that Jesus Christ stands alone in this new priesthood order. "And they [the Aaronic order] truly were many priests, because they were not suffered [allowed] to continue by reason of death: But this man [Jesus], because he continueth ever, hath an unchangeable priesthood." Verse 24 is particularly damaging to the Mormon position, for it says that Christ's priesthood is "unchangeable." This word, in the original Greek, is *aparabatos*, which means unable to change hands, or "untransferable."[73] *Thayer's Greek-English Lexicon* defines it in this way, "*unchangeable* and therefore not liable to pass to a successor."[74] In *Word Pictures in the New Testament*, Greek Scholar, Dr. A. T. Robertson explains, "God placed Christ in this priesthood and no one else can step into it."[75] The Melchizedek priesthood, then, is the peculiar possession of Jesus Christ alone. He is the only priest after the order of Melchizedek!

Mormons may claim that their Church has the restored Aaronic and Melchizedek priesthoods, but this teaching can be maintained **only by contradicting the clear teachings of the Bible.**

Other Priesthood Problems

Beyond what has already been presented, there are numerous other problems that seriously challenge the Mormon priesthood claims.

1. In Joseph Smith's *Inspired Version* of the Bible, his revision of Hebrews 7:3 indicates that he realized there was no provision for other priests in the Melchizedek priesthood. Therefore, without warrant, he inserted words at the beginning and at the end of the verse which change the meaning of the passage. The changes actually contradict the whole point of the chapter—that the Melchizedek priesthood was the peculiar possession of Jesus Christ alone. For example, Smith altered the end of the verse to read: "**And all those who are ordained unto this priesthood are** made like unto the Son of God, **abiding** a priest continually."[76]

2. There is no mention of high priests in the New Testament Christian Church. Where they are mentioned in the New Testament, they were part of the Judaic system. For instance, it was the high priest Caiaphas that helped send Jesus to His death on the cross.[77]

3. John the Baptist had authority to baptize,[78] so when he came to Joseph Smith and Oliver Cowdery, he should have baptized them. Instead, he conferred the Aaronic priesthood on them.[79] Only **after** this were Joseph and Oliver baptized. Since LDS doctrine forbids a person to receive the priesthood without baptism,[80] this ordination was not valid, nor were the baptisms that followed.

4. After their baptisms,[81] Joseph Smith laid his hands on Oliver's head and ordained him to the Aaronic priesthood. After that, Oliver ordained Joseph to the same priesthood.[82] Was the ordination they had just received under the hands of John the Baptist[83] ineffective? If that original ordination was not sufficient, then they did not have the authority to either baptize or ordain each other.[84] If John's ordination **was** authoritative, then their act of ordaining each other again was a mockery. It is true that they claimed they were commanded to do it, but if so, it shows that God did not recognize their ordination by John, creating the same problems.

5. When John the Baptist ordained Joseph and Oliver, he specifically told them that the priesthood he gave them "had not the power of laying on hands for the gift of the Holy Ghost."[85] The Holy Ghost can only be received, Mormonism teaches, by the laying on of hands by one in authority to do so.[86] Yet only three verses later, Joseph claims that they received the Holy Ghost anyway,[87] contradicting what the angel had just testified.

6. As a recent article on the LDS priesthood points out, in the Mormon Church "a worthy young man may be ordained a deacon at age 12."[88] Yet the Bible says, "Let the deacons be the husbands of one wife, ruling their children and their own houses well."[89] Clearly, the LDS version is not a restoration of the New Testament office.

7. The high priests of the Mormon Church are of the Melchizedek priesthood.[90] In the Bible, however, the high priests are found in the Aaronic priesthood.[91] The only exception is Jesus Christ Himself, but this is because He did away with the old, ineffectual priesthood service and replaced it with Himself.[92]

8. The method the LDS Church requires for the ordination of men into the Aaronic priesthood ignores the way priests were ordained in the Old Testament. The Mormon Church only ordains by "the laying on of hands."[93] If this priesthood exists today and is a true "restoration," then the Biblical method of ordaining priests should still be used. A comparison between LDS methods and Bible teachings, however, reveals a vast difference.[94]

9. The LDS *Doctrine and Covenants* says, "And without the ordinances thereof, and the authority of the priesthood ... no man can see the face of God, even the Father, and live."[95] Joseph Smith supposedly saw God the Father and Jesus Christ in 1820.[96] But he did not receive either order of the priesthood until 1829.[97] If the *Doctrine and Covenants* passage quoted above is correct, Joseph Smith could not have lived through his first vision.

10. In the Bible, there was only one active high priest at a time.[98] In the Mormon Church, however, there are literally tens of thousands of active high priests.[99]

11. Utah Senator and Mormon writer Orrin Hatch pointed out that

if the power of the priesthood (God's power) was on the earth at the time [of complete apostasy], the Church would have been spared and the Saints would not have been 'overcome.' Put another way, **if only one holder of God's priesthood had been on the earth**, since God's power or priesthood is more powerful than Satan, **the Church would have been spared.**[100]

As discussed in Chapter 3, LDS scriptures claim that the Apostle John has been living and working on the earth since the time of Jesus Christ.[101] This is an irreconcilable dilemma. Either there was no complete apostasy, since John was here with the priesthood all along; or else the revelation to Joseph Smith about John's tarrying is false. Either way, how can the Mormon claims be true?

Many additional problems concerning the "restored" priesthood could be reviewed if space permitted.[102] The LDS Church certainly has given foundational importance to its teachings about priesthood authority. But from what has been seen, it does not possess a "restored" priesthood. Instead, it employs a priesthood that has been invented, modified, retrofitted and usurped.

The True Priesthood

Mormons often ask Christians, "Where do you get your authority"? The answer is found in the Bible. It declares that all true Christians are themselves priests to God, and a royal priesthood, as a result of their redemption through Christ, who "loved us, and washed us from our sins in his own blood, And hath made us kings [a royal house] and priests unto God and his Father...."[103] This priesthood has no connections with the Aaronic priesthood. It is a royal priesthood, under Jesus Christ, the Christian's Great High Priest: "But ye are a chosen generation, a royal priesthood, an holy nation, a peculiar people...."[104]

As members of this holy priesthood, Christians are "to offer up spiritual sacrifices, acceptable to God by Jesus Christ."[105] He has given believer-priests "the ministry of reconciliation" as "ambassadors for Christ."[106] All authority has been given to Jesus Christ,[107] so as Christians act in His name and according to His will, they have all the available authority behind their actions. In fact, believers' actions should always be by Christ's direction and according to His will.[108]

"Born-again"[109] Christians need only to read their Bibles to see that there is no Scriptural justification for Mormon priesthoods, temples, ordinances, rites or ceremonies—all of which the Mormon Church claims are necessary for salvation and exaltation. Instead of relying on human works such as these, Christians have put their confidence in the completed work of our Great High Priest, the Lord Jesus Christ. He alone "is able also to save them to the uttermost [absolutely, completely] that come unto God by him, seeing he ever liveth to make intercession for them."[110]

Chapter 12
The Mormon Testimony

Joseph Smith's Claim –
I pray that the Lord may enable you to treasure these things in your mind, for I know that His Spirit will bear testimony to all who seek diligently after knowledge from Him.
– *Teachings of the Prophet Joseph Smith,* 29

Burning in the Bosom

Many LDS members have a testimony about the LDS gospel. When asked, most have an assurance of the truthfulness of Mormon teachings. They are encouraged on the first Sunday of every month to share these testimonies publicly. Almost without fail, these testimonies include the members' thoughts about Joseph Smith, the *Book of Mormon* and the current LDS leadership. They claim to know, for example, that Joseph Smith was a true prophet of God and that the *Book of Mormon* is a truthful historical record. They assure others that their current prophet is called and led by God. They know without doubt that the Mormon Church is the only true church of Jesus Christ on the earth today. How can they know these things? Because they have been assured of their truthfulness by a "burning in the bosom" experience. They firmly believe that this inner feeling they have received is assurance from the Holy Ghost of spiritual truth.

Just Pray to Know the Truth

And when ye shall receive these things, I would exhort you that **ye would ask God**, the Eternal Father, in the name of Christ, if these things are not true; and if ye shall ask with a sincere heart, with real intent, having faith in Christ, **he will manifest the truth of it unto you, by the power of the**

Holy Ghost. And by the power of the Holy Ghost ye may know the truth of all things.[1]

This passage comes from the *Book of Mormon*, and it is one that Mormon missionaries always quote when they leave a copy with investigators. They ask the person to read the *Book of Mormon*, then earnestly pray to know that it is true. They promise that God will manifest the truth of the book to them, usually through a "burning in the bosom," or some other form of inner verification. Once they receive this "feeling," they are told that they will know that the *Book of Mormon* is true, and that the Mormon Church is also true.

Admittedly, many people have done exactly that—read the book, or part of it, then prayed about it. And many receive this "burning in the bosom," just as they were promised. Here are several brief accounts:

> As you listen to my message ... look for the steps that lead to a testimony: desiring to know the truth, pondering in our hearts, then feeling and obediently following the promptings of the Holy Ghost.... **I have felt** the undeniable witness of the Spirit of God, **like a fire burning in my heart**, that the restored [LDS] gospel is true.[2]

> A true and solid testimony of the truth comes to the sincere individual through desire, faith, study, observance, fasting and prayer. By such a process the Lord, **by way of the Holy Ghost, will tell you what is true** and correct and what is false....My family and I followed these steps and we happily testify that it works.[3]

> As my commitment increased, a good friend of mine, who was not a member of the [Mormon] Church, became concerned about me. He had been researching and shared some facts on the Church I didn't know about. These facts didn't disturb me, however, because **I had prayed** about the Church **and had a testimony of the truthfulness** of our gospel.[4]

The Doctrine and Covenants confirms that when a preacher and hearer "are edified," **or feel "the Spirit of truth,"** that which they speak and hear is the truth (D&C 50:21-22). Most of us **have felt this spiritual feeling** when reading the Book of Mormon or hearing about Joseph Smith's epiphanies. **What we interpret this to mean is** that we have therefore encountered **the truth,** and we then base subsequent religious commitments **on these feelings.**[5]

Niki Payne began dating a Mormon boy.... she "had **had a burning bosom experience** and was **convinced of the truth** of the experience and of the Mormon church."[6]

In the back of *The Book of Mormon* ... it promises that if you read it with a sincere heart, and you ask the Lord if it's true, he'll manifest the truth of it unto you.... Well, **the Holy Ghost came to me** after I finished it **and showed me very strongly that this book was true.**[7]

It was a Thursday night in October, before a general conference of The Church of Jesus Christ of Latter-day Saints. I came home from work **with a peculiar feeling** growing inside me—**a feeling I had never before experienced.** I did not know what to make of it. It slowly grew in intensity. What a marvelous **feeling!**... Then came the testimony— that sureness of the missionaries that had bothered me in the past. **I knew.**[8]

Judy Robertson joined the LDS Church because she was "duly impressed with the trappings of Mormonism, **I felt sure** this was the only true church."[9] In an article in *Christianity Today,* it was reported that

> John Kunich was converted to Mormonism by this type of experience. "I had prayed about what [the missionaries] were asking me to study and **I felt like** I was being enveloped by love. It was a beautiful experience; it brought tears to my

eyes. **I felt it was spiritual confirmation** of what I had been studying."[10]

Writing about LDS missionary Hyuk Hong, the *Los Angeles Times* reported that "eight years ago [1984], while reading a Book of Mormon given to him by missionaries in Korea, **a warm, tingly sensation** filled his torso and he converted to the [Mormon] faith, Hong says: '**It was the Holy Ghost.**'"[11]

Not only is this subjective form of verification taught in the *Book of Mormon*, but also in the *Doctrine and Covenants*, which says,

> But, behold, I say unto you, that you must study it out in your mind; then you must ask me if it be right, and if it is right **I will cause that your bosom shall burn within you**; therefore, **you shall feel that it is right.** But if it be not right you shall have no such feelings, but you shall have a stupor of thought that shall cause you to forget the thing which is wrong; therefore, you cannot write that which is sacred save it be given you from me.[12]

LDS leaders also teach that this is how truth is revealed from God. Bruce R. McConkie writes,

> Logic and reason lead truth seekers along the path to a testimony, and they are aids in strengthening the revealed assurances of which a testimony is composed. But **the actual sure knowledge** which constitutes "the testimony of Jesus" **must come by "the spirit of prophecy."** This is received when the Holy Spirit **speaks to the spirit within men**; it comes when the whisperings of the still small voice are **heard by the inner man**.[13]

Robert Hales also explains how the testimony is gained. Referring to a *Book of Mormon* character named Nephi, Hales writes, "Nephi gives a clear and compelling account of the process, which includes desiring, believing, having faith, pondering, and then following the Spirit."[14]

Contradictory Manifestations

Speaking of the *Book of Mormon*, Gordon B. Hinckley writes that "it is the only book that contains within its covers a promise that by divine power the reader may know with certainty of its truth."[15] If this were true, then everyone who reads and prays about it should know it is true. But this is not the case. There are many that have read the *Book of Mormon* and prayed about it, but never received this promised confirmation. Still others have had an inner manifestation indicating that it was false! Here are a few examples:

> Mormon missionaries promise people that the Holy Ghost will bear witness of the Book of Mormon. They ask contacts to pray for that witness. **None whom I asked to do that ever got any witness, except one.** That lady said that **the Holy Ghost revealed to her that the Book of Mormon was false.** We simply denied her witness and departed.[16]

> I have made the test of Moroni 10:4-5. **The result was the strong emphasis** of five words from that passage, "**THESE THINGS ARE NOT TRUE.**"[17]

James Spencer writes,

> The missionaries pointed out a passage in the Book of Mormon promising that, if I prayed sincerely, I would receive a witness from the Holy Spirit that the Church was true. Every night I prayed, **trying to come up with a feeling or sensation** that would match what they told me to expect.... [One of the missionaries asked,] "By the way, have you gotten an answer to your prayers yet about the Book of Mormon?" "**No, I haven't.**"[18]

Speaking of his experiences while serving an LDS mission, Dr. Simon Southerton shares,

> I began like many missionaries to desire my own witness of the truthfulness of the Book of Mormon. I had never doubted that it was true but I earnestly wanted to have my own answer to prayer as Moroni promised in the last pages of the Book of Mormon.... I was a willing and diligent missionary and I felt **my desire for a witness was appropriate**. I was confident that the Holy Ghost could answer my prayers **by causing a burning or warm feeling in my heart**. I was confident that I would receive an answer.... I pleaded for a witness that the Book of Mormon was true. Again and again I asked, **but I did not receive the promised burning in the bosom**.[19]

Bernard Brady and his wife were LDS members when they were confronted with Fundamentalists' doctrines, which teach that the Salt Lake City LDS Church leadership has gone astray and is no longer the true church of Jesus Christ. He shares that "she and I both did a lot of questioning about whether it was true or not. We went through an intense period of investigating and fasting and praying. At the end **both of us were impressed that the fundamentalist message was basically true**. And if it was true, we couldn't ignore it."[20]

LDS leader Dallin Oaks reveals,

> I have heard adult members of the (Mormon) Church claim they do not have a testimony because **they have never experienced a "burning in the bosom."** (D&C 9:8.) If I thought this scriptural "burning" only referred to caloric heat, I would have to say that **I have never had a burning in the bosom either**....[21]

While Oaks goes on to clarify that he did have some form of manifestation, he freely admits that many members of the LDS Church **have not had this inner verification** of the "truth."

Ignore Verifiable Facts

The problem has often arisen that LDS members have had the "burning in the bosom" prove Mormonism true for them, only to find later that the facts and evidence have proven it false. This happened in some cases when they learned that no archaeological evidence could be found to substantiate the *Book of Mormon* as a historically accurate document.

Thomas S. Ferguson was heavily involved in archaeological research trying to prove the *Book of Mormon* true. After many years of research, he privately circulated a letter in which he concluded, "I'm afraid that up to this point, I must agree with Dee Green, who has told us that to date there is no Book-of-Mormon geography. I, for one, would be happy if Dee were wrong."[22] Ferguson was fighting to maintain his faith in spite of evidence to the contrary. Eventually, Jerald and Sandra Tanner report that "Ferguson, one of the Church's great defenders of the Book of Mormon, visited us on Dec. 2, 1970, and told us that he had spent 25 years trying to prove Mormonism, but had finally come to the conclusion that his work had been in vain."[23]

The same dilemma faced many LDS members in the 1960s when the Book of Abraham was proven to be fraudulent. Dee Jay Nelson was an elder in the Mormon Church in January of 1968 when Hugh Nibley convinced him to re-translate the papyri from which the book was taken into English.[24] The original papyri that Joseph Smith had used to produce it had recently been rediscovered and turned over to the LDS Church leaders. Retranslating the document was an effort to show that Joseph Smith was truly inspired by God and had produced an accurate rendition via his prophetic gifts. However, Nelson found that Joseph Smith had not translated a single word from the document correctly. The Tanners inform us that "as time went on, however, it became evident that Nelson was moving further from the Church."[25] Nelson was obviously struggling between his faith in the Church and the evidence showing it to be wrong. His strife lasted several years until "in 1975 he completely left the Church."[26]

Another example dates from the 1980s, when Mark Hoffman was able to deceive the LDS First Presidency and the Twelve Apostles with his forgeries. Most recently, DNA evidence has shown that the *Book of Mormon* is a fictional work, and not a true historical record.[27] Once again, it has led many LDS members to see the conflict between their subjective faith and the facts that have come to light. Dr. Southerton shares his conflict:

> I became interested in recent research on the DNA of American Indians.... For two weeks I wrestled with the research. I collected more and more research papers.... I struggled with the complete discrepancy between the research and my understanding of the Book of Mormon and the doctrine of the Lamanites.... I desperately tried to find holes in the research, but soon realised just how fruitless this was.... I became aware of the contradiction that I was faced with.... As much as I wanted the Book of Mormon to be true, I suddenly knew that it wasn't.... I had firmly believed that it was true. I had not been looking for evidence to prove it wrong. I had been looking for research that could be viewed as supportive. It was a shock to have my belief shattered so quickly.[28]

Quite often, LDS members are faced with the same dilemma: the "evidence" of their faith is contradicted by scientific, historical or other known facts. This occurs because "evidence" to most Mormon members is nothing more than a feeling, or even just a dream. Early Mormon Orson Whitney explains, "Testimony means evidence, and it may consist of divers things, fruits of the gospel's varied gifts. **Dreams, visions, prophecies, tongues** and their interpretation, healings, and other manifestations of the divine Spirit are all included in the category."[29] According to this definition, simply desiring for something to be true would qualify as "evidence" that it is true.

Jerry and Dianna Benson experienced this situation when meeting with LDS missionaries. After being shown proof that their leaders had altered documents, falsified information, and then lied about the situation, the missionaries did not seem to care. The Bensons found that "no evidence would convince them of any problem within the church that would show it was not of God. Changes didn't matter. Falsified history didn't matter. Doctrine doesn't matter. False prophecy didn't matter. All that matters is you pray and God will give you a confirmation of the truthfulness of their church."[30]

During the crisis in the Church that surrounded Mark Hoffman's forgeries, Dallin Oaks issued a statement telling the membership of the Church how to handle such conflicts. According to *The Salt Lake Tribune*, Oaks

> warned members **to rely on faith and not historical fact**.... He also cautioned Mormons to **rely not on historical facts but on faith in their beliefs** in the authenticity of the church. "Our individual, personal testimonies are based on the witness of the spirit, **not on any** combination or accumulation of **historical facts**.... If we are so grounded, no alteration of historical facts can shake our testimonies."[31]

It seems incredible that Oaks could seriously advise people to ignore factual or historical evidence in favor of their "testimonies." Certainly they need to weigh all of the facts carefully and have all the information available before jumping to any conclusions.[32] But even today, Mormons heed these instructions, and live out their faith despite historical evidence that contradicts it.

Writing in *Sunstone* magazine, John-Charles Duffy admits that "Mormonism has long emphasized that **knowledge of the truth comes through spiritual manifestations** (testimony), understood as something **apart from the intellect**...."[33] He later elaborates, "Latter-day Saints maintain **that knowledge of the truth comes ultimately through 'testimony,'** understood as spiritual manifestations that transcend normal intellectual activity. Out of this belief has grown a discourse that tends to denigrate intellectualism **and to represent reason and scholarship as irrelevant** to questions of faith."[34]

Brian Birch, director of religious studies at Utah Valley State College, writes, "Whether there is evidence or no evidence, a person still has to go through the process of reading it [the Book of Mormon] and **praying** about it.... **Evidence is irrelevant** at this point."[35] But once the facts are known and well documented, simply ignoring them in favor of a personal feeling is completely irresponsible—like a child who learns by observation that the Tooth Fairy is not real, yet chooses to believe in it anyway.

Arza Evans shares, "I have personally experienced the strange phenomenon of a testimony. I gained most of my testimony while in the Northern States Mission. Somehow I came to **'know'** that Joseph Smith was a prophet and that his *Book of Mormon* was true. I was so sure of these things that I would have given my life for my Church." After further research, he admits "that I was wrong about Smith, his gold plates, and his *Book of Mormon*." How could he have been wrong? He explains, "I realize that first I was indoctrinated, and then I was placed into a situation where I was forced to come up with a testimony for my own mental health.... **My testimony was based upon ignorance, feelings, emotions, deception, and self-deception.**"[36] People can talk themselves into believing anything, if they want to badly enough. A teaching is not true just because someone feels it is or wants it to be. Ignoring facts in preference to feelings, then, is very foolish.

Real Truth Is Always True

Why would some people receive the inner assurance, and others not? What it comes down to is that either the *Book of Mormon* is true or it is not. If everyone prays to know that it is true, and God is going to manifest its truthfulness to them, they should all get the burning confirmation in their hearts. The examples reviewed here show that some people get the feeling that it is true, some get the feeling it is false, and others get no feeling at all. But there is yet another category to consider—those who have had feelings both ways.

I (Lane Thuet) had the experience of the "burning in the bosom" about the truthfulness of the *Book of Mormon* and the Mormon Church. I prayed about them when I was a teenager and studied the *Book of Mormon* in my LDS Seminary classes. The warm inner feeling came. It was enough for me at the time. I was taught that I would only have that feeling if it were true. Since I had a feeling, I figured it must be true.

Years later, after researching the claims of the LDS Church and finding them false, I desired to have the reassurance of the Holy

Spirit again. I wanted the burning in the bosom experience to reassure me that the Church was true, in spite of the evidence to the contrary that I had seen. I received no feeling this time. All I had was the undeniable evidence from the research I had done, so I left the Church. I was once again challenged by missionaries to read the *Book of Mormon* and pray about it a few years afterward, so I did. This time, I felt "the burning in the bosom" confirm that the *Book of Mormon* and the Mormon Church were **not true**. Now I had received one "feeling" verifying its truthfulness, and another verifying that it was false. I cannot deny that I had both feelings. Clearly, we cannot rely on feelings such as these to verify the truthfulness of anything, even in prayer. No one should rely on a subjective feeling to tell them what is true.

Robert Crossfield shares that he received the verification from the Holy Ghost that the Mormon Church was true. He was then baptized into the Mormon Church. Crossfield goes on to state that some time later, the "still small voice of the Lord" came to him and revealed that he was to be "God's mouthpiece," that the leaders of the LDS Church had "cut themselves off from the voice of the Lord" and that they had betrayed some of Joseph Smith's teachings. In response, the LDS leaders excommunicated him.[37]

And yet, some Mormons who have had their faith confirmed by a "burning in the bosom" say that no matter what they discover, no matter what contrary evidence they find, they will continue believing in the LDS Church. Their personal experience has "proven" everything true for them. It does not matter that others have had different personal experiences and feelings.

In *Dialogue: A Journal of Mormon Thought*, LDS historian Dr. Richard Bushman writes,

> The question I have in my mind is how much does our faith depend on supporting historical evidence? On the one hand, we make a great deal of it.... On the other hand, **we are prone to dismiss all this as irrelevant**.... Granted that negative historical evidence would not destroy the faith of the faithful. For those blessed with it, **spiritual experience is the most compelling data**. Honesty requires that one

remain true to it even in the face of other evidence to the contrary.[38]

Pastor John MacArthur wrote of just such a situation in his book, *Reckless Faith:*

> And one person's experience is as valid as another's—**even if everyone's experiences lead to contradictory conceptions of truth.** "Truth that is true for me" might be different from someone else's truth. In fact, our beliefs might be obviously contradictory, yet another person's "truth" in no way invalidates mine. Because "truth" is authenticated by personal experience, **its only relevance is for the individual** who makes the leap of faith. **That is existentialism.**[39]

MacArthur is absolutely correct; existentialism teaches that there is no objective truth, so that a person's own **experience** is to be taken as gospel truth even though someone else's **experience** is completely different. But are these verifications really from God, or are they just subjective personal feelings?

After giving irrefutable evidence that the Book of Abraham is a completely false translation, Charles Larson makes these observations about the LDS testimony:

> Virtually every Latter-day Saint has "borne his testimony" at one time or another.... However, is such a testimony a *valid* truth test? Is it a *biblical* truth test? There is no reason to doubt that the majority of these testimonies are honest and sincere. But **this in itself is no indication they are *reliable*....** *The real power of a Mormon testimony, then, can actually be a potential trap that a person falls into by failing to realize that* **we can literally talk ourselves into anything if we want to believe it badly enough....** In the absence of valid evidence for the object of his faith, the Latter-day Saint is left with only *subjective feelings,* **which are inconclusive.** In order to be objective, one must be willing to examine the evidence both for and against religious claims.[40]

No doubt these people are entirely sincere in what they have felt or experienced, but that means nothing more than that they honestly had a feeling or experience. It cannot indicate that what they experienced taught them the truth. Ironically, even Orson Pratt verifies this, saying, "Sincerity is a good thing, and without it there can be no real Christians; but **sincerity** does not make a person a true child of God ... it **does not show that its possessor is right, or that he has received the true doctrine**; it only shows that he is sincere."[41]

Subjective Feeling, or Real Prompting?

Many Mormons would not classify their experience as a feeling, calling it a "prompting" from the Holy Ghost instead. Essentially, there is no difference between the two. Even if God is prompting someone in this way, it is still just a feeling inside the person. Oaks verifies this when he says this "burning in the bosom" experience "does not seem to refer to heat but rather to **an intensity of feeling**. For me, the witness of the Holy Ghost is **an intense feeling of serenity** or well-being."[42] Bruce R. McConkie agrees, saying, "Receipt of a testimony is accompanied **by a feeling of calm, unwavering certainty**."[43]

Speaking of the personal LDS testimony, non-Mormon Brodie Crouch correctly observes,

> If one be a faithful Mormon believing himself to be in possession of the Holy Spirit [Holy Ghost], **whatever may be the conclusion of the mind** or the substance of his "hunch" **it can be said to be the result of the direction of the Spirit**. If in the silence of reposing sleep a dream may cross the subconscious mind, and it appear to have some meaning, the person can be said to have been "divinely inspired."[44]

With this kind of verification, Mormons can convince themselves to believe that literally any conclusion is inspired by the Holy Ghost, whether it be rational, reasonable, logical, true, or not.

Not only can people talk themselves into believing anything—even into receiving a feeling they are hoping to get—but others can manipulate people into receiving such experiences, as well. It is very common in religious groups to become overwhelmed with feelings of joy, or comfort, or well-being and serenity, and even a burning in the bosom that feels as though the heart might burst. Many things can bring on these feelings: a touching story or sermon, a deeply moving song, a stirring video message, strong admiration of a person or object, or even the fact that all those in the group around them are receiving such feelings. Members of Pentecostal religious movements have these religious experiences and feelings every week in their meetings. Once again, I (Lane Thuet) have often felt these kinds of feelings in religious meetings **outside** the LDS Church. I have also felt them when visiting historical locations of interest to me, and the feelings did not differ significantly from those I received both for and against the *Book of Mormon*. Surely LDS members would not admit that these experiences I had are the inner verification of the Holy Ghost, and yet they are essentially the same as those experiences of LDS members who have had them.

Obviously, personal experience and personal feelings do not establish gospel truth. God has given us a standard that is not subjective, and He expects us to measure our experiences by that standard of truth, not the other way around. We are never told in the Bible to determine "truth" by our personal experiences, which in the case of the LDS "burning in the bosom" are clearly contradictory and inconsistent.

What Does the Bible Say?

Why is it that people experience different and contradictory feelings about the *Book of Mormon*? The only answer is that God is not verifying truth in this way. They are simply having a "feeling" about the matter. Otherwise, God is breaking His promise given in the *Book of Mormon* to verify its truthfulness to all that sincerely ask. The Bible has consistently taught that our feelings, particularly the ones we get in our hearts, are often unreliable and even deceitful. Consider the following Bible references on the subject:

And God saw that the wickedness of man was great in the earth, and that **every imagination of the thoughts of his heart was only evil continually.** (Genesis 6:5)

And the LORD smelled a sweet savour; and the LORD said in his heart, I will not again curse the ground any more for man's sake; for **the imagination of man's heart is evil from his youth**; neither will I again smite any more every thing living, as I have done. (Genesis 8:21)

There is a way **which seemeth right unto a man**, but the end thereof are **the ways of death.** (Proverbs 14:12)

This is an evil among all things that are done under the sun, that there is one event unto all: yea, also **the heart of the sons of men is full of evil,** and **madness is in their heart while they live**, and after that they go to the dead. (Ecclesiastes 9:3)

For I earnestly protested unto your fathers in the day that I brought them up out of the land of Egypt, even unto this day, rising early and protesting, saying, Obey my voice. Yet they obeyed not, nor inclined their ear, but walked every one **in the imagination of their evil heart**.... (Jeremiah 11:7-8)

The heart is deceitful above all things, and desperately wicked: who can know it? (Jeremiah 17:9)

For **this people's heart is waxed gross**, and their ears are dull of hearing, and their eyes they have closed.... (Matthew 13:15)

For from within, **out of the heart of men, proceed evil thoughts**, adulteries, fornications, murders, Thefts, covetousness, wickedness, deceit, lasciviousness, an evil eye, blasphemy, pride, foolishness: **All these evil things come from within**, and defile the man. (Mark 7:21-23)

Moreover, the heart can be filled with ideas and feelings that do not come from God. Consider the example of Ananias:

> But Peter said, Ananias, why hath **Satan filled thine heart to lie to the Holy Ghost**, and to keep back part of the price of the land? (Acts 5:3)

The Apostle Paul also verified that Satan has all kinds of powers, and that he uses "all power and signs and lying wonders" to deceive people.[45] Jesus told us that as well.[46] How foolish it would be, then, to rely upon inner feelings as a test for truth, especially when a person's eternal destiny is at stake.

Feelings Are Not the Standard for Truth

If we cannot trust the subjective feelings of our hearts in order to determine truth in every circumstance, then how can we know what is true and what is false? Scripture tells us.

> And now, O Lord God, thou art that God, and **thy words be true**, and thou hast promised this goodness unto thy servant. (2 Samuel 7:28)

> Heaven and earth shall pass away, but **my words shall not pass away**. (Matthew 24:35)

> Sanctify them through thy truth: **thy word is truth**. (John 17:17)

> These [the Bereans] were more noble than those in Thessalonica, in that they received the word with all readiness of mind, and **searched the scriptures daily, whether those things [that Paul taught] were so**. (Acts 17:11)

> **Prove all things**; hold fast that which is good. (1 Thessalonians 5:21)

All Scripture is given by inspiration of God, and **is profitable for doctrine**, for reproof, for correction, **for instruction in righteousness: That the man of God may be perfect**, throughly [thoroughly] furnished unto all good works. (2 Timothy 3:16-17)

In spite of the clear teachings of the Bible, LDS leaders teach that reliance on the Scriptures should come **only after** following feelings. This is the exact opposite of what the Apostles in the Bible taught. Robert Hales teaches that "**once we receive a witness** of the **Spirit, our testimony is strengthened through study**, prayer, and living the gospel."[47] Studying Scripture, according to him, should come **only after** obedience to the feelings of the heart—feelings that were received after merely "desiring to know the truth" and "pondering in our hearts." Yet the Bible says to ignore the evil promptings of the heart and to rely on Scripture instead. We can trust the Bible. We, like the Bereans, would be more noble if we would simply search the Scriptures to see if what the Mormon Church is teaching is true.

Sheer Numbers

Nevertheless, we are faced with a question. With over 12 million people reported to be members of the Mormon Church, how can so many of them have had this "burning in the bosom" that they believe tells them it is true? Would not the sheer number of people who have received this same feeling mean that the feeling must be right?

The Bible answers this question in Exodus 23:2, "**Thou shalt not follow a multitude to do evil....** " The *NIV* puts it this way, "Do not follow the crowd in doing wrong." The fact that a large number of people believe something does not mean it is true. For example, there are more Roman Catholics and Muslims worldwide than there are Mormons. In fact, according to the *2002 National Council of Churches Yearbook*, the LDS Church is listed **fifth in the United States** according to membership numbers,[48] so if truth is determined by sheer numbers, it falls short.

Hypnosis or Power of Suggestion?

The question remains why so many people have had this nearly identical experience since it cannot be relied upon. LDS writer Grant Palmer asks and answers this question in his book, *An Insider's View of Mormon Origins*.

> The question I will pose is **whether this is an unfailing guide to truth**. Is something true because I and others find it edifying? Hundreds of thousands of people believe in the truthfulness of their own religion because of similar confirming experiences.... American psychologist William James ... studied hundreds of people, including religious founders, who claimed to receive inspiration.... He concluded that **while their experiences and feelings were real to them, they could not be a valid source for determining truth because their claims were doctrinally incompatible**.... Doctrinal contradictions appear not only between and within Christian denominations but also within the LDS church itself.... The evangelical position of **identifying and verifying truth by emotional feelings**, which the Book of Mormon advocates, **is therefore not always dependable**.[49]

Certainly these subjective feelings are unreliable, but why have so many LDS members had them? Christian writer Larry Jonas gives one possible explanation. Speaking about his own experience with LDS missionaries, he tells us, "The Mormons did not expect that I would pray for either an affirmative or negative answer. They generally tell the inquirer to 'Pray to God and he will tell you it is true.' This is a form of positive hypnosis."[50]

We are not attempting to say with any authority what does or does not qualify as "positive hypnosis." But it is obvious that what the LDS missionaries do is definitely a form of "positive suggestion." Whether this kind of technique is called "positive hypnosis," "self-fulfilling prophecy," or just the "power of suggestion," it is still putting the idea into someone's mind, which is a form of hypnotherapy.

Hal Brickman, author of *The Thin Book*, writes about this exact principle when describing his own hypnosis techniques. He says, "The scripts use **positive suggestions or positive hypnosis** in the form of metaphors, analogies, empathy and confrontation **that contradict the effects of the unconscious mind.**"[51] Mormonism uses a similar technique to encourage a faith that is based solely upon feelings.

Jonas is quite correct to claim that Mormon missionaries do not ask someone to pray **whether or not** the *Book of Mormon* is true. While the Moroni passage does tell the potential convert to ask God whether these things are **not** true, the Mormon missionaries take a different approach. They place the seed in the investigator's mind **that it is already true**, and that God will confirm this through a feeling. In the LDS missionary manual, *Uniform System for Teaching the Gospel*, the missionary was instructed on how to lead the discussion, what to focus on, what to emphasize and quite often exactly what to say. On page 1-1 (First Discussion), the missionary was instructed as follows:

> During this discussion you need to help the investigators **feel the presence of the Holy Spirit**. This will prepare them to make the commitments that lead to conversion and baptism. During this discussion the investigators should commit themselves to— 1) Read from the Book of Mormon and **pray to know that it is true.**[52]

Even the handout given to the investigators after this discussion contains this positive suggestion:

> You Can Know the Truth.... You can know that **the Book of Mormon is the word of God.** You can know that **Joseph Smith was a true prophet.** You can know these things by reading the Book of Mormon, pondering its message and its importance for you, **and praying to know that it is true.**[53]

Other Religious Groups Not Exempt

It is not only the Mormon Church that employs "feelings," specifically feelings obtained "as an answer to prayer," to try to establish truth. Many religious groups have used a similar approach. Here as well, feelings should not be taken as truth over the authority of Scripture. After mentioning several Christian examples of this in his book, *Unholy Devotion*, Harold Bussell writes, "You will notice that the 'spiritual' is placed above the authority of the Word."[54]

This is exactly what cults do to take the emphasis off the authority of Scripture (even though Jesus clearly put it there in John 17:17 as did the Apostle Paul in 2 Timothy 3:16-17), and establish their own set of guidelines. Rather than rely on the objective truth of the Bible, they want potential converts to rely on the subjective feelings that they claim are the result of being "led by the Spirit."

Stephen B. Clark writes about this very phenomenon, though he was not speaking about Mormon Church members:

> The statement ... "led by the Spirit" can be **a way to bypass scriptural authority. This happens when someone makes the Spirit's leading a decisive factor in accepting anything as true.** When such people say they are "waiting for the Spirit's leading," they are saying that **they personally require direct revelation or inspiration in order to accept something as true**.... Such a position does not deny outright the authority of scripture, but **it does amount to such a denial in practice**.[55]

Even the sixteenth-century reformer Martin Luther had to deal with this issue. He once wrote a poem about it, in which he said, "For feelings come and feelings go, And **feelings are deceiving**; My warrant is **the Word of God, Naught else is worth believing**."[56]

Simon Southerton was an LDS member for 30 years. He eventually left the church because scientific evidence proved LDS teachings to be incorrect. Speaking on the matter of religious feelings, he writes,

I now know that those feelings that most members are conditioned to recognise as the Spirit are not the exclusive property of the Mormon Church. **All people experience strong emotions and warm feelings in their hearts, and many people feel them about their church....** Like many Mormons, however, I had invalidated the feelings of non-members, rationalising that they only feel portions of the Spirit because they have portions of the truth. If that was true, then how does a person distinguish between a portion of the Spirit and a full dose? **Why would God make so much rest on such an impossibly hard decision.** I am now convinced that He cares more about how genuinely good a person is than their ability to allow their feelings to direct their lives.[57]

Bible Support for Feelings?

Should we not be allowed to recognize our feelings or our experiences? Jesus told us that the Holy Spirit would be our teacher,[58] as did the Apostle John.[59] Two disciples even described experiencing "our hearts burn within us."[60] These scriptural teachings are absolutely true, but they **do not** tell us to abandon the Word of God in favor of them. The context of the passages must be taken into account.

We should pray to discern truth from the Holy Spirit, but we are nowhere told that verification will come as a burning sensation. Not only were the disciples given their "burning in the bosom" by Jesus (instead of by the Holy Spirit) on the Road to Emmaus, but Luke tells us the reason why they received this feeling—Jesus was explaining the Scriptures to them.[61] **In none of these passages are we relieved of the responsibility to search the Scriptures to verify what we perceive to be the answer to prayer.**

Explaining 1 Thessalonians 5:21, MacArthur writes,

> Those who are truly discerning are passionately committed to sound doctrine, to truth, and to all that is inspired by God.... He [the Apostle Paul] rules out the kind of "faith" that is driven by feelings, emotion, and the human imagination.

> Instead, we are to identify "that which is good" by examining everything carefully, objectively, rationally—using **Scripture as our standard**. No human teacher, no personal experience, no strong feeling is exempt from this objective test.... **Experience and feelings—no matter how powerful—do not determine what is true.** Rather, those things themselves must be subjected to the test.[62]

Only One Conclusion

The Apostle John tells us to "try the spirits"[63] ("**test** the spirits" – *NIV, NASB*) and Paul also warns us that "Satan himself masquerades as an angel of light" (*NIV*).[64] No experience, whether as vivid as the visit of an angel or as personal as a burning feeling in the heart, should be accepted in place of the Bible and what it declares to be true. We are to test all things by this objective, God-given test, and then stand with the revealed truth.

Many Mormons have had the "burning in their bosom" verify for them that the LDS Church is true. Many people, myself included, have also had it verify that the LDS Church is false. The only obvious conclusion is that real truth **cannot** be ascertained by this subjective feeling. Truth must be based on an objective standard. It must be based on the teachings of the Bible, which Jesus told us is the truth.[65] In the Bible, those who based their doctrine on the teachings of Scripture were said to be "more noble" than others:

> These were more noble than those in Thessalonica, in that they received the word with all readiness of mind, **and searched the scriptures daily, whether those things were so.** (Acts 17:11)

Chapter 13
The Mormon Gospel

Joseph Smith's Claim –
> Oh! I beseech you to go forward, go forward and make your calling and your election sure; and if any man preach any other Gospel than that which I have preached, he shall be cursed; and some of you who now hear me shall see it, and know that I testify the truth concerning them.
> – *History of the Church*, 6:365[1]

The Gospel, or Another Gospel?

In the introduction to this book, it was stated that many things about the LDS Church are impressive. Most Mormons are friendly, industrious people who are a credit to their communities. For the most part they are loyal, moral and generous. They honestly desire to serve God. These qualities, along with many others that could be mentioned, are commendable. Unfortunately, they do not make a person right with God. After all, the same qualities can be found among people of all religions. Even people who do not believe in God can be equally friendly, moral, industrious and generous.

To be right with God, however, requires salvation. Salvation is not acquired by man's work in an earthly dimension, but comes from the work of God in the spiritual and earthly dimensions. In this chapter, the most vital issue of all is discussed: What is the true gospel?

Most Mormons would readily accept the position that for a person to truly be a Christian, one must accept the true gospel. LDS writers have explained that according to Mormonism, the true gospel embraces all of God's laws, principles, ordinances, rites, acts, powers, keys and authorities necessary for man's exaltation to the celestial kingdom. According to them, individual salvation (or eternal life) results from belief in Christ's atonement, repentance, baptism into the LDS Church, receiving the gift of the Holy Ghost and obedience to the laws of ordinances of the LDS gospel for all of a person's life.[2] Is this gospel which Mormonism teaches the true gospel or is it "another gospel"?[3]

What Is the Gospel?

The question, "What is the gospel"? is of critical significance. As Paul states, "the gospel of Christ ... is the power of God unto salvation to every one that believeth ..." (Romans 1:16). He also teaches, "I have fully preached the gospel of Christ" (Romans 15:19), and that the gospel he preached "is not after man. For I neither received it of man, neither was I taught it, but by the revelation of Jesus Christ" (Galatians 1:11-12).

Is the Mormon gospel the same as that which Paul preached? Put simply, the answer is no (see contrast chart at the end of this chapter). To see this difference clearly, we need to examine the gospel Paul preached. The main elements are spelled out in 1 Corinthians 15:1-4. Verses 3 and 4 state: "For I delivered unto you first of all that which I also received, how that Christ died for our sins according to the scriptures; And that he was buried, and that he rose again the third day according to the scriptures." To Paul, to the early church and to mainstream Christians today, the gospel, or "good news," is not a set of laws, principles, ordinances, rites, etc. to be obeyed in order to earn our own salvation. Instead, it centers on Christ and His redemptive work, the means by which God provided salvation freely as a gift for all who simply believe.

The Bible teaches that all humans are sinners from birth.[4] Because of this sinful nature, there was nothing they could do to seek after God. Their very nature drove them away from God, instead.[5] So in order for them to be reconciled to Him, it was up to God to take the initiative. Paul understood that, writing, "For when we were yet without strength, in due time Christ died for the ungodly.... But God commendeth his love toward us, in that, while we were yet sinners, Christ died for us.... For if, when we were enemies, we were reconciled to God by the death of his Son, much more, being reconciled, we shall be saved by his life."[6] This is why Jesus told us that "no man can come to me, except the Father which hath sent me draw him...."[7]

All that is required is that we repent and believe in Jesus' sacrifice on our behalf.[8] Jesus made this clear when He said, "He that believeth on him [Jesus Christ] is not condemned: but he that believeth not is condemned already, because he hath not believed in the name of the only begotten Son of God."[9]

But what about baptism? Baptism is included as one of the "first principles and ordinances" of the Mormon gospel.[10] Often, those who hold this view will point to Mark 16:16 in support of their argument. This verse says, "He that believeth **and is baptized** shall be saved...." Baptism was certainly commanded by Jesus,[11] but it was always just an outward sign of joining with Christ in his death, burial and resurrection.[12] Paul writes: "For Christ sent me not to baptize, but to preach the gospel...."[13] Obviously, baptism is separated and distinguished from the gospel. The last half of Mark 16:16 makes this clear, for it says, "he that believeth not shall be damned." It says nothing there of "he that is baptized not." Belief is the only way to salvation.[14]

In its simplest expression, the gospel is summarized in Jesus' words in John 3:16: "For God so loved the world, that he gave his only begotten Son, that whosoever believeth in him should not perish, but have everlasting life." This gospel is the true gospel, which has been taught throughout the Bible for over 1,900 years. It has neither been removed nor needed to be restored. Jude 3 tells us that the gospel of faith was delivered **once only** to the saints, and that **for all time**. It never was and never will be taken away.

The totality of the true gospel is revealed throughout the entire Bible, for Jesus said, "Search the scriptures ... they are they which testify of me...."[15] He also asked God the Father to "sanctify them through thy truth," then clarified for us that "thy word is truth."[16]

One Mediator

Many religious people are familiar with the Bible reference, "For there is one God, and one mediator between God and men, the man Christ Jesus...."[17] Clearly, then, there is no other who can mediate besides Christ. But contrary to what the Bible clearly states, Brigham Young introduced a second mediator. He taught that

> no man or woman in this dispensation will ever enter into the celestial kingdom of God **without the consent of Joseph Smith**.... every man and woman **must have the certificate of Joseph Smith**, junior, as a passport to their entrance into the mansion where God and Christ are—I with you and you with me. I cannot go there without his consent.[18]

The LDS Church still believes this, and quoted the first sentence of Young's statement in the *Desert News* as a gospel truth in 1968.[19] The teaching continues to appear without correction or contradiction in recent LDS-published books such as *Joseph Smith: The Choice Seer* (1996).[20]

Since Jesus Christ is the "one mediator between God and men," how can Joseph Smith also be a mediator who gives "consent" or "passport" for entrance into the celestial kingdom? Certainly such a declaration comes under Paul's condemnation as "another gospel."[21] The Bible also says of Jesus Christ that "neither is there salvation in any other: for there is none other name under heaven given among men, whereby we must be saved."[22] This would include Joseph Smith.

The Plan of Salvation

Writing for the LDS Church, John Morgan states that the Mormon plan of salvation differed from that of the "sects" because the sects teachings were contrary to the Bible.[23] But this is not true. The plan of salvation taught by the vast majority of Christian "sects" is based entirely on Biblical teaching. How does the Mormon salvation message compare with that taught in the Bible? They are vastly different.

Ephesians 2:1-5 identifies everyone outside of Christ as "dead in trespasses and sins." The book of Romans verifies that without Christ, all are hopelessly lost, "There is none righteous, no, not one:... For all have sinned, and come short of the glory of God."[24] Since all are dead, lost, and unrighteous, there is no hope of ever earning salvation for themselves. They are completely helpless—unable to change their condition or their eternal destiny. Thankfully, "Christ Jesus came into the world to save sinners...."[25] Even though "the wages of sin is death ... the gift of God is eternal life through Jesus Christ our Lord."[26]

This is God's simple message: "For by grace are ye saved through faith; and that not of yourselves: it is the gift of God: Not of works, lest any man should boast."[27] It is not a person's works, then, that will save a man. Salvation is based entirely upon God's free gift.

The Bible also teaches that it is "not by works of righteousness which we have done, but according to his mercy he saved us ... being justified by his grace...."[28] Paul wrote in Romans that we are "being justified freely by his grace through the redemption that is in Christ Jesus."[29] He added that "to him that worketh not, but believeth on him that justifieth the ungodly, his faith is counted for righteousness."[30] Clearly the gospel of the Bible is not one of works-earned salvation, but that of a gift given freely by God because of His eternal love and mercy.

A good example is found in Acts 10 in Peter's sermon to Cornelius and his household. The Apostle Peter did not preach a gospel of works-oriented salvation, but one of faith, of simple belief. Verse 43 says, "To him [Christ] give all the prophets witness, that through his name whosoever believeth in him shall receive remission of sins." It is particularly important to note that these people received "the gift of the Holy Ghost" **before** baptism and **without** the laying on of hands.[31] No works had been done. They believed in Jesus Christ for salvation, and they were saved.

The faith or belief referred to in the passages cited is more than mental assent to historic fact. Even the demons believe in God,[32] but it does them no good. True faith is more than simply reciting words. It is having a deep and personal faith in the Jesus Christ of the Bible. It is believing in His death on the cross as the substitutionary payment for our sins.[33] It is trusting in Him completely for forgiveness of sin and deliverance from the penalty and power of sin.[34]

It is because of placing faith in Jesus Christ alone for salvation that Christians are able to perform the works that God has prepared for them to do.[35] Their belief is, therefore, demonstrated by the good works that follow salvation.[36] Believers work **because God loved them and saved them**, even though they were once His enemy.[37] All their work is in gratitude for Christ having fully accomplished their salvation.[38] As a result, believers have full assurance from God of their salvation.[39] They know without doubt that they are secure in Christ.[40] They know that they will live forever in heaven with God because of the sacrifice Jesus made on their behalf.[41]

What About You?

Do you have the assurance of eternal life as a present possession? Most Mormons do not have any such assurance. In fact, Spencer W. Kimball taught that the only way they can be assured of their salvation is if they are living "all of the commandments" of God. In other words, he goes on to clarify, they must be "perfect."[42]

The Bible teaches that the only perfect human was Jesus Christ.[43] No other person will ever become perfect by his or her own works. But all that have put their faith in the saving blood of Jesus Christ are now free from the condemnation they rightly deserve.[44] They are also assured that they will never be separated from God's saving grace.[45] Put your faith in the redemptive blood of Jesus' sacrifice on the cross for your salvation, and God will give you assurance of your salvation as well!

> And this is the record, that **God hath given to us eternal life**, and this life is in his Son. **He that hath the Son hath life**; and he that hath not the Son of God hath not life. These things have I written unto you that believe on the name of the Son of God; that **ye may know that ye have eternal life**, and that ye may believe on the name of the Son of God. (1 John 5:11-13)

We sincerely long for you to believe in Jesus Christ, and by so believing have eternal life.

The Mormon Gospel and the Biblical Gospel Contrasted

The Mormon Gospel	The Biblical Gospel
1. The gospel is derived from latter-day revelation through Mormon prophets.	1. The gospel is derived entirely from the teachings of the Bible.
2. Only resurrection is derived from the work of Christ. Salvation beyond that is dependent upon a man's own works.	2. The gospel is centered entirely on the completed redemptive work of Christ.
3. Man is responsible for his own sins, not for Adam's. But man is not responsible for his own sins until he reaches the age of 8.	3. We are sinners from birth, having inherited the sinful nature from Adam.
4. The Fall of Adam and Eve should be celebrated as an act of heroism. It would have been tragic if they had not disobeyed God.	4. The Fall of Adam brought a curse on all mankind and all creation.
5. In spite of our sinful nature, direct communion can be had with God in LDS temples if we are pure.	5. Our sin is what has separated us from intimate communion with God.
6. The penalty for sin can be offset through good works—specifically, obedience to all laws and ordinances of the LDS gospel.	6. The penalty required because of our sin is death.
7. All men are able to seek God.	7. The natural man will not seek God.

8. Man is responsible to earn his own salvation, and can assist in helping his ancestors achieve salvation as well.	8. Man cannot earn God's favor or his own salvation in any degree.
9. In order for man to be saved, he must obey laws and complete ordinances.	9. In order for man to be saved, God had to intervene.
10. Christ provided atonement for sin in the Garden of Gethsemane.	10. The blood of Christ provided atonement for the sins of man when it was shed on the cross.
11. The blood of Jesus is not able to save man from certain sins. Past leaders have identified theft, murder, adultery, immorality, breaking LDS covenants, marriage of a Caucasian to an African, and apostasy from the LDS Church as being just a few.	11. The blood of Jesus is sufficient to pay for all the sins of mankind.
12. Requirements for salvation include (but are not limited to) membership in the LDS Church, baptism by one in authority, laying on of hands for the gift of the Holy Ghost, receipt of temple endowments and celestial marriage.	12. All that is required of man in order to be saved is repentance and faith in the sacrifice of Jesus on his behalf.
13. Salvation is found through Christ, but belief in Joseph Smith, Jr. as a true prophet is also required.	13. There is only one mediator between God and man–Jesus Christ. Only in His name is salvation to be found.

14. Those who live celestial law fully will dwell in heaven with God and become Gods themselves. Those who do not will be placed in a lower heavenly kingdom. There is no eternal fiery hell for anyone.

15. Those who will be truly saved are members of the LDS Church and will work for their salvation and that of their ancestors. They will perfect their lives here on earth.

16. Baptism is one of the many required ordinances that must be performed in order to be fully saved in the Celestial Kingdom.

17. The gospel was lost to the earth after the original apostles died, about 100 years after Christ ascended. It was not restored until 1830 through Joseph Smith, Jr.

18. No one knows while living what his or her eternal state will be.

---

14. Those who believe in Jesus will spend eternal life with God in heaven. Those who do not will be sent to a real, eternal, fiery hell.

15. Those who are truly saved will demonstrate that fact by obedience to God's commands, turning from a lifestyle of continual sin, and confession of their belief in the saving blood of Jesus Christ.

16. Those who are truly saved publicly demonstrate their uniting with Jesus in His death, burial and resurrection by being baptized. Baptism, however, is not a requirement for salvation.

17. The gospel has been available to mankind since the time of Christ. It was never lost from the earth. Nature itself testifies to the love of God, so that all are without excuse.

18. Once saved, a person can have full assurance of salvation and eternal life with God.

| 19. Salvation, once attained, can always be taken away. | 19. Once saved, a person cannot lose salvation. |

References for the above:

From LDS Authorized Materials	From the Bible
1. *Book of Mormon*, Introduction; *History of the Church*, 1:12; *Mormon Doctrine*, 608, 646; *Doctrine and Covenants* 28:2-8.	1. Luke 24:25-27; John 5:39; Acts 10:43; Romans 1:1-5; 1 Corinthians 15:1-8; Galatians 1:8-9; 2 Timothy 3:15-17.
2. *Mormon Doctrine*, 329, 339, 641, 671; *Doctrine and Covenants* 93:18-20; *Teachings of the Prophet Joseph Smith*, 62.	2. John 3:14-18; 14:5-6; Acts 2:22-24; 4:12; 8:35; 10:36; 1 Corinthians 1:17-18; 2:7; 15:1-8; Philippians 2:8; Colossians 1:20; 2:15.
3. LDS Article of Faith #2; *Doctrine and Covenants* 68:25-27; *Journal of Discourses*, 10:192; *Mormon Doctrine*, 852-53; *Adam: Who Is He?*, 73.	3. Psalm 51:5; 58:3; Ecclesiastes 7:20; 9:3; Isaiah 53:6; Mark 7:21-23; Romans 1:18-3:23; 5:12-14; 1 Corinthians 15:22; Ephesians 2:1-3; Colossians 2:13; 1 John 1:8.
4. *The Book of Mormon*, 2 Nephi 2:25; *The Pearl of Great Price*, Moses 5:10-11; January 1994 *Ensign*, 10; November 1993 *Ensign*, 73; *The Articles of Faith*, 70.	4. Genesis 3:17-19; 5:29; Romans 3:9-20, 23; 5:12-14; 6:23; 8:20-22; 1 Corinthians 15:22, 56; Hebrews 2:14-18.

5. *Mormon Doctrine*, 780; *Doctrine and Covenants* 124:37-42; *Teachings of the Prophet Joseph Smith*, 226-27; *Journal of Discourses*, 2:45-46.

6. *Journal of Discourses*, 2:4; *Mormon Doctrine*, 669-71; *Doctrine and Covenants* 6:13; 130:20-21; *The Articles of Faith*, 149; *Gospel Truth*, 1:166; *Gospel Doctrine*, 556.

7. *Conference Report*, October 1909, 73-74; February 1927 *Improvement Era*; *Gospel Truth*, 1:304.

8. *The Miracle of Forgiveness*, 206-07; *Mormon Doctrine*, 308, 671, 822; *Doctrine and Covenants* 128:5-15; *Doctrines of Salvation*, 1:134-35; *Deseret News – Church Section*, 10 April 1993.

9. *Journal of Discourses*, 8:61; 14:133; *The Book of Mormon*, 2 Nephi 25:23; *Mormon Doctrine*, 670-71; *The Articles of Faith*, 478-81; October 1898 *Conference Report*, 47; October 1910 *Conference Report*, 53; *The Gospel Kingdom*, 327-28; *Discourses of Brigham Young*, 1.

---

5. Genesis 3:23-24; Psalm 130:3-4; Isaiah 53:6; 59:2; Romans 3:9-12; 8:6-8; Ephesians 2:1-3, 12; 4:17-19.

6. Genesis 2:17; Ezekiel 18:4, 20; John 5:24; Romans 1:32; 5:12; 6:23; Ephesians 2:1-5; James 1:15; 1 John 3:14.

7. Job 14:1-4; Psalm 14:1-3; Jeremiah 13:23; John 6:44, 65; Romans 3:10-28; 1 Corinthians 2:14.

8. Proverbs 20:9; Isaiah 64:6-7; Jeremiah 13:23; John 8:44; Romans 4:4-13; 6:20-21; 7:5; Ephesians 2:1-5; Titus 3:3-5.

9. John 6:44, 65; Romans 8:28-30; Ephesians 2:1-9; 2 Thessalonians 2:13-14; 2 Timothy 2:25-26; 1 Peter 3:18; 1 John 4:9-11.

10. LDS Bible Dictionary, "Atonement"; *Jesus the Christ,* 613-14; *Doctrine and Covenants* 19:16-18; *Gospel Principles,* 73; *Come Unto Christ,* 66; *Doctrines of Salvation,* 1:130.

10. Isaiah 53:5-6; 1 Corinthians 1:18; Colossians 1:19-22; 2:15; Hebrews 9:28; 12:1-4; 1 Peter 1:18-19; 2:24; 1 John 1:6-2:2.

11. History of the Church, 5:296; 7:597; *Journal of Discourses,* 1:97, 108-9; 4:50-51, 53-54, 219-20, 375; 3:247; 10:110; 21:82; *The Seer,* 223. **Apostasy is no longer taught to be in this category**, but the main doctrine is taught to be correct: *Doctrines of Salvation,* 1:134-37.

11. Isaiah 53:10-11; Hebrews 9:11-14; 10:4-18; 1 John 1:7, 9; 2:1-2; 4:13-16.

12. Mormon Doctrine, 257, 669-670; *Doctrine and Covenants* 20:29; *The Articles of Faith,* 478-80; *Journal of Discourses,* 14:133; *Encyclopedia of Mormonism,* 2:479.

12. Mark 1:15; John 1:12-13; 3:15-16, 18; 5:24; Acts 13:38-39; 16:31; Romans 3:21-25; 10:9-13; Ephesians 2:8-10; Hebrews 7:25; 1 John 5:1, 5, 10-13.

13. Doctrines of Salvation, 1:189-90; *Mormon Doctrine,* 670; *Journal of Discourses,* 4:271; 7:289; 8:176-177; *Gospel Truth,* 1:254-55; *Collected Discourses* 2, 16 January 1891.

13. Matthew 1:21; John 3:16-18; 5:22-24; 6:47; 14:6; Acts 4:12; 10:43; 16:31; Philippians 2:9-11; 1 Timothy 2:5-6; Hebrews 7:23-28.

14. *Doctrine and Covenants* Section 76; October 1898 *Conference Report*, 47; October 1910 *Conference Report*, 53; *Doctrine and Covenants Student Manual* (1981), 165; *The Gospel Kingdom*, 20, 327-28; *Journal of Discourses*, 9:102; 14:133; *The Articles of Faith*, 146-48; *Mormon Doctrine*, 349.

14. Matthew 8:12; 25:31-46; Luke 12:5; 13:28; John 3:14-16, 18, 36; 5:24; 6:29, 40; 11:25-26; 14:2-4; 2 Corinthians 5:1-10; 2 Peter 2:4-9; Revelation 3:12, 21; 20:13-15.

15. *Doctrine and Covenants* Section 128; *Mormon Doctrine*, 670, 822; *The Miracle of Forgiveness*, 165, 208-9; *Doctrines of Salvation*, 2:129-80.

15. Matthew 7:16-17, 21; Romans 6:1-4, 22; 7:6; 2 Corinthians 5:17; Galatians 5:16-25; Ephesians 2:10; Titus 2:14; James 2:18-20; 3:13; 1 John 2:3-6; 3:4-6.

16. LDS Article of Faith #4; *Teachings of the Prophet Joseph Smith*, 360; *Gospel Standards*, 8; *Discourses of Wilford Woodruff*, 19; *Mormon Doctrine*, 69-73; *Teachings of Lorenzo Snow*, 96.

16. Matthew 28:18-20; Luke 23:39-43; Acts 2:41; 8:12-13, 34-40; 16:14-15, 31-34; Romans 6:3-4; Ephesians 2:8-9.

17. *Gospel Principles*, 105; *The Pearl of Great Price*, Joseph Smith–History 1:18-20; *Teachings of Ezra Taft Benson*, 86; *Mormon Doctrine*, 634-37; *Encyclopedia of Mormonism*, 3:1220; *We Believe*, 800-13; *Teachings of Gordon B. Hinckley*, 548-51.

17. Matthew 16:18; 28:18-20; John 1:1-5; Romans 1:19-20; 2:1-7; 11:1-5.

18. *Doctrine and Covenants* 82:7-10; *Gospel Principles*, 292-93; *The Miracle of Forgiveness*, 360; *Repentance Brings Forgiveness*, 7, 12; *Doctrines of Salvation*, 2:14-15.	18. John 3:16-18; 5:24; 10:27-29; Romans 8:11-12, 28-39; 1 John 5:13.
19. *Doctrine and Covenants* 20:31-33; *Mormon Doctrine*, 699-700; *Miracle of Forgiveness*, 360; *Conference Report* (October 1898), 47; *Doctrines of Salvation*, 2:14-19.	19. John 3:16, 36; 5:24; 6:35-40; 10:27-30; Romans 8:1, 35-39; 1 Corinthians 1:7-9; Ephesians 4:30; 1 Peter 1:3-5; 1 John 5:11-13.

Appendix A
The Testimony of Lane Thuet*

I was born and raised in the Church of Jesus Christ of Latter-day Saints. In fact, I was a sixth-generation Mormon through my mother's lineage. I was the fourth child in my family of five. I was born in southern California, but before I was two my family moved back to Salt Lake City, Utah, where I was raised. All my life, the only religion I was taught and that I practiced was Mormonism. When I was little, I knew it was the true Church because everyone in the Church told me that it was. When I was older, I prayed about the *Book of Mormon* and had a "burning in the bosom" experience that I figured meant Mormonism was true.

When I was old enough to attend LDS seminary, I learned a little more about other religions from the Mormon perspective that they were all wrong. I was also taught incredible and awe-inspiring stories from my Church's history. Some of them were so impressive that I could not help thinking God must have had His hand in them. Details were told, videos were shown, and such heart-rending testimonies were given that I became emotionally tied to the religion as well.

It was very important to my parents that we live our religion and fulfill our obligations in it. This included going on missions[1] (for the boys) and having temple marriages.[2] I had always planned on going on a mission. Both of my older brothers had served missions, but when the time finally came for me to go, I had lost interest in doing so. My testimony[3] of Mormonism had not faltered. I still went to church faithfully and agreed with all LDS teachings. I just knew that I did not want to serve a mission at that time. This, of course, created a lot of displeasure when I tried to explain my decision to my parents. They were deeply disappointed, and did their best to talk me into going, but I refused. Still, they hoped that I might eventually change my mind and serve a mission at a later date. As it turned out, I never did go on a mission for the Mormon Church, even though at that time I still believed it was the true Church of Christ.

Once I made known to my Bishop[4] my intention not to serve a mission, he regarded my character with suspicion from then on. Because my decision was a personal one, he suspected there was a problem with my personal "worthiness," and he held me back in my regular priesthood advancement. But when confronted about this, he could not prove me guilty of any serious misdeeds. So he reluctantly made me an Elder[5] in the Church in March 1986, nearly one full year later than usual.

The following year, I met the woman that I would eventually marry. However, at the time she was not a member of the Mormon Church. I told her that I would not date her seriously unless she became a Mormon, because I did not want to marry outside of the LDS Church. She converted in April 1988, and we became engaged. Church rules dictated that she would not be allowed to go through the temple until she had been a member for a full year, so we set our wedding date for April of 1989.

Even though my fiancée was not allowed to attend the temple yet, I had a strong desire to do so. After interviews with both my Bishop and my Stake President, both agreed that I was qualified for a temple recommend—a document that is required to enter a Mormon temple.[6] On 21 September 1988, I went through the Salt Lake City temple and received my personal "endowment."[7]

I had been looking forward to this experience all my life, having been repeatedly taught that it would be the most holy and inspiring form of worship I could know. I was very eager to go, and invited my family and some friends to come with me in support. Right from the beginning, I felt humiliated by the washing and anointing ceremony, since I was required for this part to be totally naked except for a "shield" worn over my shoulders. (Basically, this was a very thin sheet, completely open on both sides, which hung down like a poncho. The style of this shield was changed in January 2005 so that it is no longer open on the sides.) I had to walk through various temple passageways in this condition and was led into a room where I was left with two strangers. These men offered prayers while touching my body at various points with a wet sponge or with oil on their fingers. (This part of the ceremony was also changed in January 2005, and is far less offensive. The washing and anointing are now done only by touching the person's head.) I was then led into another curtained room, where another stranger held my "sacred underwear" (called garments) open so that I could step into them.[8] After that, I was allowed to return to the locker room and dress in regular temple clothing,[9] and then to proceed through the main ceremony.

This part of the ceremony began by following part of the Biblical story of creation. But as it progressed, I found it more and more difficult to take seriously. The temple robes and caps seemed ridiculous, and the ceremony was something like going through a children's club ritual. I was very disappointed and wanted to leave. However, with my family and friends there, I kept quiet. They had already been through the temple, and looked as though they felt this was a holy worship experience.

The ceremony continued about two hours, and was often quite boring. As it continued, I became more concerned about the absurdity of it all. My father (who was my official temple escort that day) tried to break the tension by offering me some Pez candy at one point during the ritual. That helped me relax a little. I appreciated his understanding about how I was feeling.

After the ritual was over, I reflected on how disturbing the experience had been for me. I tried to convince myself that I just did not understand it well enough. I decided that I would probably have to experience the ceremony several more times before I could truly understand the significance of everything. In the months that followed, I went back to the temple alone several more times, reminding myself that the ceremony must be more sacred than it looked. I eventually became more accustomed to it, but it still continued to feel like nothing more than a bizarre clubhouse ritual.

I was married in the Salt Lake Temple on 14 April 1989. Since my wife had been a reluctant convert, she left the Church immediately afterward.[10] Over the next several months, she tried her best to convince me that Mormonism was false. Her brother, who was a born-again Christian, kept giving her information that might make me question my faith. I always had a reply that would brush off their questions, but it nagged at me that I never had any real answers for them. During the first year of our marriage, we experienced many difficult arguments because of my faith. My family tried to convince me that it would be best just to divorce her, but I did not listen to them. Consequently, my life was filled with a great deal of stress and tension, with no one that I felt I could turn to for help.

In the early spring of 1990, I was shown the engravings on the LDS History Museum across from Temple Square, and noticed the satanic pentagram among them.[11] There were other strange symbols around Temple Square as well, many on the temple itself. I knew what they were, and I immediately thought, "If this is the true church of Jesus Christ, then why do our Church leaders display the pentagram usually associated with Satanism on their buildings, but vehemently denounce the use of all common Christian symbols, such as the cross?" Once again, I could think of no reasonable answer, but I vowed to myself that I would find one.

No one in the Church leadership would offer any explanation about the pentagram or what meaning it held, officially, for the Church. The only clearly defined meanings I could find for the symbols were the ones associated with black magic. I searched deeper, and after researching this and some other prominent Mormon symbols, I concluded there was no acceptable reason for them to be there if the Church were truly of God. No matter what historical meanings the symbols held, currently they represent evil magic. Even though they may not have commonly held those meanings when the Salt Lake Temple was built, they certainly had them by the time the LDS History Museum was constructed. I could not see how using the symbols today was following the Apostle Paul's admonition to avoid "all appearance of evil" ("every kind of evil" [*NIV*] 1 Thessalonians 5:22). Though I was troubled by this issue, I was unwilling to leave the Church over it.

At about the same time, however, my brother-in-law confronted me with more information from "anti-Mormon" literature.[12] I was already disturbed about the pentagram, and I wanted to settle the matter finally—both to silence my brother-in-law and my wife, as well as for my own peace of mind. I knew that most of the things mentioned in the literature were not what I had been taught growing up. **I had always been told that "anti-Mormon" writers distorted the truth, told outright lies, and took quotes out of context to** prove their points. So I was unwilling to believe any of the information I had been given.

I decided that the best course of action was to go ahead and prove that the literature was wrong once and for all. I thought it would be easy, since I believed that the "anti-Mormon" writers were doing exactly what my Church leaders had told me they would do—lie and ignore context. So I looked into several of the allegations.[13] But, since I was extremely biased, I decided that I would only accept proof from pro-Mormon materials.[14] I assumed that if the LDS Church really were false, its own publications would prove it. But I was fully confident that even a long and difficult research project would ultimately prove Mormonism to be true.

I was stunned that **it took only three months of investigation in my spare time to reach an undeniable conclusion.** Unwilling to give in, I did even more intense and time consuming research—photocopying and carefully documenting everything I found along the way. **I concluded that the LDS leaders were the ones lying to me; it was the "anti-Mormon" writers who had actually been telling the truth.** Their quotes from Mormon literature **were not** out of context and the claims they made **were completely correct.**[15] I found that not only was Mormonism false, but that the **easiest** way to prove it was by examining Mormon literature. When investigated, LDS teachings can be seen to often contradict each other. What one prophet teaches as divine truth, another prophet teaches as false doctrine. Some LDS leaders even contradicted **themselves.** Most of them contradicted the basic teachings of the *Book of Mormon.* I was devastated to see these facts for myself, and found that I could not excuse them, ignore them, or explain them away.

Though I now knew Mormonism was not what it claimed to be, I still had a difficult time giving up my faith for a number of reasons. First, when I would pray for confirmation of my feelings from the Holy Spirit, I got no burning in the bosom. I did not know how to interpret this at the time.[16] Second, anytime I considered leaving Mormonism I underwent intense spiritual warfare—beyond anything I had ever heard of or seen in my lifetime.[17] Third, I knew I would risk losing my family or having them "cut-off" from me should I renounce my faith.[18] Finally, since Mormonism was all I knew, by giving it up I felt I would not have any spiritual foundation. Ultimately, I battled with myself for several weeks about whether I should just ignore the problems and remain in the Church, or leave. Eventually, I decided I could not stay in a false religion, but I continued to put off making my final decision as long as my conscience would allow. I finally compiled the information from my research into a study so I could see it all laid out before me, and the proof was overwhelming.[19] The LDS Church was not the true Church of Jesus Christ. The leaders were not truly inspired by God. They had, in fact, blatantly lied about many things on many occasions. At that point I knew I had to leave the Church permanently.

I sent my resignation letter, along with a copy of the results from my study, to the President of the Mormon Church—at the time Ezra Taft Bensen (who I am sure never saw it). The letter I received back indicated that they were unwilling to simply remove my name from their records.[20] Instead, they wanted to hold a "Bishop's Court" to review my character. Only after threatening a lawsuit did they comply, removing my name from their membership records. The verification letter stated that my name had been removed "in accordance with your request" on 23 October 1990.[21]

It was not until moving to California, and another year and a half had passed, that I looked into joining a Christian Church. During this time, I knew the facts of the gospel and continued to believe in God and in the Bible. But I had not accepted Jesus Christ into my heart as Lord and Savior. Then in April of 1992, during a membership class at the church I was attending, the full significance of the gospel message finally became clear to me, and I made that decision. I accepted Jesus as my Savior, and chose to follow Him. I knew that my baptism into the Mormon Church[22] did not fulfill the Biblical requirements for believer's baptism, so I was baptized as a believer in the true Jesus Christ of the Bible[23] in May of that year.

The difference in my life after that decision was astonishing. The spiritual warfare stopped completely. When I had followed Mormon teachings, I constantly felt discouraged as I tried to live according to all the laws required of me. No matter how hard I tried, I knew in my heart that I would never be perfect. But I also knew that perfection was the requirement, according to LDS leaders, for full salvation. Every day I wondered whether I had done enough good works to warrant entrance into the Celestial Kingdom of heaven. I never knew if I would eventually be admitted.

As a Mormon, I had received assurances from time to time that repentance would fill in whatever was missing for my salvation. I was told I just needed to work harder at living well and serving others. I knew that I was a decent person, and not anywhere near as bad as some people in the world seemed. I knew that I sinned every day, but in spite of that knowledge, I still did not see myself as a "sinner." I worked very hard at trying to earn my own salvation, only to find myself depressed and discouraged when I saw little progress. All I had was the dim hope that in the end my good works would outweigh my bad works and qualify me for heaven. It was an immense load on my shoulders.

For the first time, I truly felt the freedom promised in John 8:32-36. Once I learned the true gospel from the Bible, I understood more clearly my struggle against the flesh. I saw that there was no possible way that I could ever earn my own salvation. Thankfully, I also found that I did not have to. That was why Jesus Christ came to Earth—to provide it for me. That was also why Jesus had said on the cross, "It is finished."[24] The sacrifice was made for us! The work was completed there! All I had to do was accept that generous gift from God by putting my faith in the blood of Jesus Christ, which was shed on the cross on my behalf.[25] The load was removed. Now I am truly free—not free to sin, but free to worship God and follow his teachings with thankfulness, wonder and gratitude. Jesus loved me enough to come to earth and die on a cross so that I could be free from the penalty of my sin! I love Him because He first loved me, and I seek to obey Him in return!

It was shortly after this time that I finally understood God's work in my life back when I was 17. If I had served a Mormon mission, I know that I could have convinced many to join the LDS Church. Once I came to the knowledge that Mormonism was false, I would have been devastated that I had led them astray. Knowing that I had potentially led people away from Christ would have forever troubled my conscience. I think God knew this, and I believe that He kept me from going on a Mormon mission for that very reason.

He was working further in my life by giving me a strong desire to go through the temple, because now I am able to testify more fully of the things Mormonism teaches and believes. If I had not experienced the temple ceremony, then perhaps my witness would not be as complete. Since becoming born again, I have met with LDS missionaries on occasion. One asked me to pray again about the truthfulness of the *Book of Mormon* and the Mormon Church. I did. I got a "burning in the bosom" indicating that they were **not** true.

I know that feelings are unreliable, so I have continued to do research in the area of Mormon doctrine and history. The more I research, the more evidence I see that The Church of Jesus Christ of Latter-day Saints is **not** God's Church. I have also continued to study the Bible, learning more about salvation and the work of Christ. I have taken classes through Moody Bible Institute, and I am a certified Bible study leader for Precept Ministries International. I belong to a strong, Jesus-centered and Bible-believing Christian church. God has blessed me with three beautiful children, and I am excited to be teaching them about the true Christ of the Bible.

Having left the LDS Church, I now witness to their members about its doctrines. I know the position that Mormons are in, having been there myself; and I understand the kind of spiritual struggles they labor under. My heart aches for them to know the truth. Out of earnest love for them, I seek to show them that they are unfortunately being deceived. While they are honestly zealous for what they believe is the truth, they are basing their conclusions on lies. And although they are doing many good works, those works will never be able to save them.[26] I wish only for them to see the truth about Mormon history and doctrine, and for them to hear the true gospel message of the Bible. I long for them to know the freedom that I personally know, which is found in Jesus Christ alone. I also help equip other Christians to reach out to Mormons for Christ by showing them what the LDS Church teaches and contrasting that with what the Bible teaches. I help them learn how to share their hope with others. God has graciously permitted me to minister in this area, most notably through volunteer work with the Mormonism Research Ministry, which I have been affiliated with since 1998.

To all Mormons who may read this testimony, I beg you not to ignore the issues, nor to simply take my word alone about them. Take the time to check the facts out for yourself and see. With your eternal destiny at stake, a little time researching can prove forever valuable.

- **Appendix A Notes**

1. Mormon boys are taught from a very young age that it is their responsibility to serve a mission for the LDS Church. Mormon children even sing songs such as "I Hope They Call Me On A Mission" before they are even 10 years old. Boys will plan on leaving for a mission when they are 19. Any who decide not to serve a mission for any reason are put under strong pressure to go anyway (see Peggy Fletcher Stack, "Say No to the Mission Call and the Pressure Builds," *The Salt Lake Tribune*, 10 March 2001, C-1 to C-2). Young ladies who wish to serve a mission can do so after they reach age 21. The mission is from a year and a half to two years long. They can be assigned to preach in the United States or in any of the countries in which the Mormon Church is allowed to proselytize. If the mission requires a foreign language, the missionary spends three months in the LDS Missionary Training Center in Provo, Utah. While there, they are aggressively taught the foreign language they will need, and they are also instructed on how to make converts. They rarely witness to people on their own initiative. Instead, they are required to closely follow strict lesson plans developed and published by the leadership of the Mormon Church (in 2006, this curriculum was *"Preach My Gospel"* [Salt Lake City: The Church of Jesus Christ of Latter-day Saints, 2004]).

    This mission is supposed to be served at the expense of the missionary's family, rather than at any cost to the Church. Some families with very little income endure great sacrifices and hardship to pay for their children to go on a mission. If a child truly wants to serve a mission, but there is no possible way for the family to afford it, then the Church will cover a portion of the expense — but this is the exception rather than the rule.

The 2004 Statistical Report for the Mormon Church listed that as of 31 December 2004, there were 51,067 full-time missionaries (Conference Report, *Ensign*, May 2005, "Statistical Report, 2004," 25). This number was down by more than 5,100 from the previous year, and down by more than 10,500 from 2002 (see Conference Reports from *Ensign*, May 2004, 26 and May 2003, 25).

2. The Mormon Church teaches that couples can be married for both time and eternity. They believe marriage does not have to end at death in spite of Jesus' clear teaching (Matthew 22:30; Mark 12:25; Luke 20:34-36). But this requires that an LDS authority must perform the marriage ceremony in one of the Mormon Temples. This type of marriage is called a "Celestial Marriage," and the husband and wife are said to be "sealed" together by the ceremony. Any children born to them after being sealed are said to be born "under the covenant," which means the children are sealed to the parents in the hereafter, as well.

3. Mormons hold their personal convictions about the LDS Church as proof from God that it must be the only true Church. They are encouraged to share this "testimony" with each other and with those outside the Mormon Church. These testimonies usually consist of their personal feelings, and include any experiences that they believe prove the Mormon Church to be "true" (i.e.: the only true Church of God and Christ on earth). It is possible, and in fact very common, for a Mormon to see undeniable and logical proof that the LDS Church is false, and yet still believe it to be true simply because they have a very strong personal testimony. For more information about LDS testimonies, see Chapter 12 in this volume.

On the first Sunday of every month, the main Mormon congregational meeting is called a "Fast and Testimony Meeting." Members are urged to abstain from eating two meals on that day, and to donate the equivalent value of those meals to the Church for the purpose of helping feed underprivileged members. In addition, they do not take their final meal of the day until after this Sunday service is completed. During the service, the bulk of the time is set aside for members to stand and "bear their testimony" (i.e.: publicly share their feelings about the Church). Almost without fail, every testimony includes that the member "knows Joseph Smith was a true Prophet of God" and that they "know this [LDS] Church is true" and that their leaders are "truly called, inspired and led by God." In reality, there is no proof for these affirmations, they are most often not based on any concrete evidence (Romans 10:2). The member simply "feels deeply" that they must be true. Even their personal experiences do not qualify as substantial proof, because people from all religions and all faiths have had experiences that they believe prove their particular group to be truly led by God.

4. Mormon congregations are divided up into geographical areas. Each large area is called a "Stake," which is headed by a leader known as the Stake President. Within his Stake there are several small congregations which are called "Wards." Each Ward is headed by a Bishop. The Bishop is the local ecclesiastical leader for that congregation, much like a Pastor is the leader over a Christian church congregation.

5. An Elder in the Mormon Church is different from an Elder in most Christian denominations. It is not a position of great responsibility for a majority of Mormons; it is simply a ranking office within the "Higher Priesthood." Advancement within each Priesthood is based primarily upon age, though much is said of personal worthiness playing a factor. Experience has shown me that personal worthiness had nothing to do with many boys advancing in the Priesthood. Some advanced at the regular pace in spite of their lack of personal worthiness.

In the "Lesser" LDS Priesthood—the Aaronic Priesthood—there are three offices, or ranks: Deacons, Teachers and Priests. Most LDS boys become Deacons at age 12, but they do not function as Deacons do in Christian Churches. Their main duties are to pass the emblems of the sacrament (communion) to the congregation each week, and assist the Teachers with their duties. They become Teachers upon turning age 14. These young men do not actually teach any classes. Instead, they usher at the doors to the Chapel, assist in all the duties of the Deacons, and accompany others in visiting the members of the local Ward on a monthly basis. They also collect the tithes and offerings from the membership of the Church on the first Sunday of each month. They become Priests at age 16, but again, this is nothing like the priests of the Bible. They say the public blessing on the sacrament, and are given the "authority" to baptize people into the Mormon Church. However, before they can actually exercise this function, they must have individual authorization from their Bishop.

Young LDS men are usually given the "Higher" Mormon Priesthood—called the Melchizedek Priesthood—at age 18. This Priesthood officially consists of six offices: Elder, High Priest, Seventy, Patriarch, Apostle and Presidency of the High Priesthood (see John Widtsoe, *Priesthood and Church Government* [Salt Lake City: Deseret Book, 1939], 111-12). Most of the members who hold this Priesthood are Elders. Their primary function is to serve as missionaries, and to pass on the "gift of the Holy Ghost" through the laying on of hands. If a calling within the Church requires it, they are then made High Priests or Patriarchs. Those who become "General Authorities" over the Church are made Seventies or Apostles. The head over the whole Church is the Presidency.

6. A "temple recommend" is a certificate authorizing the recipient's entrance into a Mormon temple. To receive one, an individual must be declared "worthy" by the Bishop and Stake President, and be an active Church member for at least one year. Men must hold the Melchizedek Priesthood, though they can belong to any rank within it.

The Bishop interviews the one seeking the recommend using the following questions, each of which must be answered with a "yes:"

1. Do you believe in God, the Eternal Father, in His Son, Jesus Christ, and in the Holy Ghost? Do you have a firm testimony of the restored [i.e.: LDS] gospel?
2. Do you sustain the President of the Church of Jesus Christ of Latter-day Saints as the prophet, seer and revelator? Do you recognize him as the only person on earth authorized to exercise all priesthood keys?
3. Do you live the Law of Chastity [remaining morally pure and undefiled]?
4. Are you a full tithe payer [members are required to pay a full 10% tithe on their income]?
5. Do you keep the Word of Wisdom [a set of rules regarding physical health: i.e., abstinence from certain foods and drinks and other standards, such as not smoking and not drinking alcohol]?
6. Are you totally honest in all your dealings with others?
7. Do you earnestly strive to do your duty in the Church; to attend your sacrament, priesthood and other meetings; and to obey the rules, laws and commandments of the gospel?
8. Do you live in accordance with the teachings of the gospel?

There are two additional questions for divorced members which basically ask if they are paying a full spousal and child support in accordance with their court orders.

After the Bishop's approval, the person then meets with the Stake President, who asks the same series of questions and then usually grants the request. The recommend allows access to any LDS temple for one year. After it expires, the whole process must be repeated.

7. An LDS "Endowment" is basically a course of instruction, ordinances and covenants given in LDS temples. A member is said to have received their endowment after going through the temple ceremony for the first time. It includes a series of specific rituals. First is the "washing and anointing." Then,

special underwear is placed upon them, and they are given a new name, which is to be remembered but kept secret all their life. Then they go through a long ceremony depicting scenes from the Book of Abraham, Chapters 4 and 5; and the Book of Moses, Chapter 4. Other elements are included in the drama, as well. During the ritual, patrons are given secret words, handshakes (called "tokens") and hand signs which will supposedly allow them access into heaven after they die. However, they must remember and be able to give all of them correctly to sentinel angels in order to enter the Celestial Kingdom. This is why temple Mormons are encouraged to return and repeat the ceremony on a regular basis. The first time they experience this ceremony, they are being endowed for themselves. Every subsequent time they go through the temple, they will be endowed on behalf of someone who is dead.

8. When individuals go through the LDS temple ceremony for the first time, they "place" the sacred underwear onto their body. Since the design of the underwear does not really allow this, they do it as best they can, making it clear that placing the garment upon them is their real intent. The official name of this underwear is "The Garment of the Holy Priesthood," but most Mormons simply refer to them as their "garments."

These garments are made of a lightweight, white material (patrons have their choice of several different fabrics), and can be purchased in one piece or two piece varieties. It covers from the neck down to the knees, and can be purchased in a long or short sleeve style.

There are special marks sewn into these garments. There is a "square" over the right breast, which looks like a reverse capital "L"; a "compass" over the left breast, which looks like a capital "V"; a flat, horizontal mark over the navel, and another over the right knee. Each mark is to serve as a reminder to the LDS member.

Mormons are told that if they remain true and faithful to their temple covenants, their garments will serve as a "shield and a protection" to them. They are to wear these garments throughout the rest of their lives, only removing them for laundering or changing, and they are strongly advised not to be out of them longer than it would take to put on a new set. Realistically, most Mormons remove them for bathing, swimming, sports and having marital relations. However, there are some that take their faith in these garments to extremes and will not even remove them for these activities. Many cases have been reported of people who would take one arm or leg out of the garment, wash it, then immediately place that limb into a clean garment. Only then would they remove the next limb and follow the same procedure, so that they were never fully out of their garments for anything.

Hundreds of stories are circulated throughout the LDS Church of people who have been miraculously "preserved" by their garments. One such story I heard personally was of a woman who claimed she had been badly burned over her entire body—except for where her garments covered the skin. Another story I heard told of a person whose garments supposedly stopped a bullet. Yet for every such undocumented and unsubstantiated story, several more can be told of faithful Mormons whose garments afforded them no protection at all in similar circumstances.

All in all, to Mormons the garment has become nothing more than a sacred talisman of sorts. Yet belief in this talisman has generated millions of dollars in revenue for the Mormon Church, since the only place to purchase this sacred underwear is through their Church-owned manufacturing and distributing plant (Beehive Clothing).

9. All temple clothing is white, and is worn over the sacred garments. For men, this clothing includes regular shirts, pants, belt, socks and slippers. For women it is a simple white gown, socks and slippers.

At later points in the ceremony, patrons also put on a cap (or veil), robe, sash and apron. All are white except for the apron, which is usually green. These additional items are then worn over the temple clothing for the remainder of the ceremony, and until they change back into their street clothing when they are ready to leave the building.

Strangely enough, each temple patron's street clothing is kept in a locker in the basement of the temple, always secured with a lock while they go through the ceremony. Since only "worthy" individuals are allowed into the temple, it seems contradictory that they should need to furnish a lock to protect personal belongings while there. Yet this is provided for members in every temple.

10. Three days prior to our wedding day, she had gone through the temple to receive her own endowment. She later admitted that the entire time she was in the temple, she was uncomfortable. She felt that the whole ceremony was wrong, admitting that—to her—it did not have a godly feeling. Instead, she felt an oppressive atmosphere throughout the ceremony. This confirmed her suspicion that the LDS church was not true, but she remained a member just long enough to complete the marriage ceremony a few days later out of respect for me.

    I mention these events as matters of fact, but I do so with caution that the Bible is very clear in teaching that we are not to rely on our subjective feelings to determine what is the truth. Instead, we are to test everything by the only true standard of God—the teachings of the Bible—to determine what is truth and what is error (Genesis 6:5; Jeremiah 17:9; 1 Thessalonians 5:21; 2 Timothy 3:16-17). There are many teachings in the Bible that the Mormon temple ceremony contradicts. While I do not believe that the Mormon temples or their ceremonies are intrinsically evil in themselves, I do know that God is not their source.

11. Over the entrance to this museum, located across the street to the west of Temple Square in Salt Lake City, Utah, is a collage of engravings representing various events in the history of the LDS Church. In the upper left-hand side, above the historical engravings but off by themselves, there are two special stars carved into the granite facing. One is the satanic pentagram—an upside-down, five-pointed star in a circle. The one next to

it is commonly known in the magic world as the "goat's-head star"—also an upside-down, five-pointed star, but with the horizontal arms shortened.

Both of these symbols, I found in researching further, are frequently used in black magic and Satanism. Even some witches avoid the use of these symbols because of their association with black magic. It should be noted that the inverted pentagram has also been associated with one of the degrees of Freemasonry, but long before its association with them it was being used in Satanism and black magic.

In all my research, no LDS leader would explain what the symbols officially meant, a refusal which I found disturbing. I was a temple Mormon and privy to the secrets of the temple, yet they refused to give an explanation for publicly displaying these symbols. Other LDS writers had come to the unofficial conclusion that the "goat's-head star" was representative of the "Star of the Morning," another name in Mormonism for Jesus. One writer in particular, Matthew B. Brown, wrote an article entitled "Inverted Stars on LDS Temples" (copyrighted May 2002). By citing examples from the drawings of men who have never been known as great historical teachers of Christianity, Brown concludes that inverted stars were common Christian symbols from early times (pp. 5-8), and claims the symbol did not become associated with Satanism until the mid-1800s. Specifically, he claims that connotation came after Joseph Smith employed its use in the Nauvoo Temple design (pp. 9-10).

While I disagree with Brown's conclusions regarding the origin of the star, I agree that Smith probably never associated the star with any evil connotations. Rather, there is abundant evidence that shows he borrowed the symbology directly from Freemasonry, which employed it long before the 1800s. Joseph Smith had been initiated into the first three degrees of Freemasonry on the 15th and 16th of March 1842. Six weeks later, he instituted the full temple "endowment ceremony," undeniably patterned after the first three degrees of Freemasonry. Before then, the Mormon temple ceremonies never included washing and anointing of the body (previously it had only been a foot washing ceremony), wearing garments, use of secret words, handshakes and signs, use of the "compass" and "square," swearing oaths, wearing robes and aprons, employment of penalties or secrecy—all were essential parts of the Masonic ceremony. Smith had a vision in which he supposedly saw the symbology for the Nauvoo Temple on 5 February 1844—two years after becoming a Freemason. Until that temple was built, he had been giving the endowment ceremony to select Mormon leaders in the same room that they were using for the Freemason lodge.

Prior to this time, all Mormon buildings that featured symbology (such as the Kirtland, Ohio temple) employed ordinary geometric symbols and patterns. No stars, moons, pentagrams or other detailed symbols were used **until after** Smith became a Freemason. **Since then**, symbols common in Freemasonry have been liberally used in the construction of LDS temples and buildings. Even Mormon writer E. Cecil McGavin writes, "Masons who visit the Temple Block in Salt Lake City are impressed by what they call the Masonic emblems displayed on the outside of the Mormon Temple. Yes, the 'Masonic emblems' are displayed.... Masonic writers tell us that the Mormon Temple ritual and their own are slightly similar in some respects. Without any apologies we frankly admit that there may be some truth in these statements" (*Mormonism and Masonry* [Salt Lake City: Stevens and Wallace, 1947], 6).

No matter where the symbols originated or what meaning they have held in the past, **the fact is that current culture regards these emblems as having strong connections to black magic and even Satanism.** That a church, which claims to be the "Church of Jesus Christ," would still employ them, then, is indefensible.

12. Specifically, I was given a copy of *The Maze of Mormonism*, by Walter Martin (Ventura, Calif.: Regal Books, 1978); and *Mormonism, Mama and Me*, by Thelma Geer (Chicago: Moody Press, 1986). In addition, I was shown several pamphlets and tracts—all of which listed many of the unbiblical teachings of

Mormonism. They also compared and contrasted teachings from various prophets of the Mormon Church, showing the many contradictions between them. They pointed out contradictions between the teachings of the Mormon Scriptures and the official Church doctrines. I was asked what I thought of these materials, and my first response was that they were not telling the truth. Further investigation showed that they **were** definitely telling the truth.

13. They are listed in endnote 19.

14. I wanted to see the original teachings in books that were endorsed by and distributed through the Mormon Church. If I examined the Mormon material first-hand, in the context intended by the speakers and writers, then I would know whether these non-Mormon books were telling the truth.

   Most of the teachings and doctrines mentioned in the non-Mormon books were taken from the *Journal of Discourses,* 26 vols. (England: various publishers, 1854-1886 [photo reprint])— a set of books which contain the lectures and discourses of the early prophets and apostles of the LDS Church—and the *History of the Church of Jesus Christ of Latter-day Saints,* 7 vols. (Salt Lake City: Deseret Book Company, 1951)—an official publication ostensibly copied from the journal entries of Joseph Smith. There were various other publications mentioned and quoted, and I wanted to see the information in these materials first-hand as well.

   The problem was that I did not own most of these books. But since I was living in Salt Lake City, Utah at the time, I had access to these original publications through the University of Utah Library Archive, the Salt Lake City Public Library Archive, and the LDS Church Historian's Office Archive. Everything I checked out, I photocopied and kept in a notebook.

15. While there are some writers out there who twist the truth, I have found that most LDS critics are very honest in what they write, and accurate in the research they present. Certainly the ones I

looked into were truthful in their presentations. Since leaving Mormonism I have read the research and findings of many more writers considered to be "anti-Mormon," and, for the most part, their work is truthful and well researched. **Nevertheless, I always encourage both Mormons and non-Mormons to check out for themselves everything they read.** Even the information I present should be double-checked by anyone reading it. That way there is no question that quotations and other sources of information are accurate and in context.

16. I do now. I realized that I wanted to believe Mormonism was still true. I did not want a feeling that would confirm that my research had shown me the truth. Anything that might have served as such a feeling, I simply ignored.

17. To this day, I still find it hard to believe that some of these things happened. It almost seemed as though my wife and I were trapped in a haunted apartment, though I knew for a fact we were not. I had never believed in ghosts, spirits, or demons until then.

    The experiences ranged from the normal to the extreme paranormal. They included repeated, frightening nightmares. Voices called to us at night from empty rooms. Doors would open and close by themselves—even a sliding door we had would slowly rumble shut, then after a minute begin to slide open again. Sudden and debilitating feelings of an overpowering, evil presence would overtake us. The presence of strong odors, flashes of bright light and unexplainable temperature changes would occur in various rooms. Other unexplainable events happened so that we were terrified of being alone in the apartment or of going to sleep at night for fear of what might happen. We changed apartments to get away from these events, only to find them more frequent and more intense in the new apartment. Once we were even "visited" by a relative that had long been dead.

    The frequency of these strange happenings dropped dramatically once our names had been removed from LDS Church records. After accepting Jesus Christ into my heart as the Bible teaches, they stopped completely and have never returned. I would like to think that we only imagined these events, but since Shawna also experienced them with me and vividly remembers them as well, I cannot deny them.

I have since discovered that many of these same events are very common to those who are trying to escape the bonds of the occult. Johanna Michaelsen recalls many of the same kinds of episodes as she was struggling to leave occult bondage, and documents them in her book *The Beautiful Side of Evil* (Eugene, Oreg.: Harvest House, 1982). Dr. Kurt Koch also lists such incidents and gives many examples of them in his book *Christian Counseling and Occultism* (Grand Rapids: Kregel Publications, 1965). Thankfully, we had not gone through some of the more serious encounters that others had experienced.

Actually, I even hesitated to recount these things we experienced. But I have to admit that they really happened. I take some reassurance in the fact that we were not alone in experiencing such spiritual warfare.

18. Sometimes, when members of a family leave the LDS Church, the remaining members are counseled by the Church leadership to have nothing more to do with the "apostates." They recommend no contact of any kind between them. This is what being "cut off" from family means. One possible rationale for this is that if the dissenting members love their family more than their religious convictions, they will return to the LDS Church. If they do not, then the severed ties will keep them from convincing the rest of their family that the Church is wrong. This is a very common practice among the cults.

19. The study basically contained the following information:
    Section 1: Proof that Joseph Smith was a false prophet by examining 13 of his prophecies that failed.
    Following this opening study, the main body of the research contained 10 chapters of information. In each chapter, I documented that the doctrine was once or is currently taught in Mormonism, then show

how the Bible, *Book of Mormon*, and/or other LDS leaders contradict the teaching.

Chapter 1: The Adam-God doctrine. Joseph Smith and Brigham Young taught that the God of this world that Mormons worship was in reality Adam, the first man.

Chapter 2: Conclusive proof that the Mormon Church teaches a belief in the **plurality of Gods.**

Chapter 3: The doctrine of Adam's creation. Brigham Young taught that Adam was not made from the dust of this earth, but was rather transported here from another one.

Chapter 4: The doctrine of the birth of Jesus Christ. The *Book of Mormon* teaches that Jesus was born in Jerusalem, not Bethlehem. Brigham Young taught that Christ was conceived by a literal, physical sexual union between God the Father and Mary.

Chapter 5: The doctrine of Blood Atonement. Brigham Young and his contemporary LDS leaders taught that the blood of Christ would never atone for certain sins. Instead, sinners had to have their own blood shed to atone for their sins. This was also a part of the temple ceremony for decades, including the ceremony I experienced. These sins included: stealing, murder, adultery, immorality, breaking temple covenants, not receiving the LDS gospel when presented, marriage of Caucasians to those of African ancestry, not forsaking sins (no matter how trivial), and apostasy from the Mormon Church.

Chapter 6: The doctrine of God's progression. Mormonism teaches that God was once a man, and that He progressed in knowledge and experience until He became a God. Some leaders taught that He continues to progress. Others teach that He has gone as far as is possible. This doctrine is the foundation for the LDS belief that Mormon men can become Gods eventually.

Insert 1: This section was added at the request of several people who had read my study. It was **an actual transcript of the Mormon temple ceremony** prior to 10 April 1990. Jerald and Sandra Tanner graciously gave me permission to photocopy the transcript from their book, *Mormonism—Shadow or Reality?* (Salt Lake City: Utah Lighthouse Ministry, 1987) to put into the study.

Chapter 7: Changes to the Temple Ceremony. Since the temple ceremony was drastically changed while I was researching all the information for that study, I included a chapter examining the changes as well as previous changes that it had undergone. Since God supposedly revealed the ceremony and it was said to be necessary for salvation, the fact that it had undergone so many changes proved that these claims were untrue.

Insert 2: This was **the transcript of the then current Mormon temple ceremony**, photocopied from the Tanner's book, *Evolution of the Mormon Temple Ceremony: 1842-1990* (Salt Lake City: Utah Lighthouse Ministry, 1990). Further changes to the ceremony were made in January 2005, mainly relating to the washing and anointing ceremony.

Chapter 8: Research into pagan symbology. This chapter set forth all my findings related to the symbols found on and around Temple Square in Salt Lake City.

Chapter 9: General questions. This section listed 58 questions about LDS doctrines—most of which were my own, but some of which were used by permission from other authors—all of which have no logical answer. Some of them show that the LDS teachings make no sense, contradict other teachings, or demonstrate that the Mormon belief system is both illogical and unscriptural in many respects.

Chapter 10: This chapter was a brief exposition of the true gospel of Jesus Christ, as taught in the Bible.

Appendix: This last section included photocopies of all **written communications between me and the LDS Church** as I was seeking to have my name removed from their records.

20. Mormon Church leaders do not want a member to simply leave the church. That would generate too many questions from the remaining membership. They will wonder why the apostate left, or even ask the person for their reasons. Instead, the leadership would prefer to "excommunicate" the person. There is a very negative connotation associated with being excommunicated, because that usually does not happen unless a person is involved in a grave sin. So, when an individual wishes to have his or her name removed from Church records, the leaders immediately set up a "Bishop's Court" to hear the person's complaint. After the member airs his or her grievances, the Bishop then excommunicates the member. This way, the person is not regarded as having removed his or her name from the records voluntarily.

    My wife and I refused to attend any kind of Bishop's Court, and received verification from the Church that the only reason our names were removed was because we had requested the action. However, we had to threaten legal action to accomplish this.

21. Letter from F. Michael Watson (Secretary to the First Presidency) to Lane A. Thuet, dated 2 March 1992. The letter also stated that Shawna's name had also been removed as per our request.

22. I was baptized into the Mormon Church on 2 August 1975, at age eight. I had waited several extra months so that my oldest brother would be able to perform the ordinance for me. Eight years old is the usual age at which children in the Mormon Church are baptized. It seems strange, because the Mormon Church teaches that the main purpose of baptism is to cleanse people from their sins. Meanwhile, it also teaches that children are not account-

able for their sins until they reach that age. Realistically, then, these children are baptized to cleanse them from sins for which they are not accountable. However, a secondary purpose for the baptism is that it is a requirement for Church membership, so perhaps this is the main objective in baptizing them.

23. See Chapter 10 for a comparison between the Mormon Jesus and the true Jesus Christ of the Bible.

24. John 19:30.

25. Romans 5:9-10; Ephesians 2:13-16; Colossians 1:19-22; Hebrews 9:22-26; 1 Peter 2:21-24.

26. Romans 3:27-28; 4:4-5; Galatians 2:16; 3:10-14; Ephesians 2:8-10.

Appendix B
Short Biographies of Quoted LDS Leaders

(Listed alphabetically by last name.)
Further information is available in *The Deseret News Church Almanac*, published annually.

Bangerter, W. Grant
Born: 8 June 1918

LDS Leadership:
Assistant to the Quorum of Twelve Apostles – 4 April 1975
First Quorum of Seventy – 1 October 1976
Presidency of the First Quorum of Seventy – 30 Sept 1978 to 5 April 1980
 Again – 17 February 1985 to 1 October 1989
Emeritus General Authority – 1 October 1989

Benson, Ezra Taft
Born: 4 August 1899; Died: 30 May 1994

LDS Leadership:
Quorum of Twelve Apostles – 7 October 1943
President of Quorum of Twelve Apostles – 30 December 1973
13th President of the LDS Church – 10 November 1985

Brown, Hugh B.
Born: 24 October 1883; Died: 2 December 1975

LDS Leadership:
Assistant to the Quorum of Twelve Apostles – 4 October 1953

Quorum of Twelve Apostles – 10 April 1958
Counselor in First Presidency – 22 June 1961
(under President David O. McKay)
Second Counselor in First Presidency – 12 October 1961
(under President David O. McKay)
First Counselor in First Presidency – 4 October 1963
(under President David O. McKay)
Released back to Quorum of Twelve Apostles – 18 January 1970

Cannon, George Q.
Born: 11 January 1827; Died: 12 April 1901

LDS Leadership:
Quorum of Twelve Apostles – 26 August 1860
Counselor in the First Presidency – 8 April 1873
(under President Brigham Young)
Assistant Counselor in the First Presidency – 9 May 1874
(under President Brigham Young)
First Counselor in the First Presidency – 10 October 1880
(under President John Taylor)
First Counselor in the First Presidency – 7 April 1889
(under President Wilford Woodruff)
First Counselor in the First Presidency – 13 September 1898
(under President Lorenzo Snow)

Clark Jr., J. Reuben
Born: 1 September 1871; Died: 6 October 1961

LDS Leadership:
Second Counselor in the First Presidency – 6 April 1933
(under President Heber J. Grant)
First Counselor in the First Presidency – 6 October 1934
(under President Heber J. Grant)
Quorum of Twelve Apostles – 11 October 1934

First Counselor in the First Presidency – 21 May 1945
   (under President George Albert Smith)
Second Counselor in the First Presidency – 9 April 1951
   (under President David O. McKay)
First Counselor in the First Presidency – 12 June 1959
   (under President David O. McKay)

Corrill, John
Born: 17 September 1794; Died: 1843

LDS Leadership:
Second Counselor to Presiding Bishop Edward Partridge –
   6 June 1831 to 1 August 1837
Excommunicated – 17 March 1839

Cowdery, Oliver
Born: 3 October 1806; Died: 3 March 1850

LDS Leadership:
Apostle – May 1829
Second Elder of the LDS Church – 6 April 1830
Assistant President of the LDS Church – 5 December 1834
Assistant Counselor in the First Presidency – 3 September 1837
   (under President Joseph Smith, Jr.)
Excommunicated – 12 April 1838
Rebaptized – 12 November 1848

Grant, Heber J.
Born: 22 November 1856; Died: 14 May 1945

LDS Leadership:
Quorum of Twelve Apostles – 16 October 1882

President of the Quorum of Twelve Apostles –
23 November 1916
7th **President** of the LDS Church – 23 November 1918

Grant, Jedediah M.
Born: 21 February 1816; Died: 1 December 1856

LDS Leadership:
One of the First Seven Presidents of the Seventy – 2 December 1845
Quorum of Twelve Apostles – 7 April 1854
Second Counselor in the First Presidency – 7 April 1854
 (under President Brigham Young)

Hales, Robert D.
Born: 24 August 1932

LDS Leadership:
Assistant to the Quorum of Twelve Apostles – 4 April 1975
First Quorum of Seventy – 1 October 1976
Presiding Bishop – 6 April 1985
Quorum of Twelve Apostles – 7 April 1994

Hinckley, Gordon B.
Born: 23 June 1910

LDS Leadership:
Assistant to the Quorum of Twelve Apostles – 6 April 1958
Quorum of Twelve Apostles – 5 October 1961
Counselor in the First Presidency – 23 July 1981
 (under President Spencer W. Kimball)
Second Counselor in the First Presidency – 2 December 1982
 (under President Spencer W. Kimball)

First Counselor in the First Presidency – 10 November 1985
  (under President Ezra Taft Benson)
President of the Quorum of Twelve Apostles – 5 June 1994
First Counselor in the First Presidency – 5 June 1994
  (under President Howard W. Hunter)
15th President of the LDS Church – 12 March 1995

Holland, Jeffrey R.
Born: 3 December 1940

LDS Leadership:
First Quorum of the Seventy – 1 April 1989
Quorum of Twelve Apostles – 23 June 1994

Hunter, Milton R.
Born: 25 October 1902; Died: 27 June 1975

LDS Leadership:
Seventy – 31 August 1928
First Council of the Seventy – 6 April 1945

Hyde, Orson
Born: 8 January 1805; Died: 28 November 1878

LDS Leadership:
Quorum of Twelve Apostles – 15 February 1835
Dropped from the Quorum of Twelve Apostles – 4 May 1839
Restored to Quorum of Twelve Apostles – 27 June 1839
President of Quorum of Twelve Apostles – 27 December 1847
Repositioned lower in Quorum of Twelve Apostles –
  10 April 1875

Ivins, Anthony W.
Born: 16 September 1852; Died: 23 September 1934

LDS Leadership:
Quorum of Twelve Apostles – 6 October 1907
Second Counselor in the First Presidency – 10 March 1921
    (under President Heber J. Grant)
First Counselor in the First Presidency – 28 May 1925
    (under President Heber J. Grant)

Kimball, Heber C.
Born: 14 June 1801; Died: 22 June 1868

LDS Leadership:
Quorum of Twelve Apostles – 14 February 1835
First Counselor in the First Presidency – 27 December 1847
    (under President Brigham Young)

Kimball, Spencer W.
Born: 28 March 1895; Died: 5 November 1985

LDS Leadership:
Quorum of Twelve Apostles – 7 October 1943
Acting President of the Quorum of Twelve Apostles – 23 January 1970
President of the Quorum of Twelve Apostles – 7 July 1972
12th President of the LDS Church – 30 December 1973

Lyman, Richard R.
Born: 23 November 1870; Died: 31 December 1963

LDS Leadership:
Quorum of Twelve Apostles – 7 April 1918

Excommunicated – 12 November 1943
Rebaptized – 27 October 1954

McConkie, Bruce R.
Born: 29 July 1915; Died: 19 April 1985

LDS Leadership:
First Council of the Seventy – 6 October 1946
Quorum of Twelve Apostles – 12 October 1972

McKay, David O.
Born: 8 September 1873; Died: 18 January 1970

LDS Leadership:
Quorum of Twelve Apostles – 9 April 1906
Second Counselor in the First Presidency – 6 October 1934
    (under President Heber J. Grant)
Second Counselor in the First Presidency – 21 May 1945
    (under President George A. Smith)
President of the Quorum of Twelve Apostles – 30 September 1950
9th **President** of the LDS Church – 9 April 1951

McLellin, William E.
Born: 18 January 1806; Died: 24 April 1883

LDS Leadership:
Quorum of Twelve Apostles – 15 February 1835
Excommunicated – 11 May 1838

Monson, Thomas S.
Born: 21 August 1927

LDS Leadership:
Quorum of Twelve Apostles – 10 October 1963
Second Counselor in the First Presidency – 10 November 1985
  (under President Ezra Taft Benson)
Second Counselor in the First Presidency – 5 June 1994
  (under President Howard W. Hunter)
President of the Quorum of Twelve Apostles – 12 March 1995
First Counselor in the First Presidency – 12 March 1995
  (under President Gordon B. Hinckley)

Morgan, John
Born: 8 August 1842; Died: 14 August 1894

LDS Leadership:
Quorum of the Seventy – 8 October 1875
One of the First Seven Presidents of the Seventy –
  5 October 1884

Oaks, Dallin H.
Born: 12 August 1932

LDS Leadership:
Quorum of Twelve Apostles – 3 May 1984

Packer, Boyd K.
Born: 10 September 1924

LDS Leadership:
Assistant to the Quorum of Twelve Apostles –
  30 September 1961
Quorum of Twelve Apostles – 9 April 1970

Acting President of the Quorum of Twelve Apostles – 5 June 1994, 12 March 1995
    and 2 October 2004.

Peterson, Mark E.
Born: 7 November 1900; Died: 11 January 1984

LDS Leadership:
Quorum of Twelve Apostles – 20 April 1944

Pratt, Orson
Born: 19 September 1811; Died: 3 October 1881

LDS Leadership:
Quorum of Twelve Apostles – 26 April 1835
Excommunicated – 20 August 1842
Rebaptized – 20 January 1843
Ordained to former office in Quorum of Twelve Apostles –
    20 January 1843
Repositioned lower in Quorum of Twelve Apostles –
    10 April 1875

Pratt, Parley P.
Born: 12 April 1807; Died: 13 May 1857

LDS Leadership:
Quorum of Twelve Apostles – 21 February 1835

Richards, Franklin D.
Born: 2 April 1821; Died: 9 December 1899

LDS Leadership:
Quorum of Twelve Apostles – 12 February 1849

President of the Quorum of Twelve Apostles –
13 September 1898

Richards, LeGrande
Born: 6 February 1886; Died: 11 January 1983

LDS Leadership:
Presiding Bishop – 6 April 1938
Quorum of Twelve Apostles – 10 April 1952

Roberts, Brigham H.
Born: 13 March 1857; Died: 27 September 1933

LDS Leadership:
Quorum of Seventy – 8 March 1877
One of the First Seven Presidents of the Quorum of Seventy
 – 7 October 1888

Smith, George A.
Born: 26 June 1817; Died: 1 September 1875

LDS Leadership:
Quorum of Twelve Apostles – 26 April 1839
First Counselor in the First Presidency – 7 October 1868
 (under President Brigham Young)

Smith, Hyrum
Born: 9 February 1800; Died: 27 June 1844

LDS Leadership:
Assistant Counselor in the First Presidency –
 3 September 1837
 (under President Joseph Smith, Jr.)

Second Counselor in the First Presidency
(under President Joseph Smith, Jr.) – 7 November 1837
Quorum of Twelve Apostles – 24 January 1841
Patriarch to the Church – 24 January 1841
Assistant President of the LDS Church – 24 January 1841

Smith, Joseph F.
Born: 13 November 1838; Died: 19 November 1918

LDS Leadership:
Ordained Apostle – 1 July 1866
Counselor in the First Presidency – 1 July 1866
(under President Brigham Young)
Quorum of Twelve Apostles – 8 October 1867
Second Counselor in the First Presidency – 10 October 1880
(under President John Taylor)
Second Counselor in the First Presidency – 7 April 1889
(under President Wilford Woodruff)
Second Counselor in the First Presidency – 13 September 1898
(under President Lorenzo Snow)
First Counselor in the First Presidency – 6 October 1901, not set apart.
(under President Lorenzo Snow)
6th **President** of the LDS Church – 17 October 1901

Smith, Joseph Fielding
Born: 19 July 1876; Died: 2 July 1972

LDS Leadership:
Quorum of Twelve Apostles – 7 April 1910
Acting President of Quorum of Twelve Apostles – 30 September 1950
President of the Quorum of Twelve Apostles – 9 April 1951

Counselor in the First Presidency – 29 October 1965
(under President David O. McKay)
10th **President** of the LDS Church – 23 January 1970

Smith, William B.
Born: 13 March 1811; Died: 13 November 1893

LDS Leadership:
Quorum of Twelve Apostles – 15 February 1835
Dropped from the Quorum of Twelve Apostles – 4 May 1839
Restored to Quorum of Twelve Apostles – 25 May 1839
Patriarch to the Church – 24 May 1845
   (Rejected by Church membership 6 October 1845)
Dropped from Quorum of Twelve Apostles – 6 October 1845
Excommunicated – 19 October 1845

Smith Jr., Joseph
Born: 23 December 1805; Died: 27 June 1844

LDS Leadership:
Organized the LDS Church – 6 April 1830
First Elder (Acting President) in the LDS Church – 6 April 1830
1st **President** of the LDS Church – 25 January 1832

Snow, Lorenzo
Born: 3 April 1814; Died: 10 October 1901

LDS Leadership:
Quorum of Twelve Apostles – 12 February 1849
Counselor in the First Presidency – 8 April 1873
   (under President Brigham Young)
President of the Quorum of Twelve Apostles – 7 April 1889
5th **President** of the LDS Church – 13 September 1898

Stevenson, Edward
Born: 1 May 1820; Died: 27 January 1897

LDS Leadership:
Quorum of Seventy – 1 May 1844
One of the First Seven Presidents of the Seventy – 7 October 1894

Talmage, James E.
Born: 21 September 1862; Died: 27 July 1933

LDS Leadership:
Quorum of Twelve Apostles – 8 December 1911

Taylor, John
Born: 1 November 1808; Died: 25 July 1887

LDS Leadership:
Quorum of Twelve Apostles – 19 December 1838
President of the Quorum of Twelve Apostles – 6 October 1877
3rd **President** of the LDS Church – 10 October 1880

Taylor, John W.
Born: 15 May 1858; Died: 10 October 1916

LDS Leadership:
Quorum of Twelve Apostles – 9 April 1884
Resigned as Apostle – 28 October 1905
Excommunicated – 28 March 1911

Wells, Daniel H.
Born: 27 October 1814; Died: 24 March 1891

LDS Leadership:
Second Counselor in the First Presidency – 4 January 1857
  (under President Brigham Young)
Counselor to the Quorum of Twelve Apostles – 6 October 1877

Whitney, Orson F.
Born: 1 July 1855; Died: 16 May 1931

LDS Leadership:
Quorum of Twelve Apostles – 9 April 1906

Widtsoe, John A.
Born: 31 January 1872; Died: 29 November 1952

LDS Leadership:
Quorum of Twelve Apostles – 17 March 1921

Woodruff, Wilford
Born: 1 March 1807; Died: 2 September 1898

LDS Leadership:
Quorum of Twelve Apostles – 26 April 1839
President of the Quorum of Twelve Apostles – 10 October 1880
4th President of the LDS Church – 7 April 1889

Young, Brigham
Born: 1 June 1801; Died: 29 August 1877

LDS Leadership:
Quorum of Twelve Apostles – 14 February 1835

President of the Quorum of Twelve Apostles – 14 April 1840
Acting President of the LDS Church – 8 August 1844
2nd President of the LDS Church – 27 December 1847

Notes

• Introduction Notes

1. As of 9 November 2005, according to the LDS Church official web site (www.lds.org/ temples/chronological/0,11206,1900-1,00.html [unless otherwise noted, all web sites listed were accessible on 28 February 2006]). While the web site at that time only listed nine, two more temples planned for the Salt Lake Valley were announced by Pres. Hinckley in the 1 October 2005 General Conference.
2. Church membership at the end of 2004 was 12,275,822. Of these, 241,239 were new converts (*Ensign*, May 2005, 25).
3. After extensive research, Richard and Joan Ostling estimated tithing offerings for the Mormon Church at $5.3 billion a year, with stocks and Church-owned businesses generating an additional $600 million per year. They estimated the Church's assets at that time to be $25-30 billion and with normal appreciation, "the figure would go well beyond that" (*Mormon America* [San Francisco: HarperSanFrancisco, 1999], 115). This despite President Hinckley's 1985 assertion that "the only real wealth of the Church is the faith of its people" (www.lds.org/newsroom/page/0,15606,4032-1—-14-168,00.html).
4. Jeffrey L. Sheller, "The Mormon movement: The Church of Latter-day Saints grows by leaps and bounds," *U. S. News & World Report*, 13 November 2000, 59.
5. Jerome Kramer, "20 Books that Changed America," *Book Magazine*, July/August 2003.
6. The official Church web site reported that 120,175,500 copies of the *Book of Mormon* have been published since 1830. In 2003 alone, 4,686,231 copies of the book were distributed worldwide (www.lds.org/newsroom/page/0,15606,4034-1—-10-168,00.html).
7. There were 51,067 full-time missionaries serving for the Mormon Church in 2004 ("Statistical Report, 2004," *Ensign*, May 2005, 25).

8. Read Lane Thuet's personal testimony in Appendix A of this book.
9. The Church of Jesus Christ of Latter-day Saints is the official name of the Salt Lake City based Mormon Church. We will occasionally refer to the organization throughout this book as the LDS Church or the Mormon Church, even though they no longer find use of these short titles acceptable. See Larry Stammer, "Church Plans to Drop Use of LDS as Shorthand Name," *Los Angeles Times*, 24 February 2001, A-14.
10. 1 Thessalonians 5:21; "good" meaning that which "passes the test," is true, or is genuine. See William F. Arndt and F. Wilbur Gingrich, *A Greek-English Lexicon of the New Testament* (Chicago: University of Chicago Press, 1957), 401.
11. Charles Larson, *By His Own Hand Upon Papyrus*, rev. ed. (Grand Rapids: Institute for Religious Research, 1992), 179.

- **Chapter One Notes**

1. John 3:16-18; Revelation 20:14-15.
2. *The Doctrine and Covenants of the Church of Jesus Christ of Latter-day Saints* (Salt Lake City: The Church of Jesus Christ of Latter-day Saints, 1981), 1:30.
3. Boyd K. Packer, "The Only True Church," *Ensign*, November 1985, 80.
4. Jude 3.
5. 1 Peter 3:15.
6. In Smith's testimony in *The Pearl of Great Price* (Salt Lake City: The Church of Jesus Christ of Latter-day Saints, 1981), Joseph Smith—History, several church denominations are specifically named: Methodist, Presbyterian and Baptist (1:5). Shortly after the Nauvoo Temple was finished I. McGee Van Dusen and his wife Maria published an account of the endowment ceremony as it was at that time. He explained, "The following process is what myself and wife were personally taken through, in turn with twelve or fifteen thousand others, in the Temple, in February, 1846, said to be our reward, as revealed from God to Joseph Smith, for erecting that

splendid edifice.... After some more ceremony of not much consequence, we are conducted into another, a fifth room, which is a representation of the present Religious world. This room is darker than any of the others through which we have passed, I suppose **expressive of what the Mormons say of the sects, that they are wrong and in gross darkness....** Our attention is now attracted by an individual coming in from an adjoining room, **representing the Devil....** He says, 'Good morning **brother Methodist, Presbyterian, Roman Catholic, Baptist, Universalist, Shaking Quaker, Millerite, Campbelite,' &c., enumerating all the sects of the day, except the Mormons:** 'Come, let us drink the cup of fellowship this morning'" (*A Dialogue Between Adam and Eve, The Lord and the Devil, Called The Endowment* [Albany: C. Killmer, 1847], 4, 10).

7. This was stated by Apostle Orson Pratt: "Now let me go a little further, and say that the ordinance of **marriage is illegal among all people**, nations and tongues, unless administered by a man appointed by new revelation from God to join the male and female as husband and wife. Says one—'You do not mean to say that all marriages are also illegal, as well as our baptisms?' Yes, I do, as far as God is concerned. That is taking a broad standpoint; but I am telling you that which is my belief; and I presume, so far as I am acquainted, **it is the belief of the Latter-day Saints throughout the world, that all the marriages of our forefathers, for many long generations past, have been illegal in the sight of God.** They have been legal in the sight of men; ... but in the sight of heaven **these marriages are illegal, and the children illegitimate**" (*Journal of Discourses*, 26 vols. [England: Various publishers, 1854-1886] photo reprint, 16:175-76, 31 August 1873).

8. John R. Farkas, *Does the Mormon Church Attack Orthodox Christianity?* (St. Louis: Personal Freedom Outreach, 1988), 2-3.

9. Bill McKeever, "A Subtle Belittling?" *Mormonism Research Ministry Update*, April 2004, 3.

10. Farkas, *Does the Mormon Church Attack Orthodox Christianity?*, 3. In another book by Farkas and David Reed, the changed LDS strategy is commented upon: "In recent years, the Mormon missionaries have not given this message [that their Church is the only true church] the same emphasis as in the past. **However, it has not changed**; it is just not given the strong focus, **probably for public relations purposes**. Mormons have learned the old adage 'You catch more flies with honey than vinegar'" (John Farkas and David Reed, *Mormons: How to Witness to Them* [Grand Rapids: Baker Books, 1997], 160).
11. Jerald and Sandra Tanner, *Major Problems of Mormonism* (Salt Lake City: Utah Lighthouse Ministry, 1989), 8.
12. LaMar Petersen, *The Creation of the Book of Mormon: A Historical Inquiry* (Salt Lake City: Freethinker Press, 2000), 126. For examples, see 1 Nephi 13:5-6, 8, 26, 28; 14:3, 9-17; 22:13-14. *Doctrine and Covenants* 29:21; 88:94.
13. This portion of Smith's testimony is very close to Matthew 15:8-9, where Jesus quoted Isaiah 29:13: "This people draweth nigh unto me with their mouth, and honoureth me with their lips; but their heart is far from me. But in vain they do worship me. Teaching for doctrines the commandments of men." Jesus condemned the Pharisees and teachers of the Law as hypocrites.
14. *History of the Church of Jesus Christ of Latter-day Saints*, 2nd ed. 1980, 7 vols. (Salt Lake City: Deseret Book Company, 1951), 1:XCI.
15. See Chapter 3 for more information on this topic.
16. See the discussion of changes to the temple ceremony in Chapter 9.
17. Jerald and Sandra Tanner, *Evolution of the Mormon Temple Ceremony: 1842-1990* (Salt Lake City: Utah Lighthouse Ministry, 1990), 79-80. The Tanners explain that "this part of the temple ceremony seems to have evolved from a group representing the various sects of the day to a number of ministers. Eventually there was only a single minister who was highly paid by the Devil for preaching the orthodox Christian

religion. As the years passed, the minister's wages became ridiculously low, and finally in April 1990, the minister was entirely removed from the ceremony" (33).

The former Temple Endowment ceremony is also found in Chuck Sackett's, *What's Going On In There?* (Thousand Oaks, Calif.: Ex-Mormons for Jesus, n.d.), and in Bob Witte and Gordon H. Frazer's *What's Going on in Here?: An Exposing of the Secret Mormon Temple Rituals* (Eugene, Oreg.: Gordon Fraser publisher, n.d.). The compilers/publishers of these two booklets were former Mormons and Temple workers.

Lane Thuet personally went through the temple ceremony, first experiencing it on 21 September 1988.

18. Tanner, *Evolution of the Mormon Temple Ceremony*, 32.
19. Ibid., 33.
20. Jerreld L. Newquist, comp., *Gospel Truth: Discourses and Writings of President George Q. Cannon* (Salt Lake City: Deseret Book, 1987), 324.
21. Bruce R. McConkie, *Mormon Doctrine* (Salt Lake City: Bookcraft, Inc., 1966), 69.
22. Joseph Fielding Smith, comp., *Teachings of the Prophet Joseph Smith* (Salt Lake City: Deseret Book Co., 1976), 270.
23. *History of the Church*, 7:287, 6 October 1844.
24. *Journal of Discourses*, 5:73, 26 July 1857. The *Journal of Discourses* contains discourses (sermons) given by the General Authorities of the LDS Church and others from the later 1800's. Though they are not included among the "Standard Works," George Q. Cannon stated, "**The Journal of Discourses deservedly ranks as one of the standard works of the Church**, and every rightminded Saint will certainly welcome with joy every number as it comes forth from the press as an additional reflector of the 'light that shines from Zion's hill'" (*Journal of Discourses*, 8: Preface). Brigham Young once declared: "I say now, when they [his sermons] are copied and approved by me **they are as good Scripture as is couched in this Bible**, and if you want to read revelation read the sayings of him who knows the mind of God ..." (ibid., 13:264, 6 October 1870). On another occasion, he said,

"I have never yet preached a sermon and sent it out to the children of men, that they may not call Scripture" (ibid., 13:95, 2 January 1870).
25. Ibid., 6:176, 17 January 1858.
26. Ibid., 8:199, 7 October 1860.
27. Orson Pratt, *The Seer*, January 1854, 205. *The Seer* was a monthly publication edited by Apostle Orson Pratt. It was authorized by the First Presidency of the Church (see *The Seer*, January 1853, 2).
28. Ibid., 255 (April 1854).
29. *Journal of Discourses*, 5:89-90, 26 July 1857.
30. Ibid., 6:25, 1 November 1857.
31. Ibid., 6:167, 17 January 1858.
32. Ibid., 13:225, 6 May 1870.
33. Ibid., 22:44, 6 February 1881.
34. Ibid., 24:320, 28 October 1883.
35. Joseph Fielding Smith, *Doctrines of Salvation: Sermons and Writings of Joseph Fielding Smith*, Bruce R. McConkie, comp., 3 vols. (Salt Lake City: Bookcraft, 1956), 3:283.
36. Spencer W. Kimball, *The Miracle of Forgiveness* (Salt Lake City: Bookcraft, 1969), 54-55.
37. Ezra Taft Benson, *Teachings of Ezra Taft Benson* (Salt Lake City: Bookcraft, 1988), 164-65.
38. Ibid., 177.
39. Regional Conference, North Ogden, Utah, 3 May 1998; cited in *Ensign*, June 2004, 3.
40. The *Ensign* is "AN OFFICIAL MAGAZINE OF THE CHURCH OF JESUS CHRIST OF LATTER-DAY SAINTS" – according to the title page of the monthly magazine.
41. Kent P. Jackson, "Early Signs of the Apostasy," *Ensign*, December 1984, 9.
42. Bruce R. McConkie (d.1985) was a widely respected Apostle and prolific LDS speaker and writer. As scriptural spokesman his speeches and writings are still quoted authoritatively in LDS publications. His book, *Mormon Doctrine* was first published in 1958, with a second edition in 1966, and a 35th printing by 1991. McConkie's Preface to the second edition

states: "From the time the first copies came from the press, this compendium of *Mormon Doctrine* has found wide and gratifying acceptance among doctrinal students in all parts of the Church." McConkie is often quoted by researchers such as Bill McKeever (Mormonism Research Ministry) and other non-Mormons. Mormon apologists sometimes try to discount McConkie's statements by claiming they were "just his opinion" and not official Mormon doctrine. But as McKeever writes: "During his lifetime, Bruce Redd McConkie was probably one of the most respected LDS theologians in the Mormon Church.... I have never heard anyone with McConkie's credentials actually declare that this man's teachings should not be trusted." He certainly was not a "theological rogue." McKeever concludes: "Within the context of Mormonism, he was about as orthodox as they come" ("Bruce McConkie—Trusted General Authority or theological hack?" *Mormonism Researched*, Fourth quarter 2003, 3-4).

43. Bruce McConkie, *The Millennial Messiah* (Salt Lake City: Deseret Book, 1982), 54.
44. Bruce McConkie, *A New Witness for the Articles of Faith* (Salt Lake City: Deseret Book, 1985), 544.
45. Richard N. and Joan K. Ostling, *Mormon America: The Power and the Promise* (San Francisco: HarperSanFrancisco, 1999), 319-20. The Ostlings remind the reader that "the Mormon scriptures contain more than twenty passages denouncing the rest of Christendom as apostate" (322).

• Chapter Two Notes

1. *The Pearl of Great Price* (Salt Lake City: The Church of Jesus Christ of Latter-day Saints, 1981), Joseph Smith—History 1:7 states, "I was at this time in my fifteenth year," but verse 14 clarifies that it was the Spring of 1820, which would make Smith 14 at the time.
2. Joseph Smith—History 1:19.

3. James Allen, "The Significance of Joseph Smith's 'First Vision' in Mormon Thought," *Dialogue: A Journal of Mormon Thought*, Autumn 1966, 39.
4. G. Homer Durham, comp., *Gospel Ideals: Selections from the Discourses of David O. McKay* (Salt Lake City: Improvement Era, 1953), 85.
5. John Widtsoe, *Joseph Smith—Seeker After Truth, Prophet of God* (Salt Lake City: Deseret News Press, 1951), 19.
6. *The Salt Lake Tribune*, 7 October 2002, A-1, A-6.
7. Gordon B. Hinckley, "Four Cornerstones of Faith," *Ensign*, February 2004, 5.
8. Gordon B. Hinckley, *Teachings of Gordon B. Hinckley* (Salt Lake City: Deseret Book, 1997), 226-27.
9. Sterling McMurrin, "Introduction," B. H. Roberts, *Studies of the Book of Mormon* (Chicago: University of Illinois Press, 1985), xv.
10. Grant Palmer, *An Insider's View of Mormon Origins* (Salt Lake City: Signature Books, 2002), 240.
11. Allen, "The Significance," 30-32.
12. Fawn Brodie, *No Man Knows My History* (New York: Alfred A. Knopf, 1971), 24-25.
13. Ibid., 405.
14. Joseph Smith—History 1:22-23. Richard Lloyd Anderson tried to defend that Joseph Smith truly had this "first vision" by referring to circumstantial evidence ("Circumstantial Confirmation Of the First Vision Through Reminiscences," *BYU Studies*, Spring 1969, 373-404). However, Anderson does not even produce one source earlier than 1834 to make his case. Once again, this shows that the vision went completely unnoticed by anyone at the time it supposedly happened. According to Anderson, "By far the best independent source on Joseph's early personal life is his mother, who confirms the religious excitement about 1819 'in the surrounding country,' relates his vision, describes his ostracism afterwards, and emphasizes that his conviction that the churches were wrong prevented his following the majority..." (404). Anderson is referring to Lucy Mack Smith's book, *Biographical Sketches*

of Joseph Smith (Liverpool, England: S. W. Richards, 1853). But she did not dictate her manuscript until the late 1830s or early 40s, so her account is not early enough to prove his point. He is left with no evidence to demonstrate his claim.
15. These affidavits were published by E. D. Howe in *Mormonism Unvailed* (Painesville, N. Y.: E. D. Howe, 1834), photo reprint by Utah Lighthouse Ministry. Jerald and Sandra Tanner point out that for many years, these affidavits were considered by Mormon writers to be "corrupted" by D. P. Hurlburt. But LDS scholar Richard L. Anderson wrote an article for *Dialogue: A Journal of Mormon Thought*, in which he reports that the statements were procured "independent of Hurlburt" ("The Reliability of the Early History of Lucy and Joseph Smith," *Dialogue*, Summer 1969, 25; see Jerald and Sandra Tanner, *Mormonism—Shadow or Reality?* [Salt Lake City: Utah Lighthouse Ministry, 1987], 41).
16. Palmer, *An Insider's View*, 245.
17. Preston Nibley, *Joseph Smith the Prophet* (1944), 30; cited in Tanner, *Mormonism—Shadow or Reality?*, 145.
18. *Times and Seasons*, 1 April 1842, 748-49.
19. See discussion of Version 2 below.
20. Account found in *Book of Commandments*, 1833, Chapter XXIV:1-7; reproduced in Wilford Wood, *Joseph Smith Begins His Work* (Salt Lake City: Wilford C. Wood, 1962), vol. 2.
21. Palmer, *An Insider's View*, 235.
22. Verse 1.
23. *Book of Commandments* XXIV:1, 6-7.
24. While some might feel this "holy Angel" could be Jesus Christ, the context of the revelation makes it clear that the visitor was not Jesus. For example, in verse 9, the angel tells Joseph Smith that he will bring forth the *Book of Mormon*, describing its contents as containing "the fulness of the gospel of Jesus Christ." Had the messenger been Jesus Christ, he would have said the book contained "the fulness of My gospel." Hyrum Smith and Janne Sjodahl identify the angel in this revelation as "Moroni" (*Doctrine and Covenants Commentary* [Salt Lake City: Deseret Book Company, 1951], 100). Current editions

of the *Doctrine and Covenants* also identify the angel in this account as Moroni, though they identify this account as being a second vision rather than Smith's first.
25. Lucy Smith to Solomon Mack, Jr., 6 January 1831, LDS Church Archives; reprinted in Dan Vogel, *Early Mormon Documents*, 5 vols. (Salt Lake City: Signature Books, 1996), 1:214-17.
26. This account was first published in Dean Jessee, "The Early Accounts of Joseph Smith's First Vision," *BYU Studies*, Spring 1969, 275-94. It was also published by Jerald and Sandra Tanner in *Joseph Smith's Strange Account of the First Vision* (Salt Lake City: Modern Microfilm Co, n.d.). Account found in *Joseph Smith Letterbook 1*, pp. 1-6, in the LDS Church Historian's office; Dean Jessee, *The Papers of Joseph Smith*, 2 vols. (Salt Lake City: Deseret Book, 1989), 1:3-7; Brodie, *No Man Knows My History*, 406-07; and Vogel, *Early Mormon Documents*, 1:26-31.
27. Allen, "The Significance," 35.
28. Jessee, *The Papers of Joseph Smith*, 1:3; also Vogel, *Early Mormon Documents*, 1:26.
29. Paul R. Cheesman, "An Analysis of the Accounts Relating Joseph Smith's Early Visions," BYU thesis, June 1965.
30. Joseph Smith—History 1:18.
31. Ibid. This statement is actually contradicted by verse 10, in which Joseph said that, before he even went out to pray, he wondered if the various churches were "all wrong together" or "if any one of them be right."
32. Account in *Messenger and Advocate*, February 1835, 1:78-79. See also Jessee, *The Papers of Joseph Smith*, 1:48-54; and Vogel, *Early Mormon Documents* (1998), 2:426-30.
33. *Messenger and Advocate*, October 1834 (letter dated 7 September 1834), 1:13-16. See also Francis Kirkham, *A New Witness for Christ in America* (Salt Lake City: Utah Printing, 1960), 1:17; B. H. Roberts, *Comprehensive History of the Church*, 6 vols. (Salt Lake City: Deseret News Press, 1930), 1:78; and Joseph Fielding Smith, *Doctrines of Salvation: Sermons and Writings of Joseph Fielding Smith*, Bruce R.

McConkie, comp., 3 vols. (Salt Lake City: Bookcraft, 1956), 3:236.
34. Max H. Parkin, "Conflict at Kirtland," M. A. thesis, BYU 1966, 166; cited in Tanner, *Mormonism—Shadow or Reality?* 151.
35. *Manuscript History of the Church*, A-1, 1-187, Joseph Smith Papers, LDS Church Archives; reproduced in Jessee, *The Papers of Joseph Smith* 1:48-54.
36. *Times and Seasons*, 15 December 1840, 241-43; also Smith, *Doctrines of Salvation*, 3:236.
37. Joseph Smith—History 1:15.
38. Account in Dean C. Jessee, "How Lovely was the Morning," *Dialogue: A Journal of Mormon Thought*; Spring 1971, 87. See also Jessee, "The Early Accounts," 284; Jessee, *The Papers of Joseph Smith* 1:125-27; and Brodie, *No Man Knows My History*, 408-09.
39. Jessee, "How Lovely," 87.
40. Brodie, *No Man Knows My History*, 408.
41. Jessee, "How Lovely," 87.
42. Account in *William Appleby's Diary*, typed transcript, 30-31, LDS Archives. See also Vogel, *Early Mormon Documents*, 1:145-48.
43. William Appleby was an early LDS convert and an Elder in the Church under Joseph Smith. Later, under Brigham Young, he was made a high priest and served as a mission President.
44. *Journal of Discourses,* 26 vols. (England: Various publishers, 1854-1886), photo reprint, 2:171, 196; 6:335; 12:334; 13:78; 18:239; 20:167; 24:135.
45. Dean C. Jessee, *The Personal Writings of Joseph Smith* (Salt Lake City: Deseret Book, 1984), 84. Entry dated 14 November 1835.
46. Account published in *Pearl of Great Price* as Joseph Smith—History 1:10-20. Original in *Manuscript History of the Church*, A-1, pp. 1-240, Joseph Smith Papers, LDS Church Archives. See also *Times and Seasons*, 1 April 1842; *History of the Church of Jesus Christ of Latter-day Saints,* 2nd ed. 1980, 7 vols. (Salt Lake City: Deseret Book, 1951), 1:4-6; Jessee, *The*

Papers of Joseph Smith, 1:270-73; and Vogel, *Early Mormon Documents,* 1:54-62 (dated there as written in 1839).
47. *History of the Church,* 1:2-6.
48. Jessee, *The Papers of Joseph Smith,* 1:265; also Vogel, *Early Mormon Documents,* 1:54.
49. Account printed in *Congregational Observer* 2, dated 3 July 1841. Reprinted in *Peoria Register and North-Western Gazetteer,* 3 September 1841. See also Vogel, *Early Mormon Documents,* 1:477-80.
50. *Times and Seasons,* 15 December 1840, 241.
51. *Journal of Discourses,* 2:171, 196, 197; 10:127; 13:78, 324; 20:167.
52. Ibid., 2:171.
53. Now named the Community of Christ.
54. *The Saint's Herald,* 4 October 1884, 643. William Smith shared this information in a sermon given on 8 June 1884.
55. William Smith, *William Smith on Mormonism* (Lamoni, Iowa: Herald Steam Book and Job Office, 1883), 8.
56. Jessee, "The Early Accounts."
57. Allen, "The Significance."
58. Originally in *Times and Seasons,* 1 March 1842, 706-07. See also Jessee, *The Papers of Joseph Smith,* 1:429-30; and Vogel, *Early Mormon Documents,* 1:169-72.
59. Often referred to by Mormon scholars as "The Wentworth Letter." John Wentworth (then only 26 years old) was the editor of the weekly *Chicago Democrat,* the first newspaper in Chicago, Illinois. He had written to Joseph Smith requesting a brief sketch of the rise of the Latter-day Saints church. The sketch was to be used by a friend of Wentworth's, who was planning to write a history of New Hampshire. Joseph Smith wrote the referenced letter in reply (see Jessee, *The Papers of Joseph Smith,* 1:427-29).
60. Account published in part in Allen, "The Significance," 43. See also Jessee, *The Papers of Joseph Smith,* 1:438-44 (in its entirety); and Vogel, *Early Mormon Documents,* 1:181-82.
61. David White was then editor of the newspaper, and visited Joseph Smith at his home in Nauvoo. His purpose was to obtain

information about the "far famed kingdom of the Latter-day Saints" for an article (see Jessee, *The Papers of Joseph Smith*, 1:439-40).
62. Found in Jessee, *The Papers of Joseph Smith*, 1:445-58; and Vogel, *Early Mormon Documents*, 1:183-86.
63. Israel D. Rupp, (editor and compiler), *He Pasa Ekklesia: An Original History of the Religious Denominations at Present Existing in the United States* (Philadelphia, 1844), 404-07; cited in Jessee, *The Papers of Joseph Smith*, 1:445-58.
64. Partially printed in Allen, "The Significance," 43. Original journal in LDS Church Archives. See also Jessee, *The Papers of Joseph Smith*, 1:459-62; and Vogel, *Early Mormon Documents*, 1:189-90.
65. Alexander Neibaur was one of the first Mormon converts in England. He moved to Nauvoo, Illinois after his conversion, and practiced dentistry there. He was also one of Joseph Smith's tutors, teaching the prophet German and Hebrew (see Jessee, *The Papers of Joseph Smith*, 1:459).
66. *Book of Commandments* XXIV:1, 6-7.
67. Jessee, *The Papers of Joseph Smith*, 1:125-27.
68. *Joseph Smith Letterbook 1*, page 1, LDS Church Historian's office; cited in Jessee, *The Papers of Joseph Smith*, 1:37 and Vogel, *Early Mormon Documents*, 1:26-31.
69. *Journal of Discourses*, 6:29, 8 November 1857.
70. *Times and Seasons*, 1 April 1842, 753; 1851 *Pearl of Great Price*, 41; *Millennial Star* 3:53, 71.
71. *Messenger and Advocate*, February 1835, 1:78-79.
72. Joseph Smith—History 1:17.
73. Jessee, *The Papers of Joseph Smith*, 1:125-27.
74. Ibid., 1:3-7.
75. Ibid., 1:48-54.
76. See Version 2, above.
77. See Version 3, above.
78. See Version 6, above.
79. Ibid.
80. See Versions 1-3, above.
81. Brodie, *No Man Knows My History*, 25.

82. Lucy Smith History, "*Preliminary Manuscript*," 77-78, LDS Church Archives. See also Vogel, *Early Mormon Documents*, 1:289-91.
83. Palmer, *An Insider's View*, 240. Palmer's book is very frank and honest about the problems and contradictions in early LDS history. His book was sold in LDS bookstores for more than two years before LDS authorities realized how many difficulties the book revealed. Once they did, they stopped selling the book. Then on 12 December 2004, Palmer was disfellowshipped. Palmer was surprised that the Church took action, but felt he had come under fire because his book made academic scholarship available and understandable to average readers. Articles about his Church suspension appeared in the *Los Angeles Times* on 9 December 2004, A-34, and 13 December 2004, A-21.
84. Brodie, *No Man Knows My History*, 25.
85. Palmer, *An Insider's View*, 245-48.
86. Jessee, *The Papers of Joseph Smith*, 2:217n2.
87. Palmer, *An Insider's View*, 248, 251. Previous to Smith's renaming the Church, it had been known as "The Church of Christ," "The Church of Jesus Christ," "The Church of God" and "The Church of the Latter-day Saints" (*History of the Church*, 3:23-24fn).
88. Marvin S. Hill, "The First Vision Controversy: A Critique and Reconciliation," *Dialogue: A Journal of Mormon Thought*, Summer 1982, 39.
89. Marvin S. Hill, *Quest for Refuge: The Mormon Flight from American Pluralism* (Salt Lake City: Signature Books, 1989), 9.
90. Gordon Hinckley, "Four Cornerstones of Faith," *Ensign*, February 2004, 5.
91. Wesley Walters, "Joseph Smith's First Vision Story Revisited," *The Journal of Pastoral Practice*, vol. IV, no. 2, 1980, 109.

- **Chapter Three Notes**

1. Lloyd Sharp, "A Possible Apostasy?" *The Cross*, Summer 2002, 3.
2. *History of the Church of Jesus Christ of Latter-day Saints*, 2nd ed. 1980, 7 vols. (Salt Lake City: Deseret Book, 1951), 1:XL (Introduction).
3. Kent Jackson, *From Apostasy to Restoration* (Salt Lake City: Deseret Book, 1996), 8.
4. *The Pearl of Great Price* (Salt Lake City: The Church of Jesus Christ of Latter-day Saints, 1981), Joseph Smith—History 1:18.
5. Joseph Smith—History 1:10.
6. Marquardt and Walters explain, "The newspaper [*The Wayne Sentinel*] also followed contemporary religious events, which clearly affected young Joseph and his family.... The paper published in 1823 Asa's [Asa Wild's] claim that God told him ... 'that every denomination of professing christians had become extremely corrupt; many of which never had any true faith at all'" (*Wayne Sentinel*, 22 October 1823, 4; cited in *Inventing Mormonism* [Salt Lake City: Smith Research Associates, 1998], 46). They go on to comment that "Wild's claim that existing churches were in error would have found sympathetic ears in the Smith family. Even by the time of young Joseph's birth in 1805, both of his parents had come to rely on personal interpretation of the Bible as primary guides to religious life" (ibid.). Joseph Smith's mother wrote that she and her husband had concluded early on that all churches were in error. She writes that Smith Sr., after having had a night vision, was "more confirmed than ever, in the opinion that there was no order or class of religionists that knew any more concerning the Kingdom of God, than those of the world, or such as made no profession of religion whatever" (Lucy Mack Smith, *Biographical Sketches of Joseph Smith* [Liverpool, England: S.W. Richards, 1853], 57-58; cited in Marquardt and Walters, *Inventing Mormonism*, 49, 59n31).
7. *Book of Commandments* IV:5.

8. Letter from Joseph Smith to Colesville Saints, 28 August 1830. See Vogel, *Early Mormon Documents*, 5 vols. (Salt Lake City: Signature Books, 1996), 1:14. By 1832, the phrase "restoration of all things" had become more common, and even found its way into Joseph Smith's revelations (see *Doctrine and Covenants* 86:10). The phrase also appears in *Doctrine and Covenants* 27:6, a revelation dated August 1830, but the section containing this phrase was added to the original revelation for publication in the 1835 *Doctrine and Covenants*. See H. Michael Marquardt, *The Joseph Smith Revelations: Text and Commentary* (Salt Lake City: Signature Books, 1999), 72-80.
9. *Joseph Smith Letterbook 1*, pp. 1-6, LDS Church Historian's office; Dean Jessee, *The Papers of Joseph Smith*, 2 vols. (Salt Lake City: Deseret Book, 1989), 1:3-7; Vogel, *Early Mormon Documents*, 1:26-31.
10. Vogel, *Early Mormon Documents*, 1:28.
11. Grant Palmer, *An Insider's View of Mormon Origins* (Salt Lake City: Signature Books, 2002), 251.
12. Jerald and Sandra Tanner, *Mormonism—Shadow or Reality?* (Salt Lake City: Utah Lighthouse Ministry, 1987), 162-162A; Palmer, *An Insider's View*, 253 and fn51. Marquardt and Walters write, "In 1879 Joseph and Hiel Lewis, cousins to Joseph's first wife, Emma Hale, stated that Joseph joined the Methodist Episcopal church or class in Harmony, Pennsylvania, in the summer of 1828.... It is possible that Joseph attended class with his wife Emma because of the death of their first son on 15 June 1828. That Joseph was a member of the class was not questioned... " (*Inventing Mormonism*, 61n49).
13. Palmer, *An Insider's View*, 253.
14. *Book of Commandments* X:8, May 1829; compare *The Doctrine and Covenants of the Church of Jesus Christ of Latter-day Saints* (Salt Lake City: The Church of Jesus Christ of Latter-day Saints, 1981), 11:15-16. This was originally recorded as **a revelation given to Hyrum Smith** (*Book of Commandments* X:1; see Wilford Wood, *Joseph Smith Begins His Work*, 2 vols. [Salt Lake City: Wilford C. Wood, 1962], 2:28). When it was

republished in 1835 in the *Doctrine and Covenants*, the first 4 verses were copied verbatim into Section VIII, **but the rest of the revelation pertained to Oliver Cowdery** instead of to Hyrum Smith (ibid., vol. 2; 1835 *Doctrine and Covenants*, Section VIII, 109-11). Eventually, the revelation was restored to its original wording, but this time published as **a revelation to Joseph Smith in reference to Hyrum** (*Doctrine and Covenants* [1981 ed.] Section 11: Introduction).

15. *Book of Commandments* XV:5, June 1829; *Doctrine and Covenants* 18:6.
16. *Doctrine and Covenants* 33:2, 4, October 1830.
17. *Doctrine and Covenants* 35:7, December 1830.
18. Lucy Smith to Solomon Mack, Jr., 6 January 1831; in Vogel, *Early Mormon Documents*, 1:216.
19. *Doctrine and Covenants* 1:13, 15-16; 1 November 1831.
20. Grant Palmer concludes the two stories were not merged until 1838. He states, "During the leadership crisis of April 1838, Joseph remembered a different purpose in going to pray … he now says, 'My object in going to enquire of the Lord was to know which of all the sects was right.' While it was unnecessary to even ask this question in his 1832 report, in 1838 the matter of importance was apostasy from the only true church.... When a crisis developed around the Book of Mormon in early 1838, he [Smith] conflated several events into one" (*An Insider's View*, 252-54).
21. James E. Talmage, *The Great Apostasy* (Salt Lake City: Deseret Book, 1958), 19-20.
22. Joseph Fielding Smith, *Answers to Gospel Questions*, 5 vols. (Salt Lake City: Deseret Book, 1966), 5:36-37.
23. Kimball, Paris France Area Conference, August 1976; cited in Rulon T.Burton, *We Believe* (Salt Lake City: Bookcraft, 1994), 30.
24. Mark E. Petersen, *Conference Report,* April 1945 (first day, afternoon meeting), 43.
25. Ezra Taft Benson, *Conference Report,* October 1949 (first day, morning meeting), 27.

26. Bruce R. McConkie, *Doctrinal New Testament Commentary*, 3 vols. (Salt Lake City: Bookcraft, 1973), 3:528.
27. *Duties and Blessings of the Priesthood* (Salt Lake City: The Church of Jesus Christ of Latter-day Saints, 1996), Basic Manual for Priesthood Holders, Part A, 13.
28. *Journal of Discourses*, 26 vols. (England: Various publishers, 1854-1886), photo reprint, 16:266, 8 October 1873.
29. *History of the Church*, 1:xl.
30. Talmage, *The Great Apostasy*, iii (preface).
31. 2 Thessalonians 2:3; 1 Timothy 4:1-3; 2 Timothy 3:1-5; 4:3-4.
32. 1 John 2:18-19; 4:3.
33. Roderick Cameron, *Missionary Scripture Guide* (n.p.: Hawkes Publishing, Inc., 1984), 5. Isaiah 60:2 and Acts 20:29-30 are added to the list in Keith Marston, *Missionary Pal: Reference Guide for Missionaries and Teachers* (Salt Lake City: Quality Press, Inc., 1987), 4.
34. James P. Holding, *The Mormon Defenders* (no imprint, 2001), 129-30.
35. Talmage, *The Great Apostasy*, 25.
36. Elder Richard R. Lyman, *Conference Report*, April 1924, 140.
37. Amos 6:1 NIV ("at ease" – *KJV*).
38. Amos 6:1 NIV ("trust" – *KJV*).
39. Amos 6:8 NIV ("excellency" – *KJV*; "arrogance" – *NASV*).
40. Ezekiel 7:26; 20:1-3; Micah 3:4, 7. God had done the same thing with King Saul in 1 Samuel 28:6.
41. The literal translation of the Hebrew for this verse begins, "And I will restore the fortunes of my people Israel...." See the *New American Standard Bible* for this verse. The remainder of the passage verifies that the context is the return and restoration of all that Israel had before their captivity.
42. See the books of Ezra; Nehemiah and Esther. Ultimately, the complete fulfillment of the prophecy in Amos 9:14-15 will not be until the Millennial Reign of Christ, so again the restoration of Mormonism does not fulfill this.

43. Thomas S. Monson, *Be Your Best Self* (Salt Lake City: Deseret Book, 1979), 10.
44. Cited in Joseph McConkie and Robert Millet, *Doctrinal Commentary on the Book of Mormon* (Salt Lake City: Bookcraft, 1988), 2:57.
45. Richard Lloyd Anderson, *Understanding Paul* (Salt Lake City: Deseret Book, 1983), 376-77.
46. Ezra Taft Benson, *Conference Report*, October 1949, 26.
47. Acts 20:17.
48. John MacArthur is Senior Pastor and Teacher of Grace Community Church in Sun Valley, California. He is President of The Master's College and Seminary, and Grace To You Ministry. He is a well-respected Bible teacher worldwide and has written numerous best-selling books. He authored the notes for *The MacArthur Study Bible* (Nashville: Word Publishing, 1997), which has sold over 500,000 copies since 1997.
49. John MacArthur, Jr., *The MacArthur New Testament Commentary: Acts 13-28* (Chicago: Moody Press, 1996), 226.
50. David J. Williams was Vice Principal of Ridley College at the University of Melbourne at the time he wrote the cited quotation. He was also one of the translators for the *New International Version* of the Bible.
51. David J. Williams, *New International Biblical Commentary: Acts* (Peabody, Mass.: Hendrickson Publishers, 1990), 356.
52. Even though Mormon apologists would point to vv. 4-7 as a sign of apostasy, it could not have been a complete apostasy, since the Lord commends so much about the church in vv. 1–3.
53. Andrew Jenson, *Church Chronology: A Record of Important Events Pertaining to the History of the Church of Jesus Christ of Latter-day Saints* (Salt Lake City: Deseret News, 1914), "The Holy Priesthood."
54. Joseph Fielding Smith, *Doctrines of Salvation: Sermons and Writings of Joseph Fielding Smith,* Bruce R. McConkie, comp., 3 vols. (Salt Lake City: Bookcraft, 1956), 3:268-69.

55. 2 Thessalonians 2:2 (*NIV*).
56. John MacArthur, Jr., *The MacArthur New Testament Commentary: 1 & 2 Thessalonians* (Chicago: Moody Press, 2002), 272.
57. James Strong, *The New Strong's Exhaustive Concordance of the Bible* (Nashville: Thomas Nelson Publishers, 1990), Greek word number 646 – *apostasia*, "Greek Dictionary," 15.
58. Spiros Zodhiates, *The Complete Word Study New Testament* (Chattanooga: AMG Publishers, 1991), 891.
59. David J. Williams, *New International Biblical Commentary: 1 and 2 Thessalonians* (Peabody, Mass.: Hendrickson Publishers, 1992), 124.
60. 2 Thessalonians 2:4.
61. Such as those mentioned in 1 John 2:19, who left the early Church to follow the teachings of Gnosticism – "They went out from us, but they did not really belong to us. For if they had belonged to us, they would have remained with us; but their going showed that none of them belonged to us" (*NIV*).
62. MacArthur, *Commentary: 1 & 2 Thessalonians*, 274.
63. Marvin W. Cowan, *Mormon Claims Answered* (n.p.: Marvin Cowan, 1989), 88.
64. Bill McKeever, *Answering Mormon's Questions* (Minneapolis: Bethany House Publishers, 1991), 35.
65. Ibid., 36.
66. Holding, *The Mormon Defenders*. Holding reviews the LDS doctrines of Divine Embodiment, Christ and the Father, Pre-existence, Baptism for the Dead, Salvation for the Unevangelized, Salvation, and Human Deification–showing how each poses an insurmountable problem to the LDS claim of a complete apostasy.
67. Ibid., 129.
68. A letter from the LDS Missionary Department dated 24 April 1979 (Carlos Asay to John Juedes) states that the brochure had been revised and was still available. The pamphlet was included in the *Gospelink 2001* CD-Rom sold in LDS bookstores. Much of the material here that deals with the brochure was taken from Edmond C. Gruss and Paul Beddoe,

"Examining a Mormon Claim: Was There a Total Apostasy?" *The Discerner*, April-June 1986, 2-9.
69. LDS Tract, *The Falling Away and Restoration of the Gospel of Jesus Christ Foretold*, 1. The brochure also features the Apostle Paul (quoting 2 Thessalonians 2:23) and concludes with Peter's statement in Acts 3:20-21. Second Thessalonians 2:2-3 has been discussed earlier in this chapter. To interpret the "restitution of all things" in Acts 3:20-21 as the restoration of the gospel by divine agency through Joseph Smith is to remove it from its Scriptural context. This restoration will be realized with the Second Coming of Christ and the Messianic Age (Isaiah 65:17; 66:22; 2 Peter 3:13; Revelation 21:1).
70. Ibid., 3.
71. Ibid., 4.
72. Ibid., 5.
73. Ibid., 6.
74. Heber J. Grant, *Conference Report*, October 1910, 116-117; Ezra Taft Benson, *Conference Report*, October 1949, 27; Hugh B. Brown, *Conference Report*, October 1956, 97. At the time of this address, Brown was an official Assistant to the Twelve Apostles. He was ordained an Apostle 18 months later (David O. McKay, *Conference Report*, October 1966, 86). McKay was President of the Church during this address.
75. Benson, *Teachings of Ezra Taft Benson* (Salt Lake City: Bookcraft, 1988), 86; James Talmage, *The Articles of Faith* (Salt Lake City: The Church of Jesus Christ of Latter-day Saints, 1968), 480-81; Benson, *So Shall Ye Reap* (Salt Lake City: Deseret Book, 1960), 51; Hugh Brown, *Abundant Life* (Salt Lake City: Bookcraft, 1965), 77; Bruce McConkie, *A New Witness for the Articles of Faith* (Salt Lake City: Deseret Book, 1985), 364; B. H. Roberts, *Outlines of Ecclesiastical History* (Salt Lake City: Deseret Book, 1927), 181; LeGrand Richards, *A Marvelous Work and a Wonder* (Salt Lake City: Deseret Book, 1958), 29; David O. McKay, *Man May Know for Himself* (Salt Lake City: Deseret Book, 1967), 164.
76. Cameron, *Missionary Scripture Guide*, 6.

77. A collection of LDS works—under the sub-title "Pamphlets—LDS tracts."
78. Luther to Emperor Charles V and the Estates; cited in Ernest G. Schwiebert, *Luther and His Times* (St. Louis: Concordia Publishing House, 1950), 509.
79. John M. Todd, *Martin Luther: A Biographical Study* (London: Burns & Oates, 1964), 188. The Todd quotation is taken from Heinrich Boehmer's, *Martin Luther: Road to Reformation* (Philadelphia: Muhlenberg Press, 1946), 393. Both Todd and the LDS brochure **have left a word out** of Luther's statement as found in Boehmer: "I simply say that **true** Christianity has ceased to exist among those who should have preserved it—the bishops and scholars."
80. H. Lehmann, gen. ed., *Luther's Works* (Philadelphia: Fortress Press, 1967), 33:85.
81. Ibid., 33:86.
82. Ibid., 54:243.
83. John Wesley, *Sermons on Several Occasions* (New York: Carlton and Phillips, 1854), 2:266-273. The sermon identified in the Mormon brochure as number 89 is the same as that numbered 94 in *Sermons on Several Occasions*.
84. Ibid., 2:65.
85. Ibid., 2:110.
86. Ibid., 2:362-63.
87. William P. Barker, *Who's Who in Church History* (Old Tappan, N.J.: Fleming H. Revell, 1969), 299.
88. Edmund S. Morgan, *Roger Williams: The Church and the State* (New York: Harcourt, Brace and World, 1967), 50.
89. Ibid., 51.
90. Ibid., 55-56.
91. W. Clark Gilpin, *The Millennarian Piety of Roger Williams* (Chicago: University of Chicago Press, 1979), 57, 61.
92. Bruce R. McConkie, *Mormon Doctrine* (Salt Lake City: Bookcraft, 1966), 493.
93. Morgan, *Roger Williams*, 55. During the General Conference of the LDS Church in October 2004, LDS Apostle Jeffrey Holland again mentioned Roger Williams (who was Holland's

10th great-grandfather), claiming that Williams had preached there was no church on earth with any authority to perform any ordinances ("Prophets, Seers, and Revelators," *Ensign*, November 2004, 6-9). However, Holland had reinterpreted and added to William's quote. Holland also neglected to tell the whole story about Williams. According to Cotton Mather, Williams had once bragged that "of all the churches in the world, those of New England **were the purest**; and of all in New England, **that whereof himself was the teacher**." Williams was considered to be **eccentric** and of "**ill character**," and many New England churches refused to hire him. He often preached against the instituted government of the Massachusetts Bay Colonies, and was therefore banished. He then traveled to Rhode Island, **preaching against the churches who refused him and the government** that banished him. He and his followers became "Separatists," denouncing the Church of England. Instead of claiming there had been a total apostasy of the church of Jesus Christ, **Williams felt he alone had the proper authority to establish his own sect and administer ordinances within it**. The sect Williams founded, however, dissolved shortly afterward. Williams eventually changed his profession from preaching to politics, though in his retirement he would often preach Christianity to the Indians in his area (see Cotton Mather, *Magnalia Christi Americana* [Abridged Edition, New York: Frederick Ungar Publishing, 1970], 126-30).
94. A Socinian is one who follows the teachings of Faustus Socinus (1539-1604). Socinus denied the doctrine of the Trinity and the divinity of Christ, and believed that salvation is attained solely by practicing the virtues exemplified by Christ.
95. Adrienne Koch, *The Philosophy of Thomas Jefferson* (New York: Columbia University Press, 1943), 26-27.
96. Ibid., 34.
97. Ibid., 23.
98. Ibid., 34-35.
99. Ibid., 25.

100. Ibid., 37fn61, 62; personal letter to John Adams, Monticello, 11 April 1823.
101. Saul Padover, ed., *Thomas Jefferson on Democracy* (New York: D. Appleton-Century Co., 1939), 118; letter to Van der Kemp, 1820.
102. Moses 5:58-59.
103. McKeever, *Answering Mormon's Questions*, 36-37.
104. *The Book of Mormon* (Salt Lake City: The Church of Jesus Christ of Latter-day Saints, 1981), 3 Nephi 28, Chapter Summary, 460.
105. *Doctrine and Covenants* 7:1-3.
106. Joseph F. Smith, *Liahona*, or *Elders' Journal*, 4:46. The speech was delivered on 7 September 1895, but was printed in the 1 November 1906 *Elders' Journal*; cited in Daniel Ludlow, *Latter Day Prophets Speak* (Salt Lake City: Bookcraft, 1948), 213.
107. McConkie and Millet, *Doctrinal Commentary on the Book of Mormon* (1992), 4:211.
108. Third Nephi 28:7.
109. *Doctrine and Covenants* 7:1-3.
110. Elder John W. Taylor, *Conference Report*, Oct. 1902, 75.
111. *Journal of Discourses* 13:320, 5 September 1869.
112. Smith, *Answers to Gospel Questions*, 2:46. Many stories about visits by the Three Nephites abound. See such works as Hector Lee, *The Three Nephites: The Substance and Significance of the Legend in Folklore* (Albuquerque: Ayer Co., 1949); and Bruce Dana, *The Three Nephites and Other Translated Beings* (Springville, Utah: Bonneville Books, 2003). Oliver B. Huntington was told the names of the Nephites by Joseph Smith—Jeremiah, Zedekiah and Kumenonhi (*Journal of Oliver Boardman Huntington* [San Marino, Calif.: Huntington Library, microfilm copy], 16 February 1895).
113. McConkie and Millet, *Doctrinal Commentary on the Book of Mormon*, 4:188.
114. Marvin W. Cowan, *Mormon Claims Answered* (1975 ed.), 53.

• Chapter Four Notes

1. *The Book of Mormon* (Salt Lake City: The Church of Jesus Christ of Latter-day Saints, 1981), Mormon 6:2-11; especially verse 6.
2. Examination of the evidence shows that the story of the Golden Plates, like many of Joseph Smith's claims, was something that was developed and elaborated over time. Michael Marquardt and Wesley Walters observe, "In contrast to the account which was later told, the earliest versions linked the finding of the plates with the practice of searching for buried treasure. They also linked obtaining the plates with magical rituals traditionally associated with winning treasure from its guardian spirits" (*Inventing Mormonism* [Salt Lake City: Smith Research Associates, 1998], 89). After tracing the history of the story, they point out, "**Many aspects of the story** told in New York and Pennsylvania **were later revised**, especially the details which linked the gold plates and treasure hunting" (ibid., 105).
3. Joseph Fielding Smith, comp., *Teachings of the Prophet Joseph Smith* (Salt Lake City: Deseret Book, 1976), 71.
4. LDS Articles of Faith, article 8.
5. *History of the Church of Jesus Christ of Latter-day Saints,* 2nd ed. 1980, 7 vols. (Salt Lake City: Deseret Book Company, 1951), 4:461; also in *Book of Mormon,* Introduction.
6. Bruce R. McConkie, *Mormon Doctrine* (Salt Lake City: Bookcraft, 1966), "Book of Mormon," 99.
7. Address at Book of Mormon Symposium, Brigham Young University, 18 August 1978; cited by Ezra Taft Benson, "A New Witness for Christ," *Ensign,* November 1984, 7.
8. Orson Pratt, "Repentance," *The Seer,* March 1854, 235.
9. Orson Pratt, *Divine Authenticity of the Book of Mormon* (Liverpool, England, 1850), 1.
10. Ibid.
11. Benson, "A New Witness for Christ," 7.
12. Gordon B. Hinckley, *Teachings of Gordon B. Hinckley* (Salt Lake City: Deseret Book, 1997), 38, 41.

13. See Chapter 12 for information concerning this subjective verification standard.
14. B. H. Roberts, *Defense of the Faith and the Saints*, 2 vols. (Salt Lake City: Deseret News Press, 1907), 1:287-88.
15. Pratt, *Divine Authenticity*, 1.
16. *History of the Church*, 1:54-55.
17. While the Mormon Church officially claims that the *Book of Mormon* was translated through use of the Urim and Thummim (Joseph Smith—History 1:62), sources contemporary with Joseph Smith are agreed that most of the translating was done through use of a brown seer stone (D. Michael Quinn, *Early Mormonism and the Magic World View* [Salt Lake City: Signature Books, 1998], 171-75). This seer stone was one that Joseph Smith had found in 1822 while helping his brother dig a well for the Chase family in Palmyra, New York (ibid., 44).
18. Cited in George Reynolds, *Myth of the Manuscript Found* (Salt Lake City: Juvenile Instructor Office, 1883), 91.
19. *Journal of Oliver Boardman Huntington* (San Marino, Calif.: Huntington Library, microfilm copy), 26 February 1881. Quote also found on page 168 of typed copy at Utah State Historical Society.
20. Grant Palmer, *An Insider's View of Mormon Origins* (Salt Lake City: Signature Books, 2002), 5.
21. Joseph Fielding Smith, "The Book of Mormon, A Divine Record," *Improvement Era*, December 1961, 924.
22. Roberts, *Defense of the Faith*, 1:281.
23. John Widtsoe, *Joseph Smith—Seeker After Truth, Prophet of God* (Salt Lake City: Deseret News Press, 1951), 251.
24. Lamoni Call, *2000 Changes in the Book of Mormon* (Bountiful, Utah: Lamoni Call, 1898).
25. Roberts, *Defense of the Faith*, 1:300.
26. Brigham Young University is owned and operated by the LDS Church.
27. Sidney Sperry, *The Problems of the Book of Mormon*, 190; cited in Jerald and Sandra Tanner, *Mormonism—Shadow or Reality?* (Salt Lake City: Utah Lighthouse Ministry, 1987), 90.

28. Hugh Nibley, *Since Cumorah* (Salt Lake City: Deseret Book, 1967), 7.
29. *The Challenge* (Burbank, Calif.: Malan Industries, n.d.) pamphlet put out by the LDS Church—California Mission, point 6. When this pamphlet was revised and reprinted in 1982, this point was left out. See *What Is the Book of Mormon?* (Salt Lake City: The Church of Jesus Christ of Latter-day Saints, 1982), pamphlet published by the LDS Church.
30. Roberts, *Defense of the Faith*, 1:279.
31. Nibley, *Since Cumorah*, 6, 8.
32. Mosiah 21:28.
33. Original edition printed by photo-offset in Wilford C. Wood, *Joseph Smith Begins His Work*, 2 vols. (Salt Lake City: Publisher's Press, 1958), vol. 1.
34. Book of Mosiah, Chapter IX, p. 200.
35. Fifteen chapters are reckoned according to the current chapter and verse divisions of the *Book of Mormon*. See Mosiah 6:5.
36. 1 Nephi 20:1.
37. First Book of Nephi, Chapter VI, p. 52.
38. 2 Nephi 12:9.
39. Second Book of Nephi, Chapter VIII, p. 87.
40. Alma 29:4.
41. Book of Alma, Chapter XV, p. 303.
42. Fourth Chicago Edition, p. 319. This verse reads, "... yea, I know that he allotteth unto men, according to their will; whether ..."
43. 1920 Edition, p. 267. This verse reads, "... I know that he allotteth unto men according to their wills, whether ..." Notice some additional "mechanical" changes between these two editions—the comma after "men" had been removed; the word "will" was changed to "wills"; and the semicolon after "will" became a comma.
44. 1964 Edition, p. 267. This verse reads the same as the 1920 Edition. See Tanner, *3,913 Changes in the Book of Mormon*, 7.
45. See *Mormonism—Shadow or Reality?*, 72-81; and *The Case Against Mormonism*, 3 vols. (Salt Lake City, Utah Lighthouse Ministry, 1968), 2:72-107.

46. Tanner, *Case*, 2:87.
47. 2 Nephi 25:1. Colleen Raulson writes, "Why in the world then did the writer quote over fifteen chapters of Isaiah, up to this point (he quotes more later), if he thought it was too hard for the people to understand?" (Colleen Ralson, *Color Me Confused—the Book of Mormon* [Nauvoo, Ill.: Personal Freedom Outreach, 1988], 19).
48. Tanner, *Case*, 2:72-76.
49. Nephi (1 Nephi 1:1) is found in 2 Maccabees 1:36; Ezias (Helaman 8:20) is found in 1 Esdras 8:2. Some newer translations of the Apocrypha have changed these names. However, the translation found in Joseph Smith's Bible has them both. Reed Durham identified Joseph's copy as "an edition of the Authorized Version 'together with the Apocrypha,' ... an 1828 edition, printed in Cooperstown, New York, by H. and E. Phinney Company" (Reed Durham, "*A History of Joseph Smith's Revision of the Bible*," Ph.D. diss., BYU, 1965, 25; cited in Tanner, *Mormonism—Shadow or Reality?*, 72). Current copies of the Authorized Version of the Apocrypha still contain these names (*Apocrypha: Authorized [King James] Version*, [Great Britain: Cambridge University Press, n.d.—circa 2000], 140, 9, respectively).
50. Tanner, *Case*, 2:76-82.
51. 1 Nephi 22:15 (see Malachi 4:1); 2 Nephi 25:13 (see Malachi 4:2); 2 Nephi 26:4, 6 (see Malachi 4:1); 2 Nephi 26:9 (see Malachi 4:2). The *Book of Mormon* even cross-references to Malachi in the first two references. The *Book of Mormon* passages were supposedly written between 588-545 BC. While the exact date that the book of Malachi was written is unknown, internal evidence points to it being written about 433-424 BC (John MacArthur, *The MacArthur Study Bible* [Nashville: Word Bibles, 1997], 1359; *The NIV Study Bible* [Grand Rapids: Zondervan Publishing House, 1985], 1423). Merill F. Unger, in *The New Unger's Bible Dictionary* (Chicago: Moody Press, 1988), states, "A date around 455 B.C. or later would be probable" (806).

52. Tanner, *Case*, 2:82-107, particularly pp. 87-102. See also H. Michael Marquardt, *The Use of the Bible in The Book of Mormon* (Salt Lake City: Utah Lighthouse Ministry, 1979 – reprint of articles from *The Journal of Pastoral Practice*).
53. Compare 3 Nephi 20:23-26 to Acts 3:22-26.
54. See, for example, Sydney Sperry, *Book of Mormon Institute*, 5 December 1959; cited in Tanner, *Case*, 2:103.
55. *Book of Mormon* footnotes indicate these verses were written between 588 and 570 B.C.
56. 1 Kings 6:20-25; 7:48-51.
57. 1 Kings 7:51.
58. 1 Kings 7:14-45.
59. 1 Kings 6:15-38.
60. 1 Kings 5:14-16; 6:38.
61. Matthew 2:1, 5, 6, 8, 16; Luke 2:4, 15; John 7:42. The Bible also calls it the "land of Judah," or "land of Juda." Judea is the Greco-Roman name for Judah.
62. Micah 5:2.
63. See, for instance, the FARMS report entitled "Jesus' Birthplace and the Phrase 'Land of Jerusalem'" (farms.byu.edu/display. php?print=1&id=127&table=transcripts).
64. Matthew 2:1, 5; Luke 2:4—Judaea; Micah 5:2—Judah; Matthew 2:6—Juda. The footnote for Matt. 2:6 indicates Juda is Judah. All three words (Juda, Judah, Judaea) are interchangeable, identifying the same location.
65. Luke 2:4.
66. Micah 5:2 – Ephrath was the original name of the city (Genesis 35:19), so this town was occasionally "surnamed" Ephrath (or "Ephrathah in *NIV*). It was also located in Judea, rather than in Israel, so it was also identified by the title Judea, much like US cities are identified by city name and state name. See J. D. Douglas, ed., *New Bible Dictionary* (Downers Grove, Ill.: Intervarsity Press, 1996), 133.
67. Ruth 1:2.
68. Kenneth Barker, gen. ed., *The NIV Study Bible* (Grand Rapids: Zondervan Publishing, 1985), notes for Micah 5:2, 1376. See also Ruth 4:11 and 1 Samuel 17:12.

69. For a more detailed look at this topic, see Bill McKeever and Eric Johnson, "Was Jesus Born 'at Jerusalem'?" (www.mrm.org/multimedia/text/at-jerusalem.html).
70. George Reynolds and Janne M. Sjodahl; *Commentary on the Book of Mormon* (Salt Lake City: Deseret Book, 1959), 4: 64.
71. We see this again in Alma 48:10, supposedly one year later.
72. Acts 11:26.
73. *NIV Study Bible*, "The Spread of the Gospel" chart, 1668.
74. 3 Nephi 9:3, 9, 10-11.
75. 3 Nephi 9:4, 7.
76. 3 Nephi 9:5, 6, 8.
77. 3 Nephi 9:12.
78. Luke 19:10.
79. That was the event that supposedly caused these disasters—the crucifixion of Christ (see 3 Nephi, summary of Chapter 8).
80. According to the official *Book of Mormon* Introduction, "The crowning event recorded in the Book of Mormon is the personal ministry of the Lord Jesus Christ among the Nephites soon after his resurrection."
81. Matthew 5:17.
82. Revelation 19:11-21.
83. For a more thorough and detailed examination of major problems with the *Book of Mormon* text, we recommend H. Michael Marquardt, *The Rise of Mormonism: 1816-1844* (Longwood, Fla.: Xulon Press, 2005), Chapter 9, "Literary Dependence in the Book of Mormon: Two Studies," 167-210.
84. *The Doctrine and Covenants of the Church of Jesus Christ of Latter-day Saints* (Salt Lake City: The Church of Jesus Christ of Latter-day Saints, 1981), 20:8-9; see also *History of the Church*, 1:65.
85. Hyrum M. Smith and Janne M. Sjodahl, *Doctrine and Covenants Commentary* (Cambridge: University Press, 1951), 100.
86. McConkie, *Mormon Doctrine*, 333.

87. Ezra Taft Benson, *The Teachings of Ezra Taft Benson* (Salt Lake City: Bookcraft, 1988), 55.
88. *Gospel Principles* (Salt Lake City: The Church of Jesus Christ of Latter-day Saints, 1992), personal study guide, 303-04.
89. Bill McKeever and Eric Johnson, *Mormonism 101* (Grand Rapids: Baker Books, 2000), 121.
90. McConkie, *Mormon Doctrine*, 193.
91. Ibid., 318.
92. Ibid., 396. In *Doctrine and Covenants* 135:3 we read, "**Joseph Smith**, the Prophet and Seer of the Lord, **has done more, save Jesus only, for the salvation of men** in this world, **than any other man** that ever lived in it." George Q. Cannon, speaking of Joseph Smith, said, "He stands, therefore, at the head of this dispensation and will throughout all eternity.... **If we get our salvation, we shall have to pass by him; if we enter into our glory, it will be through the authority that he has received. We cannot get around him...**" (Jerreld H. Newquist, comp., *Gospel Truth: Discourses and Writings of President George Q. Cannon*, 2 vols. [Salt Lake City: Deseret News Press, 1957], 1:255). Brigham Young taught that "**no man or woman** in this dispensation **will ever enter into the celestial kingdom of God without the consent of Joseph Smith.... every man and woman must have the certificate of Joseph Smith, junior, as a passport to their entrance into the mansion where God and Christ are**—I with you and you with me. I cannot go there without his consent. He holds the keys of that kingdom for the last dispensation..." (*Journal of Discourses*, 26 vols. [England: Various publishers, 1854-1886], photo reprint, 7:289, 9 October 1859). Brigham Young also said, "For unbelievers we will quote from the Scriptures—'Whosoever believeth that Jesus is the Christ is born of God.' Again—'Hereby know ye the Spirit of God: Every spirit that confesseth that Jesus Christ is come in the flesh, is of God.' I will now give my scripture—'Whosoever confesseth that **Joseph Smith** was sent of God to reveal the holy Gospel to the children of men, and lay the foundation for gathering Israel, and building up the kingdom of God on

the earth, that spirit is of God; and every spirit that does **not** confess that God has sent **Joseph Smith**, and revealed the everlasting Gospel to and through him, is of Antichrist..." (*Journal of Discourses*, 8:176, 9 September 1860).
93. Jacob 1:15; 2:24.
94. *Journal of Discourses*, 11:269; 20:28-31.
95. *Doctrine and Covenants* 132:1.
96. Ibid., vv. 38-39.
97. LDS Articles of Faith, article 2.
98. McConkie, *Mormon Doctrine*, 15-16; Moroni 8:5-26; *Doctrine and Covenants* 18:42; 20:71; 29:47; 68:27; 74:7.
99. Newquist, *Gospel Truth*, 1:85; Widtsoe, *Joseph Smith—Seeker After Truth, Prophet of God*, 178; McConkie, *Mormon Doctrine*, 349.
100. "God the Father is a glorified and perfected Man, a Personage of flesh and bones..." (McConkie, *Mormon Doctrine*, 319).
101. "It is true that there may be a second chance to hear and accept the gospel.... Salvation for the dead is the system by means of which those who '*die without a knowledge of the gospel*' ... may gain such knowledge..." (McConkie, *Mormon Doctrine*, 685-86). See also *Doctrine and Covenants*, Section 128.
102. See Jerald and Sandra Tanner, *Evolution of the Mormon Temple Ceremony: 1842-1990* (Salt Lake City: Utah Lighthouse Ministry, 1990).
103. McConkie, *Mormon Doctrine*, 319-23. See also *History of the Church*, 6:474.
104. *History of the Church*, 6:476; John Widtsoe, *Discourses of Brigham Young* (Salt Lake City: Deseret Book, 1954), 388.
105. *History of the Church*, 6:305; *Journal of Discourses*, 1:93; 6:120; 11:286. "Mormon Prophets have continuously taught the sublime truth that **God the Eternal Father was once a mortal man ... He became God**—an exalted Being—through obedience to the same eternal Gospel truths that we are given opportunity today to obey" (Milton Hunter, *The Gospel Through the Ages* [Salt Lake City: Deseret Book, 1945], 104-05).

106. *Book of Mormon*, Introduction. See also *History of the Church*, 4:461.

• **Chapter Five Notes**

1. For instance, it is difficult to understand why Joshua's army was able to so easily defeat the Northern Kings at the Waters of Merom in Joshua 11:6-9. After all, the Northern Kings had chariots (Joshua 11:4) while Joshua did not. By knowing that the Waters of Merom was basically a swamp hemmed in by mountains (James Orr, gen. ed., *International Standard Bible Encyclopedia*, 5 vols. [Grand Rapids: Wm. B. Eerdman's Publishing, 1956], 3:2037), it is easy to understand that the chariots were completely useless—Joshua's victory was therefore easy.
2. An LDS apologetic group based at Brigham Young University in Provo, Utah.
3. *Conference Report*, April 1928, 13-14.
4. *Deseret News–Church Section*, 23 October 2004, 2.
5. *Journal of Discourses*, 26 vols. (England: Various publishers, 1854-1886), photo reprint, 14:10-11; 19 February 1871.
6. F. Michael Watson (on behalf of Gordon B. Hinckley) to Bishop Darrell L. Brooks, 16 October 1990, 1.
7. The so-called "Hemispheric Model" was taught in the Book of Mormon Religion class at the LDS Business College in the spring of 1988. Lane Thuet attended the class along with Shawna Burchard, his fiancée. Both recall clearly that the teachings of the Church sponsored class were that the *Book of Mormon* lands encompassed both the North and South American Continents.
8. Church Educational System, *Book of Mormon (Religion 121-122) Student Manual* (Salt Lake City: The Church of Jesus Christ of Latter-day Saints, 1981), ii, 354, 460. The possible map was presented on page 286, with *Book of Mormon* geographical references on page 287.
9. Ibid., 354.

10. See William Hamblin, "An Apologist for the Critics," (Early Latter-day Saint Views of Book of Mormon Geography) – farms.byu.edu/display.php?id=146&table=review.
11. Joseph Fielding Smith, *Doctrines of Salvation: Sermons and Writings of Joseph Fielding Smith*, Bruce R. McConkie, comp., 3 vols. (Salt Lake City: Bookcraft, 1956), 3:232-41.
12. John L. Sorensen is a former BYU Professor, former Chairman of the BYU Department of Anthropology and a board member for FARMS.
13. John Sorenson, "The Book of Mormon in Ancient America," FARMS paper, 3.
14. By making this claim, LDS apologists are saying that they do not agree with what the LDS critics point out, but at the same time they are refusing to accept the teachings of their apostles and prophets. If they do not want to listen to their own leaders, then why should anyone else?
15. This is the advice given by Apostle Bruce R. McConkie. When another professor from Brigham Young University was teaching doctrine out of harmony with the teachings of the current Church leadership, McConkie wrote to him and asserted that "it is not in your province to set in order the Church or to determine what its doctrines shall be....it is my province to teach to the Church what the doctrine is. It is your province to echo what I say or to remain silent" (Bruce R. McConkie to Eugene England, 19 February 1981, 8). Current apologists at BYU seem to have forgotten this.
16. One excellent example is a Nephite city called Manti (Alma 56:14) which Smith pinpointed geographically in Missouri (Smith, *Doctrines of Salvation*, 3:239). He also identified the remains of "an Old Nephite altar or tower" in Daviess County, Missouri (Joseph Fielding Smith, *Church History and Modern Revelation*, 4 vols. [Salt Lake City: Deseret Book, 1949], 3:117-18).
17. *History of the Church of Jesus Christ of Latter-day Saints*, 2nd ed. 1980, 7 vols. (Salt Lake City: Deseret Book Company, 1951), 2:79-80. See also Smith, *Doctrines of Salvation*, 3:238-39. Heber C. Kimball's journal verifies the event and the fact

that Joseph learned of the skeleton's identity by a "vision" from God—*Heber C. Kimball's Journal*; cited in *Times and Seasons*, 1 February 1845, 788. Also in Orson Whitney, *Life of Heber C. Kimball* (Salt Lake City: Juvenile Instructor Office, 1888), 60-61.

18. *The Pearl of Great Price* (Salt Lake City: The Church of Jesus Christ of Latter-day Saints, 1981), Joseph Smith—History 1:34.
19. *Biography and Journal of William I. Appleby*, 30-31; cited in Dan Vogel, *Early Mormon Documents*, 5 vols. (Salt Lake City: Signature Books, 1996), 1:147. Both Jaredites and Nephites are prominent people groups in the *Book of Mormon*.
20. Lehi's family came to America at the start of the *Book of Mormon*. The two main people groups of the book—Nephites and Lamanites—are named after two of his sons.
21. Franklin D. Richards and James A. Little, *Compendium of the Doctrines of the Gospel* (Salt Lake City: George Q. Cannon and Sons, 1898), 289. In the *Compendium*, "Chile" was spelled "Chili." Other sources have corrected the spelling. This revelation is also published by Fred C. Collier in *Unpublished Revelations of the Prophets and Presidents*, 2 vols. (Salt Lake City: Collier's Publishing, 1979), 1:85, Part 39. LDS scholar Robert Matthews traces the revelation back as far as 1845 via the Bernhisel Manuscript, and shows that similar statements indicate the revelation may have been received during the dedicatory services of the Kirtland Temple ("Notes on 'Lehi's Travels,'" *BYU Studies*, Spring 1972, 312-14).
22. Apostle John Widtsoe verifies that this account has been accepted as correct by the members of the Church—Widtsoe, *A Book of Mormon Treasury* (Salt Lake City: Bookcraft, 1959), 128.
23. *The Book of Mormon* (Salt Lake City: The Church of Jesus Christ of Latter-day Saints, 1981), Mormon 6:2-11; Ether 15:8-11.
24. Mormon 6:2-4.
25. Joseph Smith—History 1:34, 51-52; *History of the Church*, 2:79-80.

26. Daniel Ludlow, ed., *Encyclopedia of Mormonism*, 4 vols. (New York: Macmillan Publishing, 1992), "Cumorah," 1:346-347. See also footnotes under the picture of the hill on p. 346.
27. Jeff Call, "Faithful Follow Spiritual Path," *Deseret Morning News*, 7 March 2004, A-1.
28. Ibid., A-1, A-12.
29. See Bill McKeever and Eric Johnson, *Mormonism 101* (Grand Rapids: Baker Books, 2000), 112.
30. Videotaped interview contained in Video: *DNA vs. The Book of Mormon* (2003), Living Hope Ministries.
31. Smithsonian Institution, National Museum of Natural History, Department of Anthropology, "Statement Regarding the Book of Mormon," 1988, 1.
32. Call, "Faithful Follow Spiritual Path," A-12.
33. John L. Sorenson to James S. Lindberg, 27 May 1982, 1.
34. John Sorensen, *An Ancient American Setting for the Book of Mormon* (Salt Lake City: Deseret Book in association with FARMS), 1979 edition, p. 0/3. In the 1985 edition of that book, this statement has been changed to read "Until recently … we had neglected to pin down the location of a single city… " (xvii). Sorensen then goes on to develop a "model" of *Book of Mormon* events and travels, but in the end he still has to admit that his model has not been proven, but is instead only "plausible" (xx). Sorensen later wrote a book, *Mormon's Map* (Provo, Utah: Foundation for Ancient Research and Mormon Studies, 2000), setting forth a "comprehensive map" of *Book of Mormon* lands. But even this book (which is no longer in print) did not fix the sites mentioned to any real world locations.
35. A-21.
36. Grant Palmer, *An Insider's View of Mormon Origins* (Salt Lake City: Signature Press, 2002), 56. See also Dan Vogel, *Indian Origins and the Book of Mormon: Religious Solutions from Columbus to Joseph Smith* (Salt Lake City: Signature Books, 1986), 35-52.
37. Scott H. Faulring, ed., *An American Prophet's Record: The Diaries and Journals of Joseph Smith* (Salt Lake City: Signature

Books in association with Smith Research Associates, 1987), 9 November 1835, 51. Smith was not unique in suggesting in the *Book of Mormon* that the American Indians were descendants of Israelites. The idea had also been suggested in Ethan Smith's *View of the Hebrews* (Poultney, Vt.: Smith and Shute, 1825) as well as by others. As mentioned, it was the popular opinion of the time period. This is demonstrated by an article printed in the *Wayne Sentinel* on 11 October 1825, which quoted a Smith contemporary—Mordecai M. Noah—as saying, "Those who are conversant with the public and private economy of the Indians, are strongly of (the) opinion that they are the lineal descendants of the Israelites, and my own researches go far to confirm me in the same belief" (cited in Michael Marquardt and Wesley Walters, *Inventing Mormonism* [Salt Lake City: Smith Research Associates, 1998], 45).

38. *Messenger and Advocate*, February 1835, 1:78, 80.
39. Ibid., October 1835, 2:193.
40. Joseph Smith—History 1:34. Also in *History of the Church*, 1:183.
41. Joseph Smith, "Latter Day Saints," in I. Daniel Rupp, *He Pasa Ekklesia* (Philadelphia: J.Y. Humphreys, 1844) 404-07; cited in Dan Vogel, *Early Mormon Documents*, 1:183-86.
42. *The Doctrine and Covenants of the Church of Jesus Christ of Latter-day Saints* (Salt Lake City: The Church of Jesus Christ of Latter-day Saints, 1981), 54:8.
43. *History of the Church*, 1:183-85fn.
44. Ibid., 185. The full footnote runs from 183-85. Additional statements concerning this mission also verify that the American Indians were said to be the descendants of the Lamanites from the *Book of Mormon*:

"At the September, 1830, conference of the young Church, missionary work really began. Four elders, Oliver Cowdery, Parley P. Pratt, Peter Whitmer, Jr., and Ziba Peterson, were called to go westward into the Indian country **to tell the red men that a book about their ancestors had been revealed**" (John A. Widtsoe, *Joseph Smith—Seeker After Truth, Prophet* *of God* [Salt Lake City: Deseret News Press, 1951], 135-36. See also *Doctrine and Covenants* 32).

"And now, behold, I say unto you that you shall **go unto the Lamanites and preach** my gospel unto them; and inasmuch as they receive thy teachings thou shalt cause my church to be established among them ... Behold, I say unto you that it [the city Zion] shall be built **on the borders by the Lamanites**" (*Doctrine and Covenants* 28:8-9).

"At this time a great desire was manifested by several of the Elders respecting **the remnants of the house of Joseph, the Lamanites, residing in the west**—knowing (Of course this knowledge arose from what the brethren had learned from the Book of Mormon of the promises of God to the Lamanites) that the promises of God were great respecting that people..." (*History of the Church*, 1:118 and fn1).

45. *History of the Church*, 2:357.
46. Ibid., 2:358.
47. *Times and Seasons*, 1 March 1842, 707. See also Vogel, *Early Mormon Documents*, 1:171.
48. *Times and Seasons*, 15 November 1844, 707. See also *History of the Church*, 1:315 (entire letter traverses pp. 312-16).
49. *Journal of Discourses*, 26 vols. (England: Various publishers, 1854-1886), photo reprint, 1:106, 8 May 1853.
50. Ibid., 19:173, 2 December 1877. See also Orson Pratt; ibid., 14:10-11, 19 February 1871.
51. Leonard Arrington and Davis Bitton, *The Mormon Experience* (New York: Alfred A. Knopf, 1979), 145.
52. Richard Bushman, *Joseph Smith and the Beginnings of Mormonism* (Chicago: University of Illinois Press, 1984), 133.
53. Ibid., 169.
54. Thomas G. Alexander, *Mormonism in Transition: A History of the Latter-day Saints, 1890-1930* (Chicago: University of Illinois Press, 1986), 200.
55. Smith, *Doctrines of Salvation*, 1: preface. This is Bruce R. McConkie's preface to the book.
56. Ibid., (1990 printing) vol. 1 Dust Jacket: rear flap.

57. Ibid., 1:151.
58. Bruce McConkie, *Mormon Doctrine* (Salt Lake City: Bookcraft, 1966), 33.
59. *Gospel Principles* (Salt Lake City: The Church of Jesus Christ of Latter-day Saints, 1992), 268.
60. George D. Smith, "B. H. Roberts: Book of Mormon Apologist and Skeptic," in Dan Vogel and Brent Metcalfe, eds., *American Apocrypha* (Salt Lake City: Signature Books, 2002), 149. The *Deseret News* article repeatedly referred to the American Indians as Lamanite and Hebrew descendants.
61. Ibid., 131.
62. Brigham H. Roberts, *New Witnesses for God* (Salt Lake City: Deseret News, 1909), 3:40.
63. "BYU Gene Data May Shed Light On Origin Of Book of Mormon's Lamanites," *The Salt Lake Tribune*, 30 November 2000, B-1.
64. *The Seattle Times*, 7 December 2002; *The Los Angeles Times*, 8 December 2002.
65. *Los Angeles Times*, 8 December 2002, A-21.
66. Thomas Murphy, "Lamanite Genesis, Genealogy and Genetics," *American Apocrypha*, 47-77.
67. Ibid., 47-48.
68. Simon Southerton, "DNA Genealogies of American Indians and the Book of Mormon" (www.exmormon.org/whyleft125.htm).
69. *DNA vs. The Book of Mormon*, video. An extensive treatment of this subject is presented in the *Salt Lake City Messenger*, November 2004 (Utah Lighthouse Ministry), "Who are the Lamanites?" 1-19.
70. Smith, "'B. H. Roberts' Book of Mormon Apologist and Skeptic," *American Apocrypha*, 150.
71. *Los Angeles Times*, 8 December 2002, A-21.
72. Bill McKeever, "A Diluted Gene Pool? Not Likely." *Mormonism Research Ministry Update*, January 2003, 1.
73. *Journal of Discourses*, 17:30, 6 April 1874.
74. *Deseret News–Church Section*, 26 February 1984, 4.

75. "Another Mormon Author Facing Excommunication," 16 July 2005 KUTV News/Associated Press story. On-line at http://kutv.com/topstories/local_story_ 197205005.html.
76. Simon G. Southerton, *Losing a Lost Tribe* (Salt Lake City: Signature Books, 2004), 186.
77. Murphy, "Lamanite Genesis, Genealogy, and Genetics," *American Apocrypha*, 61.
78. Ibid., 66.
79. Ibid., 68.
80. Ibid., 69.
81. Roberts, *New Witnesses for God*, 3:40.
82. LDS sources include: Richard Anderson, *Investigating the Book of Mormon Witnesses* (Salt Lake City: Deseret Book Co., 1981); Frances W. Kirkham, *A New Witness For Christ in America* (Salt Lake City: Brigham Young University, 1942), vol. 1, Chapter XIX "Witnesses to the Book of Mormon."

    Sources that question the witnesses' testimonies include: Joel B. Groat, "Facts on the Book of Mormon Witnesses," Parts I and II (www.irr.org/mit/bomwit1.html and www.irr.org/mit/bomwit2.html); Palmer, *An Insider's View*, Chapter 6, "Witnesses to the Golden Plates"; LaMar Petersen, *The Creation of the Book of Mormon: A Historical Inquiry* (Salt Lake City: Freethinker Press, 2000), Chapter 5, "The Witnesses"; Jerald and Sandra Tanner, *The Changing World of Mormonism* (Chicago: Moody Press, 1980), "The Witnesses," 94-110; Dan Vogel, "The Validity of the Witnesses' Testimony," *American Apocrypha*, Chapter 4; David Persuitte, *Joseph Smith and the Origins of the Book of Mormon* (Jefferson: McFarland and Company, Inc. Publishers, 2000), Chapter 8.
83. Kirkham, *A New Witness for Christ*, 245-46.
84. Palmer, *An Insider's View*, 175.
85. Ibid., 175-76.
86. Ibid., 186.
87. Ibid., 189.
88. Ibid., 184-85.
89. Vogel, "The Validity," 93.
90. Palmer, *An Insider's View*, 175-76.

91. Ibid., 178.
92. Ibid., 178-79.
93. Vogel, "The Validity," 94.
94. Palmer, *An Insider's View*, 194.
95. Ibid.
96. Vogel, *Early Mormon Documents* (1998), 2:255. In a 16 March 1879 letter to James T. Cobb, John H. Gilbert recalls, "I asked Harris once if he had really seen the plates with his naked eyes? – his reply was, No, but with spiritual eyes" (ibid., 526).
97. Ibid., 255.
98. Ibid., 290-91.
99. Ibid., 289.
100. Brigham D. Madsen, "Introduction," B. H. Roberts, *Studies of the Book of Mormon* (Salt Lake City: Signature Books, 1985), 23.
101. Palmer, *An Insider's View*, 204.
102. Petersen, *The Creation of the Book of Mormon*, 84-85.
103. Ibid., 87-88. Hiram Page had a stone by which he claimed to receive revelations, and Joseph Smith wrote that "especially the Whitmer family and Oliver Cowdery, were believing much in the things set forth by this stone, we thought best to enquire of the Lord concerning so important a matter... " (*History of the Church,* 1:109-10). Joseph Smith's revelation from the Lord recorded in *Doctrine and Covenants* 28:11 states: "And again, thou shalt take thy brother Hiram Page, between him and thee alone, and tell him that those things which he hath written from that stone are not of me and that Satan deceiveth him."

Fawn Brodie writes that in mid 1837, a faction opposing Joseph Smith "had rallied around a young girl who claimed to be a seeress by virtue of a black stone in which she read the future. David Whitmer, Martin Harris, and Oliver Cowdery, whose faith in seer stones had not diminished when Joseph stopped using them, pledged her their loyalty, and F. G. Williams, formerly Joseph's First Counselor, became her scribe. Patterning herself after the Shakers, the new prophetess would dance herself into a state of exhaustion before her followers, fall upon the floor, and burst forth with revelations" (*No Man Knows My History* [New York: Alfred A. Knopf, 1971], 205).

In David Whitmer's, *An Address to All Believers in Christ* (Richmond, Mo.: David Whitmer, 1887), he writes, "If you believe my testimony to the Book of Mormon; if you believe that God spake to us three witnesses by his own voice, then I tell you that in June, 1838, God spake to me again by his own voice from the heavens, and told me to 'separate myself from among the Latter Day Saints, for as they sought to do unto me, so should it be done unto them.' In the spring of 1838, the heads of the church and many of the members had gone deep into error and blindness" (27).

104. Four of the six which questioned his honesty were:

"**Second**—For seeking to destroy the character of President Joseph Smith, Jun., by **falsely insinuating** that he was guilty of adultery....**Seventh**—For leaving his calling to which God had appointed him by revelation, **for the sake of filthy lucre**, and turning to the practice of law....**Eighth**—For disgracing the Church **by being connected in the bogus business** [counterfeiting], as common report says....**Ninth**—For **dishonestly retaining notes** after they had been paid; and finally for leaving and forsaking the cause of God..." (*History of the Church*, 3:16).

105. Petersen, *The Creation*, 85.
106. *Times and Seasons*, 15 July 1841, 482.
107. Petersen, *The Creation*, 86.
108. Ibid., 88.
109. Christopher G. Crary, *Pioneer and Personal Reminiscences* (Marshalltown, Iowa: Marshall Printing Co., 1893), 44-45; cited in Petersen, *The Creation*, 92.
110. Vogel, "The Validity," 94.
111. Petersen, *The Creation*, 89.
112. Ludlow, *Encyclopedia of Mormonism*, 2:576.
113. David Persuitte, *Joseph Smith and the Origins of The Book of Mormon*, 94.

114. Vogel, "The Validity," 99.
115. Ludlow, *Encyclopedia of Mormonism*, 3:1359-60.
116. D. Michael Quinn, *The Mormon Hierarchy: Origins of Power* (Salt Lake City: Signature Books in association with Smith Research Associates, 1994), 210-11.
117. Palmer, *An Insider's View*, 208.
118. Ibid., 209.
119. Ibid., 211.
120. Quinn, *Origins of Power*, 211.
121. Ibid.
122. Palmer, *An Insider's View*, 212-13.
123. Joel B. Groat, "Facts On The Book Of Mormon Witnesses," Part 1 (www.irr.org/mit/bomwit1.html), 1.
124. Groat, Part 2 (www.irr.org/mit/bomwit2.html), 10.
125. Ibid., 12.
126. Tanner, *The Changing World of Mormonism*, 102.
127. Ibid., 105.
128. Richard Abanes, *One Nation Under Gods: A History of the Mormon Church* (New York: Four Walls Eight Windows, 2002), 505-06n47.
129. Petersen, *The Creation*, 94.
130. Vogel, "The Validity," 79-80.
131. Ibid., 108.
132. B. H. Roberts, *Studies of the Book of Mormon*, xvi.
133. Leonard J. Arrington, "The Intellectual Tradition of the Latter-day Saints," *Dialogue: A Journal of Mormon Thought*, Spring 1969, 24.
134. Ron Bitton, "B. H. Roberts Book Stirs Controversy," *Sunstone*, December 1985, 36.
135. Ludlow, *Encyclopedia of Mormonism*, 2:690.
136. Sterling McMurrin, "Brigham H. Roberts: A Biographical Essay," in Roberts, *Studies of the Book of Mormon*, xxxi. Arrington writes, "Roberts published eight books of theology and nine of history, including the monumental six-volume *Comprehensive History of the Church* (Salt Lake City, 1930).... Roberts also wrote two volumes of biography,

three of sermons and commentaries, and one novel" ("The Intellectual Tradition," 23).
137. *Deseret Morning News 2005 Church Almanac* (Salt Lake City: Deseret News, 2004), 72. The First Council of Seventy is a position in the LDS Church directly below the Quorum of 12 Apostles in rank and authority. They are considered General Authorities for the Church.
138. Roberts, *Studies of the Book of Mormon*, Introduction, 20.
139. Ibid., 21.
140. Smith, "B. H. Roberts," 125-26.
141. Roberts, *Studies of the Book of Mormon*, 46.
142. Ibid., 47-51.
143. Ibid., 22.
144. Ibid., 23.
145. Ibid.
146. In 1979, modern Microfilm Company (now Utah Lighthouse Ministry) published *An Examination of B. H. Roberts' Secret Manuscript*, explaining that it "contains an article by Wesley P. Walters and photographs from Roberts's original manuscript." His article, "The Origin of the Book of Mormon," had been published in *The Journal of Pastoral Practice*, vol. III, no. 3, 1979.

Walters summarized the points made by B. H. Roberts. "In this landmark work Mr. Roberts presents a powerful case for the human origin of the *Book of Mormon*, based upon four important observations. (1) The book stands in conflict with what is known about the early American races from scientific investigation. (2) It, however, agrees with the *erroneous* information believed in the nineteenth-century to have been true about these early Americans. (3) Joseph Smith, Jr., had sufficient creative and imaginative powers of mind to have taken this nineteenth-century 'knowledge' and produced such a book. (4) The book evidences such blunders as would have been made by an unsophisticated nineteenth-century mind that lacked formal education as Joseph Smith, Jr. did" (122).

In 1980 Modern Microfilm Company published an incomplete copy (Chapter 2 of "Book of Mormon Difficulties" was

missing) of Roberts's material, entitled *Roberts' Manuscripts Revealed: A Photographic Reproduction of Mormon Historian B. H. Roberts' Secret Studies on the Book of Mormon.*
147. Roberts, *Studies of the Book of Mormon*, xviii.
148. "Brigham H. Roberts – Studies of the Book of Mormon – book review" (www.lds-mormon.com/sotbom.shtml).
149. "B. H. Roberts' Secret Manuscript," *Salt Lake City Messenger*, December 1979, 15.
150. Roberts, *Studies of the Book of Mormon*, 22.
151. Ibid., 29.
152. Ibid., 30.
153. Ibid.
154. Bitton, "B. H. Roberts Book," 37.
155. Brigham D. Madsen, "Reflections on LDS Disbelief in the Book of Mormon as History," *Dialogue: A Journal of Mormon Thought*, Fall 1997, 89.
156. Smith, "B. H. Roberts," 123.
157. Wesley P. Walters, "The Origin of the Book of Mormon: B. H. Roberts, Mormon Apologist, Historian and General Authority Proposes the Book of Mormon is of Human Origin," *Journal of Pastoral Practice*, vol. III, no. 3, 1979, 124.
158. Stan Larson, *Quest for the Golden Plates* (Salt Lake City: Freethinker Press, 1996), 170n55.
159. One reviewer of the book states: "*Quest for the Golden Plates* is an impressive, meticulous reconstruction of Thomas Ferguson's troubled path from true believer to disillusioned skeptic. No lawyer's brief could present the argument more convincingly" (William Mulder, Emeritus Prof. of English, University of Utah, book jacket).
160. Co-authored with Milton R. Hunter.
161. After Ferguson's death, *One Fold and One Shepherd* was revised and republished under the title *The Messiah in Ancient America* (1987), with the names Bruce W. Warren and Thomas Stuart Ferguson on the cover. Because the new edition does not represent Ferguson's more recent conclusions, the revision "offers an incomplete and misleading representation of his real views" (S. Larson, *Quest for the Gold Plates*, 273).

See S. Larson's Appendix B: "Examining the Authorship of *The Messiah in Ancient America*" (ibid., 269-74).
162. S. Larson, *Quest for the Gold Plates*, 56.
163. Ibid., 43.
164. Ibid., 44.
165. Ibid., 44, 46.
166. Ibid., 50.
167. Ibid., 58.
168. Ibid., 67.
169. Ibid., 68-70.
170. Ibid., 91.
171. Ibid., 93.
172. Ibid., 136-37.
173. Ibid., 157.
174. Ibid., 218.
175. Charles Larson, *By His Own Hand Upon Papyrus* (Grand Rapids: Institute for Religious Research, 1992), 182-87.
176. Photocopy of letter reproduced in C. Larson, *By His Own Hand*, 187.
177. Ibid. LaMar Petersen comments, "While Ferguson's initial assignment was to respond to the Norman and Sorenson geographical theories, his paper addressed more broadly what he saw as the critical difficulties in Book of Mormon archaeology. He divided these problems into four areas: the Plant-Life Test, the Animal-Life Test, the Metalurgy Test, and the Script Test. This insightful document reveals Ferguson's perception of what he termed 'the big weak spots' involved in attempting to authenticate the Book of Mormon through archaeology" (Petersen, *The Creation*, 171-72).

For Ferguson's paper and a discussion of its contents, see Petersen, *The Creation*, Appendix D, "Book of Mormon Archaeological Tests" (169-230). See also S. Larson, *Quest for the Gold Plates*, Appendix A, "Thomas Stuart Ferguson on Book of Mormon Archaeology" (235-67). In the conclusion to his paper Ferguson states: "The evidence supporting the geographical views of [V. Garth] Norman and [John L.] Sorenson, under the exacting tests laid down by the text of the

Book of Mormon, is indeed very meager.... I'm afraid that up to this point, I must agree with Dee Green, who has told us that **to date, there is no Book-of-Mormon geography.** I, for one, would be happy if Dee were wrong" (S. Larson, *Quest*, 266-67).
178. Petersen, *The Creation*, 218.
179. C. Larson, *By His Own Hand*, 185. Jerald and Sandra Tanner write: "On a number of occasions when people wrote to him, Mr. Ferguson recommended that they read our publications on Mormonism" ("Ferguson's Two Faces," *Salt Lake City Messenger*, September 1988, 5). Ferguson wrote the Tanners in 1968 commending them for their work on the Book of Abraham (ibid., 4).
180. S. Larson, *Quest*, 217.
181. "Ferguson's Rejection Of The Book Of Mormon Verified," *Salt Lake City Messenger*, November 1990, 8-9. See also S. Larson, *Quest*, 157-58; Stan Larson, "The Odyssey of Thomas Stuart Ferguson," *Dialogue: A Journal of Mormon Thought*, Spring 1990, 55-93.
182. Petersen writes, "In establishing the ambitious program for the New World Archaeological Foundation, Ferguson essentially followed the procedure outlined by Nibley, in which one **began with the assumption that the Book of Mormon was true**" (Petersen, *The Creation*, 219).
183. The Tanners explain that when he visited them on 2 December 1970, "Mr. Ferguson told us frankly that he had not only given up the Book of Abraham, but that **he had come to the conclusion that Joseph Smith was not a prophet and that Mormonism was not true**. Ferguson felt that our work was important and that it should be subsidized. He told us that he had spent twenty-five years trying to prove Mormonism, but had finally come to the conclusion that all the work in this regard had been in vain. He said that his training in law had taught him how to weigh evidence and that **the case against Joseph Smith was absolutely devastating and could not be explained away**" (*Salt Lake City Messenger*, September 1988, 4).

184. Dee F. Green, "Book of Mormon Archaeology: The Myths and the Alternatives," *Dialogue: A Journal of Mormon Thought*, Summer 1969, 77.
185. Edward H. Ashment, "Making the Scriptures 'Indeed One in Our Hands'" in Dan Vogel, ed., *The Word of God* (Salt Lake City: Signature Books, 1990), 260-61.
186. Edward H. Ashment, "'A Record in the Language of My Father,': Evidence of Ancient Egyptian and Hebrew in the Book of Mormon" in Brent Lee Metcalfe, ed., *New Approaches to the Book of Mormon* (Salt Lake City: Signature Books, 1993), 374.
187. Charles W. Carpenter, "Latter-day Skeptics," *Christianity Today*, 11 November 1991, 31-32.
188. John C. Kunich, "Multiply Exceedingly: Book of Mormon Population Sizes," *New Approaches*, 231.
189. Ibid., 252.
190. Ibid., 259.
191. Ibid., 265.
192. Wesley P. Walters, *The Journal of Pastoral Practice*, vol. II, no. 2, 1978, 94.
193. Marquardt publications include the historical monographs: "The Book of Abraham Revisited," "Joseph Smith's Diaries," "The Strange Marriages of Sarah Ann Whitney"; and the books: *Inventing Mormonism: Tradition and the Historical Record* (co-authored with Wesley Walters), *The Joseph Smith Revelations: Text and Commentary* (Salt Lake City: Signature Books, 1999), and *The Rise of Mormonism: 1816-1844* (Longwood, Fla.: Xulon Press, 2005).
194. H. Michael Marquardt, "The Use of the Bible In the Book of Mormon," *Journal of Pastoral Practice*, vol. II, no. 2, 1978, 117. Marquardt's article contains three Appendixes that further demonstrate his conclusions. Appendix I: "*The Book of Mormon Borrows from New Testament Writings Not Written in Old Testament Times*" (118-28)—with 200 examples. *Book of Mormon* accounts "were supposed to have been written between 600 B.C. and 1 B.C." (118). Appendix II: "*Prophecies from the Old Testament Period are Given in New Testament*

King James Wording" (129-32) — with 58 examples. Appendix III: "The Book of Mormon's *Use of Biblical Material for the New Testament Time Period*" (132-36). "The following list gives King James wording for the New Testament for the period between A.D. 1 and A.D. 421" — with 67 examples.

195. Marvin Hill, "The 'New Mormon History' Reassessed in Light of Recent Books on Joseph Smith and Mormon Origins," *Dialogue: A Journal of Mormon Thought*, Fall 1988, 124.
196. *Dialogue*, Spring 1989; Letters, 7-8.
197. Vogel, *Indian Origins,* 71-72.
198. http://www.peabody.yale.edu/collections/ant/
199. Michael Coe, "Mormons & Archeology: An Outside View," *Dialogue*, Summer 1973, 40-48.
200. Ibid., 41-42.
201. Ibid., 46.
202. Photocopied letter in *Mormonism Researched*, Winter 1993, 6.
203. Thomas J. Finley, "Does the Book of Mormon Reflect an Ancient Near Eastern Background?" in Francis J. Beckwith, Carl Mosser, Paul Owen, eds., *The New Mormon Challenge* (Grand Rapids: Zondervan, 2002), 339.
204. Ibid., 366.
205. Thomas D. S. Key, *A Biologist Examines the Book of Mormon,* 14th ed. (Marlow, Okla.: Utah Missions, Inc., 1995), 56.

- **Chapter Six Notes**

    1. *History of the Church of Jesus Christ of Latter-day Saints*, 2nd ed. 1980, 7 vols. (Salt Lake City: Deseret Book Company, 1951), 1:2fn. See also George Cannon, *The Life of Joseph Smith* (Salt Lake City: Deseret News, 1888), 50. H. Michael Marquardt and Wesley P. Walters write, "Folklore has it that Joseph returned the gold plates into a cave in the Hill Cumorah in Manchester, New York" (*Inventing Mormonism* [Salt Lake City: Smith Research Associates, 1998], 114n57).
    2. Apostle Anthony W. Ivins informs us, "This sealed portion of the record which came into the hands of Joseph Smith but was

not translated by him ... deposited in the Hill Cumorah, still lie in their repository, awaiting the time when the Lord shall see fit to bring them forth, that they may be published to the world. Whether they have been removed from the spot where Mormon deposited them we cannot tell, but this we know, that they are safe under the guardianship of the Lord, and that they will be brought forth at the proper time as the Lord has declared they should be, for the benefit and blessing of the people of the world, for his word never fails" (*Conference Report*, April 1928, 15).

3. While recorded in the first person in the *History*, this information actually was taken from *William Clayton's Journal*. Some may feel this exempts Joseph Smith from the events surrounding the plates, but it does not. The entry in Clayton's journal is contemporaneous with the event, and records what actually happened. Later LDS historians falsified the information for the *History* (See Chapter 9 for more information about the *History of the Church*). Clayton's 1 May 1843 entry reads, "I have seen 6 brass plates which were found in Adams County.... **Prest J. has translated a portion** and says they contain the history of the person with whom they were found & he was a descendant of Ham through the loins of Pharoah king of Egypt, and that he received his kingdom from the ruler of heaven & earth" (Jerald and Sandra Tanner, *Clayton's Secret Writings Uncovered: Extracts From the Diaries of Joseph Smith's Secretary William Clayton* [Salt Lake City: Utah Lighthouse Ministry, 1982], 18). See also James B. Allen, *Trials of Discipleship: The Story of William Clayton, a Mormon* (Urbana: University of Illinois Press, 1987), 117.

This information was recorded as Clayton's eyewitness account of Joseph Smith's statement. It can certainly be trusted, because as Joseph explained on 26 May 1844, a faithful record of events had been kept **"for the last three years** I have a record of all my acts and proceedings, for I have kept several good, faithful, and efficient clerks in constant employ: they have accompanied me everywhere, and **carefully kept my history, and they have written down**

what I have done, where I have been, and **what I have** said; therefore my enemies cannot charge me with any day, time, or place, but what **I have written testimony to prove my actions**; and my enemies cannot prove anything against me" (*History of the Church*, 6:409).
4. *History of the Church*, 5:372. The facsimiles are reproduced on pp. 374-76. A letter by Apostle Parley P. Pratt to his cousin John Van Cott dated 7 May 1843 agrees with the account recorded in the *History* (Grant H. Palmer, *An Insider's View of Mormon Origins* [Salt Lake City: Signature Books, 2002], 31).
5. *Improvement Era*, September 1962, 637.
6. Ibid.
7. Ibid., 656.
8. Ibid., 660.
9. *Times and Seasons*, 1 May 1843, 185-87.
10. Ibid., 185.
11. *History of the Church*, 5:372-379.
12. W. Fugate swore an affidavit on 30 June 1879 admitting the plates to be a deliberate hoax played on Smith by himself and two others (*History of the Church*, 5:378fn).
13. *History of the Church*, 5:379.
14. A copy of this handbill is reproduced in Palmer, *An Insider's View*, 32. The Tanners quote an article published 22 May 1844 in the *Warsaw Signal*, shortly before Joseph Smith's death, that says Smith was "busy in translating them [the Kinderhook plates]" (*Mormonism—Shadow or Reality?* [Salt Lake City: Utah Lighthouse Ministry, 1987], 125-H).
15. Fawn Brodie, *No Man Knows My History* (New York: Alfred A. Knopf, 1971), 291.
16. Palmer, *An Insider's View*, 33. While Harris' letter was written in 1855, it was not published until 1912 (ibid., 33fn72).
17. W. Wyl, *Mormon Portraits* (Salt Lake City: Tribune Printing and Publishing Co, 1886), 211. After his account, Wyl adds: "But let us return to the 'Seer' [Joseph Smith]. The plates were taken to him and he made a rough estimate that their

translation into English would make a volume of *some ten or twelve hundred pages!*" (ibid.).
18. Jerald and Sandra Tanner, *Archaeology and the Book of Mormon* (Salt Lake City: Modern Microfilm Co., 1969), 27.
19. George M. Lawrence, "Report of a Physical Study of the Kinderhook Plate Number 5"; cited in Tanner, *Archaeology and the Book of Mormon*, 28.
20. Stanley Kimball, "Kinderhook Plates Brought to Joseph Smith Appear to be a Nineteenth-Century Hoax," *Ensign*, August 1981, 66, 70; cited in Tanner, *Mormonism—Shadow or Reality?*, 125-G.
21. Daniel Ludlow, ed., *Encyclopedia of Mormonism*, 4 vols. (New York: Maxwell Macmillan International, 1992), Stanley B. Kimball, "Kinderhook Plates," 2:789-90.
22. Such as Welby Ricks's article, "The Kinderhook Plates," *Improvement Era*, September 1962, 636-37, 656, 658, 660.
23. *Manuscript History of the Church*, 19 February 1842; cited in Ivan Barrett, *Joseph Smith and the Restoration* (Provo, Ut.: Brigham Young University Press, 1973), 500-01.
24. William Berrett, *The Restored Church* (Salt Lake City: Deseret Book, 1961), 107.
25. Arthur Wallace, *Evidence in Science and in Religion* (Los Angeles: Arthur Wallace, 1966), 124.
26. Sterling McMurrin, "Brigham H. Roberts: A Biographical Essay"; cited in B. H. Roberts, *Studies of the Book of Mormon* (Chicago: University of Illinois Press, 1985), xvi.
27. B. H. Roberts, *Comprehensive History of the Church*, 6 vols. (Salt Lake City: Deseret News Press, 1930), 2:138.
28. Tanner, *Mormonism—Shadow or Reality?* (Salt Lake City: Utah Lighthouse Ministry, 1987), 302-04.
29. Charles M. Larson, *By His Own Hand Upon Papyrus: A New Look at the Joseph Smith Papyri* (Grand Rapids: Institute for Religious Research, 1992), 36.
30. Ibid., 53.
31. Klaus Hansen, "Reflections on The Lion of the Lord," *Dialogue: A Journal of Mormon Thought*, Summer 1970, 110.

32. For those interested in a complete, detailed treatment of this important topic, these materials from the Institute for Religious Research are recommended: Charles M. Larson, *By His Own Hand Upon Papyrus*; and the video, *The Lost Book of Abraham: Investigating a Remarkable Mormon Claim* (Grand Rapids: Institute for Religious Research, 2002). Web site: www.irr.org.
33. *History of the Church*, 2:236 (3 July 1835).

"On the 3rd of July [1835], Michael H. Chandler came to Kirtland to exhibit some Egyptian mummies. There were four human figures, together with some two or more scrolls of papyrus covered with hieroglyphic figures and devices. As Mr. Chandler had been told I could translate them, he brought me some of the characters, and **I gave him the interpretation**, and like a gentleman, he gave me the following certificate.

Kirtland, July 6, 1835 "This is to make known to all who may be desirous, concerning the knowledge of **Mr. Joseph Smith, Jun., in deciphering the ancient Egyptian hieroglyphic characters in my possession,** which I have, in many eminent cities, showed to the most learned; and, from the information that I could ever learn, or meet with, **I find that of Mr. Joseph Smith, Jun., to correspond in the most minute matters.** MICHAEL H. CHANDLER ..." (*History of the Church*, 2:235).
34. Selected references to Smith **translating**:

"The remainder of this month, I was continually engaged **in translating** an alphabet to the Book of Abraham, and arranging a grammar of the Egyptian language as practiced by the ancients" (*History of the Church*, 2:238).

7 October 1835

"This afternoon recommenced **translating the ancient records**" (Scott H. Faulring, ed. *An American Prophet's Record: The Diaries and Journals of Joseph Smith* [Salt Lake City: Signature Books in association with Smith Research Associates, 1987], 38).

19, 20, 24, 25 November 1835
"I returned home and spent the day in **translating** the Egyptian records" (*History of the Church*, 2:318).
"We spent the day in **translating**, and made rapid progress" (ibid., 2:318).
"In the afternoon we **translated** some of the Egyptian records" (ibid., 2:320).
"Spent the day in **translating**" (ibid., 2:320).
"Thus I have given a brief history of the manner in which **the writings of the fathers, Abraham and Joseph**, have been preserved, and how I came in possession of the same—a correct **translation of which I shall give** in its proper place" (ibid., 2:350-51).
"Warren Parish was called as a scribe to Smith for work on the Book of Abraham. In 1838 Parish wrote: 'I have set [sat] by his [Smith's] side and penned down the **translation of the Egyptian** Hieroglyphicks [Heiroglyphics] **as he claimed to receive it by direct inspiration from Heaven ...**'" (H. Michael Marquardt, *The Joseph Smith Revelations: Text and Commentary* [Salt Lake City: Signature Books, 1999], 276fn20).

4 March 1842
"I commenced publishing **my translations** of the Book of Abraham in the *Times and Seasons* as follows—" (*History of the Church*, 4:520).

8 March 1842
"Recommenced **translating** from the Records of Abraham for the tenth number of Times and Seasons..." (*History of the Church*, 4:548).

9 March 1842
"... in the afternoon continued **the translation** of the Book of Abraham ... continued **translating** and revising, and reading letters in the evening ..." (*History of the Church*, 4:548).

In a letter to Edward Hunter:
"I am now very busily **engaged in translating**, and therefore cannot give as much time to public matters as I could wish..." (*History of the Church*, 4:549, 9 March 1842).

"In the present no. [of *Times and Seasons*] will be found the commencement of the Records discovered in Egypt some time since **as penned by the hand of Father Abraham** which I shall continue to translate & publish as fast as possible till the whole is completed ..." (H. Michael Marquardt, *The Book of Abraham Revisited* [Salt Lake City: Utah Lighthouse Ministry, 1983], 102; citing "Joseph Smith to the Times and Seasons," Joseph Smith Collection, LDS Archives).

"I learned it by **translating the papyrus** which is now in my house. **I learned a testimony concerning Abraham**, and he reasoned concerning the God of heaven" (*History of the Church*, 6:476).

35. *History of the Church*, 2:236.
36. *Journal History of The Church of Jesus Christ of Latter-day Saints*, 20 July 1835; cited in Ivan J. Barrett, *Joseph Smith and the Restoration*, 334-35.
37. Marquardt, *The Book of Abraham Revisited*, 101. Marquardt cites many examples in support of his statement.
38. Ibid., 103. The current title page for the Book of Abraham states:
    "THE BOOK OF ABRAHAM. TRANSLATED FROM THE PAPYRUS, BY JOSEPH SMITH. *A Translation of some ancient Records, that have fallen into our hands from the catacombs of Egypt.—The writings of Abraham while he was in Egypt, called the Book of Abraham,* **written by his own hand,** *upon papyrus.*"
39. Jerald and Sandra Tanner, *Major Problems of Mormonism* (Salt Lake City: Utah Lighthouse Ministry, 1989), 217. According to *History of the Church*, 2:351, he claimed that he would produce "a correct translation."
40. Charles Larson, *By His Own Hand*, 145; citing William Berrett, *The Latter-day Saints: A Contemporary History of*

the Church of Jesus Christ (Salt Lake City: Deseret Book Co., 1985), 395.
41. Marquardt, *The Book of Abraham Revisited*, 105.
42. Ibid.
43. Larson, *By His Own Hand*, 5.
44. Marquardt, *The Book of Abraham Revisited*, 104. Marquardt also mentions Professor Gustavus Seyffarth, who was familiar with Egyptian who actually viewed the papyri on display in the St. Louis Museum. Seyffarth came to the same conclusion.
45. Samuel A. B. Mercer, "Joseph Smith as an Interpreter and Translator of Egyptian," *The Utah Survey*, vol. 1, no. 1, September 1913, 8. Reproduced in Tanners, *Why Egyptologists Reject the Book of Abraham* (Salt Lake City: Utah Lighthouse Ministry, n.d.).
46. F. S. Spalding, *Joseph Smith, Jr., As A Translator* (Salt Lake City: The Arrow Press, 1912), 13; reproduced in Tanners, *Why Egyptologists Reject the Book of Abraham*.
47. Spalding, *Joseph Smith, Jr., as a Translator*, 23.
48. Ibid., 24.
49. Ibid., 26-27.
50. Ibid., 27.
51. Ibid., 28.
52. Ibid., 29-30.
53. Ibid., 30-31.
54. Ibid., 29.
55. Ludlow, *Encyclopedia of Mormonism*, 1:137-38. Font styles in original.
56. *The New York Times*, Magazine Section, 29 December 1912. This article was also reproduced in *The Evangel*, March 2003, 1, 6-7. The article adds the testimony of Dr. Albert M. Lythgoe, who was head of the Department of Egyptian Art at the Metropolitan Museum. His comment on the Book of Abraham material was, "Sad copies of very familiar papyrus... and **a sadder, a much sadder, translation.**"
57. *The Utah Survey*, 4; reproduced in Tanner, *Why Egyptologists Reject the Book of Abraham*.
58. Ibid., 8, 11.

59. Ibid., 36.
60. Marquardt, *The Book of Abraham Revisited*, 105-06.
61. As Charles Larson explains, "Joseph Smith clearly took his Egyptian Alphabet and Grammar material very seriously. His numerous diary entries (recorded in the *History of the Church*) mention the considerable labor he devoted to it, and he often quoted from it to demonstrate his understanding of Egyptian before various public and private audiences. Also, Smith used many of the Egyptian 'words' from the Grammar, along with their 'interpretations,' in his inspired explanations of the facsimiles in the Book of Abraham" (C. Larson, *By His Own Hand*, 93).

Egyptologists have examined Joseph Smith's *Egyptian Alphabet and Grammar* and have concluded it bears no resemblance to the Egyptian Language. One of the authors (Edmond Gruss) gave a copy of *Joseph Smith's Egyptian Alphabet and Grammar* (reproduced by Jerald and Sandra Tanner [Salt Lake City: Modern Microfilm Co., 1966]) to an associate, Dr. R. D. Patterson, who is an expert in Near Eastern Languages, with the instruction, "Look at it and tell me what you think." His response was in three pages. Excerpts from the opening and closing statements follow:

"To prepare to comment on Joseph Smith's Egyptian Alphabet and Grammar has been **an odious and tedious task**, for even the most casual glance is enough to see immediately that **the book does not merit the time taken to evaluate it**.... There can be no doubt that **Joseph Smith neither knew nor to him was ever revealed one single word of Egyptian.** Moreover, his proposed explanations of the funerary material represented in the three illustrations of The Book of Abraham prove conclusively that **Smith simply had not knowledge whatsoever** of the culture of ancient Egypt" (Dr. R. D. Patterson, Response to Ed Gruss, circa 1966. Copy on file. Patterson became Chairman of the Department of Biblical Studies at Liberty University, Lynchberg, Va.).
62. *The Cross* (newsletter), October-November 2002, 1-2.
63. C. Larson, *By His Own Hand*, 28.

64. Stan Larson, *Quest for the Gold Plates* (Salt Lake City: Freethinker Press, 1996), 91.
65. Ferguson letter to Boyack, 13 March 1971; cited in S. Larson, *Quest for the Gold Plates*, 93. The four Egyptologists were Leonard H. Lesko (Instructor of Egyptology at the University of California at Berkeley), Henry L. F. Lutz (emeritus professor of Egyptology at the University of California at Berkeley), Klaus Baer (Egyptologist at the University of Chicago) and Dee Jay Nelson (LDS Church member and self-taught translator of Egyptian). Nelson's interaction with Ferguson on this matter ended up costing him his membership in the Mormon Church (ibid., 92-93).
66. *Encyclopedia of Mormonism*, 1:136-37. After the church received the papyri, "Three noted Egyptologists soon made translations of and commentaries on the fragments, which resulted in new attacks of Joseph Smith's 'inabilities' as a translator. The critics argued that the *Book of Breathings* bore no resemblance to the book of Abraham, which Joseph Smith apparently claimed to have translated from these very papyri. Indeed, the *Book of Breathings* is a late text, originating about the first century A.D., some 2000 years after the time of Abraham. Against criticisms such as these, **Hugh Nibley has consistently and ably defended Joseph Smith**, maintaining that the book of Abraham should be evaluated on the basis of what it claims to be—Abraham's own account of his life. Nibley's research has shown that a significant number of links exist between the book of Abraham and ancient texts related to Abraham. These similarities seem too numerous and subtle to be attributed to mere coincidence" (*Encyclopedia of Mormonism*, 1:137).

In his review of Hugh Nibley's Abraham in Egypt (Salt Lake City: Deseret Book, 1981), H. Michael Marquardt quotes Nibley where he states, "To date, not a critic has laid a finger on the book of Abraham, (1)."

He then writes, "The truth is that what was represented as a 'translation' of an ancient Egyptian papyrus made by the Mormon founder, Joseph Smith, Jr., and entitled the Book of Abraham **has been completely discredited** in the eyes of scholars by the rediscovery of some portions of that papyrus in 1967 in the Archives of the Metropolitan Museum in New York City. Dr. Nibley tries to put as much distance as possible between those papyrus fragments and Joseph Smith's Book of Abraham, because **the papyrus fragments have demonstrated beyond doubt that Joseph Smith did not have the slightest idea of what the Egyptian characters on the papyrus really said**" (Marquardt, *The Book of Abraham Revisited*, 113).

67. Stephen E. Thompson, "Egyptology and the Book of Mormon," (www.lds-mormon.com/thompson_book_of_abraham.shtml), 1. Also in *Dialogue: A Journal of Mormon Thought*, Spring 1995, 143.
68. Thompson, "Egyptology," 10. Also in *Dialogue*, Spring 1995, 160.
69. David P. Wright, "Egyptology and the Book of Abraham," (www.lds-mormon.com/dpwonboa.shtml), 1.
70. Ibid., 3-4.
71. Edward H. Ashment, "Reducing Dissonance: The Book of Abraham as a Case Study," in Dan Vogel, ed., *The Word of God* (Salt Lake City: Signature Books, 1990), 231.
72. S. Larson, *Quest for the Gold Plates*, 116. See C. Larson, *By His Own Hand* (114-40), for a review of eight explanations proposed by LDS apologists.
73. Marquardt, *The Book of Abraham Revisited*, 109.
74. Ibid., 34-35.
75. C. Larson, *By His Own Hand*, 175.

- # Chapter Seven Notes

    1. Fawn Brodie, *No Man Knows My History* (New York: Alfred A. Knopf, 1971), 118-19; see also B. H. Roberts, *History of the Church of Jesus Christ of Latter-day Saints*, 2nd ed. 1980, 7 vols. (Salt Lake City: Deseret Book Company, 1951), 1:216-17; and E. D. Howe, *Mormonism Unvailed* (Painesville, Ohio: E. D. Howe, 1834), 175-221.

2. Examples are: Oliver Cowdery (Of the nine charges brought against him in Church court, six were insubordination. Three of those were either dropped or were not sustained.); Lyman Johnson; W. W. Phelps; John Whitmer; and David Whitmer. Joseph once wrote, "The Messiah's kingdom on earth is of that kind of government, that there has always been numerous apostates, for the reason that it admits of no sins unrepented of without excluding the individual from its fellowship" (*History of the Church*, 2:22). However, anyone that did not do as Joseph requested was considered apostate.
3. A few examples are *Doctrine and Covenants of the Church of Jesus Christ of Latter-day Saints* (Salt Lake City: The Church of Jesus Christ of Latter-day Saints, 1981), Sections 5, 9, 28. See also *History of the Church*, 2:300-01.
4. *Doctrine and Covenants* 1:37-38; *History of the Church*, 1:224.
5. George Cannon, *Life of Joseph Smith* (Salt Lake City: Deseret News Press, 1888), 400.
6. Nephi Morris, *Prophecies of Joseph Smith and their Fulfillment* (Salt Lake City: Deseret Book, 1920), Preface.
7. John A. Widtsoe, *Joseph Smith—Seeker after Truth, Prophet of God* (Salt Lake City: Deseret News Press, 1951), 279-80.
8. Joseph Fielding Smith, *Doctrines of Salvation: Sermons and Writings of Joseph Fielding Smith,* Bruce R. McConkie, comp., 3 vols. (Salt Lake City: Bookcraft, 1954), 1:188.
9. "Beware of False Prophets," *Evening and Morning Star,* July 1833, 105.
10. Michael Agnes, ed., *Webster's New World College Dictionary*, 4th ed. (New York: Macmillan, 1999), "Prophecy," 1150.
11. Ibid., "Predict," 1132.
12. Ibid., "Revelation," 1226.
13. Michael Fordham, "A Non-Prophetic Report of Mormonism 101's Failing Grade." Fordham was citing the *Random House Webster's College Dictionary* (1079) for this definition. His critique was posted on a web site until the Mormonism Research Ministry posted their response. Since then, Fordham's article (along with several others critical

of the book *Mormonism 101*) has been removed. MRM's response to Fordham's critique is on-line at www.mrm.org/articles/mormonism-201/chapter-09/.
14. David Whitmer, *An Address To All Believers In Christ* (Richmond, Mo.: David Whitmer, 1887), 30-31.
15. B. H. Roberts, *A Comprehensive History of the Church of Jesus Christ of Latter-day Saints*, 6 vols. (Salt Lake City: Deseret News Press, 1930), 1:165n.
16. H. Page to W. McLellin, 2 February 1848; cited in H. Michael Marquardt, *The Joseph Smith Revelations, Text and Commentary* (Salt Lake City: Signature Books, 1999), 372 (brackets in Marquardt).
17. W. McLellin to Joseph Smith III, July 1872; cited in Marquardt, *The Joseph Smith Revelations*, 373 (brackets in Marquardt).
18. W. McLellin to J. Traughber, 7 May 1877; cited in Marquardt, *The Joseph Smith Revelations*, 373 (brackets in Marquardt).
19. Whitmer, *An Address*, 31.
20. Roberts, *Comprehensive History of the Church*, 1:165-66.
21. Whitmer, *An Address*, 31.
22. Roberts, *Comprehensive History of the Church*, 1:165-66.
23. Ibid., 1:164-66. Also cited in Davis Bitton, "B. H. Roberts as Historian," *Dialogue, A Journal of Mormon Thought*, Winter 1968, 40-41.
24. Whitmer, *An Address*, 31.
25. W. McLellin to Joseph Smith III, July 1872; cited in Marquardt, *The Joseph Smith Revelations*, 373.
26. *Doctrine and Covenants* 29:8-10.
27. Hyrum Smith and Janne Sjodahl; *Doctrine and Covenants Commentary* (Cambridge: University Press, 1951), 146.
28. *Doctrine and Covenants* 45:64-75; see also *History of the Church*, 1:158-63.
29. *Doctrine and Covenants* 84:1-5.
30. 2 Timothy 2:13.
31. *Doctrine and Covenants* 84:1-5, 31; also in *History of the Church*, 1:286-95, (22-23 September 1832).
32. *Journal of Discourses*, 26 vols. (England: Various publishers, 1854-1886), photo reprint, 9:71, 10 March 1861.

33. *Journal of Discourses*, 10:344, 23 October 1864.
34. *Journal of Discourses*, 13:362, 5 May 1870.
35. Additional references verifying that Joseph meant the generation then living can be found in *Journal of Discourses*, 17:111, 291-92; and *Times and Seasons*, 15 March 1843, 141.
36. *Doctrine and Covenants* 84:1, 114-15; *History of the Church*, 1:294-95.
37. Joseph Smith, Jr. to Emma Smith, personal letter dated 13 October 1832; Community of Christ Archives (formerly the RLDS Church); reproduced in Dean Jessee; *The Personal Writings of Joseph Smith* (Salt Lake City: Deseret Book, 1984), 252-57.
38. Smith and Sjodahl, *Doctrine and Covenants Commentary*, 523.
39. *History of the Church*, 2:464.
40. *Doctrine and Covenants* 88:86-93.
41. Calculation was as follows. From 3 January 1832 to the end of that year was 364 days (1832 being a leap year). Add to that 62,780 days (172 years x 365 days per year). Then add 43 days for the 43 leap years between 1832 and 2003. 364 + 62,780 + 43 = 63,187.
42. *History of the Church*, 1:312-16. See also Jessee, *Personal Writings*, 269-74.
43. *History of the Church*, 1:312fn.
44. *Times and Seasons*, 10 October 1844, 656; also *Evening and Morning Star*, July 1832, 17.
45. *History of the Church*, 1:400-02; see also *Doctrine and Covenants* 97:1, 18-20.
46. *Patriarchal Blessings Book*, vol. 1, 8; LDS Church Historians Office; cited in Fred Collier, *Unpublished Revelations*, 2 vols. (Salt Lake City: Collier's Publishing, 1979), 1:63-66; Part 18:1, 16, 27-28, 36.
47. Daniel Ludlow, ed., *Encyclopedia of Mormonism*, 4 vols. (New York: Maxwell Macmillan International, 1992), 3:1349.
48. Ibid.
49. *History of the Church*, 2:53.

50. *Doctrine and Covenants* 105:13-15; also *History of the Church*, 2:108-11.
51. *Reed Peck Manuscript* (Salt Lake City: Utah Lighthouse Ministry, n.d.), photo reproduction, 18 September 1839, 3; also *History of the Church*, 2:117.
52. *History of the Church*, 2:144-45.
53. Ibid., 2:180-82.
54. *Journal of Oliver Boardman Huntington* (San Marino, Calif.: Huntington Library, microfilm copy), Journal 13, 56th page, circa 1875; cited in *The Researcher*, March/April 1993, 4. Also in Maurice Barnett; *Mormonism Against Itself*, 2 vols. (Cullman, Ala.: Printing Service, 1980), 2:188. Huntington went on to record, "Joseph said 'if they shed my blood it shall shorten this work 10 years' that taken from 1891 would reduce the time to 1881 which if the true time within which the Saviour should come much must be crowded into 6 years" (Journal 13, 53rd and 54th page).
55. Robert Smith, *The Signs of the Times* (Payson, Utah: Juvenile Instructor Office, 1887), 39-40.
56. Brian H. Stuy, ed., *Collected Discourses*, 5 vols. (Woodland Hills, Utah: B. H. S. Publishing, 1988), vol. 2, 6 October 1890.
57. Ibid.
58. Such as the 6 April 1843 prophecy.
59. *Doctrine and Covenants* 111:1-4, 10; see also *History of the Church*, 2:465-66.
60. *History of the Church*, 2:466.
61. Ibid.
62. Elden J. Watson, *Manuscript History of Brigham Young, 1801-1844* (Salt Lake City: Smith Secretarial Service, 1968), August 1836, 15. LDS Church archives.
63. *Messenger and Advocate*, 3 April 1837, vol.3 no.31, 488.
64. Ibid.
65. The US Census Report for 2000-2004 gave a population estimate for Kirtland city, Ohio at "7,106" inhabitants on 1 April 2000. See web site www.census.gov/popest/cities/tables/SUB-EST2004-04-39.csv.

66. *History of the Church*, 2:478-79.
67. *Doctrine and Covenants* 114:1; *History of the Church*, 3:23.
68. *Deseret Morning News 2005 Church Almanac* (Salt Lake City: Deseret News, 2004), 62; *History of the Church*, 3:170-71.
69. *Doctrine and Covenants* 117:1, 12-15. Lane Thuet was Mormon for 23 years and never once in all that time did he ever remember hearing the name "Oliver Granger." He was certainly never taught that he should hold it in sacred remembrance.
70. Ludlow, *Encyclopedia of Mormonism*, 2:793, 955.
71. Andrew Jenson, *LDS Biographical Encyclopedia*, 4 vols. (Salt Lake City: Andrew Jenson Historical Co., 1901-1936), 2:372 (1914); 4:190 (1936).
72. *GospeLink 2001* CD-Rom (Salt Lake City: Deseret Book Co., 2000).
73. Hoyt Brewster, Jr., *Doctrine and Covenants Encyclopedia* (Salt Lake City: Bookcraft, 1988), 220.
74. Susan Black, *Who's Who in the Doctrine and Covenants* (Salt Lake City: Bookcraft, 1997), 107.
75. Byron Merrill, *The Heavens Are Open: The 1992 Sperry Symposium on the Doctrine and Covenants and Church History* (Salt Lake City: Deseret Book, 1993), 52.
76. Robert Millet, *Selected Writings of Robert L. Millet: Gospel Scholars Series* (Salt Lake City: Deseret Book, 2000), 493.
77. Robert Millet, *Within Reach* (Salt Lake City: Deseret Book, 1995), 101.
78. *Doctrine and Covenants* 121:7-8, 11-15; also *History of the Church*, 3:289-300.
79. *History of the Church*, 4:206-12.
80. Smith, *Doctrines of Salvation*, 3:94 (1956).
81. Ibid.
82. William Tew, Jr., *Conference Report*, October 1938, 119-20; Brent L. Top, Larry E. Dahl, and Walter D. Bowen, *Follow the Living Prophets* (Salt Lake City: Bookcraft, 1993), 113-14; Hoyt Brewster, Jr., *Prophets, Priesthood Keys and Succession* (Salt Lake City: Deseret Book, 1991), 138; "Read, Heed

Counsel of Church Leaders," *Deseret News—Church Section*, 10 October 1992.
83. *Deseret News—Church Section*, 23 October 2004, 4.
84. Wilford Woodruff, *Conference Report*, October 1897, 22-23.
85. *Doctrine and Covenants* 124:1, 20-21; also *History of the Church*, 4:274-76.
86. *Doctrine and Covenants* 132:46.
87. Andrew Jenson, *Church Chronology* (Salt Lake City: Deseret News 1914), 36.
88. Matthew 26:69-75; Luke 22:54-62; John 21:15-19; 2 Timothy 2:13.
89. *History of the Church*, 4:605-06.
90. Romans 3:3-4; 1 Corinthians 1:9; 2 Timothy 2:13.
91. *Doctrine and Covenants* 127:1-2.
92. *President Joseph Smith's Journal 1843*; recorded by Willard Richards; LDS Church Archives, 143; cited in Scott Faulring, ed., *An American Prophet's Record* (Salt Lake City: Signature Books in association with Smith Research Associates, 1987), 294.
93. *Doctrine and Covenants*, Section 89—given 27 February 1833.
94. For more on this subject, see LaMar Petersen, *Hearts Made Glad* (Salt Lake City: Lamar Petersen, 1975).
95. *History of the Church*, 5:336.
96. Ibid.
97. A fact we looked at under a previous prophecy dated 14 February 1835.
98. *History of the Church*, 5:393-94; also in Joseph Fielding Smith, comp., *Teachings of the Prophet Joseph Smith* (Salt Lake City: Deseret Book, 1976), 302-03; also in *The Deseret News*, 24 September 1856, front page.
99. Morris, *Prophecies of Joseph Smith*, 215.
100. Ibid., 212.
101. See further discussion of this prophecy in the next chapter for reasons why this cannot be the case.
102. *Millenial Star*, 21 July 1860, 455; also in Faulring, *An American Prophet's Record*, 432.

103. *History of the Church*, 6:116.
104. Ibid., fn.
105. *President Joseph Smith's Journal 1844*; recorded by Willard Richards; LDS Church Archives, 255; cited in Faulring, *An American Prophet's Record*, 445; see also D. Michael Quinn, *The Mormon Hierarchy: Origins of Power* (Salt Lake City: Signature Books, 1994), 642.
106. *History of the Church*, 6:197.
107. Dick Baer and Jim Robertson, "Fifty-three False Prophecies of Joseph Smith." This series ran from the October 2000 issue through February 2001.
108. July 1989 issue, 6.
109. Robert Morey, *How to Answer a Mormon* (Minneapolis: Bethany House Publishers, 1983), 116.
110. Provo School of the Prophets (1868), according to LDS Stake President Abraham O. Smoot; cited in Quinn, *Origins of Power*, 639.
111. Titles in this section indicate the highest position held in the Church during their lifetime, not necessarily the position they held when they made a listed prophecy or prediction.
112. Collier, *Unpublished Revelations*, 1:4-9, 29, Part 79, pp. 123-29.
113. John Mills Whitaker, Journal; cited in Klaus Hansen "The Kingdom of God," *Dialogue: A Journal of Mormon Thought*, Autumn 1966, 74.
114. Revelation dated 27 September 1886, Collier, *Unpublished Revelations*, vol. 1, Part 88.
115. See endnotes 82, 83 and 84.

• Chapter Eight Notes

1. *Doctrine and Covenants of the Church of Jesus Christ of Latter-day Saints* (Salt Lake City: The Church of Jesus Christ of Latter-day Saints, 1981), Section 89.
2. Joseph Fielding Smith, comp., *Teachings of the Prophet Joseph Smith* (Salt Lake City: Deseret Book, 1976), 302-03.
3. *Doctrine and Covenants*, Section 87.

4. B. H. Roberts, *History of the Church of Jesus Christ of Latter-day Saints*, 2nd ed. 1980, 7 vols. (Salt Lake City: Deseret Book Company, 1951), 5:85.
5. Hyrum Smith and Janne Sjodahl, *Doctrine and Covenants Commentary* (Cambridge: University Press, 1951), 571.
6. *Doctrine and Covenants* 89:9.
7. Ibid., 89:6.
8. Ibid., 89:17.
9. Ibid., 89:7.
10. Ibid., 89:12-13.
11. Ibid., 89:16-17.
12. The *Encyclopedia of Mormonism* states, "The practice of abstaining from all forms of ALCOHOL, TOBACCO, COFFEE, and TEA ... derives from this revelation. ... Hot drinks (later defined as coffee and tea) were not for "the body or belly" (Daniel Ludlow, ed., *Encyclopedia of Mormonism*, 4 vols. (New York: MacMillan Publishing Co., 1992), 4:1584.
13. For example, Joseph Fielding Smith writes, "SALVATION AND A CUP OF TEA ... 'surely the Lord will forgive me if I drink a cup of tea.' Yes, he will forgive you, because he is going to forgive every man who repents; but ... if you drink coffee or tea, or take tobacco, are you **letting a cup of tea or a little tobacco stand in the road and bar you from the celestial kingdom of God?** ... 'Oh, it is such a little thing' ... Well, **there is not anything that is little in the way of sinning**" (Joseph Fielding Smith, *Doctrines of Salvation: Sermons and Writings of Joseph Fielding Smith*, Bruce R. McConkie, comp., 3 vols. [Salt Lake City: Bookcraft, 1955], 2:16).
14. *Journal of Discourses*, 26 vols. (England: Various publishers, 1854-1886), photo reprint, 12:158, 8 February 1868.
15. *The Des Moines Daily News*, 16 October 1886; cited in Jerald and Sandra Tanner, *Mormonism—Shadow or Reality?* (Salt Lake City: Utah Lighthouse Ministry, 1987), 406.
16. Leonard Arrington, "An Economic Interpretation of the 'Word of Wisdom,'" *BYU Studies*, Winter 1959, 39-40; cited in Tanner, *Mormonism—Shadow or Reality?*, 406.

17. Kirtland, Ohio was where Joseph Smith lived at the time, and where he received this revelation.
18. Whitney Cross, *The Burned-Over District* (New York: Cornell University Press, 1965), 211-12; cited in Tanner, *Mormonism—Shadow or Reality?*, 406.
19. *Doctrine and Covenants* 89:4; 18-21.
20. Nephi Morris, *Prophecies of Joseph Smith and their Fulfillment*, 2nd ed. (Salt Lake City: Deseret Book, 1920), 213.
21. Ibid., 200-01.
22. Ibid., 200fn.
23. This meeting may have even been the catalyst that originally put it into Joseph Smith's mind to run for US President–an intention that he formally announced on 29 January 1844, just 8 months after this meeting with Judge Douglas. See D. Michael Quinn, *The Mormon Hierarchy: Origins of Power* (Salt Lake City: Signature Books, 1994), 117-20; Scott Faulring, ed., *An American Prophet's Record* (Salt Lake City: Signature Books in association with Smith Research Associates, 1987), 443; and *History of the Church*, 6:188.
24. Morris, *Prophecies of Joseph Smith*, 201.
25. The early Mormon Church was well known for "bloc-voting," in other words, whomever Joseph Smith wanted them to vote for, the majority of the Church would vote for that candidate. See Quinn, *Origins of Power*, 105-10. Quinn notes that "Illinois politicians were dismayed that the Mormon bloc vote had become the key to the state's national politics" (ibid., 120). With their voting tactics so well known, it is hardly a stretch to understand that Judge Douglas would want the support of the Mormon Prophet and seek his favor in a meeting to discuss political ambition.
26. Current LDS Patriarchs demonstrate this same technique when giving Patriarchal Blessings to Mormon members. The Patriarch meets with the member and asks general questions for 30 to 60 minutes in an interview. He learns the member's hobbies, likes, dislikes, talents, etc. Following the interview, the Patriarch then gives the formal prayer, prophesying certain

events and blessings upon the individual that are based upon their faithfulness to God. Inevitably, these supposed prophetic promises are rooted in information the Patriarch gleaned during the prior interview. Lane Thuet and Shawna Derry (at that time his fiancée) both went through this exact process in the Mormon Church for their Patriarchal Blessings—Lane on 2 May 1983, and Shawna on 6 November 1988. It is not a far stretch to see that Joseph Smith may have done the same thing; promising certain prophetic events based upon the three-hour discussion he had with Douglas preceding the "revelation."

27. Facts on Stephen Arnold Douglas were obtained from the following web sites: "Illinois and the Civil War" (www.illinoiscivilwar.org/douglas-sa.html); "Stephen Arnold Douglas" (www.spartacus.schoolnet.co.uk/USAdouglas.htm); "Wikipedia—Stephen A. Douglas" (www.wikipedia.org/wiki/Stephen_A._Douglas).
28. Morris, *Prophecies of Joseph Smith*, 213.
29. *Doctrine and Covenants* 87:1.
30. Morris, *Prophecies of Joseph Smith*, 21.
31. Ibid., 40.
32. "The American Civil War" (www.swcivilwar.com/cw_causes.html); "The Age of Jackson and Ante-Bellum Reform Timeline" (www.pinzler.com/ushistory/timeline4.html).
33. Bill McKeever informs us that "the fact is, not far from Smith's Kirtland, Ohio headquarters, a newspaper called the *Painesville Telegraph* printed a story from the *New York Courier* and *Enquirer* entitled '*The Crisis.*' The article spoke of the '*probabilities of dismemberment*' stemming from discontent in South Carolina and Georgia over states rights. It is interesting to note that the date of this article is Friday, December 21,1832, just four days before Smith received his alleged 'prophecy'" (Bill McKeever, "Joseph Smith's Prophecy on War" [www.mrm.org/multimedia/text/civilwar.html]). *The Boston Daily Advisor and Patriot* (10 December 1832) also carried an article about the rebellion in South Carolina. Jerald and Sandra Tanner point out that, interestingly enough, Orson Hyde had been in Boston during the

time this article was printed. He returned to Kirtland, arriving on 22 December 1832 (*Journal of Orson Hyde*, typed copy, 56-57). Joseph's prophecy was given three days later (see *Mormonism—Shadow or Reality?*, 190-92).
34. Charles Dickens, *American Notes for General Circulation* (London, England: Chapman and Hall, 1842).
35. Alexis DeTocqueville, *Democracy in America* (London, England: Saunders and Otley, 1836). While the first volume of that work was not published until 1835—two years after Joseph Smith gave his prophecy—DeTocqueville's travels in America were in 1831. After that visit, he went back to France and started writing this book. Obviously, conditions in America in 1831 were volatile enough that this foreigner expected a civil war that would divide the northern and southern states.
36. Morris, *Prophecies of Joseph Smith*, 38.
37. Alice Smith McKay, "A Psychological Examination of a Few Prophecies of the Early Founders of Mormonism;" Master's thesis; University of Utah, 15; cited in Tanner, *Mormonism—Shadow or Reality?*, 191.
38. McKay, "A Psychological Examination," 19; Tanner, *Mormonism—Shadow or Reality?*, 191.
39. *Doctrine and Covenants* 87:1.
40. Daniel Ludlow, ed., *Encyclopedia of Mormonism*, 4 vols. (New York: Maxwell Macmillan International, 1992), 1:288; B. H. Roberts, *A Comprehensive History of The Church of Jesus Christ of Latter-day Saints*, 6 vols. (Salt Lake City: Deseret News Press, 1930), 1:294. While this may be the case, neither writer gives any evidence to prove the claim.
41. *Times and Seasons*, 1 November 1844, 688.
42. *Millenial Star*, 3 July 1852, 289-96; 10 July 1852, 305-19.
43. B. H. Roberts informs us that "**the revelation and prophecy on war, of December 25th, 1832, was not immediately published**. The elders engaged in the missionary work of the church, however, obtained manuscript copies of it, and in their journeys carried it with them and read it to their congregations in various parts of the United States. In Vol. XIII of

the *Millennial Star,* published in 1851, pp. 216 and 217, is an advertisement of a new church publication to be called the *Pearl of Great Price*. In the announced contents is named **this revelation of December, 1832, with a statement that it had 'never before appeared in print.**' Subsequently, but in the same year, the *Pearl of Great Price* with this prophecy in it, was published by Franklin D. Richards, in Liverpool, England" (*A Comprehensive History,* 1:294).

44. See *The Deseret News* for 15 June 1850 and 22 March 1851 for examples.
45. *Mormonism Researched,* Summer 1991, 4.
46. *History of the Church,* 5:85.
47. Richard Poll, gen. ed., *Utah's History* (Provo, Utah: Brigham Young University Press, 1978), 114. See also "Declaration of the Twelve Apostles" 24 September 1845; cited in Richard Abanes, *One Nation Under Gods* (New York: Four Walls Eight Windows, 2002), 216 and 552n58.
48. Poll, *Utah's History,* 124.
49. Abanes, *One Nation Under Gods,* 209-10.
50. Ludlow, *Encyclopedia of Mormonism,* "Handcart Companies" 2:571-73. Poll, *Utah's History,* states that over the forty years of the organized Mormon migration, "an estimated 6,000 died along the way" (125).
51. This was the original name of Salt Lake City, Utah. Mormons are credited with settling or helping to settle such places as Cedar City (1851) and Saint George (1861) in Southern Utah; Las Vegas (1855) and Carson Valley (1851) in Nevada; San Bernardino (1851), Los Angeles (1847), San Diego (1847), and Yerba Buena (now San Francisco—1846) in California. See Poll, *Utah's History,* 730. "About Carson Valley" (www. canyoncreekrealty.com/valley.html – web page removed, last accessed October 2003. Copy on file). "History of Las Vegas" (www.lasvegasnevada.gov/ FactsStatistics/history. htm). "California Firsts" (www.ldssocal.org/history/ califirst. htm – web page removed, last accessed October 2003. Copy on file). "Los Angeles Area Timeline" (www.cagenweb.com/ re/losangeles/langetim.htm). "Human History in St. George"

(www.stgeorgeutah.net/history.html). "Yerba Buena Walk" (www.sfgenealogy.com/sf/history/hgybw.htm).
52. Morris, *Prophecies of Joseph Smith*, 130-31.
53. T. B. H. Stenhouse, *Rocky Mountain Saints* (New York: D. Appleton and Co., 1872), 146.
54. Ibid. See also Faulring, *An American Prophet's Record*, 446-47, 20 February 1844.
55. Morris, *Prophecies of Joseph Smith*, 139.
56. Tanner, *Mormonism—Shadow or Reality?*, 135.
57. Vol. D-1, p. 1362; reproduced photographically in Tanner, *Mormonism—Shadow or Reality?*, 134.
58. Tanner, *Mormonism—Shadow or Reality?*, 126-42D.
59. Dean C. Jessee, "The Writing of Joseph Smith's History," *BYU Studies*, Summer 1971, 456-58, 469-70.
60. Morris, *Prophecies of Joseph Smith*, 139.
61. Ibid., 132 and fn.
62. Jessee, "The Writing of Joseph Smith's History," 469-70.
63. Ibid., 470.
64. *The Deseret News*, 7 November 1855, p. 273. This issue printed the *History* from the end of July 1842 through 11 August 1842. The Rocky Mountain Prophecy was contained under the date of 6 August 1842.
65. Tanner, *Mormonism—Shadow or Reality?*, 135.
66. Circular: to the Whole Church of Jesus Christ of Latter Day Saints, Nauvoo, October 1845. BYU archives, available on-line at: http://library.byu.edu/~imaging/into/ lvnauvoo/ 13circfs.html.
67. Orson Whitney, *History of Utah* (Salt Lake City: Cannon, 1893), 239; cited in Morris, *Prophecies of Joseph Smith*, 137.
68. *Heber C. Kimball's Journal* (Salt Lake City: Modern Microfilm Co., n.d.), photomechanical reprint of dates 21 November 1845 through 7 January 1846, 139.
69. Tanner, *Mormonism—Shadow or Reality*, 135; letter originally in *Prologue*, Spring 1972, 29.
70. J. H. Beadle, *Polygamy, or the Mysteries and Crimes of Mormonism* (Philadelphia: National Publishing, 1882), 118.

Beadle goes on to say "they finally fixed indefinitely upon 'some valley in the Rocky Mountains.'"
71. This was in February 1846. M. R. Werner, *Brigham Young* (New York: Harcourt, Brace and Co., 1925), 228.
72. Beadle, *Polygamy*, 114.
73. Werner, *Brigham Young*, 206.
74. Major Howard Egan, *Pioneering the West: 1846 to 1878—Major Howard Egan's Diary*, William Egan, comp. and ed. (Salt Lake City, Skeleton Publishing Co., 1917), 14. The editor of the diary adds that there were "undefined plans" from Joseph Smith of migrating to the midst of the Rocky Mountains, but this editorial comment was added for the printing of the book in 1917, well after the Mormons were already settled in the Great Salt Lake Valley. The prophecy had been widely published by that point.
75. Beadle, *Polygamy*, 116.
76. One stanza states, "The Upper California, O that's the land for me! It lies between the mountains and the great Pacific Sea … Upper California—O, that's the land for me!" See Ann-Eliza Young, *Wife No. 19* (Hartford, Conn.: Dustin, Gilman and Co., 1875), 111, 116-17; also Werner, *Brigham Young*, 210.
77. Elder W. W. Riter, "Correct Placing of the Monument, Pioneer View," *Improvement Era*, September 1921.
78. *Journal of Oliver Boardman Huntington* (San Marino, Calif.: Huntington Library, microfilm copy), 16 October 1846.
79. Werner, *Brigham Young*, 229.
80. John Krakauer, *Under the Banner of Heaven: A Story of Violent Faith* (New York: Doubleday, 2003), 109.
81. Poll, *Utah's History*, 124.
82. Werner, *Brigham Young*, 228.
83. This decision could well have been based upon the fact that Young had contracted Mountain Fever, and was very ill by the time they reached the Salt Lake Valley. He would not have wanted to continue traveling further because of the illness (see Stenhouse, *Rocky Mountain Saints*, 259; Werner, *Brigham Young*, 227-28). Major Howard Egan, who traveled with Young, recorded in his journal that Young first came

down with the illness on 12 July. As they progressed, the journey often was too much for Young. On the evening of 12 July, Egan writes, "President Young not being able to go on, brother Kimball's three wagons remained behind." Again on 17 July, Egan notes, "The reason of our stopping so soon was in consequence of President Young being taken quite ill, and could not endure to travel any further today." After getting somewhat better and traveling a bit further, Egan shares that on 21 July, "Brother Young was not able to travel today, being much fatigued by yesterday's travel" (*Pioneering the West: 1846 to 1878*, 95-99). Young entered the Salt Lake Valley a few days later. According to his own account, Young was unable to get out of the carriage and view the Great Salt Lake Valley when he arrived there. He ordered Wilford Woodruff, who was driving him, to **turn [the carriage] half way round so that I could have a view** of a portion of Salt Lake Valley" (William Harwell, ed., *Manuscript History of Brigham Young* [Salt Lake City: Collier's Publishing, 1997], 61; 23 July 1847). Woodruff recalls, "On the twenty-fourth I drove my carriage, **with President Young Lying on a bed in it**, into the open valley.... When we came out of the canyon into full view of the valley, I turned the side of my carriage around, open to the west, and **President Young arose from his bed** ... he said: 'It is enough. This is the right place. Drive on.' So I drove to the encampment..." (cited in B. H. Roberts, "Monument at Pioneer View," *Improvement Era*, September 1921). The *Journal of Mormon History* records that as an adult, Brigham weathered "a tick-borne 'mountain fever' from which **he was still prostrate at the time of his momentous arrival** in the Great Salt Lake Valley..." (Lester Bush, Jr., "Brigham Young in Life and Death: A Medical Overview," vol. 5 [1978], 79). One of the travelers behind Young, W. W. Riter, recalls, "I doubt if Brigham Young himself, **when he was on this spot—prostrated with mountain fever** ... realized just what the power was that was with him" (Elder Riter, "Correct Placing of the Monument").

84. Transcript of journal entry in Morris, *Prophecies of Joseph Smith*, 140.
85. Michael Fordham, "A Non-Prophetic Report of Mormonism 101's Failing Grade." Fordham's critique was posted on a web site until the Mormonism Research Ministry posted their response. Since then, his article (along with several others critical of *Mormonism 101*) has been removed. MRM's response to Fordham's critique is on-line at www.mrm.org/articles/mormonism-201/chapter-09/.
86. Fordham, "A Non-Prophetic Report," text for footnote 61. Originally in a signed affidavit by Paulina Elizabeth Phelps Lyman, witnessed on 31 July 1903 by James Jack, notary. Notice that this affidavit was given well after the Mormon Church had already been established in the midst of the Rocky Mountains, it was not given before the fact.
87. Ibid., text for footnote 62. The autobiography was not published, typescript in BYU Library Special Collections. The manuscript was probably written after the Church was already established in the Salt Lake valley, because Joseph Smith was never known to have used the phrase "Great Salt Lake."
88. Ibid., text for footnote 63. Original from G. Homer Durham, *Discourses of Wilford Woodruff* (Salt Lake City: Bookcraft, 1946), 38-39. Woodruff made these comments in April of 1898, once again well after the facts were established.
89. G. Homer Durham, ed., *Discourses of Wilford Woodruff* (Salt Lake City: Bookcraft, 1969), 38-39.
90. From an unpublished paper; cited in Jerald and Sandra Tanner, *The Changing World of Mormonism* (Chicago: Moody Press, 1980), 406.
91. Deuteronomy 18:22.
92. David Whitmer, *An Address to All Believers in Christ* (Richmond, Mo.: David Whitmer, 1887), 31; also *History of the Church*, 1:165.

• Chapter Nine Notes

1. Daniel Ludlow, ed., *Encyclopedia of Mormonism*, 4 vols. (New York: Maxwell Macmillan International, 1992), 3:1270. Blaine Hatch writes, "... a vital characteristic of the living Church is **continuous revelation**" ("God Speaks With Man Today As He Did In Past; He Favors All Equally," *Deseret News—Church Section*, 12 September 1992). See also *Seventeen Points of the True Church* (LDS missionary handout, n.d.), point 13.
2. "I am the LORD, **I change not**..." (Malachi 3:6). "Jesus Christ is **the same yesterday, and to day, and for ever**" (Hebrews 13:8). Even LDS scriptures teach this same concept: "... I say unto you he **[God] changeth not**; if so he would cease to be God..." (*The Book of Mormon* [Salt Lake City: The Church of Jesus Christ of Latter-day Saints, 1981], Mormon 9:19). "For I know that **God is not** a partial God, neither **a changeable being; but he is unchangeable from all eternity to all eternity**" (Moroni 8:18). "... there is a God in heaven, who is infinite and eternal, from **everlasting to everlasting the same unchangeable God**..." (*Doctrine and Covenants of the Church of Jesus Christ of Latter-day Saints* [Salt Lake City: The Church of Jesus Christ of Latter-day Saints, 1981], 20:17). "From **eternity to eternity he is the same**..." (*Doctrine and Covenants* 76:4).
3. *Deseret News—Church Section*, "Our Unchangeable Deity," 5 June 1965, First Presidency Editorial.
4. B. H. Roberts, *History of the Church of Jesus Christ of Latter-day Saints*, 2nd ed. 1980, 7 vols. (Salt Lake City: Deseret Book Company, 1951), 5:501-07; *Doctrine and Covenants*, Section 132.
5. See Fawn Brodie, *No Man Knows My History* (New York: Alfred A. Knopf, 1971), 297-308.
6. John Widtsoe, *Joseph Smith—Seeker After Truth, Prophet of God* (Salt Lake City: Deseret News Press, 1951), 233.
7. Brigham Young, *Deseret News*, 6 August 1862, 41.

8. *Journal of Discourses*, 26 vols. (England: Various publishers, 1854-1886), photo reprint, 11:128, 18 June 1865.
9. Ibid., 11:269, 19 August 1866.
10. Ibid., 20:28-31, 7 July 1878.
11. Orson Whitney, *Life of Heber C. Kimball* (Salt Lake City: Juvenile Instructor Office, 1888), 328fn2.
12. Revelation dated 27 September 1886, written in John Taylor's own handwriting. John Taylor Papers, LDS Church Historian's Office; cited and photo-reproduced in Fred Collier, *Unpublished Revelations*, 2 vols. (Salt Lake City: Collier's Publishing, 1979), 1:145-46 and 177-83, Part 88.
13. *Doctrine and Covenants*, Official Declaration 1.
14. 6 October 1890; Sixty-first Semiannual General Conference of the Church. Reported in *Deseret Evening News*, 11 October 1890, 2.
15. Remarks from Cache Stake Conference, 1 November 1891. Reported in *Deseret Weekly News*, 7 November 1891. Partially cited in John Widtsoe, *Evidences and Reconciliations* (Salt Lake City: Bookcraft, 1960), 105-06. Full quote in James Clark, comp., *Messages of the First Presidency*, 6 vols. (Salt Lake City: Bookcraft, 1966), 3:226-27.
16. Widtsoe, *Joseph Smith—Seeker After Truth*, 233.
17. Ludlow, *Encyclopedia of Mormonism*, "Polygamy," 3:1109.
18. John Stewart, *Brigham Young and His Wives* (Salt Lake City: Mercury Publishing, 1961), 14. This practice continues in the Church today under careful guidelines, though not taught openly. For example, a Mormon man can be married in the temple any number of times, under certain conditions (such as after a legal divorce from a previous wife, or by becoming a widower). Then he will have that total number of wives "sealed" to him for eternity, though he had only one living wife at a time legally. A Mormon woman, however, can only have a second temple marriage if the first marriage ended with a temple divorce. She will then only have one husband in eternity.
19. Bruce McConkie, *Mormon Doctrine* (Salt Lake City: Bookcraft, 1966), 578.

20. Ibid.
21. Such as in Leviticus, chapters 1-7.
22. Hebrews 10:5-7.
23. It should be noted that the LDS Church currently believes their temples are a true restoration of those built and used by Israel in the Old Testament. However, no ceremonies or sacrifices that were performed in those ancient Jewish temples are performed in modern Mormon temples. They are not, then, a true restoration.
24. Hebrews 9:23-10:4.
25. Luke 22:19-20.
26. Such as at the city of Jericho (Joshua 6:21).
27. Genesis 9:4-6.
28. *Doctrine and Covenants* 132:63.
29. See M. R. Werner, *Brigham Young* (New York: Harcourt, Brace & Co., 1925), 398-405.
30. D. Michael Quinn, *The Mormon Hierarchy: Extensions of Power* (Salt Lake City: Signature Books in association with Smith Research Associates, 1997), 246-47.
31. Richard Abanes, *One Nation Under Gods* (New York: Four Walls Eight Windows, 2002), 232.
32. *Journal of Discourses* 4:43-45, 21 September 1856.
33. Ibid., 4:52-54, 21 September 1856.
34. One example is found in Ludlow, *Encyclopedia of Mormonism*, "Reformation," 3:1197.
35. Ann Young, *Wife No. 19* (Hartford, Conn.: Dustin, Gilman and Co., 1875), 306-08.
36. Bill Hickman, *Brigham's Destroying Angel: Being the Life, Confession, and Startling Disclosures of the Notorious Bill Hickman, The Danite Chief of Utah* (Salt Lake City: Shepard Publishing Cop., 1904).
37. R. N. Baskin, *Reminiscences of Early Utah* (n. p.: R. N. Baskin, 1914), 154.
38. Juanita Brooks, *The Mountain Meadows Massacre* (Norman, Okla: University of Oklahoma Press, 1950). See also the video: *Burying the Past: The Legacy of the Mountain Meadows*

Massacre (Salt Lake City: University of Utah, Brian Patrick Productions, 2003).
39. Orson Pratt, *The Seer*, March 1853, 42.
40. Stuart Martin, *The Mystery of Mormonism* (London: Odhams Press, 1920), 256; A. J. Montgomery, pub., *Temple Mormonism* (New York: A. J. Montgomery, 1931), 18; J. H. Beadle, *Life in Utah; or The Mysteries and Crimes of Mormonism* (Philadelphia: National Publishing Co., 1870), 494; *The Salt Lake Tribune* 12 February 1906, 2.
41. Montgomery, *Temple Mormonism*, 20; Beadle, *Life in Utah*, 495; Martin, *The Mystery of Mormonism*, 259-60; *The Salt Lake Tribune*, 12 February 1906, 2.
42. Montgomery, *Temple Mormonism*, 20; Beadle, *Life in Utah*, 496; Martin, *The Mystery of Mormonism*, 260; *The Salt Lake Tribune*, 12 February 1906, 2.
43. Jerald and Sandra Tanner, *Mormonism—Shadow or Reality?* (Salt Lake City: Utah Lighthouse Ministry, 1987), 468.
44. When Lane Thuet participated in the Mormon Temple Ceremony in 1988 and 1989, this "execution of the penalty" was still a part of the temple ceremony.
45. Thumb drawn across the breast for the Second Token of the Aaronic Priesthood (Tanner, *Mormonism—Shadow or Reality?*, 470); thumb drawn across the belly for the First Token of the Melchizedek Priesthood (ibid., 470-71).
46. Joseph Fielding Smith became the tenth President of the LDS Church after being an Apostle for nearly 60 years. See Appendix B for specifics.
47. Joseph Fielding Smith, *Doctrines of Salvation: Sermons and Writings of Joseph Fielding Smith*, Bruce R. McConkie, comp., 3 vols. (Salt Lake City: Bookcraft, 1954), 1:137.
48. Ibid., 1:131.
49. Ludlow, *Encyclopedia of Mormonism*, 1:131.
50. Jerald and Sandra Tanner, *Evolution of the Mormon Temple Ceremony: 1842-1990* (Salt Lake City: Utah Lighthouse Ministry, 1990), 7-8.
51. *Journal of Discourses*, 1:50, 9 April 1852.
52. Ibid., 2:6, 23 October 1853.

53. Ibid., 3:319, 20 April 1856.
54. Ibid., 7:286, 9 October 1859.
55. Ibid., 13:271-72, 24 July 1870.
56. Martin, *The Mystery of Mormonism*, 262.
57. Montgomery, *Temple Mormonism*, 21.
58. Smith, *Doctrines of Salvation*, 1:90.
59. *The Pearl of Great Price* (Salt Lake City: The Church of Jesus Christ of Latter-day Saints, 1981), Abraham 1:20-27.
60. McConkie, *Mormon Doctrine* (1958 ed.), 102.
61. Ibid., 477.
62. Mathias Cowley, *Wilford Woodruff, His Life and Labors* (Salt Lake City: Woodruff Family Association, 1909), 351; quoted in Arthur Richardson, *That Ye May Not Be Deceived*, 8; both cited in Tanner, *Mormonism—Shadow or Reality?*, 266.
63. *Journal of Discourses*, 2:143, 3 December 1854.
64. Ibid., 7:290-91, 9 October 1859.
65. Ibid., 11:272, 19 August 1866.
66. Joseph Fielding Smith, *The Way To Perfection* (Salt Lake City: Genealogical Society of Utah, 1949), 101-02.
67. Ibid., 110.
68. Lund, *The Church and the Negro* (no imprint, 1967), 45-46.
69. Ibid.; cited in Tanner, *Mormonism—Shadow or Reality?*, 291.
70. John Stewart, *Mormonism and the Negro* (Orem, Utah: Community Press Publishing, 1960), 19.
71. Letter from LDS First Presidency to Dr. Lowry Nelson; 17 July 1947; cited in Stewart, *Mormonism and the Negro*, 46-47.
72. Statement by the First Presidency of the Church of Jesus Christ of Latter-day Saints on the Negro Question, 17 August 1951; cited in Stewart, *Mormonism and the Negro*, 16-18. See also Byron Merril, "Heavens are Open," 1992 Sperry Symposium, 196. Some writers have dated this document 17 August 1949 (Lester E. Bush, Jr., "Mormonism's Negro Doctrine," *Dialogue: A Journal of Mormon Thought*, Spring 1973, 67n199). One of the authors (Lane Thuet) went to the LDS Church Archives and asked to see a copy of the original

statement. **Files were pulled for August 1949 and August 1951, but the statement was not found in either location.** He then wrote a letter to the Church Historian's Office on 13 April 2005, requesting the correct date. In the official reply, they state: "Published sources that I have consulted show the date both as 17 August 1949 and 17 August 1951. **We have not been able to locate an original** letter that shows either the 1949 or the 1951 date to be correct" (Reference Librarian Ronald Read to Lane Thuet, 20 May 2005).

73. *Doctrine and Covenants*, Official Declaration 2, 30 September 1978.
74. First Presidency Letter to the Church, 8 June 1978, quoted in *Doctrine and Covenants*, Official Declaration 2.
75. Widtsoe, *Joseph Smith—Seeker After Truth*, 249.
76. *Journal of Discourses*, 2:31, 6 April 1853.
77. Ezra Taft Benson, *The Teachings of Ezra Taft Benson* (Salt Lake City: Bookcraft, 1988), 250-52.
78. *Deseret News—Church Section*, "Our Unchangeable Deity," 5 June 1965, 14.
79. W. Grant Bangerter, quoted in the *Deseret News—Church Section*, "Temple Work Blesses Living," 16 January 1982, 10.
80. *History of the Church*, 4:208.
81. "Mormons Drop Rites Opposed By Women," *The New York Times*, 3 May 1990, A-1, A-22.
82. "LDS Leaders Revise Temple Endowment," *The Salt Lake Tribune*, 29 April 1990, B-2.
83. Brodie, *No Man Knows My History*, 176-80.
84. Ibid., 278-83.
85. Tanner, *Evolution of the Mormon Temple Ceremony*, 109.
86. These changes were reported by a temple worker. This information was published by Mike Norton on his web site: http://josephlied.com on 19 January 2005.
87. Benjamin McGuire, "The Temple," *Mormonism 201*, Chapter 15. When Mormonism Research Ministry (MRM) posted their reply to McGuire, his article (along with several others critiquing *Mormonism 101*) was removed from the

web site. MRM's response to this chapter was prepared by Lane Thuet, and is available on-line at: www.mrm.org/articles/mormonism_201/chapter_15/.
88. Brigham Young, quoted in *Diary of L. John Nuttall*, 7 February 1877; cited in Hyrum Andruss, *God, Man, and the Universe* (Salt Lake City: Bookcraft, 1968), 334. The journal page is photographically reproduced in Tanner, *Mormonism— Shadow or Reality?*, 178-D. See also *Journal of Discourses*, 2:31, 6 April 1853.
89. Tanner, *Evolution of the Mormon Temple Ceremony*, 77, 86, 89.
90. Ibid., 93.
91. Additional changes in reference to the LDS Godhead can be found in Chapter 10. These include: the teaching and later denial of the Adam-God doctrine; the change from teaching God's eternal progression to teaching that He no longer changes; and the change in doctrine from monotheism to polytheism.
92. *Deseret News—Church Section*, 5 June 1965, LDS Leadership Editorial.
93. Boyd K. Packer, "Revelation In A Changing World," *Ensign*, November 1989, 15-16. This speech was obviously given to prepare the membership for the Temple ceremony changes a few months later.
94. Ezra Taft Benson, who later became the thirteenth president of the Mormon church, says, "The living Prophet is more important to us than a dead prophet.... Therefore the most important prophet so far as you and I are concerned is the one living in our day and age to whom the Lord is currently revealing His will for us.... Beware of those who would pit the dead prophets against the living prophets, for the living prophets always take precedence" (*Fourteen Fundamentals in Following the Prophets*, BYU Devotional Assembly, 26 February 1980).
95. Jerald and Sandra Tanner have done extensive research into the changes made in numerous LDS works, publishing their findings through Utah Lighthouse Ministry. We are indebted

to their detailed work for some of the information presented here.
96. *The Chicago Manual of Style* (Chicago: The University of Chicago Press, 2003), 458-64. *Webster's New World College Dictionary* (New York: Macmillen USA, 1999), "**ellipsis**," "**ellipsis points**," 462.
97. *History of the Church*, 1:iii.
98. Ibid., 1:v-vi.
99. Ibid., 1:vi.
100. Smith, *Doctrines of Salvation*, 2:199 (1955).
101. Widtsoe, *Joseph Smith—Seeker After Truth*, 256-57.
102. Ibid., 297.
103. Jerald and Sandra Tanner, *Changes in Joseph Smith's History* (Salt Lake City: Utah Lighthouse Ministry, n.d.), 2.
104. Ibid.
105. Early LDS references often make reference to the *Documentary History of the Church*, and also to the *Comprehensive History of the Church*. These are two different works. What used to be identified as the *Documentary History* is what is commonly known today as the 7-volume *History of the Church*.
106. J. Reuben Clark statement, 8 April 1943; cited in D. Michael Quinn, *On Being a Mormon Historian* (Salt Lake City: Utah Lighthouse Ministry, 1982), 8-9.
107. Davis Bitton, "B. H. Roberts as Historian," *Dialogue: A Journal of Mormon Thought*, Winter 1968, 30-32.
108. Samuel Taylor, *Nightfall At Nauvoo* (New York: Macmillan, 1971), 383; quoted in Tanner, *Falsification of Joseph Smith's History*, 21.
109. *Times and Seasons*, 1 April 1842, 749.
110. *History of the Church*, 1:9.
111. Ibid., 5:85.
112. See Tanner; *Mormonism—Shadow or Reality?*, 135. For a thorough discussion on this "prophecy," see Chapter 8.
113. Examples: Joseph Smith breaking the Word of Wisdom (Tanners, *Changes in Joseph Smith's History*, 52-53, 84, 86); changing the name of an angel (*Changes*, 12); Joseph Smith swearing (*Changes*, 3, 84); and the story from the

murder of Joseph Smith (*Changes*, 87. See also Tanners, *Mormonism – Shadow or Reality?*, 141-42; and B. H. Roberts, *A Comprehensive History of the Church of Jesus Christ of Latter-day Saints*, 6 vols. [Salt lake City: Deseret News Press, 1930], 332-37).

114. Dean C. Jessee, "Has Mormon History Been Deliberately Falsified?," *Mormon Miscellaneous Response Series*, #2 (Salt Lake City: Mormon Miscellaneous, 1982), 1, 5.
115. Smith, *Doctrines of Salvation*, 2:198.
116. Benson, *The Gospel Teacher and His Message* (Salt Lake City: Church Educational System, 1976), 10. Also in Benson, *The Teachings of Ezra Taft Benson*, 128.
117. Quinn, *On Being a Mormon Historian*, 21.
118. Klaus Hansen, "Reflections on the Lion of the Lord," *Dialogue: A Journal of Mormon Thought*, Summer 1970, 107.
119. *History of the Church*, 1:Title page. "By Himself" is capitalized in the original.
120. "Extracts from Heber C. Kimball's Journal," *Times and Seasons*, 1 February 1845, 788.
121. *History of the Church*, 2:80.
122. Ibid., fn8.
123. Dean Jessee, "The Writing of Joseph Smith's History," *BYU Studies*, Summer 1971, 466.
124. Tanner, *Falsification of Joseph Smith's History*, 22.
125. For example, Benson taught that "if you feel you must write for the scholarly journals, you always defend the faith. **Avoid expressions and terminology which offend the Brethren** [i.e.: the Twelve Apostles and the First Presidency] **and Church members**" (Ezra Taft Benson, "The Gospel Teacher and His Message," address to religious educators, 17 September 1976; pamphlet version, 11). D. Michael Quinn wrote that Ezra Taft Benson and Boyd K Packer spearheaded an effort to try and keep religious educators and writers about Church history from telling all the facts. They advocated telling only those things that were "faith promoting" when writing and teaching. Quinn concluded, "**This is Accommodation History** for consumption by the weakest of the conceivably

weak Saints..." (*On Being a Mormon Historian*, 20). Benson has said, for example, "I hope there **will never be any time when teachers** in our own institutions **will ever propose any theory or program, or present as fact anything that will tend to destroy the faith** of our young people" (*Teachings of Ezra Taft Benson*, 308).

126. Tanner, *Mormonism—Shadow or Reality?*, 13-A to 13-B.
127. Tanner, *Changes in Joseph Smith's History*, 9.
128. Hansen, "Reflections," 110.
129. T. Edgar Lyon, "How Authentic Are Mormon Historic Sites in Vermont and New York?" *BYU Studies*, Spring 1969, 349-50. While Lyon was speaking specifically about the reliability of historical locations, his words are equally as true regarding the presentation of an authentic history.
130. For a thorough evaluation, see Jerald and Sandra Tanner, *3,913 Changes in the Book of Mormon* (Salt Lake City: Utah Lighthouse Ministry, n.d.).
131. Jerry and Dianna Benson, "Mormonism Challenged," *Out of Darkness* (El Cajon, Calif.: Challenge Ministries Newsletter), October 2004, 3.
132. See Tanner, "Change, Censorship and Suppression," *Mormonism—Shadow or Reality?*, 5-13.
133. Joel Groat, "Changes to Latter-day Scripture," fn1. On-line at: www.irr.org/mit/ CHANGINGSCRIPS.html.
134. Alma 29:4, "… I know that he [God] allotteth unto men, yea, decreeth unto them decrees which are unalterable…."
135. *Manuscript History* [1839 Draft], Book A-1:51. Dean Jessee, *The Papers of Joseph Smith*, 2 vols. (Salt Lake City: Deseret Book, 1989), 1:260; cited in Marquardt, *The Joseph Smith Revelations: Text and Commentary* (Salt Lake City: Signature Books, 1999), 18.
136. Smith to Phelps, 31 July 1832, LDS Archives; cited in Marquardt, *The Joseph Smith Revelations*, 18.
137. *Doctrine and Covenants*, Explanatory Introduction, 3.
138. This discussion of the changes does not include *Doctrine and Covenants*, Sections 65-136 or 138, since they were not origi-

nally included in the *Book of Commandments*. Section 137, though added in 1976, will be discussed in this chapter.
139. *History of the Church*, 1:173fn.
140. Marquardt, *The Joseph Smith Revelations*, Introduction: xv.
141. H. Michael Marquardt and Wesley Walters, *Inventing Mormonism* (Salt Lake City: Smith Research Associates, 1998), 159. They reference Chapters XVII-XXII of the 1833 *Book of Commandments*, comparing them with Sections 45-46 from the 1835 *Doctrine and Covenants* (ibid., 168n36).
142. Richard Van Wagoner, *Sidney Rigdon: A Portrait of Religious Excess* (Salt Lake City: Signature Books, 1994), 129n5.
143. J. B. Turner, *Mormonism in All Ages: or the Rise, Progress, and Causes of Mormonism* (New York: Platt and Peters, 1842), 226; cited in Marquardt, *The Joseph Smith Revelations*, 18.
144. Letter from David Whitmer; *Saints Herald*, 5 February 1887, 92.
145. *The Doctrine and Covenants*, Explanatory Introduction.
146. Peter Crawley, "A Bibliography of the Church of Jesus Christ of Latter-day Saints in New York, Ohio, and Missouri," *BYU Studies*, Summer 1972, 486.
147. See Fitzgerald, "A Study of the Doctrine and Covenants," Master's thesis, BYU, 1940; cited in Tanner, *Mormonism—Shadow or Reality?*, 14.
148. Melvin J. Petersen; "A Study of the Nature of and Significance of the Changes in the Revelations as Found in a Comparison of the Book of Commandments and Subsequent Editions of the Doctrine and Covenants," Master's thesis, BYU, 1955; cited in Tanner, *Mormonism—Shadow or Reality?*, 14.
149. Petersen, "A Study of the Nature and Significance," 118; cited in Tanner, *Mormonism—Shadow or Reality?*, 17.
150. Diary entry for 21 January 1836. See Scott Faulring, comp., *An American Prophet's Record* (Salt Lake City: Signature Books in association with Smith Research Associates, 1987), 118-19.
151. *Doctrine and Covenants* 107:54.
152. *Doctrine and Covenants* 8:6-7.

153. Hyrum M. Smith and Janne M. Sjodahl, *Doctrine and Covenants Commentary* (Cambridge: University Press, 1951), 43-44.
154. Daniel H. Ludlow, *A Companion to Your Study of the Doctrine and Covenants,* 2 vols. (Salt Lake City: Deseret Book Co., 1978), 1:78.
155. *Book of Commandments* VII:3. See Wilford Wood, *Joseph Smith Begins His Work,* 2 vols. (Salt Lake City: Wilford C. Wood, 1962), vol. 2, 21st page after the Affidavit.
156. Deuteronomy 18:10-11; Ezekiel 21:21; Hosea 4:12.
157. D. Michael Quinn explains: "Church authorities published Cowdery's 'rod of nature' revelation (D&C 8) in 1832 and again in 1833. After Eber D. Howe's 1834 *Mormonism Unvailed* ridiculed the Smith family's previous use of divining rods, **the 1835 edition of the *Doctrine and Covenants* changed these references to the euphemistic 'gift of Aaron'**" (Quinn, *Early Mormonism and the Magic World View* [Salt Lake City Utah: Signature Books, 1998], 256).
158. D. Michael Quinn, *The Mormon Hierarchy: Origins of Power* (Salt Lake City: Signature Books, 1994), 1.
159. Ibid.
160. Ibid., 622-23.
161. Quinn, *Early Mormonism,* 256-57 (204-06 in 1987 ed.).
162. Marvin Hill, "Brodie Revisited: A Reappraisal," *Dialogue: A Journal of Mormon Thought,* Winter 1972, 78.
163. Quinn, *Origins of Power,* 637.
164. Ibid., 645. See also Quinn, *Early Mormonism,* 257 (205 in 1987 ed.).
165. Quinn, *Origins of Power,* 659.
166. Ibid., 559.
167. Quinn, *Early Mormonism* (1987 ed.), 206.
168. Quinn, *Early Mormonism* (1998 ed.), 258.
169. Ibid.
170. Kimball, *Heber C. Kimball: Mormon Patriarch and Pioneer,* 248; cited in Tanner, *Mormonism—Shadow or Reality?,* 49-C.
171. *Doctrine and Covenants* 107:53-55; 116 and 117:8.

172. Smith, *Doctrines of Salvation*, 3:74 (1956).
173. Ivan J. Barrett, *Joseph Smith and the Restoration: A History of the LDS Church to 1846*, rev. ed. (Provo: Brigham Young University Press, 1973), 373.
174. *Journal History of the Church*, 15 March 1857; cited in Sandra Tanner, "Was the Garden of Eden in Missouri?," 5 (www.utlm.org/onlineresources/gardenofeden.htm).
175. *Journal of Discourses*, 10:235.
176. Joseph Fielding Smith, *Answers to Gospel Questions*, 5 vols. (Salt Lake City: Deseret Book Co., 1958), 2:93-95.
177. Kenneth Barker, gen. ed., *The NIV Study Bible* (Grand Rapids: Zondervan Publishing, 1985), Introduction: Genesis.
178. In the LDS published Bible, the title page of Genesis identifies it as "the First Book of Moses called Genesis." In the same volume, the Bible Dictionary (under "Genesis") adds that "among other things, latter-day revelation certifies to Moses as the original author of Genesis."
179. 1 Nephi 5:11.
180. Remember that Moses had been raised and schooled in the Pharaoh's Palace (Acts 7:21-22), and as such was given the best education available at the time.
181. *KJV*—"compasseth"—where it marks the boundary of something (vv. 11 and 13), and "goeth"—where it proceeds (v. 14). Both of these Hebrew words are Qal Participle Active words, indicating an action that is current and continuing at the time of writing. See Spiros Zodhiates, *The Complete Word Study Old Testament* (Chattanooga, Tenn.: AMG Publishers, 1994), "Grammatical notations," 2282.
182. *Pearl of Great Price* (1831 ed.), Explanatory Note.
183. James R. Harris; "A Study of the Changes in the Contents of the Book of Moses ..."; M.A. thesis, 224-26; cited in Tanners, *Flaws in the Pearl of Great Price* (Salt Lake City: Utah Lighthouse Ministry, 1991), 3.

- **Chapter Ten Notes**

1. Orthodox Christianity teaches that God the Father is fully God, Jesus Christ is fully God, and the Holy Spirit is also fully God. Each are individual beings, nevertheless, there is only one eternal God. This mystery of three distinct beings comprising only one God is the Christian doctrine of the "Trinity." See Robert Morey, *The Trinity: Evidence and Issues* (Grand Rapids: World Publishing, 1996); E. Calvin Beisner, *God in Three Persons*, Wheaton, Ill.: Tyndale House Publishers, 1984); and Robert Letham, *The Holy Trinity: In Scripture, History, Theology, and Worship* (Phillipsburg, N. J.: P & R Publishing, 2004).
2. An excellent examination of the LDS theology of the Godhead can be found in Bill McKeever and Eric Johnson, *Mormonism 101* (Grand Rapids: Baker Books, 2000), Chapters 1-3.
3. Bruce McConkie, *Mormon Doctrine* (Salt Lake City: Bookcraft, 1966), 317.
4. *Uniform System for Teaching the Gospel* (Salt Lake City: The Church of Jesus Christ of Latter-day Saints, 1986), Discussion 1, "The Plan of our Heavenly Father," 1-4.
5. Joseph Smith taught, "**God himself was once as we are now**, and is an **exalted Man**, and sits enthroned in yonder heavens. That is the great secret.... I am going to tell you **how God came to be God**. We have imagined and supposed that God was God from all eternity, **I will refute that idea.... he was once a man like us**; yea, that **God himself** the Father of us all, **dwelt on an earth** the same as Jesus Christ himself did ..." (*Journal of Discourses*, 26 vols. [England: Various publishers, 1854-1886], photo reprint, 6:3).
6. Milton Hunter, *The Gospel Through the Ages* (Salt Lake City: Deseret Book, 1945), 104-07; *Journal of Discourses*, 1:123, 6 October 1853.
7. *Journal of Discourses*, 1:123, 6 October 1853; James Talmage, *The Articles of Faith* (Salt Lake City: The Church of Jesus Christ of Latter-day Saints, 1968), 430.

8. *Doctrine and Covenants of the Church of Jesus Christ of Latter-day Saints* (Salt Lake City: The Church of Jesus Christ of Latter-day Saints, 1981), 130:22; Parley Pratt, *Key to the Science of Theology* (Salt Lake City: Deseret Book, 1965), 44; Talmage, *The Articles of Faith*, 42; McConkie, *Mormon Doctrine*, 319; *Journal of Discourses*, 6:3, 6 April 1844.
9. John A. Widtsoe, *Evidences and Reconciliations* (Salt Lake City: Bookcraft, 1960), 76-77; *Journal of Discourses*, 6:345, 31 July 1859; McConkie, *Mormon Doctrine*, 359; Talmage, *The Articles of Faith*, 42-43.
10. Apostle Orson Hyde said, "We believe in a God who is **Himself progressive ... a Being who has attained His exalted state** by a path which now His children are permitted to follow..." (*Journal of Discourses*, 1:123, 6 October 1853).
11. Hunter, *The Gospel Through The Ages*, 114-15. The preface to Hunter's book states, "the volume has been **written and published under the direction of the General Authorities**" (p. vii). See *Mormonism Researched* (March /April 2005) for a discussion on this teaching's functioning place in LDS theology today.
12. McConkie, *Mormon Doctrine*, 516-17; *Gospel Principles* (Salt Lake City: The Church of Jesus Christ of Latter-day Saints, 1992), 11; Joseph Fielding Smith, *Man: His Origin and Destiny* (Salt Lake City: Deseret Book, 1954), 355.
13. Orson Pratt, *The Seer*, March 1853, 38-39; *Journal of Discourses*, 4:216, 8 February 1857.
14. James Talmage, *Jesus the Christ* (Salt Lake City: The Church of Jesus Christ of Latter-day Saints, 1973), 148; *Doctrine and Covenants* 88:36-39; McConkie, *Mormon Doctrine*, 433; Pratt, *Key to the Science of Theology*, 45; *Journal of Discourses*, 13:140-41, 11 July 1869.
15. McConkie, *Mormon Doctrine*, 589-90; *Doctrine and Covenants* 93:33; Daniel Ludlow, ed., *Encyclopedia of Mormonism*, 4 vols. (New York: Maxwell Macmillan International, 1992), 2:868-69; Joseph Fielding Smith, comp., *Teachings of the Prophet Joseph Smith* (Salt Lake City: Deseret Book, 1976), 350-52; *History of the Church*, 3:387.

16. *Doctrine and Covenants* 93:30-31; 98:8; McConkie, *Mormon Doctrine*, 26-28; *The Book of Mormon* (Salt Lake City: The Church of Jesus Christ of Latter-day Saints, 1981), 2 Nephi 2:27; 10:23; Helaman 14:31.
17. Genesis 21:33; Psalm 90:2; 93:2; Isaiah 41:4; Habakkuk 1:12; Romans 16:26.
18. Numbers 23:19; Deuteronomy 30:20; Job 9:32; 10:12; 33:4; Psalm 36:9; Isaiah 40:18; John 5:26.
19. Genesis 1:2; 1 Kings 8:27; John 4:24; Colossians 1:15; 1 Timothy 1:17; 6:16; 1 John 4:12.
20. 1 Kings 8:27; Psalm 139:7-10; Isaiah 66:1; Jeremiah 23:23-24; Acts 7:48-50; 17:27-28; Revelation 3:20.
21. 1 Samuel 2:2; Isaiah 40:18; Matthew 5:48; 1 Timothy 1:17; 1 John 1:5.
22. Genesis 1:1-26; Job Chs. 38-39; Psalm 33:6-9; 148:5-6; Acts 17:24-28; Romans 4:17; Hebrews 11:3.
23. Psalm 115:3; Jeremiah 32:17, 27; Matthew 3:9; 19:26; Luke 1:37; Romans 1:20; 8:28-39; 9:16-18; Ephesians 1:11.
24. Genesis 18:14; Exodus Ch. 14; 1 Kings Ch. 17; Job 42:2; Psalm 104; Isaiah 38:5-8; Jeremiah 32:17; Matthew Ch. 14; Luke 1:37.
25. See Chapter 9 for more information about this topic.
26. *The Book of Mormon*, Introductory page.
27. *The Pearl of Great Price* (Salt Lake City: The Church of Jesus Christ of Latter-day Saints, 1981), Joseph Smith—History 1:34.
28. *Book of Mormon*, Title page.
29. *Book of Mormon*, Testimony of Three Witnesses.
30. 2 Nephi 31:21.
31. Alma 11:26-35.
32. Alma 11:44.
33. Mosiah 7:27.
34. Mosiah 15:1-5.
35. Mosiah 16:15.
36. Alma 11:38-40.
37. Ether 3:14.
38. *Doctrine and Covenants* 20:19.

39. Ibid., v. 28.
40. Moses 1:6.
41. Moses 1:20.
42. Moses 2:3-6. Numerous other examples can be cited in Moses 2:7-3:22 and throughout the rest of that book.
43. B. H. Roberts, *History of the Church of Jesus Christ of Latter-day Saints*, 2nd ed. 1980, 7 vols. (Salt Lake City: Deseret Book Company, 1951), 1:324.
44. Mark 12:32 *JST*. "*JST*" stands for *Joseph Smith's Translation of the Bible*. Also commonly called the *Inspired Version* (Independence, Mo.: Herald Publishing, 1991), since **Joseph never actually did any translating** to come up with his changes to the text. It should be noted that Joseph Smith made several additions and corrections to this chapter of the New Testament in his *Inspired Version*, yet the verse teaching that there is only one God was left unaltered.
45. 1 Timothy 2:5-6 *JST*.
46. *History of the Church*, 2:236.
47. Ibid., 4:517-18, 548.
48. LDS Scholar Van Hale wrote that Joseph Smith was publicly teaching a plurality of gods doctrine as early as 1832 (see "The Doctrinal Impact of the King Follett Discourse," *BYU Studies*, Winter 1978, 224). However, some of his proofs are somewhat ambiguous. Smith claimed that the doctrine had been preached in the LDS Church since 1829 (*History of the Church*, 6:474), but the evidence shows that this doctrine evolved over time, most notably between 1835 and 1842.
49. *Times and Seasons*, 1 September 1842, 905. Joseph Smith took over as editor for this paper on 1 March 1842.
50. *Journal of Discourses*, 6:3-5, 6 April 1844.
51. *History of the Church*, 6:474-76, 16 June 1844.
52. *History of the Church*, 3:386-87, 2 July 1839. Also in Smith, *Teachings of the Prophet Joseph Smith*, 157.
53. *History of the Church*, 3:35, 19 May 1838. Also in Smith, *Teachings of the Prophet Joseph Smith*, 122.

54. Joseph Smith, quoted in *Destiny Magazine*, December 1953, 1. Also in John Henry Evans, *Joseph Smith—An American Prophet* (New York: Macmillen Company, 1933), 179-80.
55. *Journal of Discourses*, 1:50-51, 9 April 1852.
56. *Millenial Star*, 10 December 1853, 801-02.
57. Ibid., 31 March 1855, 195.
58. Ibid., 5 August 1854, 482.
59. Ibid., 26 August 1854, 530.
60. *Journal of Discourses*, 5:331, 7 October 1857.
61. *Miscellaneous Sermons of Brigham Young*, handwritten manuscript by G.D. Watt. Date unknown. LDS Church Archives. Photocopy on file.
62. *Deseret Weekly News*, 18 June 1873, 308. The actual sermon was given on 8 June 1873.
63. Personal letter from LDS Apostle Bruce McConkie to BYU Professor Eugene England, 19 February 1981, 4, 6.
64. *Deseret News—Church Section*, 9 October 1976, 11.
65. *History of the Church*, 6:305.
66. *Journal of Discourses*, 1:93, 13 June 1852.
67. *Journal of Discourses*, 11:286-87, 13 January 1867.
68. Pratt, *The Seer*, August 1853, 117-18.
69. *Journal of Discourses*, 6:120, 6 December 1857.
70. *Journal of Discourses*, 4:126-27, 26 October 1856.
71. Bruce McConkie to Eugene England, 19 February 1981, 6.
72. Ibid.
73. Bruce McConkie, "The Seven Deadly Heresies," Fireside speech 1 June 1980. McConkie quotes himself in his letter to Eugene England, 19 February 1981, 2.
74. Joseph Fielding Smith, *Doctrines of Salvation: Sermons and Writings of Joseph Fielding Smith*, Bruce R. McConkie, comp., 3 vols. (Salt Lake City: Bookcraft, 1954), 1:7-8.
75. Ibid., 2:35 (1955).
76. *Deseret News—Church Section*, "Our Unchangeable Deity," 5 June 1965, First Presidency Editorial.
77. *Journal of Discourses*, 18:290, 12 November 1876; *Doctrine and Covenants* 76:23-24, 93:21-23; *Gospel Principles*, 11.

78. *Journal of Discourses*, 13:282, 30 October 1870; McConkie, *Mormon Doctrine*, 192; *Doctrine and Covenants* 76:25-27.
79. Evans, *Joseph Smith—An American Prophet*, 308, 341; *Gospel Principles*, 11; McConkie, *Mormon Doctrine*, 750-51.
80. *Journal of Discourses*, 1:50, 9 April 1852; 8:211, 2 September 1860.
81. *Gospel Principles*, 17-19.
82. McConkie, *Mormon Doctrine*, 193.
83. *Journal of Discourses*, 1:50-51, 9 April 1852; 3:319, 20 April 1856; 8:115, 8 July 1860; 8:211, 2 September 1860; Smith, *Doctrines of Salvation*, 1:18; McConkie, *Mormon Doctrine*, 547; Widtsoe, *Jesus the Christ*, 81; *Family Home Evening Manual* (Salt Lake City: The First Presidency of The Church of Jesus Christ of Latter-day Saints, 1972), 126. President Joseph F. Smith said, "We must come down to the simple fact that **God Almighty was the Father of His Son Jesus Christ**. Mary, the virgin girl, who had never known mortal man, was his mother. **God by her begot His son Jesus Christ**.... Now, my little friends, I will repeat again in words as simple as I can, and you talk to your parents about it, that **God, the Eternal Father, is literally the father of Jesus Christ**" (ibid.). This explanation was followed by a diagram that showed: "Daddy + Mommy = You; **Our Heavenly Father + Mary = Jesus**."
84. Brigham Young taught, "The infidel world have concluded that if what the Apostles wrote about his father and mother be true, and the present marriage discipline acknowledged by Christendom be correct, then Christians must believe **that God is the father of an illegitimate son, in the person of Jesus Christ!** The infidel fraternity teach *that* to their disciples" (*Journal of Discourses*, 1:50, 9 April 1852).
85. *Journal of Discourses*, 6:95-96, 29 November 1857; Bruce McConkie, *Doctrinal New Testament Commentary*, 3 vols. (Salt Lake City: Bookcraft, 1973), 3:238; McConkie, *Mormon Doctrine*, 257.
86. *Journal of Discourses*, 1:345-46, 7 August 1853; 2:82, 6 October 1854; 2:210, 18 March 1855; 4:259-60, n. d., circa March 1857. Elder Jedediah M. Grant said, "**The grand reason**

of the burst of public sentiment in anathemas upon Christ and his disciples, causing his crucifixion, **was evidently based upon polygamy....A belief in the doctrine of a plurality of wives caused the persecution of Jesus** and his followers. We might almost think they were 'Mormons'"(ibid., 1:346, 7 August 1853).

87. *Journal of Discourses,* 2:80-82, 6 October 1854; 2:210, 18 March 1855; Pratt, *The Seer,* November 1853, 172; Kevan and Terri Clawson, *Obtaining Your Calling and Election* (South Jordan, Utah: Walking the Line Publications, 2001), 10-11. The Clawsons apparently believe the familial line of Jesus came down through the House of del Acqs and into the line of King Arthur of England. Thus, they conclude, the search for the "Holy Grail" is not a search for the cup of Christ, but actually the search for the blood descendants of Jesus Christ. They also suggest that Joseph Smith could have been a blood descendant of Jesus (ibid., 11-12).

88. Talmage, *Jesus the Christ,* 613-14; *Doctrine and Covenants* 19:16-18; *Gospel Principles,* 73; *Come Unto Christ* (Salt Lake City: The Church of Jesus Christ of Latter-day Saints, 1986), 66; *Conference Report* (October 1947), 147-48. President Joseph Fielding Smith taught, "A great many people have an idea that when he was on the cross, and nails were driven into his hands and feet, that was his great suffering. His great suffering was before he ever was placed upon the cross. It was in the Garden of Gethsemane ..." (Smith, *Doctrines of Salvation,* 1:130).

89. McConkie, *Mormon Doctrine,* 520; *Journal of Discourses,* 3:247, 16 March 1856; 4:219-20, 8 February 1857. President Joseph Fielding Smith contradicted this by claiming, "So I say **there never was a sin committed that was not atoned for**" (Smith, *Doctrines of Salvation,* 1:131). But he then went on two pages later to claim "*there are certain sins that **man may commit for which the atoning blood of Christ does not avail***" (ibid., 133). Which conflicting teaching is the true one is never pointed out.

90. McConkie, *Mormon Doctrine,* 670-72. McConkie tells us "the mere fact of **resurrection is called** *salvation by grace*

alone.... Salvation in the celestial kingdom of God, however, **is not salvation by grace alone.** Rather, **it is** *salvation by grace coupled with obedience...*" (ibid., 671).

91. *History of the Church,* 6:408-9; *The Salt Lake Tribune* (2 September 1989 – Dr. Lee letter to the First Presidency); cited in Jerald and Sandra Tanner, *Excommunication of a Mormon Church Leader* (Salt Lake City: Utah Lighthouse Ministry, 1989).

92. John 1:1-3, 14; 8:58; 1 Corinthians 8:6; Ephesians 3:9; Colossians 1:16-18; Hebrews 1:2.

93. Job 1:6; Psalm 148; Isaiah 14:12-23; Ezekiel 28:11-19; John 1:1-3; Colossians 1:16-18; Revelation 12:9.

94. Isaiah 7:15; Matthew 1:18-25; Luke 1:27, 34-35.

95. 2 Corinthians 5:21; Hebrews 4:15; 7:26; 1 Peter 2:22; 1 John 3:5.

96. There is no Bible reference or inference that Jesus ever married. John 2:1-11 speaks of Jesus being at a wedding, but verse 2 says He was an invited guest. One of the metaphors for the Church in the New Testament pictures Christ as a husband and the Church as His bride (Revelation 19:7-9). Revelation 19:7 makes the announcement for the future event: " ... for the marriage of the Lamb [Christ] is come, and his wife [the Church] hath made herself ready." And verse 9 adds, "blessed are they who are called unto the marriage supper of the Lamb."

97. There are no references in the Bible that speak of Jesus having sired children. The *NIV* translation for Isaiah 53:8 and Acts 8:33 states, "... who can speak of his descendants? ..." *The NIV Study Bible* notes for this verse add, "To die without children was considered a tragedy" (2 Samuel 18:18 cf. also v. 10). But they mention that the word for "descendants" could also mean those of Jesus' current generation (Kenneth Barker, gen. ed., *The NIV Study Bible* [Grand Rapids: Zondervan Publishing, 1985], 1095n53:8 and text notations).

98. Isaiah Ch. 53; 1 Corinthians 1:18; Ephesians 2:14-16; Colossians 1:19-22; Hebrews 9:28; 10:10; 1 Peter 2:24.

99. Mark 3:28-29; 1 Corinthians 6:9-11; Titus 2:14; Hebrews 9:24-28; 1 John 1:7-9; 2:1-2.
100. John 3:15-18, 36; 5:24; 6:40; 10:11, 24-29; 17:1-11, 20, 24-26; Acts 2:28; Romans 8:32-34; Hebrews 2:17; 3:1; 9:15, 28; 1 John 5:11-12; Revelation 5:9.
101. John 3:14-18, 36; 14:6; Acts 4:12; 10:43; Romans 5:12-21; 6:23; Philippians 2:5-11; 1 Timothy 2:5-6; 1 John 5:11-12; Revelation Ch. 5.
102. McConkie, *Mormon Doctrine*, 359; Smith, *Doctrines of Salvation*, 1:39; Joseph Fielding Smith, *Answers to Gospel Questions*, 5 vols. (Salt Lake City: Deseret Book, 1958), 2:145-48.
103. *Gospel Principles*, 37; McConkie, *Mormon Doctrine*, 358.
104. *Gospel Principles*, 37, McConkie, *Mormon Doctrine*, 358-59; Smith, *Doctrines of Salvation*, 1:38.
105. McConkie, *Mormon Doctrine*, 358; *Gospel Principles*, 37.
106. *Gospel Principles*, 37-38.
107. *Journal of Discourses*, 1:50, 9 April 1852; 4:218, 8 February 1857; 8:115, 8 July 1860; 11:268, 19 August 1866; Smith, *Doctrines of Salvation*, 1:18-19; Pratt, *The Seer*, October 1853, 158; McConkie, *Mormon Doctrine*, 547.
108. Alma 7:10
109. "What is the gift of the Holy Ghost? Nothing more nor less than **the right to the companionship** of the Holy Ghost. As President Joseph F. Smith says: '**He does not have to dwell with one constantly**'" (Smith, *Doctrines of Salvation*, 1:40).
110. Ibid., 1:42-43.
111. McConkie, *Mormon Doctrine*, 238-39, 575-76.
112. Smith, *Answers to Gospel Questions*, 2:145-48; Smith, *Doctrines of Salvation*, 1:39.
113. The *King James Version* uses the term "Holy Ghost" 91 times (some examples are Matthew 1:18; John 20:22; Acts 4:8; Romans 15:13). The term "holy Spirit" is used in the *KJV* four times (Luke 11:13; Ephesians 1:13; 4:30 and 1 Thessalonians 4:8). However, the *KJV* also refers to Him merely as the "Spirit" about 132 times.
114. McConkie, *Mormon Doctrine*, 358-59.

115. Ibid., 361, 752-53.
116. Ibid., 752.
117. John A. Widtsoe, Osborne Widtsoe, Albert Bowen, F. S. Harris and Joseph Quinney, comps., *Gospel Doctrine: Sermons and Writings of President Joseph F. Smith* (Salt Lake City: Deseret News, 1919), 73.
118. Parley Pratt, *Key to the Science of Theology*, 46, 105.
119. McConkie, *Mormon Doctrine*, 752.
120. Psalm 139:7-10; John 14:16-17.
121. Isaiah 40:13-14; 1 Corinthians 2:10-11; 12:7-11.
122. Job 33:4; Romans 8:11; 15:19; 1 Corinthians 12:9-11.
123. Hebrews 9:14.
124. Genesis 1:1-2.
125. Matthew 1:18, 20; Luke 1:35.
126. Matthew 3:16; Luke 3:22; Acts 10:38.
127. Luke 24:49; John 14:26; Acts 1:4-8.
128. Acts 2:1-4, 10:44-48.
129. 2 Samuel 23:2; Acts 1:16; 1 Corinthians 2:9-13; 2 Timothy 3:16-17; 1 Peter 1:12; 2 Peter 1:21.
130. Romans 8:9; 1 Corinthians 3:16; Ephesians 2:22.
131. 1 Corinthians 12:4-11.
132. Galatians 5:22-23; Ephesians 5:9.
133. John 14:26; 15:26; 16:13-14; Acts 5:32; Hebrews 10:15; 1 John 2:27.

- **Chapter Eleven Notes**

1. John Widtsoe, *Priesthood and Church Government* (Salt Lake City: Deseret Book, 1939), Preface, V.
2. Gordon B. Hinckley, *Teachings of Gordon B. Hinckley* (Salt Lake City: Deseret Book, 1997), 474.
3. Ezra Taft Benson, *Teachings of Ezra Taft Benson* (Salt Lake City: Bookcraft, 1988), 219.
4. LDS records give no official account, nor a date for this restoration.
5. *Ensign*, May 2004, 123.

6. Joseph Fielding Smith, comp., *Teachings of the Prophet Joseph Smith* (Salt Lake City: Deseret Book, 1976), 180.
7. Bruce McConkie, *Mormon Doctrine* (Salt Lake City: Bookcraft, 1966), "Priesthood," 594-95.
8. Edward Kimball, ed., *The Teachings of Spencer W. Kimball* (Salt Lake City: Bookcraft, 1982), 494.
9. James Talmage, *The Articles of Faith* (Salt Lake City: The Church of Jesus Christ of Latter-day Saints, 1968), 187-88. Also in Widtsoe, *Priesthood and Church Government*, 25-26.
10. Benson, *Teachings of Ezra Taft Benson*, 215.
11. Gordon Hinckley, "The Cornerstones of Our Faith," General Conference address October 1984; cited in *Ensign*, November 1984, 52-53. Also in Hinckley, *Teachings of Gordon B. Hinckley*, 473.
12. For more information on this topic, see Chapter 3.
13. Kimball, *Teachings of Spencer W. Kimball*, 494.
14. McConkie, *Mormon Doctrine*, 468.
15. Widtsoe, *Priesthood and Church Government*, 45.
16. David Whitmer, interview by Zenas Gurley, Jr., 14 January 1885; cited in Grant Palmer, *An Insider's View of Mormon Origins* (Salt Lake City: Signature Books, 2002), 217; and also Dan Vogel, ed., *Early Mormon Documents*, 5 vols. (Salt Lake City: Signature Books, 2003), 5:137.
17. William E. McLellin to J. L. Traughber, 25 August 1877; cited in Palmer, *An Insider's View*, 224.
18. William E. McLellin to D. H. Bays, 24 May 1870; cited in Palmer, *An Insider's View*, 224.
19. William E. McLellin to Joseph Smith III, July 1872; cited in Palmer, *An Insider's View*, 225.
20. "The Church of Christ" was the original name of the LDS Church when organized in 1830 (B. H. Roberts, *History of the Church of Jesus Christ of Latter-day Saints*, 2nd ed. 1980, 7 vols. [Salt Lake City: Deseret Book Company, 1951], 1:74-78). For quite some time, the official name of the LDS Church was "The Church of the Latter-day Saints" (*History of the Church*, 2:62-63). Though occasionally called by the current

full name "The Church of Jesus Christ of Latter-day Saints," this was not the official name of the Church until April 1838 (*Doctrine and Covenants of the Church of Jesus Christ of Latter-day Saints* [Salt Lake City: The Church of Jesus Christ of Latter-day Saints, 1981], 115:3-4).

21. David Whitmer, *An Address To All Believers In Christ* (Richmond, Mo.: David Whitmer, 1887), 64.
22. Ibid., 35.
23. For example, on one occasion, Brigham Young described events connected with the restoration of the Melchizedek priesthood which would date it in February 1832, and on another occasion as February 1831 (D. Michael Quinn, *The Mormon Hierarchy: Origins of Power* [Salt Lake City: Signature Books in association with Smith Research Associates, 1994], 26, 288n126). Further evidence shows that Young was wrong in stating both of these dates.
24. The Bible, the *Book of Mormon*, Joseph Smith's revelations, and the 1833 *Book of Commandments*.
25. Palmer, *An Insider's View*, 223-24. See also Lamar Petersen, *Problems in Mormon Text* (Salt Lake City: LaMar Petersen, 1957).
26. *History of the Church*, 1:64-70; see also *Doctrine and Covenants* 20:64-70.
27. *Doctrine and Covenants* 20:67. See also *History of the Church*, 1:68fn.
28. Petersen, *Problems in Mormon Text*, 8.
29. Quinn, *Origins of Power*, 15.
30. Petersen, *Problems in Mormon Text*, 7-8.
31. Vogel, *Early Mormon Documents* (1998), 2:400.
32. *Kirtland Council Minute Book*, 27, LDS Church Archives; cited in Vogel, *Early Mormon Documents* (1996), 1:32. Notice that at this time, Joseph was only claiming that one angel had ordained him.
33. *Patriarchal Blessing Book* 1:8-9, LDS Church Archives; cited in Vogel, *Early Mormon Documents* 2:452-53.
34. Cowdery's signed statement, 13 January 1849; cited in Vogel, *Early Mormon Documents*, 2:499.

35. Whitmer, *An Address*, 46, 49-62.
36. When the *Book of Commandments* was updated and republished in 1835, it was renamed the *Doctrine and Covenants*. It has kept this later name through subsequent updates and publishings.
37. *The Evening and Morning Star*, March 1833, 6. A total of 459 words were added to this revelation since the first published account.
38. Quinn, *Origins of Power*, 16.
39. Robert J. Woodford "The Historical Development of the Doctrine and Covenants," 3 vols. (Ph.D. diss., BYU, 1974), 1:288; cited in Quinn, *Origins of Power*, 18.
40. Vogel, *Early Mormon Documents* (2002), 4:277.
41. *History of the Church*, 1:60-61.
42. Quinn, *Origins of Power*, 15.
43. Brian Q. Cannon and *BYU Studies* Staff, "Priesthood Restoration Documents," *BYU Studies*, Winter 1995, 166.
44. Larry Porter, "The Restoration of the Aaronic and Melchizedek Priesthoods," *Ensign*, December 1996, 34.
45. *History of the Church*, 1:40fn.
46. Widtsoe, *Priesthood and Church Government*, 110.
47. Palmer, *An Insider's View*, 229.
48. Quinn, *Origins of Power*, 20.
49. Ibid., 19.
50. *History of the Reorganized Church of Jesus Christ of Latter-day Saints*, 4 vols. (Independence, Mo.: Herald House, 1952), 1:64-65. Also in Hal Hougey, *Latter-day Saints—Where Did You Get Your Authority?* (Concord, Calif., 1982), 16-17; and LaMar Petersen, *The Creation of the Book of Mormon* (Salt Lake City: Freethinker Press, 2000), 147.
51. Ibid. Porter writes, "Evidence suggests a date within the 13-day period from 16 May to 28 May 1829." See also Daniel Ludlow, ed., *Encyclopedia of Mormonism*, 4 vols. (New York: Maxwell Macmillan International, 1992), 2:885-86.
52. *Journal of Oliver Boardman Huntington* (San Marino, Calif.: Huntington Library, microfilm copy), 13 January 1881. In this entry, Huntington claims that Joseph and Oliver had actually

escaped from the jail during the trial with the assistance of their attorney. Huntington repeated the same information two years later under the date of 17 February 1883, page 18 of the typed copy at Utah State Historical Society. Also cited in Ogden Kraut, *Stories of Faith* (Salt Lake City: Pioneer Press, 1996), 10. This citation in Kraut's book places the ordination in 1829, but the trial in question took place "a few months after the organization of the Church" (John Widtsoe, *Joseph Smith—Seeker After Truth, Prophet of God* [Salt Lake City: Deseret News Press, 1951], 73). Fawn Brodie also places this trial after the organization of the Church (*No Man Knows My History* [New York: Alfred A. Knopf, 1971], 87), as does George Q. Cannon—who dates the event June 1830 (*Life of Joseph Smith* [Salt Lake City: Deseret News, 1888], 64-66).

53. *History of the Church*, 1:84-85, 92-94.
54. Wesley P. Walters, *Joseph Smith's Bainbridge, N.Y., Court Trials* (Salt Lake City: Modern Microfilm Co., n.d.; reprint from *Westminster Theological Journal*, Winter 1974), 125.
55. Quinn, *Origins of Power*, 25. Quinn presents his evidence in 22-26.
56. Anthon H. Lund diary, 30 March 1897; cited in Quinn, *Origins of Power*, 25, 287n121.
57. Smith claimed they were forced to keep the circumstances of the Priesthood conferral "secret" due to persecution (*History of the Church*, 1:43-44), but the lack of any mention of it in any source demonstrates that it was a retroactive addition, and that this statement was given to try and reconcile its conspicuous absence.
58. "Priesthood Restoration Documents," *BYU Studies*, Winter 1995, 167.
59. Whitmer, *An Address*, 64.
60. *History of the Church*, 1:175-77.
61. *Journal of Discourses*, 26 vols. (England: Various publishers, 1854-1888), photo reprint, 11:4, 15 November 1864.
62. John Corrill, *A Brief History of the Church of Christ of Latter Day Saints* (St. Louis: John Corrill, 1839), 18. Corrill goes on to inform us that after this priesthood was conferred for the

first time at the meeting, "some doubting took place among the elders, and considerable conversation was held on the subject" (ibid.).

63. Petersen, *The Creation of the Book of Mormon*, 141.
64. Palmer, *An Insider's View*, 228-30.
65. Exodus 28:1-4, 43; 29:9, 44; Leviticus 6:19-23; Numbers 3:5-6; 18:1-7.
66. Numbers 18:1.
67. Exodus 2:1-8 (cf. Exodus 28:1-2).
68. Joseph Fielding Smith wrote, "Joseph Smith, unto whom the record of the Nephites was delivered, and who translated it, is of the tribe of Ephraim. The Lord so revealed it. So are most of those who have received the gospel in this dispensation" (*A Book of Mormon Treasury: Selections from the Pages of the Improvement Era* [Salt Lake City: Bookcraft, 1959], 194). On another occasion, he wrote, "At this present time most of those who are receiving the gospel are of the tribe of Ephraim" (Joseph Fielding Smith, *Answers to Gospel Questions*, 5 vols. [Salt Lake City: Deseret Book, 1966], 5:70).
69. Matthew 27:51; Mark 15:38; Luke 23:34; Galatians 3:19-25; Hebrews 6:19-20; 9:7-17; 10:1-10, 19-23.
70. The Levitical and Aaronic are two names representing the same Priesthood. See McConkie, *Mormon Doctrine*, 10; *Doctrine and Covenants* 107:1, 6.
71. Hebrews 7:17. The *KJV* spelling for Melchisedec in this passage is slightly different from the LDS spelling (Melchizedek).
72. Joseph Thayer, *The New Thayer's Greek-English Lexicon* (Lafayette, Ind.: Book Publisher's Press, 1981), 405; also Spiros Zodhiates, *The Complete Word Study Dictionary: New Testament*, rev. ed. (Chattanooga: AMG Publishers, 1992), 967, word number 3331—*metathesis*.
73. James Strong, *Strong's Exhaustive Concordance* (Nashville: Thomas Nelson Publishers, 1990), Greek Dictionary, 13, word number 531—*aparabatos*.
74. Thayer, *The New Thayer's Greek-English Lexicon*, 54.
75. A. T. Robertson, *Word Pictures in the New Testament* (Nashville: Holman Reference, 2000), 570.

76. Joseph Smith, Jr., *The Holy Scriptures Inspired Version* (Independence, Mo.: Herald Publishing, 1991), Hebrews 7:3. Words in bold for this verse were either added or altered by Joseph Smith.
77. John 11:49.
78. Matthew 3:13-16.
79. *The Pearl of Great Price* (Salt Lake City: The Church of Jesus Christ of Latter-day Saints, 1981), Joseph Smith—History 1:68-69.
80. *Doctrine and Covenants* 20:25, 37. See also *Duties and Blessings of the Priesthood* (Salt Lake City: The Church of Jesus Christ of Latter-day Saints, 1996), Part B, Lesson 4, 26-38.
81. See additional problem number 3.
82. Joseph Smith—History 1:71 and footnote.
83. Ibid., 1:68-69.
84. *Doctrine and Covenants* 84:21.
85. Joseph Smith—History 1:70.
86. "The great promise the Lord has given to all who humbly repent, is that they shall receive the guidance of the Holy Ghost. Of course **this cannot come to them unless they are confirmed by the laying on of hands by one in authority**" (Joseph Fielding Smith, *Church History and Modern Revelation*, 4 vols. [Salt Lake City: Deseret Book, 1946], 1:143).
87. Joseph Smith—History 1:73.
88. "Priesthood Restored," *Ensign*, April 2004, 18.
89. 1 Timothy 3:12.
90. Ludlow, *Encyclopedia of Mormonism* explains that "the term 'high priest' refers to an office in the MELCHIZEDEK PRIESTHOOD" (2:587).
91. Leviticus 21:1, 10; 2 Chronicles 26:16-18. Bruce McConkie admits this in *Mormon Doctrine*, 356: "When these high priests served under the law of Moses, they were ordained priests of the Aaronic order...." See also Ludlow, *Encyclopedia of Mormonism*, 2:588.
92. Hebrews 7:11-16. Also vv. 23-24, which state, "Now there have been many of those priests, since death prevented them

from continuing in office; but because Jesus lives forever, he has a permanent priesthood" (*NIV*).
93. Bruce R. McConkie explains, "God's ministers are ordained. They have the holy priesthood **conferred upon them and are ordained by the laying on of hands** to officiate in specific offices and callings" (*Doctrinal New Testament Commentary*, 3 vols. [Salt Lake City: Bookcraft, 1965], 1:748).
94. Exodus 29; Leviticus 8.
95. *Doctrine and Covenants* 84:21-22. Also 1 John 4:12 states, "No man hath seen God at any time." Joseph altered this verse when he dictated his *Inspired Version*, adding, "except them who believe." By the time he made this revision, the story of the first vision had become fairly well developed and the Church was more aware of it. Thus, he needed to justify how he could have seen God when the Bible said no one could.
96. Joseph Smith—History 1:7, 17.
97. According to LDS sources (*Doctrine and Covenants* 13). As already shown, however, this date is unlikely.
98. Numbers 35:25-28; Joshua 20:6; 2 Kings 12:10; 23:4; Nehemiah 3:1; John 11:49-51.
99. While the exact number of LDS High Priests is not usually published by the Church, most administrative duties within the leadership of the Church as a whole, and on each of the local levels, is handled by men who have been ordained high priests. In his book on the LDS priesthood, John A Widtsoe records, "We have a quorum of High Priests, and **there are a great many of them**" (Widtsoe, *Priesthood and Church Government*, 122).
100. Orrin G. Hatch, *Higher Laws: Understanding the Doctrines of Christ* (Salt Lake City: Deseret Book, 1995), 99.
101. *Doctrine and Covenants* 7:1-8
102. An excellent resource documenting the many insurmountable problems with the LDS concept of Priesthood authority is found in Hougey, *Latter-day Saints—Where Do You Get Your Authority?*
103. Revelation 1:5-6.
104. 1 Peter 2:9.

105. 1 Peter 2:5.
106. 2 Corinthians 5:17-20.
107. Matthew 28:18.
108. Matthew 12:50; 28:19-20; Mark 3:35; Romans 6:13-14; 12:1-2; Hebrews 6:3.
109. John 1:13; 3:3-7; 1 Peter 1:23.
110. Hebrews 7:25.

• Chapter Twelve Notes

1. *The Book of Mormon* (Salt Lake City: The Church of Jesus Christ of Latter-day Saints, 1981), Moroni 10:4-5.
2. Apostle Robert Hales, "Receiving a Testimony of the Restored Gospel of Jesus Christ," Conference address, 4 October 2003; cited in *Ensign*, November 2003, 28, 30.
3. Martin Cawley, Letter to the Editor, *The Signal* [Newhall California], 21 May 2003, A-10.
4. James K. Walker, *I Bear You My Testimony* (Pamphlet – Garland, Tex.: American Tract Society, 1985), 1.
5. Grant Palmer, *An Insider's View of Mormon Origins* (Salt Lake City: Signature Books, 2002), 131.
6. Leslie Reynolds, *Mormons in Transition* (Grand Rapids: Baker Books, 1998), 111.
7. Robert Crossfield; quoted in Jon Krakauer, *Under the Banner of Heaven: A Story of Violent Faith* (New York: Doubleday, 2003), 72.
8. Jerry McKean, "Just Cut My Hair and Don't Preach!" *Ensign*, April 1990, 65.
9. Judy Robertson, *No Regrets: How I Found My Way Out Of Mormonism* (Light and Life Communications, 1997), 27.
10. "Latter-day Skeptics," *Christianity Today*, 11 November 1991, 32.
11. *Los Angeles Times*, 2 September 1992, E-1.
12. *Doctrine and Covenants of the Church of Jesus Christ of Latter-day Saints* (Salt Lake City: The Church of Jesus Christ of Latter-day Saints, 1981), 9:8-9.

13. Bruce McConkie, *Mormon Doctrine* (Salt Lake City: Bookcraft, 1966), 785.
14. Robert Hales, *Ensign*, November 2003, 30.
15. *Ensign*, August 2005, 4.
16. Lewis Price (former LDS missionary), *The Testimony of a Former Mormon Missionary* (La Mesa, Calif.: Utah Christian Tract Society, n.d.), 2.
17. O. Jay Swanson, typed personal testimony, undated, 2. Copy on file.
18. James Spencer (former Mormon), *Beyond Mormonism: An Elder's Story* (Grand Rapids: Chosen Books, 1984), 40-41.
19. Dr. Simon Southerton (former Mormon), "DNA genealogies of American Indians and the Book of Mormon," 17 March 2000, 3. Online at www.exmormon.org/ whylft125.htm.
20. Quoted in Krakauer, *Under the Banner of Heaven*, 82.
21. "Recognize Spirit When It Is Manifest," *Deseret News— Church Section*, 29 April 1989, 14. The portion of this article quoting Oaks was from an instructional speech he gave at the Missionary Training Center on 21 June 1988.
22. Thomas Stuart Ferguson, 28-page response "to the Norman & Sorenson Papers"; cited in Jerald and Sandra Tanner, *Mormonism—Shadow or Reality?* (Salt Lake City: Utah Lighthouse Ministry, 1987), 125-J.
23. Tanner, *Mormonism—Shadow or Reality?*, 125-I. See Chapter 5 for a more thorough discussion of Ferguson's studies and conclusions.
24. These were the original documents Joseph Smith used to "translate" the current Book of Abraham in the *Pearl of Great Price*.
25. Tanner, *Mormonism—Shadow or Reality?*, 309.
26. Ibid.
27. See Chapter 5 for a thorough examination of this subject.
28. Simon Southerton, "DNA genealogies ...," 7-8.
29. Orson F. Whitney, 7 June 1925; cited in *Ensign*, December 2003, 6.

30. Jerry and Dianna Benson, "Mormonism Challenged," *Out of Darkness* (Challenge Ministries Newsletter), October 2004, 2.
31. "Elder Decries Criticism of LDS Leaders," *The Salt Lake Tribune*, 18 August 1985, B-2; reproduced in Charles M. Larson, *By His Own Hand Upon Papyrus* (Grand Rapids: Institute for Religious Research, 1992), 170.
32. Such was the case here. Mr. Oaks was trying to prevent the people from abandoning the Mormon Church because of the "White Salamander Letter," which had just been made public knowledge. The letter cast serious doubts upon the first vision story given by Joseph Smith. This particular letter eventually was shown to be a forgery. However, many other historical facts have irrefutably shown Mormon teachings and beliefs to be in error.
33. John-Charles Duffy, "Defending the Kingdom, Rethinking the Faith," *Sunstone*, May 2004, 22.
34. Ibid., 29.
35. Jeff Call, "Faithful Follow Spiritual Path," *Deseret News*, 7 March 2004, A-12.
36. Arza Evans, *The Keystone of Mormonism* (St. George, Utah: Keystone Books, 2003), 119.
37. Quoted in Krakauer, *Under the Banner of Heaven*, 72-75.
38. Richard Bushman, "The First Vision Story Revived," *Dialogue: A Journal of Mormon Thought*, Spring 1969, 91-92.
39. John MacArthur, Jr., *Reckless Faith* (Wheaton, Ill.: Crossway Books, 1994), 25.
40. Larson, *By His Own Hand Upon Papyrus*, 176-77.
41. *Journal of Discourses*, 26 vols. (England: Various publishers, 1854-1886), photo reprint, 16:175-76, 31 August 1873.
42. *Deseret News—Church Section*, 29 April 1989, 14.
43. McConkie, *Mormon Doctrine*, 785.
44. Brodie Crouch, *The Myth of Mormon Inspiration* (Shreveport: Lambert's Book House, 1968), 63.
45. 2 Thessalonians 2:9.
46. Matthew 24:24.

47. Robert Hales, "Receiving a Testimony of the Restored Gospel of Jesus Christ," *Ensign*, November 2003, 30.
48. Reported in *Deseret News*, "LDS Church Now 5th Largest in U.S.," 16 February 2002, A-1, A-6.
49. Palmer, *An Insider's View*, 131-33.
50. Larry Jonas, *Mormon Claims Examined* (Grand Rapids: Baker Book House, 1961), 66.
51. Hal Brickman, *The Thin Book: Hypnotherapy Trance Scripts for Weight Management* (Phoenix: Zeig, Tucker and Co., 2000), preface. **We do not agree with Brickman's methods, nor condone his writings**. But what he says here is essentially correct. Hypnosis in any form is contrary to Biblical teaching.
52. *Uniform System for Teaching the Gospel* (Salt Lake City: The Corporation of the President of The Church of Jesus Christ of Latter-day Saints, 1986), Discussion 1, 1-1.
53. *The Plan of Our Heavenly Father* (Pamphlet – *Uniform System for Teaching the Gospel* [Salt Lake City: The Corporation of the President of The Church of Jesus Christ of Latter-day Saints, 1986]), Study Guide 1, 5.
54. Harold Bussell, *Unholy Devotion* (Grand Rapids: Zondervan Books, 1983), 32.
55. Steven Clark, *Man and Woman in Christ* (Ann Arbor: Servant Books, 1980), 360; cited in Bussell, *Unholy Devotion*, 32.
56. Walter B. Knight, *Knight's Master Book of 4,000 Illustrations*, 704; cited in Donna Morley; *A Christian Women's Guide to Understanding Mormonism* (Eugene, Oreg.: Harvest House Publishers, 2003), 80.
57. Simon Southerton, "DNA genealogies ...," 15.
58. John 14:26.
59. 1 John 2:27.
60. Luke 24:13-32.
61. Luke 24:32.
62. MacArthur, *Reckless Faith*, 77-78.
63. 1 John 4:1.
64. 2 Corinthians 11:14 (*KJV* – "Satan himself is transformed into an angel of light").

65. John 17:17.

• Chapter Thirteen Notes

1. See also Alma Burton, comp., *Discourses of the Prophet Joseph Smith* (Salt Lake City: Deseret Book Co., 1977), 157.
2. LDS Articles of Faith, articles 3 and 4.
3. Galatians 1:6-9.
4. Genesis 8:21; Psalm 51:5; 58:3; 1 Kings 8:46; Ecclesiastes 7:20; Romans 3:23; 1 John 1:8.
5. Romans 3:10-20.
6. Romans 5:6, 8, 10.
7. John 6:44. See also John 6:65 and 1 Corinthians 2:14.
8. John 1:12-13; 3:15-16.
9. John 3:18.
10. LDS Articles of Faith, article 4.
11. Matthew 28:19.
12. 1 Peter 3:21. Just as the flood symbolizes baptism, baptism is itself a symbol of salvation. It pictures the death, burial and resurrection of Christ, and our identification with Him in these experiences. Romans 6:4-5 explains, "Therefore we are buried with him by baptism into death: that like as Christ was raised up from the dead by the glory of the Father, even so we also should walk in newness of life. For if we have been planted together in the likeness of his death, we shall be also in the likeness of his resurrection."
13. 1 Corinthians 1:17.
14. Also, as the *NIV* explains, "The most reliable early manuscripts and other ancient witnesses do not have Mark 16:9-20" (*The NIV Study Bible* [Grand Rapids: Zondervan, 1985], 1530). Since this section of scripture cannot be verified as authentic, no doctrines or practices should be extrapolated from it without corroborating evidence from reliable sources.
15. John 5:39.
16. John 17:17.
17. 1 Timothy 2:5.

18. *Journal of Discourses*, 26 vols. (England: Various publishers, 1854-1886), photo reprint, 7:289, 9 October 1859.
19. *The Deseret News*, 2 November 1968, 14.
20. Robert Millet and Joseph McConkie, *Joseph Smith: The Choice Seer* (Salt Lake City: Bookcraft, 1996), prologue.
21. Galatians 1:6-9.
22. Acts 4:12.
23. John Morgan, *The Plan of Salvation*, Pamphlet (Salt Lake City: Deseret Book, 2000), 1 (*GospeLink 2001* CD-Rom).
24. Romans 3:10, 23.
25. 1 Timothy 1:15.
26. Romans 6:23.
27. Ephesians 2:8-9.
28. Titus 3:5-7.
29. Romans 3:24.
30. Romans 4:5.
31. Acts 10:44-48.
32. James 2:19.
33. Colossians 1:19-22; Hebrews 10:14.
34. John 1:12; 3:16.
35. Ephesians 2:10.
36. James 2:17-18.
37. 1 John 4:10; Romans 5:10.
38. John 19:30.
39. John 5:24; 1 John 5:11-13.
40. John 6:47; Romans 8:1, 35-39.
41. Colossians 3:3-4.
42. Spencer Kimball, *The Miracle of Forgiveness* (Salt Lake City: Bookcraft, 1969), 208-9.
43. Hebrews 4:14-15. Cf. Romans 3:9-20.
44. Romans 8:1-2.
45. John 10:27-29; Romans 8:38-39.

Select Bibliography

Mention of a source in this bibliography indicates that relevant information can be found therein. It does not necessarily indicate our agreement with or endorsement of all material presented. **It is up to the reader to research the claims made and determine whether the information presented is correct** and if the conclusions and statements of the authors are valid. A number of additional sources of helpful information are found in the endnotes for each chapter.

Books

Abanes, Richard. *Becoming Gods: A Closer Look at 21st-Century Mormonism*. Eugene, Oreg.: Harvest House Publishers, 2004.

_____. *One Nation Under Gods: A History of the Mormon Church*. New York: Four Walls Eight Windows, 2002.

Ankerberg, John, and John Weldon. *Everything You Ever Wanted to Know About Mormonism*. Eugene, Oreg.: Harvest House Publishers, 1992.

_____. *Behind the Mask of Mormonism*. Eugene, Oreg.: Harvest House Publishers, 1992.

Bagley, Will. *Blood of the Prophets: Brigham Young and the Massacre at Mountain Meadows*. Norman: University of Oklahoma Press, 2002.

Banister, S. I. *For any Latter-day Saint: One Investigator's Unanswered Questions*. Fort Worth: Bible Publications Inc., 1988.

Beckwith, Francis J., Norman Geisler, Ron Rhodes, Phil Roberts, Jerald and Sandra Tanner. *The Counterfeit Gospel of Mormonism.* Eugene, Oreg.: Harvest House Publishers, 1998.

_____, Carl Mosser, Paul Owen, gen. eds. *The New Mormon Challenge.* Grand Rapids: Zondervan, 2002.

Brodie, Fawn M. *No Man Knows My History.* 2nd ed. New York: Alfred A. Knopf, 1971.

Brooks, Juanita. *The Mountain Meadows Massacre.* Norman, Okla.: University of Oklahoma Press, 1962.

Cares, Mark J. *Speaking the Truth in Love to Mormons.* 2nd ed. Milwaukee: WELS Outreach Resources, 1998.

Cowan, Marvin W. *Mormon Claims Answered.* Rev. ed. Salt Lake City: Marvin W. Cowan, 1989. Also available in Spanish.

Farkas, John R., and David A. Reed. *Mormons: How to Witness to Them.* Grand Rapids: Baker Books, 1997.

_____. *Mormonism: Changes, Contradictions, and Errors.* Grand Rapids: Baker Books, 1995.

Harris, Ethan E. *The Gospel According to Joseph Smith: A Christian Response to Mormon Teaching.* Phillipsburg, N.J.: Presbyterian and Reformed, 2001.

Holding, James Patrick. *The Mormon Defenders: How Latter-day Saint Apologists Misinterpret the Bible.* No imprint, 2001.

Larson, Charles M. *By His Own Hand Upon Papyrus: A New Look at the Joseph Smith Papyri.* Rev. ed. Grand Rapids: Institute for Religious Research, 1992.

Larson, Stan. *Quest for the Gold Plates: Thomas Stuart Ferguson's Archaeological Search for The Book of Mormon.* Salt Lake City: Freethinker Press, 1996.

Marquardt, Michael H. *The Rise of Mormonism: 1816-1844.* Longwood, Fla.: Xulon Press, 2005.

_____. *The Joseph Smith Revelations: Text and Commentary.* Salt Lake City: Signature Books, 1999.

_____, and Wesley P. Walters. *Inventing Mormonism: Tradition and the Historical Record.* Salt Lake City: Smith Research Associates, 1994.

McKeever, Bill. *Answering Mormons' Questions.* Minneapolis: Bethany House, 1991.

_____, and Eric Johnson. *Questions to Ask Your Mormon Friend.* Minneapolis: Bethany House, 1994.

_____, and Eric Johnson. *Mormonism 101: Examining the Religion of the Latter-day Saints.* Grand Rapids: Baker Books, 2000.

Morley, Donna. *A Christian Women's Guide to Understanding Mormonism.* Eugene, Oreg.: Harvest House Publishers, 2003; Reprint, Faith & Reason Press, forthcoming.

Ostling, Richard N. and Joan K. *Mormon America: The Power and the Promise.* San Francisco: HarperSanFrancisco, 1999.

Palmer, Grant H. *An Insider's View* of *Mormon Origins.* Salt Lake City: Signature Books, 2002.

Persuitte, David. *Joseph Smith and the Origins of The Book of Mormon.* Jefferson, N.C.: McFarland and Co., Inc., 2000.

Petersen, LaMar. *The Creation of the Book of Mormon: A Historical Inquiry.* Salt Lake City: Freethinker Press, 1998.

Quinn, D. Michael. *The Mormon Hierarchy: Origins of Power.* Salt Lake City: Signature Books in association with Smith Research Associates, 1994.

_____. *The Mormon Hierarchy: Extensions of Power.* Salt Lake City: Signature Books in association with Smith Research Associates, 1997.

_____. *Early Mormonism and the Magic World View.* Salt Lake City: Signature Books, 1998.

Reed, David A., and John R. Farkas. *Mormons Answered Verse by Verse.* Grand Rapids: Baker Book House, 1992.

Reynolds, Leslie. *Mormons in Transition.* 2nd ed. Grand Rapids: Baker Books, 1998.

Rhodes, Ron, and Marian Bodine. *Reasoning From the Scriptures with the Mormons.* Eugene, Oreg.: Harvest House Publishers, 1995.

Roberts, R. Philip, with Tal Davis and Sandra Tanner. *Mormonism Unmasked: Confronting the Contradictions Between Mormon Beliefs and True Christianity.* Alpharetta, Ga.:Broadman & Holman, 1998.

Robertson, Judy. *Out of Mormonism.* Minneapolis: Bethany House, 2001.

Southerton, Simon G. *Losing a Lost Tribe: Native Americans, DNA and the Mormon Church.* Salt Lake City: Signature Books, 2004.

Sundholm, Sandra and Conrad. *Understanding Mormonism: Mormonism and Christianity Compared.* Milwaukie, Oreg.: Truth Publishing, 1996.

Tanner, Jerald and Sandra. *Mormonism—Shadow or Reality?* 5th ed. Salt Lake City: Utah Lighthouse Ministry, 1987.

_____. *The Changing World of Mormonism.* Chicago: Moody Press, 1980.

_____. *Major Problems of Mormonism.* Salt Lake City: Utah Lighthouse Ministry, 1989.

Van Gorden, Kurt. *Mormonism.* Grand Rapids: Zondervan Publishing House, 1995.

Walters, Wesley P. *New Light on Mormon Origins From the Palmyra New York Revival.* El Cajon, Calif.: Mormonism Research Ministry, 1997.

White, James R. *Is the Mormon My Brother? Discerning the Differences Between Mormonism and Christianity.* Minneapolis: Bethany House Publishers, 1997.

Videos

Southern Baptist Convention. *The Mormon Puzzle: Understanding and Witnessing to Latter-day Saints.* (North American Mission Board, Alpharetta, Ga: Broadman and Holman Publishers, 1997).

Institute for Religious Research. *The Lost Book of Abraham: Investigating a Remarkable Mormon Claim.* (Grand Rapids: Institute for Religious Research, 2002). Also available in Spanish.

Living Hope Ministries. *DNA vs. The Book of Mormon.* (Brigham City, Utah: Living Hope Ministries, 2003). Also available in Spanish.

_____. *The Bible vs. The Book of Mormon.* (Brigham City, Utah: Living Hope Ministries, 2005).

Brian Patrick. *Burying the Past: Legacy of The Mountain Meadows Massacre.* (Salt Lake City: University of Utah, 2003).

Ministries Involved with Mormonism

All web sites accessible as of 28 February 2006.

Ministries Witnessing in Utah

H.I.S. Ministries
Dennis and Rauni Higley
P.O.Box 900415, Sandy, UT 84090
www.hismin.com

Mormonism Research Ministry
Bill McKeever
P.O.Box 1746, Draper, UT 84020
(801) 572-2153
www.mrm.org

Utah Lighthouse Ministry
Jerald and Sandra Tanner
P.O.Box 1884, Salt Lake City, UT 84110
(801) 485-8894
www.utlm.org
Bookstore Location: 1358 South West Temple, Salt Lake City, Utah 84115

Utah Christian Publications
Marvin Cowan
P.O.Box 71052, Salt Lake City, UT 84171
(801) 943-3035
www.utahchristianpub.org

Utah Partnerships for Christ
Russ and Tammy East
P.O.Box 150571, Ogden, UT 84415
(801) 737-1708
www.upfc.org

Ministries Witnessing Outside Utah

Alpha and Omega Ministries
James White
P.O.Box 37106, Phoenix, AZ 85069
(602) 973-0318
www.aomin.org

Ankerberg Theological Research Inst.
John Ankerberg
P.O.Box 8977, Chattanooga, TN 37411
(423) 892-7722
www.johnankerberg.org

Berean Christian Ministries
John Farkas
P.O.Box 1091, Webster, NY 14580
(716) 872-4033
www.bcmmin.org

Challenge Ministries
Jerry and Dianna Benson
P.O. Box 20195, El Cajon, CA 92021
www.challengemin.org

Christian Apologetics and Research Ministry
Matthew Slick
P.O.Box 995, Meridian, ID 83680
www.carm.org

Christian Research Institute
Hank Hanegraaff
P.O.Box 8500, Charlotte, NC 28271-8500
(888) 700-0274
www.equip.org

Concerned Christians
Jim Robertson
P.O. Box 18, Mesa, AZ 85211-0018
(480) 833-2537
www.concernedchristians.org

Evangelical Ministries to New Religions
James Bjornstad
913 Huffman Road, Birmingham, AL 35215
(205) 833-2858
www.emnr.org

Evidence Ministries
Keith and Becky Walker
P.O. Box 690371, San Antonio, TX 78269
(210) 340-TRUE
www.evidenceministries.org

Faith & Reason Forum
Brian and Donna Morley
The Master's College, 2176 Placerita Canyon Rd., Box 16, Santa Clarita, CA 91321
www.faithandreason.org

Institute for Religious Research
Luke Wilson
1340 Monroe Ave. NW, Grand Rapids, MI 49505
(616) 451-4562
www.irr.org

Ministry of John L. Smith
John L. Smith
226 W. Main, P.O. Box 9, Marlow, OK 73055
(580) 658-7359
www.mormonerror.com

Mission to Mormons
Seven Dealy
P.O. Box 365, Nauvoo, IL 62354
(217) 845-4036
www.mission2mormons.org

Nauvoo Christian Visitor's Center
Colleen Ralson
1340 Mulholland, Nauvoo, IL 62354
(217) 453-2372

Personal Freedom Outreach
M. Kurt Goedelman
P.O. Box 26062, St. Louis, MO 63136
(314) 921-9800
www.pfo.org

Reach Out Trust
Doug Harris
24 Ormond Road, Richmond, Surrey TW10 6TH (ENGLAND)
+44 (0) 870 770 3258
www.reachouttrust.org

Reasoning from the Scriptures Ministries
Ron Rhodes
P.O. Box 80087, Rancho Santa Margarita, CA 92688
(214) 853-4370
http://home.earthlink.net/~ronrhodes

Truth-in-love Ministries
Conrad and Sandra Sundholm
2135 River Heights Circle, West Linn, OR 97068
(503) 786-6201

Utah Gospel Mission
Kurt VanGordon
P.O.Box 1901, Orange, CA 92856
www.utahgospelmission.org

Watchman Fellowship Inc.
James K. Walker
P.O.Box 13340, Arlington, TX 76094
(817) 277-0023
www.watchman.org

Word for the Weary
Sharon Lindbloom
P.O.Box 46571, Eden Prairie, MN 55344
(952) 937-0934
www.answeringlds.org

Printed in the United States
105089LV00001BC/37/A